WITHDRAWN

Bundu is an anomaly among the precolonial Muslim states of West Africa. Founded during the *jihāds* which swept the savannah in the eighteenth and nineteenth centuries, it developed a pragmatic policy, unique in the midst of fundamentalist, theocratic Muslim states. Its founder, Makik Sy, set the state on a distinctive course, and the ruling Fulbe group kept its distance from subsequent Islamic revolutionary movements, and tolerated the diverse religious and social practices of its Soninke, Malinke and Wolof subjects. Located in the Upper Senegal and with access to the Upper Gambia, Bundu played a critical role in regional commerce and production and reacted quickly to the stimulus of European trade.

Drawing upon a wide range of sources both oral and documentary, Arabic, English and French, Dr Gomez provides the first full account of Bundu's history. He analyses the foundation and growth of an Islamic state at a cross roads between the Saharan and trans-Atlantic trade, paying particular attention to the relationship between Islamic thought and court policy, and to the state's response to militant Islam in the early nineteenth century.

PRAGMATISM IN THE AGE OF JIHAD

AFRICAN STUDIES SERIES 75

GENERAL EDITOR
J. M. Lonsdale, *Lecturer in History and Fellow of Trinity College, Cambridge*

ADVISORY EDITORS
J. D. Y. Peel, *Professor of Anthropology and Sociology, with special reference to Africa, School of Oriental and African Studies, University of London*
John Sender, *Lecturer in Economics, School of Oriental and African Studies, University of London*

Published in collaboration with
THE AFRICAN STUDIES CENTRE, CAMBRIDGE

AFRICAN STUDIES SERIES

A list of books in this series will be found at the end of this volume

PRAGMATISM IN THE AGE OF JIHAD

The precolonial state of Bundu

MICHAEL A. GOMEZ
Department of History, Spelman College, Atlanta

Published by the Press Syndicate of the University of Cambridge
The Pitt Building, Trumpington Street, Cambridge CB2 1RP
40 West 20th Street, New York, NY 10011–4211, USA
10 Stamford Road, Oakleigh, Victoria 3166, Australia

© Cambridge University Press 1992

First published 1992

Printed in Great Britain at the University Press, Cambridge

A catalogue record for this book is available from the British Library

Library of Congress cataloguing in publication data
Gomez, Michael Angelo, 1955–
Pragmatism in the age of Jihad: the precolonial state of Bundu / Michael A. Gomez.
  p. cm. – (African studies series)
Includes bibliographical references.
ISBN 0 521 41940 9 (hardback)
1. Boundou (Senegal) – History. I. Title. II. Series.
DT549.9.B68G66 1992
966.3 – dc20 91-43273 CIP

ISBN 0 521 41940 9 hardback

CE

To Samuel Williams, Sr. (1946–86).
Beloved friend and uncle.
May God grant you peace.

Contents

	List of maps	page x
	Acknowledgements	xi
	List of abbreviations	xii
	Notes on spelling	xiii
1	Introduction	1
2	Malik Sy and the origins of a pragmatic polity	32
3	Consolidation and expansion in the eighteenth century	52
4	External reforms and internal consequences: Futa Toro and Bundu	74
5	The reassertion of Sissibe integrity	86
6	Structure of the Bundunke almaamate	100
7	Struggle for the Upper Senegal Valley	110
8	Al-hajj Umar in Bundu	120
9	The age of Bokar Saada	137
10	Mamadu Lamine and the demise of Bundu	152
11	Conclusion	175
	Appendices	183
	Notes	199
	Bibliography	230
	Index	241

Maps

1. Western Sudan and western Sahara in the eighteenth century *page* 18
2. Bundunke towns in the nineteenth century 94
3. Areas inside Bundu in the late nineteenth century 102
4. Regional perspective in the nineteenth century 139

Based on drawings by Jeff McMichael, Department of Geography, Georgia State University

Acknowledgements

The journey towards this publication began in graduate school, and I am grateful to God that the work has now come to fruition. I should like to acknowledge a few individuals who provided help along the way. Ralph Austen served as my principal advisor and has been very supportive throughout. John Hunwick and Fred Donner were also very helpful. John Works and David Robinson agreed to read progressive drafts of the manuscript, and I thank them for their input. While Philip Curtin did not read the manuscript, my exchanges and correspondence with him were always instructive.

On the other side of the Atlantic, Boubacar Barry was gracious to a fault in his hospitality and assistance. I thank all of my informants and interpreters, especially the very charming M. Issaga Opa Sy. Thanks in particular to Moussa Diallo, Lassana Malo Diallo, Boubacar Diop, Moussa Camara, and Ni Van Nguyen, who helped me during my first trip to Bakel.

This project would not have been possible without a 1987-88 Fulbright postdoctoral award through the Council for International Exchange of Scholars. Funding for earlier trips was provided by the CIC Fellowship Program in 1984 and a Washington University (in St. Louis) Overseas Research Grant in 1986.

Finally, my family's encouragement and patience have meant everything. My wife Mary (who accompanied me twice); my daughters Sonya, Candace, and Jamila; my mother, father, and grandparents and my Aunt Bonnie were all magnificent. I am particularly indebted to my Uncle Larry for his generosity, example, and lifelong support. May God richly bless you all.

Abbreviations

ANF	Archives nationales de la France, Paris
ANF-OM	Archives nationales de la France, section outre-mer, Paris
ANS	Archives nationales du Sénégal, Dakar
BCEHSAOF	Bulletin du Comité d'Etudes Historiques et Scientifiques de l'Afrique Occidentale Française
BIFAN	Bulletin de l'Institut Fondamental d'Afrique Noire, Dakar
BSOAS	Bulletin of the School of Oriental and African Studies, London
CC	Curtin Collection of Oral Traditions of Bundu and Gajaaga
CEA	Cahiers d'Etudes Africaines
FC	Fonds Curtin
IJAHS	International Journal of African Historical Studies
JAH	Journal of African History
JHSN	Journal of the Historical Society of Nigeria
NAG	National Archives of the Gambia, Banjul
PRO	Public Record Office, London
RHCF	Revue de l'Histoire des Colonies Françaises
Supplement	Philip C. Curtin, Economic Change in Precolonial Africa (Madison, 1972), Volume 2.

Notes on spelling

Concerning place names, the designations of various states are anglicized. However, in an effort to avoid confusion, the names of Bundunke towns, villages, and areas within Bundu retain their French form, in conformity with the maps of the Institut géographique national.

The names of all living people, or of those who have recently died, are spelled as the individuals themselves spell them. With regard to historical figures, the Pulaar, Malinke, or Soninke forms are used, except when an individual is more widely recognized by the purely Arabic designation. Thus, the Arabic form is employed for *al-ḥājj* Umar, while the Pulaarized "Bokar Saada" is used instead of Abu Bakr Sa'd. Proper names are unaccompanied by diacritical marks.

The plural forms of all Arabic nouns are anglicized (e.g., *imāms* or *jihāds*). Adjectives derived from Arabic terms are simply anglicized without italicization (e.g., jihadists).

1
Introduction

West Africa in the eighteenth and nineteenth centuries witnessed the eruption of several major "holy wars" across the wide expanse of its savannah, from the Senegal River to Lake Chad. Each holy war, or *jihād*, represented the emerging interests of a militant, rural Islamic community, and resulted in both substantial conversion of the peasantry and widespread social change. The leaders of the holy wars were renowned clerics who were committed to the comprehensive Islamization of their respective societies; that is, they endeavored to bring government and social order into conformity with Islamic law (*sharīʿa*). While these movements constitute a dominant theme during this period, it is important to note that there were concurrent exceptions to these expressions of militant Islam. The Kunta religious scholars (*shaykhs*) are one example, as they provided leadership for the Qadiriyya brotherhood (*ṭarīqa*) from their base near Timbuktu, and used that influence to support the descendants of one jihadist (Amadu Sheku of Maasina) against the claims of another (*al-ḥājj* Umar). A second example can be found in the policies of the clerical leader al-Kanemi of Bornu, who militantly opposed the expansion of the Sokoto Caliphate in the name of holy war.

The polity of Bundu, located in what is now eastern Senegal along the border with Mali, also ran counter to the grain of jihadic activity. Established in the late seventeenth century, and ostensibly maintaining its form of government until 1905, Bundu was the creation of the confluent or convergent forces of Islam and commerce in Senegambia, but its particular synthesis is unique for its regional and historical context. This is because it was established by Muslim clerics during the jihadic phase as a land of Islam; yet, this was not achieved through the vehicle of holy war. And although the clerical leadership of the state was rural, its behavior more closely approximated that of urbanized clerics. As a result, the principal factor in the development of state policy was that of pragmatism. As it applies to Bundu, this concept must be understood within the context of Senegambian developments from the late seventeenth through the nineteenth centuries, and it relates to both external and internal affairs of state. Regarding the former, pragmatism is a policy in which the pursuit of commercial and agricultural advantage supercedes all other considerations, to the extent that alliances and rivalries with both neighboring polities and European powers are determined by economic expediency, and are subject to rapid and frequent realignment. Foreign policy is not formulated on the basis of advancing the claims of Islam within the region. Concerning domestic affairs, pragmatism promotes a climate of tolerance towards non-Muslims, and seeks neither their conversion nor the rigid implementation of Islamic law in the governance of the ascendant Muslim constituency.

There are several reasons for the emergence of Bundu as a rural yet pragmatic Islamic society within the dominant context of rural, militant Islam. One has to do with the circumstances surrounding its origins, and the character of the individuals associated with its founding. A second cause concerns the nature of the territory itself, as it assumed a frontier-like quality over which it was difficult to impose a normative set of ideological guidelines. These are factors which will be investigated more fully in chapters 2 and 3. But the more salient reason for the moderate posture of the Bundunke *almaamies* (the plural of the dynastic title *almaami*, itself a Pulaarized form of the Arabic *imām*), and one that can be partially addressed at this juncture, was the crucial importance of both commerce and related agricultural productivity. That is, the fortunes of the Bundunke state were so tied to the successful conduct of trade and cultivation of crops (for internal consumption and export), that in their collective wisdom, the Bundunke rulers determined that pragmatism was essential to the state's well-being. Militant Islam represented change, disruption, and uncertainty, and was therefore eschewed.

The role of commerce is of particular importance to the development of Bundu. Indeed, the overall theme of trade is inextricably interwoven into the fabric of West African Islam. Trading networks, established before the introduction of Islam into West Africa *c.* 800 C.E., were expanded during Islam's early development. The forest, savannah, and desert zones became more extensively interconnected, as the majority of long-distance traders were Muslims. The Juula merchants were the principal agents of exchange from the savannah to the forest, and from Senegambia to the Upper Niger Valley. The regional market provided for the exchange of such commodities as salt, cattle products, cereals, fish, and shea butter. Gold and cotton textiles were also among the more sought-after items. The North–South axis, linking West Africa to the Maghrib (North Africa) and beyond, was particularly lucrative. The legendary grandeur of Mali, Songhay, and Kanem-Bornu was to a large extent the consequence of the northern focus of the Sudanic empires' trading policies.

The coming of the European gradually affected this commercial activity. Beginning in the fifteenth century, European merchants established a series of trading posts or factories along the West African coast. By the late seventeenth and early eighteenth centuries, the Atlantic frontier was in competition with the Sahara as a principal medium of West African international trade. The procurement and exportation of human cargo was a primary industry, but Europe was also interested in such raw materials as gum and beeswax. In exchange, Africans imported firearms, gunpowder, iron, textiles (especially Indian cloth), rum and brandy, horses, brassware, silver, glass beads, and semiprecious stones. As a result of the growth of the Atlantic commercial frontier, new trading networks were established along East–West axes, co-existing with the older routes leading to the Maghrib. New towns evolved into new states, stimulated by both transatlantic and transsaharan exchange. In fact, it is possible to argue that several of the *jihāds* of the eighteenth and nineteenth centuries were either directly or indirectly encouraged by the emergent Atlantic frontier.

Bundu was strategically important to both the Atlantic and Saharan commercial frontiers. While it was a major supplier of rice, maize, sorghum, millet, indigo, and cotton in the Upper Senegal Valley, its principal attribute was its location relative to both the sahel (*sāḥil* or "shore," where the Sahara and the savannah meet) and the Atlantic. Bundu maintained a series of trade routes, over which local products were exported, and across which resources and products of adjacent polities passed en route to either the Maghrib or to the European factories along the coast. To the immediate east of Bundu, across the Faleme, lay the fabled goldfields of Bambuk. Further east was Kaarta, to which the salt of the Saharan regions of the Tagant and the Hodh was carried for subsequent distribution in the savannah. Still further east was the Upper Niger Valley, with its renowned commercial centers such as Segu, Jenne, and Timbuktu. European powers repeatedly attempted to establish ties with both Bambuk and the Niger floodplain well into the nineteenth century, convinced that these areas contained immeasurable wealth, principally in gold. Towards the end of the nineteenth century, peaceful overtures were superceded by military conquests. Up until that point, Bundu was an important gateway to the east. The success of trading expeditions, whether heading east or west, depended upon the good favor of the Bundunke *almaamies* and their ability to preserve order and tranquility throughout the realm.

Another aspect of Bundu's strategic importance was that its northern and southern reaches straddled the Upper Senegal and Gambia Rivers. Kola was cultivated in the densely forested territories astride the Upper Gambia, an important element in the pursuit of religion, medicine, and social etiquette throughout Muslim West Africa. The trade in kola from the Gambia north into the sahel necessarily passed through Bundu in great measure, and reinforced its key role in the commerce of Senegambia. The introduction of groundnut cultivation along the Upper Gambia towards the middle of the nineteenth century would further stimulate Bundu's interest in the area. In time, the Senegal and Gambia Rivers would become the exclusive preserves of the French and the British respectively. Bundu was critical to both powers in their determination to dominate Senegambian trade, and Bundu would continually seek to exploit their rivalry.

Pragmatism in the age of Jihad

In light of the foregoing, it can be argued that Bundu, together with Futa Jallon and Futa Toro, were in fact novel West African experiments in Islamic government. For while Takrur and Silla (in the Lower Senegal Valley) were militant Muslim polities in the eleventh and twelfth centuries, they were not led by clerics, and were a consequence of the Almoravid movement, as opposed to representing the culmination of autochthonous concerns. Similarly, reformers such as *Askia* Muhammad Ture of Songhay, *Sarki* Muhammad Korrau of Katsina, and *Mai* Dunama Dibbalemi of Kanem tended to limit their efforts to the confines of court life, and in any event their reforms did not affect the larger society. There emerged in Bundu and the two Futas, however, for the first time in West African history, subsaharan Islamic governments administered by clerics and resulting in, by the late eighteenth century, overwhelmingly Muslim societies. The creation of the Bundunke experiment was assisted by elements in both Futa Toro and Futa Jallon, with which the Bundunke leadership enjoyed familial and religious ties. The fledgling Bundunke state would in the course of the eighteenth century repeatedly require the aid of the two Futas to survive various crises. In turn, the success of Bundu as an Islamic polity did not escape the attention of reformers in the Futas, and possibly contributed to their eventual decision to perform *jihād* in their respective homelands.

Notwithstanding the foregoing, the rise of militant Islam in Senegambia, first in Futa Jallon in the 1720s, next in Futa Toro in the 1760s, and then under the leadership of *al-ḥājj* Umar in the mid-nineteenth century, presented a conundrum for the Bundunke rulers. Intent upon maintaining an atmosphere conducive to the uninterrupted flow of commerce, Bundu could not afford the disruption that would inevitably follow the attempt to implement Islamic law throughout its environs. At the same time, the state could not insulate its constituency from the penetration of powerful and persuasive views emanating from the militant reformers of the two Futas. As a result, Bundu would experience considerable social and political upheaval during the ascendancy of Abdul Qadir and *al-ḥājj* Umar, who both intervene directly in Bundu's internal affairs. In each instance, the fervor for reform within Bundu will dissipate with the decline of either man's fortunes. The ephemeral nature of militant activity in Bundu strongly suggests that, although there were those who were genuinely committed to reform as defined by the movements in the Futas and Maasina, there was no ongoing, self-sustaining tradition of reform within Bundu itself. The majority of the ruling elite subscribed to the policy of pragmatism. However, the involvement of both Abdul Qadir and *al-ḥājj* Umar in Bundu would have lasting repercussions for the polity's social and political order. Relations between the two ruling branches would become severely strained in the aftermath of Abdul Qadir's tenure. Power and succession struggles between the two branches would also find expression in divergent economic policies. In time, these differences would result in regional divisions within the state itself, as the two camps underwent a physical polarization consonant with their distinct interests.

Further complicating the internal schisms within Bundu was the intense competition among indigenous states for control of the Upper Senegal Valley's commerce. Bundu's alliances reflected the frequent changes in the political fortunes of the various states; at times those alliances were politically expedient but religiously unpalatable. Eventually the Bundunke political fabric tore at the seams: two civil wars and unending external hostilities were among the consequences.

Moving to the late nineteenth century, Bundu would be directly affected by the reform movement of Mamadu Lamine. Having suffered through the ravages of war under *al-ḥājj* Umar, Bundu was simply unable to withstand another all-consuming conflict. The devastation of the Lamine period brought the era of Bundu's significance to an end.

Precedents exist in both the Islamic and African contexts for the factional disputes which characterized Bundu's history. In Islam, there is the example of the Alfaya and Soriya ruling branches of Futa Jallon, representing the moderate and militant camps respectively. In like manner, the history of late nineteenth-century Kaarta represents a variation of the same theme, as "war" and "peace" parties emerged according to divergent economic interests, culminating in internecine warfare among the offspring of *al-ḥājj* Umar. The central Islamic world also provides an example in the form of eleventh/twelfth century Nishapur. There, the seemingly religiously motivated Hanafi–Shafi'i struggle was actually more of a political conflict. Finally, the competing commercial claims of European powers operating within Senegambia dramatically affected the Bundunke state. John Yoder has demonstrated that nineteenth century Dahomey also experienced the consequences of shifting British trade policies, which resulted in intensified factional strife.[1]

Secondary literature

For the purposes of this study, secondary literature is to be distinguished from primary information in that the former is compiled by scholars who are not themselves witnesses to any of the events they describe, nor did they live during the time of said events. Their approach to the subject matter is within the parameters of modern social scientific inquiry. In contrast, primary data is that information left by either the participants, their descendants, or those collectors who witnessed some aspect of the history they purport to narrate. With this distinction in mind, the present monograph is the first comprehensive analysis of Bundu's history. There are, however, several studies which relate to Bundu and its involvement in both regional and Islamic developments. The most recent and important is the work of Boubacar Barry (1988) on the region of Senegambia, a cogent examination of those political, economic, social and religious forces which coalesced to bind the region together via a shared historical experience. Barry's emphasis on the deleterious effects of the Atlantic commercial frontier's emergence is related to his dissatisfaction with the earlier work of Philip D. Curtin (1975), itself a study of commercial activity in Senegambia that tends to ignore Europe's culpability in the underdevelopment of the region. A critical issue concerns the relative importance and impact of the slave trade in the region, for which Barry allows a much more prominent role than Curtin. Abdoulaye Bathily's work on Gajaaga (1989) is in some sense also a rejoinder to Curtin's inadequate treatment of the regional slave trade, and in any event is a significant contribution to the monographic materials. Cissoko Sékéné-Mody has likewise made a study of the regional role of Khasso (1986). Useful theses at the monographic level include those of John Hanson (1989) on Kaarta, and Abdel Wedoud ould Cheikh on Mauritania (1985).

Beyond political syntheses and works focusing on individual polities, there are the studies of the Jakhanke (Malinke clerical communities), who maintained an extensive presence in Bundu. Lamin Sanneh (1979), Thomas Hunter (Ph.D. thesis, 1979), and Pierre Smith (1968) have all worked on the Jakhanke within Bundu, and Curtin has also published his findings concerning their activities (1971).

The larger theme of Islam has benefited from the recent discussion of rural-versus-urban categories by Nehemia Levtzion (1987), which provides a useful framework for the present study. Regarding the impact of the eighteenth and nineteenth century jihadists on developments within Bundu, Robinson (1985; 1975), Bathily (1989; 1970), Saint-Martin (1970), and Nyambarza (1969) are the most germane. However, an adequate analysis of the Futa Jallon *jihād* has yet to appear, to the detriment of all scholarly activity relating to Senegambia.

Primary sources

This section will initially focus on categorizing the various types of sources available for the history of Bundu, and will essentially be descriptive in nature. Upon completion of an adequate framework of organization, an analysis of the reliability of the sources will follow. The discussion at this juncture will turn upon such matters as the conditions of transmission and the period of collection of information, as these issues directly impact upon the utility of the data base.

In his work on *al-ḥājj* Umar, Robinson has effectively demonstrated the need to categorize primary materials with regard to their relative proximity to the subject matter.[2] That is, documents, whether oral or written, should be distinguished on the basis of whether they represent the indigenous perspective, or whether they are the observations of non-participatory witnesses. The resulting divisions of internal, external, and "mixed" bodies of information are much more useful to a critical analysis of the data than the customary dichotomy of oral and written sources, often a false (or at least misleading) distinction. In view of this persuasive approach to source materials, I have divided the primary sources on Bundu into endogenous, exogenous, and intermediate genres. Endogenous materials include indigenous Arabic documents and oral recordings, the latter ranging from interviews with informants of varying social backgrounds, to the highly stylized accounts of oral historians. Also included in this category are the traditions of singular episodes or individuals found within traveler accounts. In such cases, the traditions stand out in bold relief vis-a-vis the preceding and ensuing text – the recorder has simply written down the tradition. Any personal commentary is duly noted, and is easily dissociated from the tradition itself. The time frame is not a determinant in selecting the data for this category, as it all tends to reflect the view (collective, individual, or elitist) of the Bundunkobe ("people of Bundu").

Exogenous documents concern the observations of individuals from outside of the community in question, who do not attempt to represent that community's historical self-perception; rather, such individuals seek only to report on the community as external, non-participatory witnesses. This category is largely filled by French materials, consisting of reports filed by people either passing through Bundu on special assignment, or by officials residing in such fortified posts as Bakel and Senoudebou. Although necessarily informed by members of the community, the documents of this genre nevertheless reflect the opinion, assessment, and conclusions of the external observer, with all of the attendant problems of bias, ignorance, and misinformation which are a matter of course.

The intermediate variety of source materials is the most challenging in that it consists of witnesses who have both recorded local accounts of historical events, and who have then proceeded to complement that data with either exogenous materials, their personal observations, or both. An attempt is made to investigate persons or events from a variety of informants, and to then present their statements in synthesized form. The obvious problem concerns the process of separating the original transmission from the subsequent reflections of the recorder. In some instances the recorder clearly indicates when he is adding his own commentary. In all cases it is necessary to compare these traditions with others of the same type, and with those of the endogenous genre, to achieve a sufficient level of control. Differences between intermediate and endogenous traditions are overwhelmingly the result of varying times and conditions of transmission. Singular traditions, either uncorroborated or at variance with the view presented by a preponderance of other primary sources, must necessarily be approached with great caution.

Andre Rançon (1894) is by far the most prominent example of this genre. His ethnography of Bundu has been critical to any subsequent study of the area. In addition to Rançon, the records of Moussa Kamara, the early twentieth century scholar of Futa Toro, must also be placed into this category. More will be said about these two individuals later.

Endogenous materials. The relative scarcity of clerical writings on Bundu's history suggests that the Bundunkobe regard their history as the proper preserve of oral historians, or *griots*, of whom the *awlube* (s. *gawlo*) are principal in Bundu. This is entirely consistent with a widespread, time-honored conviction throughout subsaharan Africa that the past is to be experienced and relived through the spoken word.[3] Indeed, the past expressed orally is shared by all, whereas the written word has certain mystical properties understood by only a select few.[4] The use of letters is consequently often limited to areas such as religious legal texts and amulets (protective charms). With this in mind, the first one hundred years or so of Bundu's existence is largely revealed through oral sources.

The oral materials of the endogenous variety were recorded for posterity in various languages, including Pulaar, Soninke, and French. The earliest accounts derive from European travelers passing through the area, who took an interest in the Bundunkobe, and proceeded to record traditions of singular events or persons, especially those revolving around the probable founder of the Bundunke state, Malik Sy (d. *c.* 1699). The first to do this in any systematic way was Anne Raffenel (1847; 1843), who was followed by Carrère and Holle (1855). Although their accounts are brief and their sources unspecified, what they have written is very consistent with later, better substantiated collections. Two additional collections were made just prior to the colonial era: Bérenger-Feraud (1885), and Diakité (published in 1929, but gathered in 1891). During the colonial period, four more collections of oral data were accomplished: Adam (1904), Djibril Ly (1938), Brigaud (1962), and Dieng Doudou (quoted in Brigaud). Finally, the postcolonial period saw the assembly of two collections: Curtin (1966) and Alfa Ibrahim Sow (1968).

It is not always known where the traditions were recorded, nor from whom they were taken.[5] Curtin's collection was for the most part made in Bundu, with some interviews held in Saint Louis, Bakel, and Dakar. His data cover a wide range of topics over a vast period of time. Interviews were conducted in Pulaar, Soninke, and Malinke with informants from a variety of social strata: *awlube*, clerics, Sissibe (descendants of Malik Sy and the ruling dynasty of Bundu), and members of traditional occupational castes (e.g., a leather worker, or *gayahke*). The informants were all celebrated for their knowledge of the Bundunke past. Curtin is careful to give the status of his informants and the circumstances of the interviews. Many of his informants were well advanced in age (some of their parents were either eyewitnesses of or participants in the wars of Mamadu Lamine towards the end of the nineteenth century), but the problem of senility is never encountered, whereas faulty memories can be assisted with other, more established materials. The basic form of the accounts was a presentation lasting from ten minutes to one hour; the *awlube* were accompanied by the *hoodu* (musical instrument in Fulbe areas) or the *kora* (in Malinke-speaking areas).

Of the precolonial accounts, Mamadou Aissa Kaba Diakité was a Soninke cleric living in Nioro, and was descended from a family originally living in the Bakel area.[6] He himself is a source, his accounts having been produced at the request of a Commander Claude in the *cercle* of Nioro in 1891. Ten years later, at the age of 36, Diakité recounted the story of Malik Sy to Adam, so that both of these sources hail from outside of Bundu.[7] For the colonial collection, the account of Djibril Ly originated from Futa Toro, where he was the principal interpreter at Kaedi.[8] In contrast, Brigaud was informed by Sy Amadou Isaaga, a grandson of Abdul Sega, one of Rançon's sources.[9] It is in Brigaud that we also find Dieng Doudou's account; nothing is said concerning Doudou's background.

As for my own 1984/87–88 collection of oral data, for which I spent eight months in Senegambia (and most of that time in Bundu itself), I approached informants with the conviction that the existing corpus of oral materials, collected by Rançon, Kamara, Curtin, and others, provides the larger, stylized, more sweeping accounts of the Bundunke past. I was therefore more interested in either accounting for the historical lacunae created by these collections, or with investigating specific, unresolved issues arising from said collections. All of my informants were associated with the court in one way or another, a reflection of the emphasis of my research at the time. For the most part, I confined my inquiries to the second half of the nineteenth century, and focused on the reign of Bokar Saada. At the same time, most of the Bundunkobe preferred to talk about Malik Sy, who retains a place of prominence in the Bundunke collective memory.

All of my interviews were conducted in French. In the large towns (e.g., Goudiry and Bakel), many informants spoke French, so that the need for an intermediary was minimal. However, in smaller villages such as Gabou and Kidira, intermediaries were indispensable. In the smaller villages, it was difficult to arrange exclusive sessions with informants – this was possibly the result of the brevity of my visits (two to three days on average), which tended to attract considerable attention. On the other hand, it was much easier to limit the number of people present during the interview in the larger towns, and the length of the sessions tended to be shorter due to the fact that many of the Sissibe hold important government posts and so maintain busy schedules. All of the sessions were tape-recorded, and complemented with written notes. The most useful interviews are listed in the bibliography.

The Bundunkobe express wariness in the matter of sharing their historical traditions with outsiders. In a number of villages and towns, it was remarked that others had preceded me, asking similar questions for similar purposes, never to be heard from again. It is therefore probable that these earlier experiences conditioned the responses of informants, especially in areas of heightened sensitivity. In particular, questions concerning Bokar Saada's relations with *al-ḥājj* Umar produced noticeable discomfort, even more so in cases where an associate of the court was answering queries in the presence of Sy family members. In some instances, individuals actually said that they did not know the answer to a given question; in others, informants were evasive. Given that such lines of inquiry constituted my primary interest, my own data is most effectively employed in conjunction with other supportive sources. Otherwise, in cases where there is conflict between my sources and the archival records, I have sided in most instances with the contemporary accounts. This decision is both in light of the preceding discussion, and for reasons which will become clear at subsequent points. A lack of confidence in some of my informants' replies has necessarily created the need to carefully distinguish between what informants said and what I deem credible.

The majority of Arabic documents retrieved from Bundu belong in the endogenous category, and are to be found in the *Fonds Curtin*. Interestingly, I uncovered no such documentation in the Fulbe towns of Bundu, with the exceptions of Senoudebou and Koussan. Even then, as was true of the various libraries in the Jakhanke villages of southern Bundu, the documentation consists primarily of genealogies and *tā'rīkhs* ("histories") of the Jakhanke clans, shedding little light on the larger Bundunke context, and in any event are represented in the *Fonds Curtin*.

The scarcity of Arabic documentation is a reflection of several factors. First, writing within the West African Muslim community tended to focus on matters of religion – treatises and commentaries; such matters were not of immense importance to the ruling elite of Bundu. Second, there is no evidence that much effort was expended to create records regarding tax revenues, judicial rulings, and the like. Third, even the Jakhanke Arabic documentation only dates back to the latter quarter of the nineteenth century, and most of it was written in the twentieth. The latter quarter of the nineteenth century in Bundu saw a great deal of destruction and ruin; Bundu was severely depopulated for significant stretches of time. The catastrophic experiences of the state could therefore also account for the absence of written records.

Notwithstanding the foregoing, some of the Arabic manuscripts are useful. Several concern the emigration of the Jakhanke to the Upper Gambia, following the flight and demise of Mamadu Lamine, and thus indirectly give some information on Bundu during this period. Other documents list Bundu's heads of state and their respective tenures in chronological order.

Exogenous materials. Most of the documentation in this category consists of archival records produced by European travelers and officials who made little attempt to transmit the indigenous view of Bundu's history or society, but who rather sought to record their own observations. To be sure, this involved the use of informants, but the substance of the reports clearly conveys the opinions and sentiments of the foreign observer, to the virtual exclusion of internal assessment and perspective. Such records become much more substantial, as would be expected, in the nineteenth century. With regard to traveler accounts, those of David (1744), Rubault (1786), and Mungo Park (1795) tend to be the more useful for the eighteenth century, as they do reveal somewhat careful observation of and interaction with the Bundunkobe. Mollien (1818), and Gray and Dochard (1818–19) also attempted to describe early nineteenth century Bundunke towns. None of these travelers, in either century, bothered to record local traditions.

In addition to traveler accounts, there also exists a body of reports on the Upper Senegal Valley by officers of French commercial and military posts. Prior to 1820, the French were able to monitor events in the Upper Senegal from their posts in Gajaaga (or Galam, directly north of Bundu along the Senegal River). With the establishment of French forts at Bakel (1820) and Senoudebou (1845), information reaching the French concerning activity within Bundu greatly increased. As was the case with the travel literature, much of the information obtained by the French posts was filtered through local agents. However, because an official would sometimes spend several years at a given post, he would be less dependent on the discretion of such sources than would someone simply passing through the area. The official could cultivate more substantial relationships, and come to a more refined appreciation of the politics and customs of the people. At the point that the official, or the traveler for that matter, began to record traditions to the degree that they are identifiably autochthonous, or began to create a synthesis of personal observation and internal perspective, is the point at which his contribution would be categorized as either endogenous or intermediate.

Intermediate materials. The sources in this category represent the first attempts to develop a coherent history of Bundu. Lamartiny (1884) and Roux (1893) produced brief narratives of Bundu's past, in which traditions and synthesis are interspersed. Of the two, Roux is the more important, having served as commander of the French fort at Bakel, during which time he conducted interviews. Concerning Lamartiny, it can be assumed that he spent some time gathering data in Bundu itself, since he was commissioned to write a monograph on Bundu by the Société de géographie commerciale de Paris. But Rançon's contribution to this genre is the most critical, as he toured the Upper Senegal and Gambia Valleys twice towards the end of the nineteenth century. He benefitted from the work of Roux and Lamartiny, citing them extensively, and combining their accounts with official reports emanating from the various posts of the Upper Senegal. But Rançon also collected oral data of his own, his principal source having been Abdul Sega, a Sissibe leader from Koussan in Bundu. The French ethnographer creates an encompassing blend of all these sources as he writes on the Bundunke past; he is also the first to discuss the larger Bundunke society and culture, in which some attention is given to the role of Islam. In short, his is a more complete picture of the whole.

Having stated the foregoing, it should be made clear that there are several serious shortcomings in Rançon's work. First of all, he has a tendency to uncritically accept the testimony of Lamartiny and Roux, and to even "borrow" numerous passages from their efforts without benefit of citation. This is important in that it reveals a mindset that is more interested in synthesis than analysis. By extension, it would follow that this uncritical attitude would be true of his approach to the reports of the trading posts.

Secondly, in discussing various aspects of eighteenth century Bundu, Rançon is quite unspecific about the precise mix of his sources. That is, in those passages in which it is evident that he is not conveying traditions as he received them, it is conversely no longer evident as to where he has obtained his information. From comparing such passages with Lamartiny, Roux, and other traveler accounts, it is possible to reduce the possibilities to either unpublished reports from the posts, or to anonymous informants. The problem at this point is distinguishing such sources from Rançon's own opinion.

Thirdly, as Rançon has taken it upon himself to render a detailed and complete historical statement, he fails to account for European commercial and political policies in the region (the latter a function of the former). We get little sense of the relationship between the metropole and the periphery, and therefore of how Senegambia in general, and Bundu in particular, are adversely affected by decisions made in Paris/London via Saint Louis/ Bathurst. There is no attempt to identify the forces which conspire to create the condition of underdevelopment in the region, of which Bundu is a part. Consequently, we witness the rise of the state in the early eighteenth century and its demise in the nineteenth, in the absence of any effort to explain these developments beyond the internal politics and issues of the region.

Finally, this category also features the important collection of oral data on Bundu by *Shaykh* Moussa Kamara of Futa Toro, which is contained in his *Zuhūr al-Basātīn fī Tā'rīkh al-Sawādīn* ("Flowers of the Gardens Concerning the History of the Blacks," 1924), and translated into French by N'Diaye (1975). Kamara (1864–1945) was a contemporary of the period, his family having maintained cooperative relations with the French. However, Kamara remained a son of the soil and a Muslim. He developed a principled stance against the waging of *jihād* (he is particularly critical of the effects of *al-ḥājj* Umar's campaigns), and declined an invitation to participate in the *jihād* of Mamadu Lamine. In his challenge to the reformist position, he would be especially interested in emphasizing the adverse impact of the various *jihāds* upon the Bundunke state. His account of these movements, and of the political factions within Bundu, must therefore be employed with care.

Kamara's overall work is a unique blend of traditional and, to a lesser extent, archival elements interpreted from the perspective of an indigenous scholar. On the basis of the analysis of his work elsewhere, it would appear that his reputation for integrity would preclude any deliberate falsification of the historical record. However, it is not always known from whom he received his information on Bundu, and it is not uncommon for his account of a particular period or person to be at considerable variance from the consensus of the other sources. One could surmise, then, that his section on Bundu was largely derived from a modicum of informants.[10]

The issue of reliability. All three types of source materials – endogenous,

Introduction

exogenous, and intermediate – must necessarily be examined for dependability. It is especially true of the endogenous and intermediate genres, and to a lesser extent the exogenous, that the question of reliability is in turn a function of at least three determinants: the purpose and perspective of the informant; the process and context of transmission; and the experience, orientation, and intent of the observer. The following comments are applicable to all of the sources consulted in this study, and serve as instruments by which the data can be properly and successfully utilized.

With regard to the first determinant, the purpose and perspective of the informant, information from the ruling circles would constitute the primary source from which the various categories were supplied. This source consisted of both members of the leading families, and more importantly those *awlube* for whom the elite served as patrons. The second category comprised the merchant community, which in the interest of maintaining cordial commercial ties with any and all trading partners (including the European *tubaab*, or "foreigner"), was probably the most accessible group for those seeking information. A third source of intelligence came from those Africans who were directly in the employ of colonial powers: those who fought in the Senegalese Riflemen's Corps under the command of French officers, and from whom, due to their outsider and humble status (many having formerly been slaves), only a minimum of reliable information could flow concerning the host society; and the interpreters, laborers, couriers, and others who served colonial administrators in the network of fortified trading posts. The first two categories of informants were consistently available to foreign observers throughout the history of Bundu, and supplied the preponderant amount of information on its development and society. Concerning the third type of informant, it is evident that those who served for extended periods of time at the fortified entrepots provided the more valuable insights into the surrounding area. This was especially true of the interpreter. Likewise, the testimony of the African soldier was of some utility in describing the wars of *al-ḥājj* Umar and Mamadu Lamine in the nineteenth century. Such testimony is of negligible value, however, in the matter of interpreting the policies of the Bundunke court.

A fourth type of informant concerns those descendants of eyewitnesses, who in my scheme qualify as primary sources. While these would operate at a disadvantage due to their displacement in time, that same displacement could to an extent liberate them from the need to present a certain class (or caste) view consistent with that of their ancestors.

In light of the above comments, these various categories of informants obviously did not constitute a monolithic community or coherent perspective. Their purposes and vantage points would necessarily differ. There were those who sought to put the best face on the activities of the rulers, and who deemed it appropriate to conceal those policies which may have caused friction with either the French or the British. These observations would expressly apply to the members of the Sissibe family, along with their closely associated clerical staff and *awlube*. Such matters qualifying for concealment would include trade agreements with alternative powers (i.e., Bundu sometimes sought to hide from the French the full extent of its commercial relations with the British). Such informants served as apologists for the moderate posture of the Bundunke rulers in any religious controversy, and would therefore be unreliable sources of information with regard to disputes between Bundunke Muslim factions during the periods of Abdul Qadir and *al-ḥājj* Umar. Due to their close association with the court, the *awlube* would not be able to discuss, or would at least be reticent to address, any politically sensitive issues with a sufficient degree of objectivity or forthrightness.

In sum, the ruling family members and attendant *awlube* and clerics could only reflect the values and vantage point of the minority ruling class, as opposed to the majority of the Bundunkobe, the herding and farming peasantry. The multiethnic character of the state also suffers from inadequate representation in the court-oriented sources, as the latter promoted the interests of the Fulbe. The use of non-Fulbe informants, several of whom were consulted by Curtin, and who are further represented in the data from Diakite and Adam, helps to balance such ethnocentricity, and serves as an important check on the views of the Sissibe.

The second criterion by which reliability is judged concerns the process by and context in which information is transferred. Concerning the process, a number of variables are therein operative and must be considered in assessing the validity of the data transfer. One variable would be the possibility of mistranslation, ranging from insignificant errors to serious inaccuracies, depending upon the skills of the interviewers and translators involved. A second variable concerns the deliberate alteration of the data by the recorder. Reasons for altering or tampering with received traditions would include the desire to create a favorable slant on a given event in order to promote an individual career; conversely, the uncovering of politically embarrassing information (to either the metropole or the individual) could also result in changes in the record. A third variable concerns the role of the informant, and involves the matter of misinformation, or selective transfer of information. In this instance, in order to protect the interests of the court, or to conceal embarrassing revelations, the informant either avoids full disclosure or declines to give a factual account. Finally, a fourth variable concerns the problem of human error. For any number of reasons (e.g., the recorder being ill on the day of an interview, or in a state of haste), the recorder could misplace the emphasis in a given account, or simply misrecord the data.

Regarding the context of transmission, while scholars tend to emphasize the penultimate transmission, i.e., the relay of data from the indigenous source to the recorder, the relay of information within the indigenous community over a period of time is just as critical in the determination of validity. Unfortunately, it is rarely possible to know the chain of attestors and, based upon that gauge, the veracity or authenticity of the tradition.

Given that this is necessarily so, one can only make certain qualified deductions about a particular set of traditions with respect to another such set collected during an earlier or subsequent time, or within a different setting. More specifically, in the absence of any insight into the identity or background of the informants, any differences between two sets of traditions concerning the same subject can either be attributed to a difference in the process or the time/space context, or both. In fact, with regard to context, it is reasonable to expect that social, political, and economic factors operating at the time of transmission will affect that transmission in such a way that wholly unrelated periods and aspects of history will suffer some distortion. A good example of this concerns the person of Malik Sy. With two exceptions, all of the traditions which speak of him range some 200 to almost 300 years after his death. The autocratic, ruthless, and duplicitous behavior of nineteenth century Bundunke rulers is projected back into the late seventeenth, where it is employed to characterize the conduct of Malik Sy. The truth is that very little is really known about Malik Sy's personality, so that the traditions seize upon contemporary models to fill the void. If used sagaciously, however, such traditions which purport to reveal the person of Malik Sy can tell us something about those in power during the time of transmission.

By the same token, one must be careful to identify those issues producing social tension or conflict at the time of data transfer. History is a powerful tool of affirmation or condemnation, and can be manipulated by the ruling elite to justify or legitimize its policies. This is accomplished by simply relocating the present conflict in an earlier context, within which it is resolved by esteemed ancestors in a way that is consistent with the contemporary policy. An example of this would be the story of Malik Sy's son and successor Bubu Malik Sy, and the building of "Kumba's well." Much more will be stated about this in chapter 3; suffice it to say that nineteenth century traditions make the claim that this particular well was made operational by Bubu Malik Sy, which within the cultural symbolism of the time meant that by this feat he had become the rightful owner of the land. This, in turn, indicates that there was considerable conflict between various groups over ownership of the land during the period of Bundu's expansion in the eighteenth century; hence, the need for extrapolation.

In addition to the purpose and perspective of the informant, and the process and context of transmission, the experience, orientation, and intent of the recorder is fundamental to assessing the reliability of the sources. It should be noted at the outset that the purpose of the French in producing the monographical material was to acquire data on the region in order to facilitate commerce (through the mid-nineteenth century) and to inform proto-colonial rule (from the mid-nineteenth century). In order to accomplish these objectives, it was important to understand something of the structure of indigenous governments, the location of major trade routes, and the nature of regional politics.

With such goals in mind, the French observer set out to study the region.

Most of these external investigators could not converse in the languages of the region. It will be argued here that the limitation to French translation has not, however, substantively diminished the credibility of the materials. Of greater concern was the reliance of some observers upon only one or two informants. This is obviously a constraint to developing a full picture of Bundu's past, or even a segment thereof. However, the multiplicity of versions bearing upon a given aspect of Bundunke history provides a requisite counterweight to such an imbalance.

Notwithstanding the aforementioned objectives, the ethnocentric (usually gallocentric) arrogance of many external observers, combined with an ignorance of Islam, led to such deliberate distortions in the process as the tendency to exaggerate the numerical forces of the anti-French armies in an effort to add to the victories of individual military commanders; the accounts of Gallieni and Frey are particularly suspect in this regard. More importantly, this tendentious approach has resulted in a number of adverse consequences for the study of Bundu, for which a scholastic remedy is difficult to achieve. To be more precise, these dual deficiencies of arrogance and ignorance created a mindset that evinced little interest in the issues and controversies associated with Islam in the area; or for that matter, in the social significance of Islam in general. Religious figures were viewed with great hostility, not for the simple reason that many such leaders eventually wound up fighting against the French, but also because the external observers were uneducated in Islam, so that they did not and could not understand the Muslim perspective. Furthermore, the limited view of such observers meant that they lacked the consciousness to investigate the policies of the Bundunke state, or those of neighboring states, with the result that Bundu's history is presented as a series of unrelated developments, episodic interludes, and spasmodic reactions to various stimuli from beyond Bundu's borders. From this view, the state has no clear political direction. Such historical writing fails to consider the long term development of the state. It also fails, as did Rançon, to ponder the devastating impact of metropolitan decisions upon the Senegambian economy and society over time.

Plan of utilization. In light of the foregoing discussion of reliability, it is clear that a careful assessment of the sources for this study is critical. For the period before the mid-nineteenth century, the principal sources are Rançon, Kamara, Roux, Diakité, Lamartiny, and Curtin. After this period, data from the trading posts, in addition to Frey and Gallieni, serve to supplement the accounts of Kamara and Rançon. My own interviews are used to both corroborate existing accounts and to fill the voids they create.

With regard to informants, the preponderance of the information on the pre-1850 period reflects the views and interests of the ruling elite; non-Fulbe groups do not have much voice, and the peasantry is rarely discussed. Consequently, the non-court perspective must either be deduced from the court-centered materials of Rançon and Roux, or derived from the compilations of Diakité, Adam, and Curtin. A careful treatment of Kamara, given

Introduction

his probable preference for the more moderate faction in Bundunke politics, yields additional insight into the politics of the court. Post-1850 data emanate from more diverse sources, such as trading agents and those in the employ of the French, and therefore help to balance the Sy-oriented view so consistently represented by Rançon.

Concerning the process and context of transmission, it should be assumed that one or more variables of the process have influenced all genres of sources: endogenous, intermediate, and exogenous. Further, varying contexts have resulted in differing versions of the same events. In order to successfully use the sources, therefore, it is necessary to approach them with the goal of determining consensus, plausibility, and internal logic. Accounts exhibiting high levels in all three categories can be viewed as relatively reliable, as will be demonstrated in the discussion of Malik Sy and Bubu Malik Sy. Given the greater number of contemporary accounts after the mid-nineteenth century, the variable of context diminishes as a factor. However, corroboration among as many sources as possible remains essential to the establishing of factual accounts.

The intention and orientation of the recorder, as gallocentric and religiously uninformed as it is, affects all of the major sources. The counterweight to this problem can only be a reasoned speculation, drawing upon the geopolitical realities of the time, into the strategies of the Bundunke state and the role of Islam therein, thus compensating for the lack of such a perspective in the literature. However, intermediate and exogenous materials, particularly after the mid-nineteenth century, remain important sources for such data as the places and dates of military and political events.

Finally, it is unavoidable that certain events and scenarios will be premised upon the authority of singular accounts. In such instances, the likelihood and logic of the matter in question will play major roles in determining its potential significance.

The physical setting

The boundaries of Bundu were subject to both steady expansion during the eighteenth century and to frequent fluctuations in the nineteenth, so that its precise locality is somewhat elusive. During parts of the eighteenth century Bundu included territory beyond the eastern bank of the Faleme River, encroaching upon Bambuk. By the nineteenth century, however, the Faleme River had become the established boundary between Bundu and Bambuk. By the end of the nineteenth century, Bundu had reached the apex of its territorial expansion, having an estimated longitude of 12° 20' to 13° 30' west, and a latitude of 13° 12' to 14° 45' north.[11] Measuring 190 kilometers from east to west, and 170 kilometers from north to south, Bundu contained a surface area of almost 33,000 sq. km. Bounded on the east by the Faleme, the Senegal River from Tiyaabu to the Faleme confluence provided the northern limit. To the west lay the vast Ferlo area, a mostly dry plain

Pragmatism in the age of Jihad

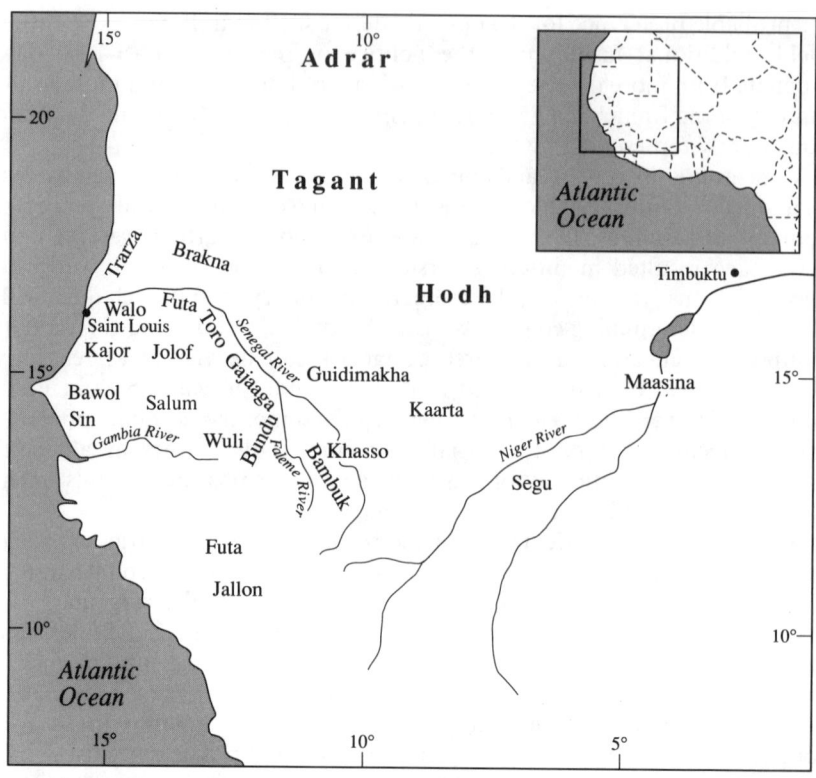

Map 1 Western Sudan and western Sahara in the eighteenth century

sparsely occupied by trees and shrubs. The southern reaches of the realm would either expand or contract according to the political fortunes of the state, but they never extended beyond the kingdoms of the Upper Gambia.

The reference to Bundu's southern border indicates that while the northern and eastern perimeters were relatively stable, most of the state's growth beyond the eighteenth century took place at the expense of peoples further south. This observation suggests the existence of a core area and a periphery. Roughly speaking, Bundu's core extended from Gabou in the north to Didecoto to the south, and from the Faleme in the east to the Ferlo in the west. The eastern sector of the core was the polity's agricultural focus, although at various times this sector also served as the site of the court. Beyond this lay a combination of tributary states (to the south) and largely wasteland (to the west), over which Bundu exercised fluctuating control throughout the nineteenth century. To the north, the important Soninke entrepot of Bakel experienced pressures from Bundu, but was never fully integrated into the state or under its firm control.

Surrounding Bundu were a number of states of varying size and power, which were more or less involved in the politics of the Upper Senegal. To the immediate north, along the banks of the Senegal River, were the Soninke states of Gajaaga (Galam) and Guidimakha. Gajaaga, to the south of the Senegal, was of considerable antiquity, and was a collection of relatively sizeable commercial towns along with smaller centers of political authority. The political centers were controlled by the warrior class, over which ruled a king (*Tunka*) from the Bacili clan. Merchants held power in the trading centers, and from their profits they accumulated large holdings in cattle, land, and slaves. With regard to religion, the Soninke boasted of well-established clerical lineages. Mosques and schools were financed by the merchants, who were Juula (and therefore Muslim). Concerning Guidimakha, it lay north of the Senegal, and its inhabitants were nominally Muslim. Guidimakha was sparsely populated by agriculturalists, although trade villages were also present. There was no central government, a fact which contributed to Guidimakha's inability to defend itself from the raids of the Moors.

The Moors were to the north of the Soninke states, in what is now southern Mauritania. They were principally engaged in pastoralism and trade. By the end of the seventeenth century, the Banu Maghfar had established both the Trarza emirate (north of the Lower Senegal) and the Brakna emirate (north of the Middle Senegal), while the Banu Ma'quil had created an emirate in the Hodh area (to the north of Nioro). These polities, together with other parts of Senegambia, would fall under the influence of the Moroccan Sultan Mawlay Isma'il (reigned 1672–1727), an influence that would directly affect both Bundu and the reform movement in Futa Toro. Finally, the Idaw 'Aish would take control of the area between the Brakna and Hodh emirates in the last quarter of the eighteenth century.

It is sufficient here to note that the densely-populated Middle Senegal Valley was controlled by the Muslim Fulbe of Futa Toro, and that their involvement with Bundu was crucial, as will be demonstrated by subsequent investigation. Further to the east, the Lower Senegal had for centuries been the stronghold of the Wolof states: Jolof, Walo, Cayor (Kajor), and Baol (Bawol), which were largely non-Muslim until well into the nineteenth century. In contrast to Futa Toro, there is little evidence of significant relations between Bundu and the Wolof governments.

Turning to the east, between the Faleme and the Niger floodplain, several kingdoms would have a profound impact upon Upper Senegal developments. In particular, the partially Islamized Fulbe–Malinke kingdom of Khasso was significant. Straddling both banks of the end of the navigable Upper Senegal, Khasso placed a greater emphasis on agriculture and animal husbandry than commerce. The Fulbe dynasty, established by the seventeenth century, was eventually weakened by succession disputes, and was forced to witness the extension of Kaartan influence over its northern half. Only Medine and villages in its immediate vicinity remained firmly under the ruling family's control. Concerning the powerful, non-Muslim Bambara state of Kaarta, established by the Massassi in 1754, its interests and activities in Senegambia are fundamental to understanding the history of the region, and will be discussed in greater detail.

Bambuk, wedged between Bundu and Khasso, was a sparsely-populated but numerous series of small and autonomous villages inhabited by non-Muslim Mandinka. The mountainous terrain provided ideal havens of refuge for political outcasts, absconded slaves, and other asylum-seekers. The Bambuk states were never able to forge an effective alliance among themselves, and were thus prey to the more powerful polities throughout the eighteenth and nineteenth centuries. The availability of gold at or near surface level allowed for labor-intensive mining during the dry season, and helped to compensate for the poverty of the soil.

Further to the south, well beyond the Upper Gambia, was the large, Islamically militant Futa Jallon empire, nestled in the highlands of what is now Guinea.[12] Relations between Bundu and Futa Jallon were extensive, and will receive subsequent treatment, as the two states periodically coordinated their foreign policies, especially in the matter of exploiting the Malinke lands of Wuli and Tenda in the Upper Gambia. These territories were in effect caught in a vise, between Bundu in the north and Futa Jallon in the south, with the former exercising greater control over the embattled area.

The founders of the state of Bundu were quite astute in selecting the site of their new polity. Bundu was placed at the very core of Senegambia, and hence at the center of the region's commercial nexus. A significant proportion of the region's trade, conducted both internally and with the English and the French, would necessarily flow through Bundu. The merchants of Bambuk, Khasso, Kaarta, and the Upper Niger, in trading with the Upper Gambia or the Middle Senegal and points further west, traveled in large measure through Bundu, and vice-versa. The Soninke of Gajaaga and Guidimakha, in their commercially reciprocal relations with the Malinke of the Upper Gambia, maintained those relations largely via Bundunke territory. Therefore, as a consequence of its very location, the economic imperative that would shape Bundu's government policy was all but inescapable.

Traveling through Bundu in December of 1795, Mungo Park observed: "Bundu, in particular, may literally be pronounced 'a land flowing with milk and honey'."[13] Mollien passed through the area in 1818, remarking that the "kingdom is but one vast forest" resembling a bow.[14] In fact, Bundu is not a vast forest, but rather a land of four physically distinct zones. Towards the southern portion of the state, one experiences dense growth and undulating hills, along with extreme heat and humidity. As one proceeds from south to north, the land gradually flattens out into an increasingly sparsely covered plain, characterizing the central and northern sections of the realm, and constituting a single, second zone (in the north, towards the Senegal River, the land becomes somewhat hilly again, and the climate more arid). The third zone consists of the western portions of the state, towards the Ferlo, which increasingly assumes the placid character of that "wilderness" as it is approximated. This is in sharp contrast to the eastern fringes, along the Faleme and its tributaries, where the land is quite fertile and green with crops and trees. Startlingly picturesque, this fourth zone was clearly the productive center of Bundu.[15]

The Faleme River flows through Bundu for approximately 150 kilometers.[16] During the rainy season, boats are capable of navigating up the river from Falou Falls, but in the dry season, only lighter boats with flat bottoms, or canoes, can make the trip. Pascal, who explored Bambuk in 1859, said of Falou Falls: "The great trees which adorn its shores, the noise of the water that falls in cascades, and the rocks which obstruct its course, make this passage one of the most beautiful sites of the Faleme."[17]

The rainfall pattern for Senegambia changes dramatically from the Senegal River to the Casamance, and is a function of the Inter-Tropical Convergence Zone, itself a consequence of two other major air masses, the Tropical Maritime and the Tropical Continental.[18] As a result, the average rainfall for northern Bundu, 800 mm per year, is twice that of the Lower Senegal Valley (400 mm per year). In central Bundu the average is 900 mm, and in southern Bundu it reaches 1000 mm per annum. In the southern section of Bundu, the rains begin as early as the latter part of May, lasting until the beginning of November.[19] In northern Bundu, the rainy season is much shorter. This period is marked by daily storms and high winds, culminating in torrential downpours.

An important consequence of both the rainfall and the proximity to the Faleme is the production of a second annual crop.[20] The Faleme, as is the case with the Senegal, has its source in the Futa Jallon mountains, where the average rainfall is greater than 2,500 mm per year. These conditions insure a dependable water supply. With the onset of the annual rains, the river rises and floods the adjoining land; crops can be sown on that land, sustained by the residual water throughout the dry season. As a result, both rainfall and floodland agriculture are possible and productivity greatly enhanced.

In Bundu, the land used for rainfall cultivation is called *jeeri* or *seeno*, whereas floodland is referred to as *waalo*, usable in the dry season. In Bundu, the floodplain of the Faleme is narrower than that of the Middle Senegal, resulting in less *waalo*. But since rainfall in Bundu is greater, *jeeri* is more valuable, and much more economically vital. Whereas millet and sorghum were almost exclusively grown in the Middle Senegal, crops with longer growing seasons could be sown in Bundu: rice along the tributaries, maize, cotton, tobacco, and indigo.[21] On higher land groundnuts, sorghum and millet were cultivated. Western hemispheric crops such as maize, groundnuts, and tobacco were introduced into the area sometime before the 1720s, although millet remained the principal export crop until the mid-nineteenth century. Groundnuts were domestically consumed, and never approximated the level of production along the Upper Gambia after the mid-nineteenth century.[22] Bundu was also an important center of cotton production and weaving, and an exporter of raw and woven cotton; cotton was also used internally as currency.[23] Mollien and Gray, who both visited Bundu around the same time, mention these crops as well as watermelons, sorrel, onions, and pepper.[24] Both men also agree that the proportion of cultivated land was small.[25] In Bundu, as was basically true of Futa Toro, ownership of the land belonged to the man who first cleared it and made it productive, as well as to his descendants.[26]

Besides an occasional reference to "wild" and "ferocious" beasts abounding in Bundu, cattle and horses were raised domestically.[27] The horses were considered excellent, a mixture of "Arabian and African." Of course, the Middle Senegal was the center of the pastoral industry, and nomads were not as numerous as in Bundu.[28] But there was no impediment to breeding cattle in the area, especially in the absence of the tsetse fly.[29]

The people and society

Bundu's own traditions state that the Sissibe were not the original inhabitants of the land. Rather, they emigrated from Futa Toro to what would become Bundu, where they encountered existing communities of other ethnicities. The Sissibe were subsequently able to usurp political power and to expand their authority over the area. When Gray and Dochard visited Bundu in 1819, they found the population a mixture of "Foolahs, Mandings, Serrawollies, and Joloffs," with the culture and language of the first dominant.[30] That is, Bundu was an ethnically heterogeneous society made up of Fulbe, Malinke, Soninke, and Wolof elements. The *lingua franca* of the society was Pulaar, a member of the West Atlantic language family and closely related to Sereer and Wolof.[31]

The precise order in which the various ethnicities came to inhabit Bundu cannot be established with absolute clarity. The Malinke and Soninke populations certainly antedate the Fulbe in Bundu, and the Wolof clearly preceded the Sissibe. However, the Sissibe were only one of a number of Fulbe families which migrated from Futa Toro (and to a lesser extent Futa Jallon) to Bundu, and it is not certain that the Wolof preceded these other Fulbe groups (more will be said about these groups in chapter 2). Furthermore, various subgroups within the broader ethnic divisions continued to come and go over the centuries. As will be examined more thoroughly, these migrations were both rapid and gradual, and could be numerically substantial or insignificant, depending upon the causes of change. Given the particular period in question, the Fulbe population could be either greater or smaller than the others, but they always controlled the political fortunes of the state. The Jakhanke, those Manding clerical communities who followed the religious tradition of *al-ḥājj* Salim Suware (d. 1525), and who constituted an integral part of the realm, exercised a disproportionate level of economic and religious influence upon the society, as will be discussed.

The Fulbe as a distinct people apparently originated just above the sahel between Mauritania and Mali, and over the centuries migrated throughout the savannah of West Africa as far as the Lake Chad area. One of the areas they settled was the Middle Senegal Valley. The middle valley people refer to themselves as *Haalpulaar'en* (s. *Haalpulaar*, "speaker of Pulaar"), whether they are pastoralists or cultivators. It was the nineteenth century French ethnographers who divided these people into distinct groups: the largely non-Muslim pastoralists were called "Peuls," while the mostly Muslim agriculturalists were referred to as "Toucouleur." English travelers to the Sokoto Caliphate (in present-day Nigeria) adopted the Hausa word for the Fulbe there, "Fulani," while the English in the Gambia used the word "Fula," a Malinke loan. The result was that four terms were being employed to refer to essentially the same ethnic group, with English scholars adopting the French designations, and vice-versa.

Senegambian societies were as a rule highly stratified, and Bundu was no exception. The various ethnicities both within and without Bundu mirrored one another in the almost ubiquitous tripartite division of their societies. It should therefore be kept in mind that, with the exceptions of religion and inheritance practices, the following discussion of the Fulbe is also applicable to the social organization of the Soninke, the Malinke, and the Wolof alike.

Fulbe society was divided into the free men (Pulaar, *riimbe*), the caste groups (*neenbe*), and the slaves (*maacube*).[32] Numerous substrata existed within the three major categories and, in general, those at the top of the caste and servile categories possessed greater wealth and power than did those in the lower levels of the *riimbe* classification. Being "free," then, was simply a "zero point," a ground floor. Kinship was all important, and to belong to a noble lineage guaranteed a higher status. The Fulbe were patrilineal (inheritance and identity passed through the male line), having switched over from matriliny (passing inheritance and identity through the female line) with conversion to Islam. Included within the *riimbe* were the cultivators, herders, fishermen, and Muslim traders and clerics. It was not necessary to be Fulbe in order to be part of the nobility, but such was usually the case.

The *neenbe* included endogamous occupational groups such as the *awlube*, blacksmiths, leatherworkers, fashioners of wood, cloth, pottery, and so on. Curtin argues effectively that these groups were not so much "lower" or inferior in the social hierarchy as they were outside of it. While sexual relations with the *neenbe* were regarded as defiling, social interaction was perceived differently. In the case of the *awlube*, the nature of their craft led to client–patron relations with the nobility and ruling elite. Blacksmiths were feared and respected for their ability to communicate with tree spirits, necessary for making charcoal. Woodworkers and leatherworkers were shunned, however, in that they either worked extensively with trees, the repository of dead spirits, or they violated blood taboos when preparing the skins of animals.

The third category, the *maacube*, constituted the servile community. They were not slaves in the western, proprietary sense, but were such in that they were separate from the host society; they were foreigners who did not "belong." This group can be further broken down into three subdivisions: trade slaves, who had been either captured or purchased, and had no rights whatsoever; slaves born in captivity, who acquired a subordinate, fictive tie to the master's family; and royal slaves, who frequently served in administrative or military positions. Such royal slaves were often positioned to exercise authority over the non-elite *riimbe*. By 1904, according to one estimate, two-thirds of Bundu's population were enslaved.[33]

Turning to the other constituent communities of Bundu, the Soninke, like the Fulbe, were also stratified into *hooro* (free peasants), *namaxala* (caste groups), and *komo* (slaves).[34] The Soninke were patrilineal and largely Islamized by the late eighteenth century. In fact, one could speculate that Bundu's proximity to Gajaaga, the heartland of the Soninke, caused the Soninke of Bundu to maintain their deep reverence for the old and very influential maraboutic families of the Darame, Silla, Ture, Saaxo, and Sisse clans. However, any political ties to the ruling elite of Gajaaga must have necessarily weakened to the point of insignificance with the expansion and consolidation of the Bundunke state.

The Mande-speaking (or Malinke) communities were similarly patrilineal. While they were probably non-Muslim towards the beginning of Bundu's history, the evidence would suggest that they converted to Islam in increasing numbers during the latter part of the eighteenth and throughout the nineteenth centuries. They also maintained a hierarchical structure consisting of the *foro* (peasants), the *namaxala* (or *nyamaxala*, castes), and the *joon* (slaves). The Mande speakers were largely concentrated along the Faleme River and to the south towards the Upper Gambia, and proved to be the most resistant to the expansion of Sissibe authority into their territory. Along with the Soninke, they would constitute the majority of the Bundunke population after the second half of the nineteenth century.

The much smaller Wolof population was similarly divided into the *baadoolo* (literally, "the people without power"), *neeno* or artisan castes, and the servile *jaam* groups. In the Wolof states along the Atlantic coast, the legendary *ceddo* warrior class emerged from within the *jaam*, as they were originally royal slaves. However, there is no evidence that elements of the Wolof *ceddo*, who became a branch of the ruling elite in the Wolof states, ever migrated to Bundu. Concerning religion, and in contrast to the Soninke and Malinke communities in Bundu, the sources suggest that the Wolof in Bundu (referred to as the "Fadube") were mostly non-Muslim. Because of an ancient pact between the Sissibe founders of Bundu and the early Wolof community that respected the latter's cultural autonomy, the Wolof were able to resist Islam without state harassment until the *jihāds* of the nineteenth century, when they became subject to periodic abuse. Even so, the sources suggest that in Bundu the Wolof remained mostly non-Muslim as late as the 1890s. While it is possible that the few who did convert to Islam adopted patriliny, it should be noted that important clans in the Atlantic Wolof states did not change their lineage system upon conversion to Islam.

Introduction

As previously stated, the Soninke, Malinke, and Wolof communities in Bundu are all older than those of the Sissibe. Evidence relating to the founding of the state clearly indicates that the Soninke and the Wolof were already resident in the sparsely inhabited land by the time of Malik Sy's arrival in the vicinity, while the presence of the Malinke along the Faleme, bordering Bambuk, is a well-established fact. Prior to the advent of the Fulbe in significant numbers, contact between the other three communities was most likely minimal, as they were located in three different areas of what would become Bundu. The Soninke lived in the north, approaching the Upper Senegal; it is probable that the Wolof occupied an area to the south of the Soninke; while the Malinke were concentrated along the Faleme. With the establishment of the Bundunke polity, there was an additional influx of ethnicities due to the tolerant policies of the government. At the same time, however, the evidence suggests that the previous Soninke and Malinke populations along the expanding periphery of the state were either absorbed or gradually displaced in the course of the eighteenth century; repeated references to warfare to the north and along the Faleme support this assertion. The displacement was a consequence of the decision within these communities to reject the political claims of the new polity. At the same time, the sources consistently describe relations between the Fulbe and the Wolof as cordial (until the nineteenth century *jihāds*), a reflection of the aforementioned accord between the founders of Bundu and the Wolof, the specifics of which will be discussed in chapter 2.

Those Malinke communities which accepted Sissibe rule, along with other Soninke, Wolof and Fulbe populations, proceeded to form numerous homogeneous villages and several heterogeneous towns within Bundu. In the latter case, members of an ethnic group and clan lived together in the same ward (in adjacent compounds) of a given town, and had their interests represented before government officials by the oldest member of the ward. The clans were linked by a perceived common ancestor and a common surname (*yetoode* in Pulaar, *jaamu* in Malinke, and *sant* in Wolof). Among non-Muslim populations, identity was also derived from common, dual totemic animals: one animal was associated with the ancestors and served as a unifying symbol and source of protection for the clan, whereas the corresponding animal functioned to repel those who did not belong to the clan. These totemic markers of identity would fall into disuse with conversion to Islam, but not completely.

It is probable that very few representatives of the nobility from any of these communities remained in (or migrated to) Bundu, and those few who did, if they were to retain upper class prerogatives within the context of the Bundunke polity, probably joined the *Torodbe* community, from which emerged Bundu's political leadership (and about which more will be said in chapter 2). In any case, it is difficult to imagine how the nobility of separate ethnic groups could have maintained their existence in the face of a newly constituted state with its own ruling and noble classes.

As will be discussed subsequently, the diversity of Bundu's initial population was an important consideration in the formation of a pragmatic domestic policy. Notwithstanding the commonalities, the cultural differences (in such matters as language, religion, and kinship) between the various ethnicities mitigated against the imposition of religious prescription.

The early, liberal policy of the state was partially responsible for attracting immigrants of varying backgrounds to relocate in Bundu. The nineteenth century, however, would witness the increasing domination of the state and its economy by the Fulbe, reaching its apex under the reign of Bokar Saada, who would target non-Fulbe groups, in particular the Soninke, to bear the brunt of increased taxation. It is in the last quarter of the nineteenth century, then, that this heretofore successful experiment in multiethnic relations turns sour, and a definitive anti-Fulbe sentiment develops.

Concerning population figures, a 1976 census found that 87,566 people resided in the *département* of Bakel, an area that includes the former state of Bundu.[35] For reasons to be discussed later, it is probable that Bundu's population in the period under review never exceeded 30,000, and that it neared this upper limit shortly before the mid-nineteenth century.

Although Bundu was relatively fertile, the evidence indicates that the area was only lightly populated prior to the foundation of the Bundunke state. This was due to several factors, the most important having been that the major trade routes did not lead through the area before the eighteenth century. The combination of religious and political turmoil in the Middle Senegal, along with the arrival of the French in the region as traders, greatly stimulated the immigratory and centralization processes.

Islam in Bundu

From the time that Malik Sy founded the state, the official religion of Bundu; that is, the religion of the nobility and ruling class, has always been Islam. Moreover, from the latter part of the eighteenth century on, the majority of the inhabitants have followed Islam. Prior to this point, there is evidence of significant numbers of non-Muslims in Bundu. But with the expansion of the Muslim rulers' power, Islam became firmly entrenched. To have lived in Bundu in the late eighteenth century was to have lived as a Muslim.

Having stated that Bundu was a Muslim land, it must be kept in mind that the political leadership was pragmatic. The available evidence is not sufficient to preclude the possibility that Bundu's government sought to regulate itself in strict accord with Islamic law, but the data strongly suggest that the elite by and large resisted the call to conform to the emerging theocratic examples of Futa Jallon and Futa Toro. However, there is no question that Islam was a powerful and ubiquitous force throughout the society, and that the policies of the Bundunke rulers represented an attempt to strike a balance between the claims of militant Islam and the demands of commercial profitability.

In all of the travel literature on Bundu, it is never suggested that the majority of Bundunkobe were anything other than Muslims. Mungo Park maintained that the people of Bundu differed from those of the adjacent Manding lands

> ... chiefly in this, that they are more immediately under the influence of the Mahomedan laws: for all the chief men ... and a large majority of the inhabitants of Bondou, are Mussulmen, and the authority and laws of the Prophet, are every where looked upon as sacred and decisive.³⁶

Raffenel even went so far as to favorably compare religion in Bundu with that in Futa Toro: "The Mohammedan religion is practiced in Bundu with more loyalty and sincere faith than in Futa ... "³⁷ What Raffenel may have been referring to was what Mollien described as Bundu's clearly established Muslim character, yet its lack of "fanaticism," a characteristic attributed to Futa Toro.³⁸

Islam in Bundu gradually evolved into the pervasive force that it was by the beginning of the nineteenth century. By that time, the clerical community was divided, according to Lamartiny and Raffenel, into three classes: the *imāms* (literally, "leaders of the prayers"), the *tamsirs* (a corruption of *tafsīr*, or Qur'anic exegesis), and the *ṭālibs* (literally, "students").³⁹ According to them, the *ṭālibs* were in fact educators who ran the schools and led the public prayers. The *imāms* ceremonially presided over successions and served as judges; the *tamsirs* were intermediate judges between the *imāms* and the *Almaami* (head of the Bundunke state), and presided over courts of appeal. Qur'anic schools were found in a majority of the towns, where classes were in session from four to six in the morning, and again from seven to nine in the evening. Small boards were provided for the students to write their Qur'anic verses in Arabic. At least so far as the Jakhanke system was concerned, students began Qur'anic school at age three or four, where they first learned the alphabet.⁴⁰ They then progressed to Qur'an memorization, a process which usually took five years. Most left Qur'anic school at this point, but some went on to study *tafsīr*. From there, the few who continued their training had to search out the various scholars wherever they could be found, and with whom they could advance their knowledge of *tafsīr*, *tawḥīd* (theology), *ḥadīth* (traditions of the Prophet), and *fiqh* (Islamic jurisprudence).

Lamartiny, seconded by Rançon, observed that both between and after classes, the students went into the villages seeking alms, and that this was their primary method of paying their instructors.⁴¹ If this was indeed the established practice in Fulbe villages, Jakhanke schools were financed differently. Beyond their sometimes large slave holdings, Jakhanke clerics also required their pupils to work in the clerical fields to pay for their instruction, food, and lodging.⁴² At the completion of the instruction, it was customary to give the instructor a slave, or his or her equivalent.⁴³ Such remuneration implies that the Jakhanke trained primarily the elite, who could afford the "tuition," while the less fortunate had to settle for whatever was available locally.

More advanced education and scholarship took place within the larger Senegambian context. The entire region was interconnected, where *shaykhs* ("teachers") and students interacted across hundreds of miles, regardless of ethnic or state affiliation. A prime example of this was the education of Karamoko Ba (d. 1836), the founder of Touba (Toubacouta, or "new Touba") in Futa Jallon, on the south bank of the Koumba River, in the upper valley of the Rio Grande.[44] Born in Bundu, he studied in several villages in Khasso, including Goundiourou.[45] Among his instructors in Khasso were *al-Shaykh* Ibrahim Jane, Fudi Mahmud Jawari, and Fudi Gassama Gaku.[46] He then went on to fabled Jenne, where he studied under Alfa Nuh, his most important instructor, as well as Alfa Hatib, Alfa Raji, Umar "the Grammarian," Muhammad Tumane, Muhammad al-Kharashi, Muhammad Ghali, Muhammad Kumasat, and Muhammad al-Taslimi.[47] At the same time that he was studying in Jenne, he was being sought out as a *shaykh* by pupils from all over West Africa, including Bundu, Futa Toro, Gajaaga, and Kaaba.[48] It is entirely possible that the particular case of Karamoko Ba represents an exaggeration in the effort to embellish his image. Notwithstanding this, the account of his travels remains highly useful in documenting the interconnectedness of the Senegambian educational and religious communities.

Not everyone was as illustrious as Karamoko Ba, but many had to travel outside of their native lands to complete their studies. This was the nature of the *shaykh*-student educational system. But where that education was completed was not uniform for everyone. Bubu Malik, Malik Sy's son and successor, went to Futa Jallon, whereas *Almaami* Abdul Qadir of Futa Toro studied in southern Mauritania. Mamadu Lamine went to Bakel to sit at the feet of the Darame *shaykhs*; *al-ḥājj* Umar spent several years in Futa Jallon before going on to Maasina and Sokoto.

Robinson has already noted that scholarship in Futa Toro, and by extension in Bundu, was of a limited nature and not to be compared with the intellectual centers of Timbuktu, Sokoto, or Jenne.[49] Such works as the *Mukhtaṣar* (*fiqh*) of Khalil b. Ishaq (d. 776/1374) and the *Maqāmāt* (poetry) of al-Hariri (d. 516/1122) were part of Karamoko Ba's curriculum in Khasso.[50] In Jenne he studied the *Shifā'* (Maliki law) of *al-Qāḍī* 'Iyad (d. 544/1149), and the *Ṣaḥīḥ* (*ḥadīth*) of al-Bukhari (d. 256/870). Besides these, it is not beyond reason that such works as the *Muwaṭṭa'* (*fiqh*) of Malik b. Anas (d. 179/795), the *Risāla* (*fiqh*) of Ibn Abu Zayd (d. 386/996), and the *Ṣaḥīḥ* (*ḥadīth*) of al-Muslim (d. 261/875) were also familiar to the clerics of Bundu, as they are West African favorites. Mungo Park had the privilege of being shown a library in which there were numerous Arabic manuscripts, but he was unable to identify them.[51]

Jakhanke and Sissibe

As early as 1725, the French viewed Bundu as basically a theocratic power, in which the clerical community enjoyed great esteem and influence.[52] Nearly one hundred years later, the power of the Bundunke clerics was still considered second only to that of the *Almaami*.[53] Preeminent among this group were the Jakhanke, a Malinke (or Soninke) clerisy identified by their rejection of *jihād* and their non-involvement in political affairs. The various communities throughout Niani, Wuli, Dentilia, Futa Jallon, and Bundu all trace their lineages back to *al-ḥājj* Salim Suware (d. 1525). At least fifteen Jakhanke villages were located in what would become Bundu.[54] Two of those villages may have been established during the time of Malik Sy, although they were not incorporated into the expanding state until after the first quarter of the eighteenth century.[55] Those which followed were attracted by the new Muslim state and, as Curtin maintains, the proximity of the Bambuk goldfields.[56] According to Jakhanke traditions, Malik Sy was in the habit of seeking the prayers and amulets of Muhammad Fudi, who had established a school in Safalou (in Diakha province, in what later became southern Bundu), at which there were nearly 500 students at any given time.[57] Because of the efficacy of his amulets, Malik Sy gave Muhammad Fudi his daughter Fatima in marriage.[58] The union produced Muhammad Fatima (d. *c.* 1772), who founded the town of Didecoto ("old Medina") eleven miles southeast of Koussan (a Bundunke capital). Didecoto immediately began attracting significant numbers of Jakhanke from Diakha Ba in Bambuk. Muhammad Fatima was celebrated for his great learning, and became a *shaykh* and *qāḍī* (judge) to the Bundunke ruler.[59] He left seven sons, one being the aforementioned Karamoko Ba.[60]

In reviewing the Jakhanke traditions, it is doubtful that Malik Sy conceded the superiority of Jakhanke amulets, given his own preeminent reputation in the field. However, it is very possible that Fulbe clerics such as Malik Sy and Jakhanke clerics developed cordial relations. The prospect that Muhammad Fudi may have allied himself with Malik Sy through marriage, given the Jakhanke disavowal of politics, is an indication that Malik Sy was not perceived as a reformer bent on waging *jihād*. But Muhammad Fatima's subsequent involvement with the politically oriented Sissibe was a clear violation of the Suwarian ideology, and such alliances may have been a principal reason for Karomoko Ba's departure to Touba, so far removed from his native Didecoto. Whatever the truth of the specific relationship between Malik Sy and the Jakhanke, the traditions point to a general closeness and compatibility between the Sissibe and the Jakhanke before the latter half of the nineteenth century, when these relations began to deteriorate under Bokar Saada. In light of the fact that such traditions were recorded after the definitive break in relations between the two groups under Mamadu Lamine, it is all the more probable that cooperation did indeed exist in earlier times. In any event, the traditions are consistent in identifying the Jakhanke as the principal advisors to the Bundunke rulers.⁶¹

The close association between the Sissibe clerical leaders of the state and the Jakhanke clerical advisors to the state resulted in a mutual reinforcement of the pragmatic nature of Bundu's government. Moreover, the preeminence of the Jakhanke clerical reputation surpassed that of the Sissibe, and probably encouraged, in conjunction with other factors, the abandonment of scholarly pursuits by the descendants of Malik Sy. The Sissibe, while remaining Muslim, began to gravitate towards a political posture more in keeping with the examples of the surrounding traditional monarchies: the Denyanke of Futa Toro, the Bacili of Gajaaga, etc. At the same time, the reputation of the Jakhanke as teachers and producers of amulets continued to grow.⁶² There were other clerics in Bundu: Wolof, Fulbe, and Malinke, who knew the *bāṭin* ("secret") sciences. But the amulets of the Jakhanke were the most highly prized. Amulets were among the more concrete expressions of faith; they were used for medicine, for protection from wild beasts, for seeking political power, and so on.⁶³ They were especially important to warriors, who wore as many as they could for protection against injury. The Jakhanke did a thriving business in producing these charms for those engaged in war, so that they became the premier source of both amulets and education in Bundu.⁶⁴ The growing political and commercial agenda of the Sissibe, combined with the religious superiority of the Jakhanke, further explains the court's moderate posture, and its inability to embrace the Islamic revolutions of Futa Jallon and Futa Toro.

Jihād

The history of Bundu is filled with the details of military campaigns. Given that the principal means of conducting legal warfare for Muslims is via *jihād*, the Bundunke *almaamies* were careful to characterize their various wars and expeditions as holy wars (as did the leaders of Futa Jallon), even though they were often only punitive or extractive raids.⁶⁵ While the concept of *jihād* will be examined more closely in chapter 2, suffice it to say that these "*jihāds*" are to be clearly distinguished from the movements of Usuman dan Fodio, *al-ḥājj* Umar, and Abdul Qadir, whose efforts were greater, conducted legally, and had further-reaching consequences. An example of the Bundunke perception of their activities is given by Fox, who advised the *Almaami* Saada Amadi Aissata against going to war in 1838, protesting it was a sin to kill. The *Almaami* responded that

> ... it was not the good people they should kill, it was those only who did not pray to God; and for doing this the Almighty would be well-pleased, and would reward him; and that if he himself fell in the contest, he should go to heaven ...⁶⁶

Fox went on to state that "the almamy, and in fact, all Mohammedan chiefs, consider they have a Divine right for making war upon the Pagans, ... "⁶⁷

That the *Almaami* regarded his campaign as prescriptive is substantiated by the theological discussion that developed with Fox. The Wesleyan missionary was asked if his teaching was the same as Muhammad's, to which Fox replied in the negative, "adding that I did not find such a name in my Bible. This led to a number of other questions, such as, 'Do you face the east when you pray?'"[68] Fox took the opportunity to explain the tenets of Christianity; the *Almaami* politely rejected his claims, incredulous that God could have a son, or that such could suffer death. The *Almaami* walked away from the encounter convinced of the superiority of his religion, and that he was operating wholly within its framework.

The furious assaults on Wuli and Tenda in the nineteenth century were also perceived by the Bundunkobe as holy war. Rançon comments that the frequent campaigns against Tenda were "under the pretext of making war against the infidels to convert them to Islam, ..."[69] Even *Almaami* Bokar Saada (1857–85) viewed his activities as religiously justified. Asked the reason for his attacks on the "pagans" of the south, while maintaining good relations with the French, he responded that the Christians were *dhimmis* (non-Muslims who were to be protected).[70] For all of his questionable actions, Bokar Saada never saw himself as anything other than a Muslim. His attitude typified the handling of the jihadist ideology by Bundu's rulers: they were aware of its theological claims, and exploited those claims when it benefitted their own imperialist designs; but they steadfastly resisted the reformist implications of the jihadists' activities within their own domain.

With this sketch of Bundunke society in hand, a discussion of Bundu's evolution is now possible. We will begin with an examination of Malik Sy, and the circumstances surrounding the foundation of Bundu.

2
Malik Sy and the origins of a pragmatic polity

The Bundunke sources are unanimous in their claim that Malik Sy, progenitor of the Sissibe ruling dynasty, was the actual founder of the state. He is thus the most highly venerated figure in the collective memory of the Bundunkobe, surpassing others of his descendants whose reigns were far longer and whose accomplishments were arguably far greater. To this day, the name of Malik Sy is revered; inhabitants of the area continue to make annual pilgrimage to the site of his purported tomb (at the base of a mountain at Wuro Himadou). It is therefore quite essential and appropriate to attempt an approximation of the historical figure, so laden with the vestments of embellishment and anachronism.

It should be noted at the outset that it is not possible to establish with absolute certainty that Malik Sy founded Bundu. However, the weight of the evidence points in that direction. Such evidence will be examined in the course of this chapter, as it is an issue for the history of the Bundunkobe. But more important than the question of who founded the state is a consideration of the circumstances and forces operative in the area during Malik Sy's period, circumstances and forces which early on conspired to channel the nascent policy towards a pragmatic posture. That is, the early period of the state proved to be a formative one, establishing a paradigm from which subsequent rulers did not seek to deviate. Directly related to this formative period is the person of Malik Sy, whose background and career require some reconstruction.

Sources

In order to achieve a credible approximation of Malik Sy's life and accomplishments, it is necessary to employ the filter of the preceding chapter's analytical framework. That is, the dependability of sources relating to the historicity of Malik Sy must be essayed according to such instruments of measure. After a proper assessment, a plan of utilization specific to the case of Malik Sy can be outlined.

The vast majority of sources concerning Malik Sy reflect a perception of him developed by his descendants, the Sissibe. Whether communicated through the medium of court-affiliated *griots*, or spoken directly by a scion of the Sy family, the principal objective of these traditions is to honor the name of the founder of the state, and to bestow upon him the requisite attributes of greatness. As such, the resulting perception of Malik Sy is very much the self-perception of the Sissibe; his glory is carefully cast to further the self-interests of the ruling elite, interests which could only be contested by those outside of the circles of power. Hence, the traditions must make it clear that those who wield power do so by way of superior endowment and divine approbation.

Having established that the preponderance of the Malik Sy materials project the interests of the court, it next becomes necessary to examine the context of the traditions' transmission. At this juncture it is critical to observe that Malik Sy is wholly known to us through oral data; there are no contemporary accounts of him. Some twenty-six more or less complete versions of his life exist, collected throughout the late precolonial, colonial, and postcolonial periods. Of that number, seven were collected prior to 1900, and only two before 1855.[1] In other words, most of the accounts of Malik Sy were recorded at least 200 years after his death; even the two earliest collections are separated from him in time by approximately 150 years. Such accounts tend to be riddled with issues and ideas current during the late eighteenth and nineteenth centuries, rather than the late seventeenth. Late eighteenth and nineteenth century Sissibe rulers were employed as models to form an image of what Malik Sy must have been like. In addition, the lacunae in the various Malik Sy stories were filled with episodes whose purpose was to explain or legitimize subsequent social and political realities. As a consequence, we cannot be absolutely certain about the specifics of Malik Sy's life. We can be reasonably assured of the fact that he is indeed an historical figure, that he emigrated from Futa Toro to what became Bundu, and that he was the progenitor of the ruling dynasty.

Beyond the context of time, there is a consideration of space. At least six of the Malik Sy collections were recorded outside of Bundu: Diakité (1929), Roux (1893), Adam (1904), Ly (1938), a number of the Curtin interviews (1966), and Sow (1968). In turn, Rançon (1894) depends in part upon the data acquired by Roux, so that at least some of his material does not emanate from within Bundu. The consideration of spatial context also partially addresses the initial issue of court-oriented materials: these six collections can be used to adjust for the elitist perspective of the remaining twenty.

With regard to the process of transmission, some of the penultimate informants are known. For example, Rançon cites Abdul Sega Sy of Koussan as a major source, and Brigaud (1962) received his information from Sy Amadou Isaaga, Abdul Sega Sy's grandson. Diakité, the Soninke cleric, was a source for his own account and that of Adam. The sources of Curtin and Gomez are clearly identified. Beyond these exceptions, the majority of the penultimate informants are unknown, and the various chains of transmission irretrievable. The anonymous nature of these sources mitigates their authority, and means that earlier accounts are not necessarily more reliable than subsequent collections.

Finally, it is assumed that the various observers made errors in their reconstructions. The inaccuracies result from both the self-interests of the ruling elite and inadequate methodology and comprehension on the part of the observers.

Altogether, the problems of self-serving traditions, unidentified sources, and observer error raise the pertinent question of how to critically use such information. Notwithstanding the deficiencies, the collections of Rançon, Roux, Lamartiny, Kamara, Sow, Bérenger-Feraud, Brigaud, Doudou, Adam, Diakité, and Curtin constitute the core of the most important data because of their breadth and detail, as they are largely whole traditions of Malik Sy from birth to death. There are other accounts, such as Raffenel, and Carrère and Holle, which serve to supplement the more comprehensive collections.

These accounts, taken from a number of sources and collected over a 150-year span, form a very rich and diverse reservoir of information. While much of the data reflects the Sissibe perspective, variations of the common themes do occur. Such variations are not only the function of differing periods of time and space; contemporary observers also produce differing versions of the same story.

In light of the foregoing observations, it is essential to approach the sources with the objective of establishing consensus, plausibility, and internal logic. By employing this methodology, several major phases of Malik Sy's life can be discerned, concerning which a significant number of the sources more or less agree. The probable historicity of these phases is enhanced by accounts originating from outside of Bundu, but which are nonetheless consistent with the view from within. In this way, data from Diakité (hence Adam), Curtin, and Kamara became especially useful. Isolated vignettes, outside of the consensus and thus impossible to corroborate, cannot be relied upon as foundations for recreating the broad contours of Malik Sy's life. However, such dissident voices retain anecdotal value, and are judiciously employed in exploring the plausibility of explanations at variance with the consensus. Matters of contemporary relevance, not at issue during Malik Sy's tenure, must be identified and dissociated from the historical period.

Of the twenty-six accounts of Malik Sy, nineteen feature recurrent episodes, but no single episode is found in all twenty-six accounts.[2] The most common episode is a reference to Malik Sy conducting some form of warfare in Bundu, found in fifteen of the twenty-six narratives.[3] A second common theme concerns the establishment of the border between Gajaaga and Bundu, repeated in fourteen accounts. The third most frequent theme is the story of Kumba's well, which has to do with the origin of the name "Bundu."

Beyond this, a substantial number of the sources discuss Malik Sy's early life and training, journeys to Gajaaga and Diara, and eventual settlement in Bundu. Upon a thorough examination of these themes, we will have formed the most probable reconstruction of the life of Malik Sy.

Background and relationship to the Torodbe

Malik Sy was born in the town of Suyuma (Sonima, Souima, Soimna, or Sonyma), a few kilometers from Podor in Futa Toro.[4] Although Bérenger-Feraud states that he was of Manding origin, all other sources maintain that he was Fulbe.[5] The year of Malik Sy's birth is unknown, but based upon Rançon's itinerary, it would have been around 1637.[6] N'Diaye's dating of Malik Sy to 1512 is a singular instance and can be discounted.[7]

Rançon was the first to provide insight into Malik Sy's background. According to his sources, the family of Malik Sy was very old, descendant from a cleric named Ibnu Morvan (a corruption of Marwan), a *sharīf* (descendant of Muhammad).[8] Ibnu Morvan would be Malik Sy's great-grandfather, a person identified by Moussa Kamara as Taim Sy Hamme-Mishin.[9] According to the latter source, Taim Sy Hamme-Mishin came from a Mauritanian town named "Suyumma"; following a personal conflict with another party, he reestablished himself in Futa Toro, founding a new village which he named "Suyuma."

Rançon's informants state that Ibnu Morvan and his Fulbe wife produced a son named Hamet, who became "chief of a Toucouleur tribe of Toro."[10] Hamet is referred to as Bakar by Moussa Kamara.[11] Hamet in turn had two sons and two daughters: N'Diob-Hamet and Dawuda-Hamet, and Maty-Hamet and Tieougue-Hamet.[12] The oldest, N'Diob-Hamet, produced a large family which later became a critical source of aid for the progeny of Malik Sy. One of the daughters, Maty-Hamet, married an important cleric who later moved to Futa Jallon, and whose sons assisted Malik Sy. The other son, Dawuda-Hamet, was Malik Sy's father. He reportedly became "one of the great marabouts" in the land, and is referred to as Dawda, B'our Malick, Ben Malik, and Bokar Diam Hamet Misin Habiballah in the other sources.[13] Dawuda-Hamet is also described as being the head of the village.[14] How "great" Dawuda-Hamet was is questionable: Diakité states that the whole family was erudite, whereas Adam, whose source was Diakité, records that Suyuma was an "agglomeration of little importance, consisting of only about thirty dwelling units, all occupied by marabouts."[15] The fact that Malik Sy is described as an "obscure marabout" by an independent source lends credence to the relative insignificance of Suyuma.[16] The fact that the corpus of data on Malik Sy's ancestry is so limited also argues against Dawuda-Hamet's importance.

The descendants of Malik Sy are referred to as the "Sissibe" (plural of "Sy"), and they constitute a clan or lineage designation equivalent to other Fulbe clans such as the Wane, Kane, Tal, Bal, Ly, Dia, Thiam, etc.[17] But the

Sissibe were also part of a collection of families known as the *Torodbe*. The *Torodbe* would eventually emerge from rather humble origins to form an elite social stratum within the Middle and Upper Senegal Valleys; Sissibe membership in this restricted grouping served to bolster their claims to political power, and was critical to their success in fending off periodic challenges to their right to rule.

According to Moussa Kamara, the term *Torodbe* (singular *Torodo*) simply signifies people from Toro.[18] On the other hand, Robinson points out that the term comes from the verb *tooraade*, which means "to ask for alms"; Willis defines it to mean "imploring Allah."[19] What this implies is that the *Torodbe* were at one time dispersed communities of Muslims, closely identified with the necessity of begging by outsiders.[20] Rançon states that they were descendants of manumitted slaves in Futa Toro: "The origin of the Torodos, according to my friend Captain Roux, ..., is none other than the application of a prescription of the Koran, which says that 'whoever gives freedom to a believing slave will be rewarded'."[21] Whatever their actual origin, the *Torodbe* apparently occupied an inferior position within the Futanke strata early in their existence, an element distinguishing Futa Toro society from others in Senegambia. As the community developed, its members came to be distinguished by four basic features: they were erudite in the Islamic sciences; they were Pulaar-speakers but Arabic-writers; they could not be fishermen, smiths, weavers, tanners, *griots*, or participate in any other caste-occupation; and they disavowed the nomadic lifestyle.[22] At some time after a formative period, non-Fulbe individuals joined the ranks of the *Torodbe*, who became the functional equivalent of the Moorish *zwāya* (clerical communities).

According to oral tradition, the Sissibe were one of the last clans to become *Torodbe*.[23] The implication of the various sources, notwithstanding the discrepancies, is that Malik Sy's great-grandfather Ibnu Morvan was the first to enter the *Torodbe* ranks. If one allows thirty years for each generation, then this person was born sometime in the 1540s. That the *Torodbe* existed prior to Ibnu Morvan means that they could have been in existence as early as the fifteenth century. Rançon's sources claim that the Ly and Tal clans of the *Torodbe* are descendant from a first/seventh century relative of one of the Companions, who participated in an invasion of Futa Toro.[24] It is difficult to determine what this "invasion" actually refers to in the historical record. However, the conquest of Futu Toro by the Denyanke in the latter part of the fifteenth century may explain the drop in social status of the *Torodbe*, or indeed their creation as a self-conscious, stigmatized group of clerical villages.

Early years

Suyuma was for all practical purposes a clerical village. Malik Sy's first instruction came from his father, under whom he studied Arabic based upon recitation, memorization, and copying of the Qur'an.[25] Education for children attending Qur'anic school (*madrasa*) usually began after circumcision, around five years of age, and lasted until age thirteen or fourteen.[26] Malik Sy was no different, remaining under his father's tutelage until age fifteen.[27] Upon completion of this phase, he earned the title *tierno*.[28]

At this point Malik Sy left Suyuma to study elsewhere. It is very likely that he went into southern Mauritania.[29] Depending upon the precise section of southern Mauritania, he would have either concentrated on the *Mukhtaṣar* of Khalil b. Ishaq (d. 776/1374), or *ash'ar* (poetry) and *naḥwa* (grammar).[30] Following his formal training, he returned to Suyuma.[31] By this time he was twenty years old, and three years later his father died. Malik Sy became the head of the family. He married at age twenty-seven, and three years later his first wife bore a son, Bubu Malik. By another wife he had two more sons: Tumane Malik and Mudi Malik. Not long afterwards, he went to Gajaaga (or Galam) where he produced amulets for the *Tunka* at Tiyaabu; he remained there for the next three years. While in Gajaaga, he would often visit the *Torodbe* who had already emigrated to southern Gajaaga (which later became Bundu). It was during this period that Malik Sy began thinking about moving with his family to southern Gajaaga. In exchange for his services to the *Tunka*, he received gifts of cattle and slaves, with which Malik Sy returned to Suyuma. Two years later, he set out for the east, passing through Gajaaga and Khasso.

It is very probable that, as four of the nineteenth and three of the twentieth century sources testify, Malik Sy went next to Diara, another Soninke stronghold (as was Gajaaga) in the sahel.[32] Diara had been founded by the Nyakhate clan, who were later overthrown by a new dynasty, the Diawara, towards the end of the fourteenth century. The capital at Kingui was a commercial center, whose vitality was a principal reason for the state's expansion at the expense of old Mali. By 1754, however, the Bambara of Kaarta were successful in extending their hegemony over neighboring Diara.[33]

Beyond a high level of consensus, the internal logic of the Diara trip is sound. The sources are careful to distinguish between the Diawara dynasty and the Bambara of Kaarta. Because of the extensive relations between Bundu and Kaarta since the eighteenth century, it would have been easy to place the Bambara in Diara during the seventeenth. The plausibility of the venture is also very credible. Diara, besides being an important center of trade, was noted for fielding an impressive army. Armies in West Africa were in turn noted for their usage of amulets. For a cleric who was trying to make a living by creating these amulets, Diara would have been an ideal market.

With the commercial nature of Diara in mind, it is probable that Malik Sy left Futa Toro (at first temporarily, then permanently) primarily for the purpose of making money to help alleviate the stressful conditions of his family's finances; part of the stress was related to exorbitant taxation levied by the Denyanke regime, about which more will be said in chapter 3.

However, it should be recognized that multiple explanations have been forwarded regarding the reason for his departure; the issue is fundamental to understanding the subsequent development of Bundu. For example, according to Rançon, Malik Sy was simply adventurous, a statement influenced, no doubt, by the exploits of the nineteenth century *Almaami* Bokar Saada.[34] Such a contention is hardly satisfactory in explaining Malik Sy's overall behavior. Two other explanations are related to Islam. One is that Malik Sy was a missionary, a kind of successor to the sixteenth-century figure al-Maghili, in that he was primarily interested in converting rulers. According to this version, he traveled from the Middle Senegal all the way to Segu making converts. Having heard that the *Tunka* of Gajaaga was a just man, although an unbeliever, he decided to rectify the situation: "Malik-sy, who lived for the triumph of Islam, said to himself: it is proper that a man as wise as the Tunka of Goye not remain a kafir (an idolater) until his death; it is necessary that his subjects not vegetate perpetually in the obscurities and the practice of animism."[35] The other religious explanation is that Malik Sy was an itinerant *'alim* (scholar), touring various lands "functioning as the reader of sacred manuscripts, commenting on the Koran and living on alms ..."[36] While it is possible that Malik Sy performed both of these services, it is doubtful. The evidence indicates that he was not perceived as a scholar.

It is conceivable that factors not mentioned by the sources could have influenced Malik Sy's decision to leave Suyuma. For example, the gradual development of the Atlantic slave trade was impacting the Senegambian interior, such that the failure of the Denyanke dynasty to protect the inhabitants of Futa Toro was one likely reason for the Islamic revolution of the 1760s. In light of both the Atlantic trade and the continuation of the trade into Mauritania, Malik Sy may have experienced pressure to protect himself and his family. Another possibility is that, as a member of the *Torodbe*, Malik Sy would have been aware of the tense relations between that clerisy and the Denyanke ruling elite.[37] Presumably, such tension was related to the former's perception that the Denyankobe had failed to properly observe the tenets of Islam. Some *Torodbe* communities had already emigrated to southern Gajaaga and Futa Jallon for asylum. Consequently, in view of the developing crises of the slave trade and Denyanke hostility, it is entirely plausible that Malik Sy would have had sufficient cause to leave Futa Toro.

However, the various traditions indicate that as many as fourteen years elapsed between the initial travels of Malik Sy (after his studies were finished), and the time when he finally removed his family from Futa Toro.[38] The question becomes, if the aforementioned pressures were so great, why did Malik Sy leave his family behind in Suyuma? The answer to this query lies in the probability that Malik Sy was fundamentally motivated by other concerns. The sources overwhelmingly indicate that the primary and original cause of his departure was financial in nature; the rather humble circumstances of the *Torodbe* condition strengthen this observation. Because of the financial strains on his family, he went to the commercial town of Diara to earn money, principally by writing amulets; sustained economic pressures, possibly including insufferable taxation, would lead to his permanent departure. Ly records that he sought to make a living by selling "charms and amulets, which had great success in the country of the Sarrakolets (Soninke) in this land of the east," who were unbelievers and "dominated by the sorcerers."[39] He reportedly acquired great influence due to the virtue of his amulets and the "realization of certain of his predictions."[40] N'Diaye records that Malik Sy led a holy life, and attained the title *waliyu*, which in Bundu signified a person who had a thorough knowledge of the Qur'an, the ability to predict the future, and was capable of supernatural feats.[41] An early tradition concerning Malik Sy confirms N'Diaye on this point: "He (Malik Sy) was everywhere the object of an eager reception, because of both his reputation for holiness, and for the superb amulets that he made."[42]

The various sources, separated by time and space, are almost all agreed that Malik Sy was renowned for the efficacy of his amulets. Even when the primary reason for his leaving Futa Toro is given as something else, the benefits of his being an amulet-maker are also mentioned. An example of this is Bérenger-Feraud, who after portraying Malik Sy as a missionary, in the same breath stated that he made excellent *gris-gris* (amulets) to guard against "all the dangers which are able to assail a man."[43] Perhaps Rançon said it best when he wrote: "He desired to see a little of the world, and to make a fortune."[44]

Diara and the sword of power

According to Rançon, Malik Sy was at least thirty-five years old by the time he set out for Diara.[45] He passed through Gajaaga and Khasso, lands "infested with brigands," where he spent some time "predicting the future and giving away amulets, and was thus able to reach Diara without having suffered too much."[46] Malik Sy supposedly arrived at Diara during the tenure of *Fari* Mamadou Ben Damankalla (or Fie Mamadou, or Faregne).[47] However, estimates on the reign of Mamadou range from the late fourteenth century to the middle of the fifteenth. The attempt on the part of traditionalists to render Malik Sy a contemporary of Mamadou reflects the fact that both men were the progenitors of novel dynasties: Malik Sy founded the Sissibe, whereas Mamadou initiated the Diawara. Notwithstanding this method of etiological embellishment, the Diara trip retains sufficient credibility for the aforementioned reasons.

The sources are agreed that Malik Sy was well-received by the ruler, who was probably *Fari* Ntiangulai (c. 1597–1679).[48] His services to the *Fari* included producing amulets and predicting future events. As payment, Malik Sy was given substantial wealth. He was also given a house next to the ruler's, and because of his sagacity and knowledge, was honored by the residents of Diara with the title *Eliman* (literally "leader of the prayers," a corruption of the Arabic *al-Imām*).⁴⁹ That this title may have been given before Malik Sy settled in southern Gajaaga is important, and will be addressed later when the nature of the *imāmate* is discussed.

Of the many services Malik Sy reportedly performed for the *Fari*, his most dramatic involved his causing the *Fari*'s previously barren wife, Dongo, to become pregnant and bear a child.⁵⁰ In return, he was permitted to examine a certain magical sword, upon which was inscribed an unspecified but potent Arabic formula. However, after seeing the sword, he was asked to leave Diara by the *Fari*, out of fear that his experience with the sword had made Malik Sy too powerful and, hence, a threat.

The tale of the sword is clearly a vehicle of legitimization: Malik Sy, formerly a poor, obscure cleric with no trace of royal or noble blood, is now invested with the stuff of political power. The sword symbolizes the conveyance of the right to both territorial conquest and temporal rule; such imagery is not uncommon in matters involving the contesting of political authority (i.e., the "sword of truth" of Usuman dan Fodio, scholar, leader of *jihād*, and founder of the Sokoto Caliphate *c*. 1804 in northern Nigeria). The sword is from Mecca, containing Arabic inscriptions, and was once in the possession of Sunjaata himself (founder of the Malian empire *c*. 1230). It therefore follows, in the view of the Sissibe, that the political authority eventually wielded by Malik Sy in Bundu was doubly sanctioned: for those concerned with Islam, the sword came from the center of the Muslim world, thus demonstrating divine approval. For those not necessarily impressed with the tenets of Islam, the sword was formerly the possession of one of the most illustrious rulers of all time. By implication, the right – indeed, the mandate – to create empire in the spirit and likeness of Sunjaata is now conferred upon Malik Sy. The latter aspect of the sword's significance, its association with Sunjaata, would be especially useful in justifying Bundu's territorial expansion at the expense of the Malinke and Soninke, who once belonged to the Malian empire. Thus, the tale of the sword of power has as its purpose the establishment of Malik Sy as a temporal ruler. It would be left to another tale, the "Tale of the Walk," to determine the land and people over which Malik Sy was to exercise this right of dominion.

Implicit in the sources is Malik Sy's desire to rule, and that he consciously sought to realize his ambitions. He is portrayed as willingly employing deception to achieve his goals. The characterization of Malik Sy as politically ambitious comes up again and again; it is argued here that this portrayal is heavily informed by the behaviour of the nineteenth century descendants of Malik Sy. Because expansionist policies were pursued by later *almaamies*, it is assumed that such tendencies originated with Malik Sy.

It is extremely interesting that the magic sword is at Diara. The sword could have been placed anywhere. The fact that Diara was chosen draws attention to the close relations maintained between Kaarta and Bundu in the eighteenth and nineteenth centuries. Around 1754 the Massassi of Segu emigrated to Kaarta as a result of a civil war with the Kulubali. The region of

Kaarta borders the realm of the Diawara, and from 1754 to 1777 the Massassi and the Diawara lived in peace.[51] In 1777, the Diawara had become the clients of the Massassi, and were given the northern province of Kaarta. Therefore, the Diara episode can be viewed as not only an attempt to legitimize Malik Sy's position as a ruler, but also to justify Bundu's relations with non-Muslim Kaarta. This use of legal fiction would help quell the subsequent protests of those in Bundu who, influenced by external reform movements, objected to maintaining such alliances.

Settlement in southern Gajaaga

Most of the sources agree that when Malik Sy left Diara, he returned to Tiyaabu, the capital of Gajaaga. The *Tunka* belonged to the Bacili dynasty, and apparently was not a Muslim.[52] The various other towns in Gajaaga, such as Makhana and Kotere, were also under rulers called *Tunkas*. The head *Tunka* for all of Gajaaga would change from time to time, so that the *Tunka* of a given town may have been *Tunka* of Gajaaga as well. In the late seventeenth century, Tiyaabu was the seat of the head *Tunka*. Once again, Malik Sy is depicted as serving in the royal court, primarily writing amulets. The *Tunka* is described as having had many virtues, but he lacked the military courage possessed by the Fulbe and the Moors.[53] He consequently asked Malik Sy for the ability to overcome this shortcoming; Malik Sy complied, giving the *Tunka* an amulet that assured victory in war.[54] The purpose of this anecdote is to explain Bundu's inability ever to subjugate Gajaaga. The Sissibe "have often made war against the Bakiris, but they have never had serious success, because the amulet given to the Tunka of Tuabo by Malik Sy retained its protective virtue."[55]

As payment for his services, Malik Sy asked the *Tunka* for "a small corner of land in this fertile country" in which to settle.[56] Some of the sources indicate that the *Tunka* immediately set into motion the means of establishing the boundaries between Gajaaga and Bundu.[57] Others indicate that at first Malik Sy was only interested in maintaining a village, and that after his community of followers had grown, he requested more land from the *Tunka*.[58] The elements of consensus, internal logic, and plausibility are sufficiently high to make this episode credible. It must be kept in mind that southern Gajaaga often served as a political refuge; the *Satigi* of Futu Toro had fled there during the *tubenan* takeover (to be discussed later), as had the *Buur-ba-Jolof*.[59] That Malik Sy would request and be granted land in the same area is entirely consistent with Gajaaga's previous policy.

Malik Sy sent for his family in Suyuma. In addition to his family, Malik Sy is said to have had numerous followers.[60] Lamartiny claims that it was because he had so many students that he required more land.[61] Among his followers were three close companions: Sevi Laya (or Layal), a *gawlo*; Tamba Kunte, a smith; and Keri Kafo (or Terry Tafo), a slave.[62] These three are traditionally viewed as the ancestors of the caste and servile groups which developed in Bundu.

Where Malik Sy settled is also an issue in the sources. Moussa Kamara states that he first settled in a place called Wajini, then moved on to Dyunfung on the other side of the Faleme.[63] It is Diakité's contention, reflected in Adam as well, that Malik Sy founded Boulebane. Carrère and Holle also support this view.[64] On the other hand, both Dieng Doudou and Brigaud state that Malik Sy settled at Guirobe, eight miles northwest of Senoudebou, and Rançon says that he built the village of Wuro-Alfa ("village of the *alfa*") near Guirobe.[65] It is unlikely that Malik Sy settled across the Faleme River in Bambuk. Boulebane is usually described as an eighteenth-century construction. Since Guirobe was already established by *Torodbe* before Malik Sy came to southern Gajaaga, it is likely that he first went to Guirobe, then built a settlement nearby.

In the late seventeenth century, the population of southern Gajaaga was both sparse and heterogeneous. The earliest inhabitants were the Fadube, the Badiar, the Wualiabe, and the "Bakiri" (the Jakhanke would arrive during or after the tenure of Malik Sy).[66] The first two groups were culturally akin to the Badiaranke, the Coniagui or Conadjis, and the Bassari who currently live further south along the Senegal–Guinea border.[67] Regarding the Fadube, they were Wolof cultivators and herdsmen who had been forced to leave Jolof because of the oppression they experienced under the *Buur-ba-Jolof*.[68] Having sought exile with the *Tunka*, they were sent to southern Gajaaga. After Malik Sy had settled at Wuro-Alfa, Adam says that he encountered a people "who resembled animals more than men, in the manner of their dress and how they walked."[69] They introduced themselves as the Fadube. Malik Sy returned the introduction, stating that he had been under the impression that the country was unpopulated. He then pledged that he would never disturb their affairs, on the condition that they live peacefully in their caves.[70]

N'Diaye similarly records that when Malik Sy came to southern Gajaaga, the Fadube, or Wolof, owned the land. They lived in the ground, and had tails. In responding to the preaching of Malik Sy, however, they came out of their holes and had their tails cut off.[71] The clear implication in both of these anecdotes is that the Fadube were uncivilized – practically subhuman, and that they had failed to make productive use of the land. As a result, even though they were the first to inhabit the land, they did not deserve to own or control it. Once again, this characterization is employed to justify the seizure of territory by referring to the supposedly inferior culture of the "natives." As a result of the civilizing influence of Malik Sy, the indigenous inhabitants actually experience marked improvement in the quality of their lives, which compensates for the loss of their autonomy and control over their land.

Amadi Bokar Sy maintains that Malik Sy converted the Fadube to Islam; similarly, Curtin and Skinner, in commenting on the preceding story, suggest that the emergence from the subterranean lifestyle and the removal of tails imply conversion to Islam and circumcision.[72] The theme of conversion facilitates the overall efforts of these authorities to portray Malik Sy as a reformer, but other sources, closer to the period, do not support the interpretation. Rançon states:

> The Fadoube were thus established there and maintained very intimate relations with the Guirobe; but they always remained separated from them [the Guirobe] by their tastes, their manners, and their religion. They were pagans and superstitious, and had strange practices and customs. The darkest forests served as their places of seclusion. They often sacrificed victims at the feet of old trees, staining the trunk with the blood; and eating the flesh of animals having died from sickness, without having bled them. They also ate pork.[73]

Roux relates that Malik Sy signed a treaty with the Fadube; he would be their ruler and cleric, and in return they would be allowed to continue eating pork.[74] Notwithstanding this testimony, it is doubtful that the Fadube became Muslims at this time. Indeed, Roux, writing in the nineteenth century, went on to add: "Today they submit themselves to the common custom and construct dwellings, but they have kept from their barbaric past the habit of eating the flesh of pork, in spite of the formal interdiction of the Koran."[75] Because of their intransigence to Islam, they repeatedly were the targets of the jihadists of the nineteenth century.[76] In contrast to the attitude of the nineteenth century jihadists, Malik Sy is depicted by most of the sources as compromising with the unbelieving element for political gain.

As for the Badiar, they were Malinke in origin.[77] By the time of Rançon's study, they had completely disappeared from Bundu.[78] The Wualiabe were also Malinke from Bambuk, who maintained a few villages along the west bank of the Faleme River. They were chased from Bundu by the *almaamies*, and went on to establish the state of Wuli, on the Gambia River. Tambacounda, the large community in Wuli, was supposedly established by Malinke immigrants from Bundu.[79] Of course, the "Bakiri" were the Bacili, the Soninke rulers of Gajaaga.

As previously stated, by the time Malik Sy arrived in southern Gajaaga, some *Torodbe* groups had already settled there. One of these communities was that of the Guirobe, a name taken from their village of Guirobe. Otherwise, they are referred to as the N'Guenar, reflecting their origin in the similarly named province of Futa Toro.[80] The other group were the Tambadunabe, or the Bambadu, whose chief village was Wuro-Dawuda, northwest of Senoudebou.[81] Beyond the *Torodbe*, it is also possible that the Jakhanke established communities around the period of Malik Sy's residence there.[82]

The Tale of the Walk

We have already introduced the notion that Bundu was a heterogeneous society. Carrère and Holle maintain that Bundu became a refuge for *Torodbe*

"Peuls," immigrants from Jolof, and "Sarracoclet" (Soninke) and Diawara groups chased out by Kaarta.[83] While Bérenger-Feraud is not specific, he states that Malik Sy followed a deliberate policy of incorporating disparate elements into a larger collective: "Malik-si made of the country that was granted to him by the Tunka a place of refuge; therefore, in a short time, he had a numerous population made up of people from many countries who were needy and often without [necessities], or else they had committed crimes."[84] The conclusion is that from the outset, Bundu was characterized by a variety of ethnic communities.

As a result of the *tubenan* failure, southern Gajaaga experienced accelerated growth in the latter part of the seventeenth century. Population density in Futa Toro also contributed to emigration. This is reflected in the account of how southern Gajaaga became independent of the *Tunka* at Tiyaabu, and how the border was established between the two states. After initially settling at Wuro-Alfa, Malik Sy's community of followers is said to have increased to such an extent that "he had to request an increase in the concession [of land] in order to lodge all of his proselytes."[85] Adam, in an interesting contrast, states that Malik Sy requested independence for the whole region, not just Wuro-Alfa and its environs.[86] The *Tunka* agreed to the more modest option and proposed the following procedure: "Return to your camp at Guirobe. Set out again tomorrow as soon as day breaks. Likewise, I will leave from my end at Tuabo, and the spot where we meet will be the boundary between my states and the lands that I will give you."[87] The account of the "Walk" is found in all of the nineteenth century versions except for Diakité, and in eight of the remaining nineteen versions from the twentieth century.[88] A few versions state that on the morning of the scheduled walk, the *Tunka* rose late, procrastinated until noon, and walked slowly towards the south.[89] The *Tunka* "had barely walked five hundred paces when he encountered Malik-si..."[90] They met very close to Tiyaabu, and the *Tunka* is made to say: "You Fulahs, you have more energy than we do. You come to take from me a part of my domain; but I have given my word, I know that I have to keep it: henceforth, here will be the line of demarcation between your country and mine."[91] Implicit in these versions is the reason why the *Tunka* was unhurried: he believed Malik Sy. It was therefore the *Tunka*'s fault that he lost so much territory, because he was naive to put faith in Malik Sy. This in turn suggests that Malik Sy was less than trustworthy.

On the other hand, the majority of the pre-1966 accounts state that the boundary between Bundu and Gajaaga was established deceitfully.[92] A certain day was designated for the mutual march, and both men were to begin walking toward each other that morning. Whereas the *Tunka* kept the agreement and began at dawn, Malik Sy took off during the previous night. They met four or five kilometers south of Bakel, not far from Tiyaabu.[93] The *Tunka* is made to be furious with the cleric: "'What!', he said to him. 'I had confidence in you, but you deceived me, and I am disappointed at that! But a ruler only has his word. Therefore, I will faithfully keep the promise that I gave you'."[94]

The "Tale of the Walk," within which is an account of the formation of the Bundu-Gajaaga border, is clearly designed to explain the genesis of Sissibe control over Bundu. As such, its function is similar to other such stories describing the origins of various states and dynasties (e.g., Queen Dido and the founding of Carthage). The previous story of the "Sword of Power" established Malik Sy's right to rule; the "Walk" addresses the specific territorial application of that right. Secondarily, the "Walk" seems to account for the proximity of the Bundu frontier to Tiyaabu.[95] Equally important, however, is the portrayal of Malik Sy. He is a deceiver, a power-hungry trickster who betrays a trust. The underlying issue here is the right of sovereignty; southern Gajaaga belonged to the Bacili of Tiyaabu, and it somehow became the property of the Sissibe. The transfer is related in mythical terms, suggesting that the reality it seeks to represent is in fact more complex and difficult to explain. For the reality is that what began as a small group of clerical communities became, by the middle of the eighteenth century, a predatory state. The story communicates that this transformation was illegal and a usurpation of legitimate authority.

It becomes almost impossible to discern what the historical Malik Sy was really like, as the mythical figure has been made a composite of the expansionist tendencies of subsequent *almaamies*. By the time Rançon made his collection, Bundu was seven generations removed from Malik Sy, and in the absence of any contemporary accounts, he was for all practical purposes a remote and legendary figure. By contrast, Bokar Saada had just died; under his leadership Bundu reached its maximum territorial expansion, and he left a lasting impression for all posterity after a thirty-year reign. In many ways, the story of Malik Sy is a commentary on his successors.

The death of Malik Sy

In discussing events surrounding Malik Sy's death, the sources make a transition from semi-mythology to an attempt at straightforward narrative. There are no supernatural swords, subhuman creatures, or flying dragons involved. A number of the sources do not mention the manner of Malik Sy's death at all.[96] Of those which treat his death, all agree that Malik Sy died violently.

That the issue of sovereignty was creating conflict between Malik Sy's adherents and the *Tunka* is supported by the key nineteenth-century sources. Roux writes that Malik Sy had succeeded in conquering some Malinke strongholds in southern Gajaaga, and that the *Tunka* was anxious to regain control of these areas.[97] Lamartiny states that Malik Sy was covetous of the *Tunka*'s domain, and was awaiting an opportunity to seize it.[98] According to Rançon, the *Tunka* gradually became aware of Malik Sy's "profound ambition" which, if unchecked, would cause great damage to the realm.[99]

Rançon adds that Malik Sy had taken command of both sides of the Faleme River, and was claiming the land just south of Tiyaabu itself.[100] All of this reinforces the view that Bundu had not become territorially defined during Malik Sy's time; that, in fact, Gajaaga had not ceded any territory to Malik Sy with the understanding that he was to create a state.

As a result of heightened tensions, war broke out between Malik Sy and the *Tunka*. Commanding an army of 2,000 men, Malik Sy reportedly captured three villages in a march on Gajaaga, killing all of the men and enslaving the women.[101] He then crossed the Faleme River at Senoudebou, and marched north to the Senegal River. He stopped near Arondou, about two kilometers east of the Faleme's mouth.[102] There he was engaged by the superior forces of the *Tunka*. Alfa Ibrahim Sow recounts the events:

>They arrived at the deep waters of
Bodogal which no one had ever crossed by
fording.
>
>Keri-Kafo came to himself and declared:
Maliki-Dawouda, what is then the meaning
of this day?
>
>I came here with you and I do not see a
passage;
>
>an army is coming and we do not have the
force to defeat it.
>
>Maliki-Dawouda replied:
have faith in God.
>
>He took for himself the magic fire and
with it struck the water.
>
>A passage of land appeared,
A ford appeared,
Maliki-Dawouda crossed.
>
>The horses of the pursuers had to wait
for someone:
the river!
>
>His companions said to him:
Maliki-Dawouda, stop!
>
>Cease from lengthening your course; you
are well leading us to the
Place-without-name;
the price of dignity, it is death.
>
>Maliki-Dawauda took the reins of his
horse.
>
>They sent out the Axe-of-torments to him
to cut off
the head.
>
>At the place where the head fell, it
cried out:

> Silamfan, satanfan!
> The faint-hearted died, the brave died.
> The most capable bodies to suffer the
> injury of the blows
> and the men best-endowed with powerful
> muscles,
> there they remained with the power.
> Maliki Si the son of Dawauda-Hamme,
> son of Manti-Ali, of Eli Bana-Musa
> did not feel the pain.[103]

The Battle of Arondou was fiercely contested; in spite of his bravery and vigor, Malik Sy was forced to beat a hasty retreat. He was pursued by the *Tunka*, who surrounded his position at Dialiguel on the Faleme. After a pitched battle, Malik Sy was mortally wounded. He managed to escape the scene of hostilities, only to die shortly thereafter at Goumba-Koko, near Selen on the Faleme. The probable year was 1699.[104]

In the aftermath of his demise, Malik Sy rose from relative obscurity to a place of unequalled esteem in the traditions of the Bundunke people. His effort to establish Bundu is a major reason for his revered memory, but there are others. His fight against localized opposition was a portent of Bundu's subsequent struggles for power within the region, and would be drawn upon both to inspire and to legitimize such struggles. Secondly, his example of moderate clerical governance would be used by his descendants to defend against unfavorable comparisons with the reformist leadership of the two Futas. Finally, the political crises following his death and that of his successor Bubu Malik Sy were ultimately resolved to the advantage of the Sissibe. However, in order to further strengthen their claims, the Sissibe would begin to promote and embellish the traditions of Malik Sy to the exclusion of all others, and in this way effectively exploit a critical vehicle of justifying the monopoly of political power.

On the creation of a pragmatic state

While it cannot be established with absolute certainty that Malik Sy established the state of Bundu, the weight of the evidence leans in this direction. The fact that he assumed the title *Eliman*, a designation usually associated with religious functions, is of some utility, as it suggests accepting the political leadership of a Muslim land.[105] However, it is possible that he received this title in Diara, not in Bundu, which would support the notion that the title simply recognized his clerical leadership. Reinforcing this view is the fact that the Jakhanke leaders also carried such titles as *alkali* (from *al-qāḍī*) and *imām*; Ayuba Sulayman Diallo, otherwise known as Job Ben Solomon and about whom more will be said in chapter 4, reported that this father was called "*alfa*" in Bundu early in the eighteenth century.[106]

Notwithstanding the foregoing, the traditions are unrelenting in their

Pragmatism in the age of Jihad

assertion that Malik Sy founded the state. Rançon writes that Malik Sy concluded treaties with both the Fadube and the Guirobe, or N'Guenar, and then began collecting taxes from both groups.[107] After his death, both Bubu Malik Sy and Maka Jiba were compelled to return to Bundu from Futa Jallon and Futa Toro respectively to fight for the preservation of the polity. Their behavior implies that a prior investment had been made; they could have remained in the Futas. While the evidence is not particularly strong, it is such that no other alternative has sufficient plausibility. Malik Sy is the most likely original investor in the Bundunke polity.

Assuming that Malik Sy founded the state, he did not do so in a political vacuum. That is, he must have had certain ideas relative to the organization and function of government, and those ideas were in all probability influenced by existing forms of government in the region. If the foregoing is plausible, then it would appear that Malik Sy and his successors made a conscious decision to adopt a pragmatic approach to government. There are a number of reasons for the adoption of such an approach, but it is necessary to begin with a consideration of what was probably the most influential factor in the unfolding of events in the Upper Senegal, the wars and enduring legacy of Nasir al-Din. Given the magnitude of Nasir al-Din's movement, and the far-reaching, albeit short-lived, consequences of his activities and influence for the region in general and Bundu in particular, it is not possible to pass over its critical history without giving it adequate consideration.

I have argued elsewhere that Malik Sy does not represent the continuation of the jihadist tradition in North-West Africa, begun by the Almoravids in the eleventh century and inherited by the illustrious Nasir al-Din in the seventeenth.[108] Malik Sy was not involved in Nasir al-Din's movement; in fact, he was busy traveling during the period of the struggle. There is absolutely no mention of Nasir al-Din in any of the Malik Sy traditions, and the evidence suggests that Malik Sy died in the course of fighting a defensive war, rather than leading a *jihād*. To state it succinctly, there is no evidence for any linkage between Nasir al-Din and Malik Sy.

However, to say that Malik Sy did not emulate Nasir al-Din is not to say that the latter's movement was without significance for what would become the polity of Bundu. On the contrary, the militant struggle of Nasir al-Din helped to create those conditions which led to the creation of Bundu, and it also contributed to the character of the state. To fully appreciate this contribution, a succinct summary of the movement is in order.

Some time during the second half of the seventeenth century, and most likely between the years 1666 and 1674, a war erupted between the *zwāya* (clerical) community led by Nasir al-Din, and the warrior Hassaniya in southern Mauritania.[109] Ould Cheikh has characterized this conflict as a "lutte de classement" between the two protagonists, as each represented contrasting interests and cultural values.[110] From this view, the conflict in late seventeenth century Mauritania, otherwise called the "Shurrbubba," was primarily the consequence of long-standing enmity between the religious emphasis of the *zwāya* and the warrior mindset of the Hassaniya.[111]

At the head of the *zwāya* faction, Nasir al-Din first launched the *jihād* in the region south of the Senegal River, where it became known as the *tubenan* movement, from the Arabic *tawba*, or "repentance." He then turned his attention north of the Senegal, where the Shurrbubba was initiated, but proved short-lived. Nasir al-Din was killed in battle in 1674, and the Shurrbubba was quickly lost to the Hassaniya. The defeated followers of Nasir al-Din renounced all political pretensions and use of arms, began paying tribute to the Hassaniya, and returned to what they had previously been, *zwāya*.

Before his death, Nasir al-Din's *jihād* to the south, the *tubenan*, had succeeded in overthrowing the governments of Futa Toro, Walo, Jolof, and Cayor. These were replaced with clerics, who collected *zakāt* from a supposedly majority Muslim population, recently converted through the *tubenan*. The clerical governors appointed lesser clerics throughout the ranks of their administrations, with ultimate allegiance to Nasir al-Din. In this way, not only did the fame and ideas of the reformer traverse the waters of the Senegal, but so did his tangible political overlordship. As a consequence, both the *Satigi* of Futa Toro and the *Buurba* of Jolof were forced into exile in Gajaaga.[112] It appeared that a new chapter in the development of militant Islam was in the making.

But with Nasir al-Din's death, the political gains in the south rapidly dissipated. Under the preaching of Nasir al-Din and his envoys, the Senegambians, and in particular the Wolof, had been persuaded that a supernatural harvest was forthcoming, and that there was no need to engage in agricultural activity.[113] When Nasir al-Din was killed, and the inevitable famine set in, the Senegambians interpreted the millenialism of the *tubenan* as a ruse. Beginning with Walo, the Wolof states revolted against clerical rule one by one, and by 1677, Futa Toro was once again under the rule of the Denyanke. The *Satigi* permitted some of the clerics to remain in Futo Toro, but their political influence was greatly diminished. In the Wolof states, however, the reaction against the *tubenan* was much stronger. A once popular movement was now decidedly unpopular; the militant clerisy was not simply suppressed, it was expunged.

The movement of Nasir al-Din impacted the whole of Senegambia, having produced political revolution, religious fanaticism, and widespread suffering. Given its ultimate defeat, Nasir al-Din's legacy is necessarily composed of irreconcilable contradictions. His successes were greatly mitigated by his failures. He was a rightly guided *imām*, who led a far-reaching *jihād*. However, he was an early casualty in that same struggle. He was widely regarded as a miracle-worker, but his most ambitious attempt, the creation of a theocratic empire, ended in utter disaster. It is this total legacy that was remembered decades after the events themselves, not just those aspects which were momentarily successful.

With regard to the impact of the *tubenan* on southern Gajaaga, its failure was of greater significance than its brief ascendancy. *Torodbe* refugees, who in all probability sided with the *tubenan* reformers, began to emigrate elsewhere, including southern Gajaaga. Malik Sy's family may have also been affected by the reformers' demise, as they reportedly suffered some type of abuse by the *Satigi* while they lived in Suyuma.[114] The N'Guenar and the Tambadunabe were two early *Torodbe* groups in southern Gajaaga, and are possible examples of those who fled the political crisis of the Middle Senegal. With the total legacy of the *tubenan* experience as a recent memory, neither these *Torodbe* communities nor Malik Sy expressed the slightest interest in continuing the militant tradition of Nasir al-Din and the Almoravids. On the contrary, their exodus from the Middle Senegal indicated their desire to escape political entanglements. This search for a more tranquil, secure lifestyle helped to fashion an anti-militant posture for the emergent Bundunke state, and what was most likely a prime determinant in the Sissibe decision to develop a pragmatic approach to governance.

A second factor contributing to Bundu's pragmatism, and in conjunction with the recoil of the *Torodbe* to the *tubenan* failure, was the active involvement of the Jakhanke clerisy. Their early presence in the area, combined with their extensive ties to Malik Sy and influence over subsequent *almaamies*, helps to explain the gravitation towards a moderate policy. The Jakhanke were renowned for their anti-militant, apolitical ideology; and, at least in the Bundunke context, very active in commercial affairs. Their preeminent status as religious leaders no doubt reinforced the moderate orientation of their counsel in matters of state. From every available indication, the Bundunke *almaamies* heeded much of their advice, and pursued centrist policies which were in opposition to the reformist demands of the regional militants. The ingredients for this ongoing relationship between the Jakhanke and the Sissibe were present early on in the life of the state, and provide an additional reason for the formation of a pragmatic polity in nascent Bundu.

The third factor in the creation of a moderate Bundunke government involves the nature of southern Gajaaga during the late seventeenth century. Sparsely inhabited by a heterogeneous population comprised of refugees, social outcasts, and miscreants, the area assumed a frontier-like atmosphere.[115] Communities were self-sufficient, spatially separate, politically autonomous, and fully expectant that these circumstances would extend into the future. It would have been problematic indeed to have attempted to impose, without sufficient force, reformist Islam on such a disparate patchwork of villages. It would be far better to solidify their allegiance by offering security, increased prosperity, and a measure of continued local autonomy. And in fact, this is precisely the tactic adopted by Malik Sy in his agreement with the Fadube. The precedent established, Bundu's population was augmented by a steady influx of newcomers who were attracted by the relative tolerance of the state. While the religious character of the polity would gradually change and become predominantly Muslim, concomitant with the expansion and consolidation of Sissibe authority, this early existence of a frontier mentality would continue well into the eighteenth century, and thus play a role during the critical, formative stage of Bundunke pragmatism.

In light of the above, there were sufficient influences within nascent Bundu which were compatible with the adoption of a moderate administrative philosophy. It is highly probable that Malik Sy, having served for years in the royal courts of Diara and Tiyaabu, was familiar with the practical perspective and values of the ruling elite. The contrast between the models before him, of which he could not have been ignorant, were striking: a failed experiment in militant Islam in Mauritania and throughout Senegambia, the repressive Denyanke regime of Futa Toro, and the relatively successful, prosperous monarchies of Tiyaabu and Diara. In his desire to realize financial profit and to secure political asylum, but in full view of his Islamic convictions, it is very possible that he chose the most appealing aspects of the existing alternatives. As such, he launched a new concept in statecraft, in which Islam would be preeminent, and over which clerics would govern, but throughout which tolerance of and cooperation with diverse groups would provide the principles of the collective venture. In short, a pragmatic Muslim polity.

3

Consolidation and expansion in the eighteenth century

During the first quarter of the eighteenth century, the fledgling state of Bundu faced two major, existence-threatening challenges. The initial crisis developed after Malik Sy's unexpected fall in battle; not only was there the question of succession, but the very viability of the polity was at issue. The second challenge to the realm came after the death of Bubu Malik Sy, Malik Sy's son and successor, and resulted in a temporary dissolution of the state. These crises together underscore the difficulties involved in launching a wholly new political entity in the midst of established, well-defined states. Neighboring hostility, ill-defined laws of succession, and the failure to find a satisfactory formula for power-sharing among Bundu's various groups were the key issues exposed by the deaths of these two men.

While this early period was difficult and filled with uncertainty, it was also formative in that the agricultural base of the state gradually expanded; at the same time, the commercial orientation of the realm began to take form. The latter development was largely a response to neighboring markets, but at the same time the entire region was experiencing the growing stimulation of the French and English trading presence along the Senegal and Gambia Rivers respectively.

Following the demise of Bubu Malik Sy, Bundu was characterized by a brief period of decentralization. The state's reconstitution under Maka Jiba (1720–64) took place during a period of significant change within the wider context of Senegambia. To the south, in the lofty highlands of Futa Jallon, the forces of militant Islam were successful in creating a theocratic government via a protracted *jihād*. The accomplishment would reverberate throughout West Africa, and would have far-reaching implications for the region's subsequent development. For Bundu, the rise of a reform government represented both an opportunity and a challenge to the ruling elite to develop in a similar direction. By the end of Maka Jiba's reign, however, pragmatism continued to provide the principles by which the government was organized and policies determined.

It was also during the tenure of Maka Jiba that the pace of the slave trade quickened. The establishment of a new Bambara dynasty at Segu under

Marmari Kulubari (1712–25) resulted in a marked increase in the number of Malinke captives available for sale along the Atlantic coast. Much of this increased traffic passed from the Upper Niger through the Upper Senegal and Gambia Valleys en route to the coast; Bundu therefore took measures to position itself to tax the wayfaring caravans. This necessarily involved territorial expansion and warfare, with which Maka Jiba was primarily occupied.

In conjunction with the slave trade, there was an elevation in European interest in the goldfields of Bambuk. The British in particular made a greater effort at accessing these fields, with the result that polities within the area began to contest both the source of the gold and the routes leading from the source to the Upper Gambia. Bundu was likewise involved in the competition, but was unable to achieve a clear advantage in this arena.

The sources for the period from Bubu Malik Sy through the interregnum (1700–20) are much more limited in number and scope than those pertaining to Malik Sy. That is, while many of the Malik Sy materials contain information on his successors, such information tends to be sketchy. The focus is clearly on the progenitor; the accomplishments of Malik Sy's descendants, even though far greater than his own in some instances, consequently suffer from a lack of attention.

In view of the foregoing, the accounts of Rançon, Roux, and Lamartiny constitute the basis for what is known about Bundu during this stretch of time. There is useful information from Diakité, Adam, and Kamara, but the perspective is overwhelmingly that of the court. The process and context of the sources are no different from those applicable to the Malik Sy materials; this observation holds true regarding the experience, orientation, and interest of the observer as well.

The significance of the preceding observations is that the vehicle of consensus, so critical in the discussion of Malik Sy, cannot be utilized for this initial period. Internal logic, plausibility, and informed speculation become much more important in the attempt to approximate the historical reality. The consequence is an emphasis on general patterns of development, as opposed to more detailed information on specific episodes and principals, about which there can be little certainty.

In contrast to information on Bubu Malik Sy, the sources for the reign of Maka Jiba represent a subtle shift from primarily oral, endogenous materials to a combination of such materials and exogenous, independent observations recorded by travelers (David, Bayol, and others) and Europeans posted at the *comptoirs* (settlements) of the Upper Senegal. That is, the European presence in the upper valley slowly increased during the reign of Maka Jiba, making it possible to corroborate the endogenous sources with independent data. However, the endogenous materials continue to constitute the major reservoir of information for the period.

Regarding the endogenous sources, Rançon's collection of oral data is far more substantive than any other, although Roux and Lamartiny offer some insight into Bundu during this time. The recordings of Curtin and Gomez help to create a more complete picture of the realm. The Sy-centric perspective presents an even greater challenge than it did concerning Bubu Malik Sy, as there is a dearth of information on Maka Jiba from non-Fulbe sources. However, the issues of process, context, and observer status remain unchanged from the discussion pertaining to Bubu Malik Sy.

The exogenous records concerning Maka Jiba make it possible to substantiate certain indigenous accounts by employing external observations. For example, it is with Maka Jiba that the first encounter between an *Eliman* of Bundu and a European (David) is recorded. At the same time, however, the value of the observations made by Europeans either passing through Bundu or stationed at an area trading settlement at this time is mitigated by their shallow acquaintance with the region; their writings reflect little comprehension of the geopolitical realities of the period. Consequently, while Europe begins to compile firsthand knowledge of Bundu during Maka Jiba's reign, such records are only exploratory, and therefore fragmentary and ambiguous.

In approaching the sources for Maka Jiba's reign, it is essential that informed speculation and the corroboration of independent observers be used to balance the indigenous record. As was true for the data for Bubu Malik Sy, the brevity with which the endogenous sources treat the tenure of Maka Jiba makes reconstruction via consensus impossible. General patterns of the reign can be discerned from the endogenous genre. There can be no certainty regarding specifics, however, unless verified by external observation. In turn, the outside perspective can aid in the effort to elucidate developments within the court, but cannot be relied upon to provide definitive answers.

The return of Bubu Malik Sy (reigned 1699–1715)

According to our key sources, Bubu Malik Sy had been sent to Futa Jallon several months prior to the outbreak of hostilities between Malik Sy and the *Tunka* of Tiyaabu.[1] He had previously spent some time studying in Futa Jallon, and was returning for the purpose of obtaining aid from his cousins, the sons of Malik Sy's aunt, Maty Hamet, in anticipation of the struggle with Tiyaabu.[2] His recruiting demonstrates the early and relatively close ties between Bundu and Futa Jallon; Bubu Malik's son, Maka Jiba, would go on to study with Karamoko Alfa, the principal leader of the Futa Jallon *jihād*. Notwithstanding these ties, it is also possible that this recruitment story was concocted in order to excuse Bubu Malik of any culpability in the death of Malik Sy: he could not prevent it, because he was not there.

Bubu Malik, according to the limited sources, was successful in recruiting assistance in Futa Jallon, but by the time he returned to Bundu, the conflict with Gajaaga had already commenced, his father an early casualty. As Lamartiny relates the story, Malik Sy had become "impatient," and decided to attack; but the idea that he had sent for help months prior to the war, and yet was unable to wait for it, indicates that he was forced into battle by an attack from the Bacili. As the tale goes, Bubu Malik finally returned with a "numerous" army, but had to take a detour in order to obtain water. It was an unfortunate decision, if the tradition can be believed. No sooner had Bubu Malik reached Bundu, than Malik Sy expired at Goumba-Koko.[3]

Leading an army of supposedly 1,000 men, armed with spears, bows and arrows, Bubu Malik did what Malik Sy could not do with 2,000.[4] While the *Tunka* was celebrating his victory at Tiyaabu, Bubu Malik proceeded to attack Gajaaga at Kounguel, Golmy, Arondou, and other villages. By the time this "belle et rapide" campaign was over, he had reportedly burned and pillaged from twenty to thirty villages, enslaving the survivors.[5] The effect of his exploits was to demonstrate the viability of the newly-born polity, even in the absence of the charismatic leadership of Malik Sy.

While the foregoing scenario cannot be established, all of the Malik Sy traditions are emphatic that Bubu Malik both assumed authority upon the death of his father, and provided some stability and direction for the newly formed state. This emphasis supports the Sissibe contention Malik Sy had previously staked out a territorial claim in what was southern Gajaaga, and that this claim was defended under successive leadership.

The early court

His objective accomplished, Bubu Malik returned to Wuro Alfa. He took the title *Eliman* and became the head of state, but in apparent violation of the pact between his father, the N'Guenar, and the Fadube.[6] In that "constitution," it was agreed that the leading individual (based upon age, and distinction in piety, wisdom, and war) from among the Sissibe and the N'Guenar would succeed Malik Sy as *Eliman*, while the Fadube would remain outside of the circle of power in perpetuity. The Jakhanke are nowhere mentioned with respect to this arrangement, suggesting that while they may have been in the vicinity, they were either not yet under Bundunke political rule, or their numbers did not warrant inclusion in the negotiations. There are few details on the other aspects of the "constitution," which suggests that it was fundamentally a compromise between two Fulbe communities on how executive power would be shared. But the circumstances surrounding Malik Sy's death were such that an abrogation of the pact was easily achieved through a show of military force. On the strength of his Futa Jallon support, Bubu Malik undermined the succession process and seized power. His action would have serious repercussions in the near future, as a violent struggle over political power between the N'Guenar and the Sissibe erupted. In the end, the Sissibe would emerge with exclusive rights to executive power, while the N'Guenar would settle for comprising the middle and upper strata of the nobility.

With regard to the sovereign power, the early role of the state centered upon the defense of the realm and the oversight of its economic growth to ensure viability. The *Eliman* was head of a non-standing military, mustered in times of crisis. Taxes were collected, a process begun under Bundu Malik, although the particular forms of taxation are unspecified. It is likely that at this early juncture, there was no substantive distinction between what the Muslim Fulbe and non-Muslim Fadube paid to the state, although the former was probably referred to as *zakāt* (obligatory alms), while non-Muslims paid *jizya* ("secular" revenue in recognition of protective and other services rendered by the Muslim government). It is possible that certain religious functions were performed by the *Eliman*, given Bubu Malik's period of study in Futa Jallon. It is also possible that he may have led the collective prayers on special occasions. As will be discussed in more detail later, the *Eliman* constituted the court of last appeal; this practice could have started as early as Bubu Malik.

Concerning the matter of justice as a whole, ordinary complaints were heard at the village level and according to customary law during the early part of the eighteenth century. As the polity grew, and interaction between villages and towns resulted in unavoidable disputes, the growing Jakhanke community would have led the Muslim clerisy in adjudicating the more important cases according to Islamic law.

The principal imperative in the policy of the early court was the acquisition of a larger and more fecund agricultural base. To that end, Bundu's initial policy was centered upon territorial expansion into the fertile plains of the Faleme River, at the expense of its Malinke inhabitants. The establishment of such a base strengthened the power of the nobility, who heretofore premised their claims to such a status solely upon membership in the ranks of the *Torodbe*. Internal slavery was therefore stimulated, as increased land necessitated greater numbers of cultivators.

Kumba's well and the name "Bundu"

When Bubu Malik took power, Bundu consisted of a handful of villages, including Wuro-Alfa, Guirobe, Fissa-Tamba, and Bubuya.[7] It was in Bubuya ("house of Bubu"), northwest of Senoudebou, that Bubu Malik fixed his permanent residence. While many of the recruits from Futa Jallon returned there after Bubu Malik was safely in power, others remained with him in Bundu, helping to ensure his reign and Sissibe succession.

It is during Bubu Malik's tenure that the name "Bundu" began to be applied to the area. According to Lamartiny, there was a very old legend, known only to a few aged men, that the area was once called "Babawuama-taguifama."[8] The first two letters stood for the Bacili of Gajaaga; the second "ba" stood for the Badiar; "wua" represented the Wualiabe; the "ma" recalled the Malinke from Bambuk; the "ta" related to the people of Tamba; the Guirobe were represented by the "gui" and the Fadube by the "fa"; and the final "ma" was added for Malik Sy. The legend is obviously a construct, but it is very useful in that it underscores the diversity and decentralized character of the area, and possibly represents the order of settlement by ethnicity.

While it is clear that it took some time before the area came to be known as "Bundu," its earlier designation is uncertain. Besides the names Gajaaga and Bambuk (or Bambuhu), the section that became southeastern Bundu was at one time called "Combegoudou," whereas the Faleme Valley was identified as "Contou."[9]

The term "bundu" means "well' in Soninke, and is traditionally believed to have come from a well found at Bubuya.[10] There are several stories relating to this well. According to one version, the followers of Malik Sy repaired a well (*bundu*) belonging to a woman named Kumba. The well was therefore called "Bundu-Kumba." Bubu Malik also had to repair the well, after which it was called "Bundu Bonadu Malik Sy," or the "well repaired by Bubu Sy." By extension, the name of the well was applied to all of the territory subjugated by the Sissibe.[11] A second version has Malik Sy digging a well in front of Wuro-Alfa, which was then given the name "Bunda Ba," or the "Great Well," and was subsequently used for the name of the area.[12]

In nine of the thirteen versions recorded by Curtin, the story of Kumba's well is repeated.[13] N'Diaye's account differs from the others, however, in that it maintains that the Fadube dug the well, but were unable to line it due to the *jinn* (spirits) living in nearby trees. Malik Sy prepared an *aaye* (amulet, from the Arabic *āya*), which consisted of writing Qur'anic verses on a board, then washing the board in water.[14] He then sprinkled the water on the trees and cut them down. Bubu Malik was able to finish the well later.[15] Curtin points out that the right to own land went to the one who first cleared it and dug a well, meaning that the Fadube did not have clear title to the land, whereas the Sissibe established their claim via the well.[16] N'Diaye's version seeks to justify the Sissibe domination of the area, and does not address the issue of how it came to be called Bundu. But the two ideas are closely related: Kumba's *bundu* became functional because of the Sissibe, which is a symbolic way of saying the Bundu became productive and thriving because of the Sissibe, whereas before their settlement it was unproductive and unimportant. It is not surprising that a well would be chosen to convey these claims, as it is an indispensable resource in the pursuit of pastoral and agricultural activities in a hot, relatively dry climate such as characterizes Bundu.

It is probable that the Soninke name "Bundu" was not the innovation of the Sissibe. However, implicit in the name is the idea of increased agricultural productivity and pastoralism, and the adoption of the name for the state reflected an increase in population and land under cultivation and pastoral use. In turn, this increased productivity became noticeable while Bubu Malik was in power, thus the usage of "Bundu" is attributed to his period.

The story of Kumba's well not only concerns agriculture and pastoralism, but also the manner in which the state was created. It is noteworthy that most of the sources credit Bubu Malik, not Malik Sy, with finishing the well. This reflects the fact that Malik Sy was prevented from completing the foundation of Bundu by the war with the Bacili. Bubu Malik was able to regain power, and to create a form of stability for the realm.

Expansion to the south and east

At the outset of Bubu Malik's reign, it is unlikely, given the limited collection of villages which made up Bundu at this time, that the state had any productive or distributive economy worth mentioning. This would rapidly change as the eighteenth century unfolded. At this early stage, Bubu Malik identified lands to the south and east as possessing the greatest potential for immediate growth.[17] This emphasis was possible because of a temporary lull in the violence with Gajaaga, apparently a reflection of some internal problems within that realm which prevented the continuation of hostilities with the upstart Bundu.[18] With his northern border momentarily peaceful, Bubu Malik turned his attention to the south and east. The first step he took was defensive: he constructed the *tata*, or "fortress," at Fena, in close proximity to Koussan.[19] He placed his son Maka Jiba at the head of the fortified post, under whom served a large number of Malinke slaves. This accomplished, Bubu Malik soon commenced the expansion to the east, targeting the Malinke villages above Bubuya, along the Faleme River.[20]

To what extent these southern and eastern moves were influenced by the English presence along the Upper Gambia is unclear. To be sure, the English were firmly established at James Island by 1661, having operated there as early as 1588. Into the region the English brought iron bars, copper basins, knives, inexpensive textiles, gunpowder and firearms, coral and crystal beads, amber, woolens, French brandy, and West Indian rum. Re-exports included east Indian cottons, calicoes and prints; Swedish and German iron and copper; and Baltic amber.[21] In exchange for these goods, the English were interested in the slaves, gold (from Bambuk), and gum trade of the region. It is inconceivable, then, that the early Bundunkobe were oblivious to the English presence.

Having stated the foregoing, there were certainly other reasons for Bubu Malik's southern and eastern strategies. First of all, the state needed to expand territorially, and given the strength of Gajaaga's forces to the north, it was only logical to expand into areas of lesser resistance. Secondly, he wanted to control the fertile *waalo* or floodplain of the Faleme, upon which a productive economy could be premised. Concomitant with territorial expansion and more cultivable land was the need for a larger population; the importation of slaves would partially fulfill this demand for labor. Finally, it was from the south that the valuable kola nut originated; Bundu's gravitational direction indicates that the *Eliman* was very much interested in benefitting from that commerce. This was to be accomplished by taxing the

Consolidation and expansion in the eighteenth century

caravans passing through the area, but this could not be achieved unless control over the area's trade routes could be established. Thus, the need to develop both productive and distributive capacities greatly stimulated the growth of early Bundu, and was important to the development of a pragmatic perspective in the court.

Stirrings along the north-west frontier: the Upper Senegal

The power of Gajaaga along the Upper Senegal precluded for the moment any bid by Bundu to contest the former's control of that area's trade. In time, however, the commerce of the Upper Senegal would prove to be an irresistible attraction for the Bundunke ruling elite, causing it to commit itself to almost perpetual war. This was a consequence of the expansion of the French up the Senegal. Having founded Saint Louis at the mouth of the Senegal in 1659, the French had established *comptoirs* (settlements) at Arguin, Saint Joseph, Goree, Joal, Albreada, Bintan, and Bisseaux by 1700. The French presence along the Senegal gave them access to the valued gum trade.[22] The gum trees are located both to the north of the Senegal, in the steppe, as far east as Guidimakha; and also to the south of the Senegal, in the Ferlo. The gum was harvested from March until the beginning of the rainy season, usually June or July. The gum was then taken to the various towns along the river and subsequently transported to Saint Louis for sale.[23] According to Cultru, the "trade in gum was always the most important of those [commodity exchanges] which were conducted at our settlements in West Africa."[24] The European demand for gum continued to increase from the 1740s through the early twentieth century.[25] Because of its location, Bundu was in a position to benefit from the gum harvests on both sides of the Senegal.

According to Delcourt, following gum, the French were mostly interested in slaves, then gold, beeswax, and ivory.[26] It is Bathily's position that the number of captives from the Upper Senegal has been seriously underestimated, and thus the impact of the slave trade on the region not fully understood.[27] Given that the regional slave trade was probably more important than previously understood, and that Bundu maintained domestic slaves and became a major commercial power in the region, it is necessarily the case that it directed war and raid captives to the *comptoirs* of the French. However, the extent of this activity in the first twenty years of the state's existence is difficult to ascertain. It would appear that its own need for labor during this period superceded export demands.

In addition to gum and slaves, the French had an abiding interest in Senegambian gold.[28] Specifically, the Bambuk region was famous for its goldfields, having supplied the ancient kingdom of Ghana with its resources. Six hundred years after the demise of Ghana, the "golden trade" of the Gambia River continued to be supplied by Bambuk gold, and was a major reason European factories were placed along the Senegambian coast in the seventeenth century.[29] For their part, the French launched three projects between the latter seventeenth and nineteenth centuries to exploit the Bambuk mines. All three were disappointing failures.[30] Bundu, established adjacent to Bambuk, would soon realize the value of its strategic position. It is quite possible that the *waalo* lands along the Faleme were also seized by Bubu Malik because of their proximity to the Bambuk fields; it is more likely, however, that the issue of controlling the flow of gold from Bambuk was more of a preoccupation with his successors.

The French, in pursuit of commercial gain, established posts deep in the interior of the upper valley, at Kounguel (1697); Fort Saint Joseph, east of the Senegal–Faleme confluence (1700–58); Boulam (1700–5); Fort Saint Pierre on the Faleme River (1714–20); Kainura, near Senoudebou (1725); Farabana (1726); Sirimana (1728); and Cagnou Island near Felou Falls (1744).[31] The intent was to divert all commercial traffic away from the English along the Gambia and towards the Senegal. However, the French never succeeded in shutting down the trade to the Gambia, and this was largely because of the strategically placed polity of Bundu, which insisted upon conducting trade with both European powers. This policy of trading with both the French and the English began with the reign of Bubu Malik, and continued on despite the demands of reformers in subsequent years to curtail that trade for reasons which will become clear in subsequent chapters.

In pursuit of his southern strategy, Bubu Malik made the fatal decision to attack Samba N'Gala, a Malinke village between Goundiourou and Didecoto, east of Koussan. The *Elliman* was mortally wounded in the chest, and died en route to Wuro-Alfa near a small village called Wassa (also near Goundiourou).[32] The sources are by no means agreed as to the length of his reign, but the date of 1715 is a reasonable approximation, based upon several considerations.[33]

The interregnum (1716–1720)

At Bubu Malik's death, the forces of decentralization were immediately set into motion. From without, the Malinke states bordering Bundu began to counterattack the young upstart, in retaliation for the latter's expansionist policies. From within, the fragile compact between the Sissibe, the N'Guenar, and the Fadube fell apart. Fulbe immigrants loyal to the Denyanke of Futa Toro had never recognized Sissibe claims in the first place. The N'Guenar, still smarting from Bubu Malik's usurpation of power and upset over his imperialist objectives, declared both their independence from the Sissibe and their intention to henceforth rule Bundu. At the same time, the other *Torodbe* communities exerted their autonomy, so that there was no central authority in place. "In a word, the most complete anarchy reigned in Bundu."[34]

In light of these developments, Bubu Malik's descendants "found themselves defenseless."[35] All of the Sissibe reportedly fled to Futa Toro except for Maka Jiba, who found refuge with the *Torodbe* at Fissa-Tamba for five years, until he declared his candidacy for the leadership of Bundu.[36] Mudi Malik and Tumane Malik, Bubu Malik's brothers, never returned to Bundu. From his sanctuary in Fissa-Tamba, Maka Jiba maintained a low profile and carefully observed the activities of the N'Guenar. The latter constituted a relatively important power in an otherwise decentralized context, as the previously cohesive modicum of villages now experienced virtual autonomy. Rançon maintains that the N'Guenar "abhorred" the Sissibe, and that they sought to systematically eliminate them. Such animosity may have indeed characterized relations between the N'Guenar and the Sissibe immediately following Bubu Malik's death. However, the resumption of Sissibe power within Bundu would also involve the acceptance of the N'Guenar as part of the nobility. This means that the Fulbe in this instance were able to agree that reconciliation was more advantageous than continued strife, particularly if the state was to prosper and to survive the hostility of its neighbors.

The dating of the interregnum, is problematic. Rançon gives the period as 1718 to 1728.[37] Curtin, in turn, believes it lasted until 1731 or 1735.[38] The reason he lengthens the period is because of the failure of Ayuba Sulayman Diallo (or "Job Ben Solomon") to mention the Sissibe. However, since Ayuba Sulayman Diallo was captured and exported to North America as a slave in 1731, and Maka Jiba was definitely in power when Thomas Hull visited Bundu in 1735, Maka Jiba must have taken the reins between 1731 and 1735 at the latest.[39]

The evidence indicates, however, that Maka Jiba came to power even before 1731. A critical portion of this evidence is a report written by the Commandant of Fort Saint Joseph in April of 1725, describing the country of Gajaaga. According to this document, Gajaaga was divided into two social groups: "marabouts" and "commoners."[40] The clerics were involved in commerce, exerting great control over trade and legal matters, and even influencing the royal court. To the northwest of Gajaaga was the "Royaume des Siratiques," a reference to Futa Toro. To the southwest was the "republique de Bondou." It was composed of three "estates." The first was that of the clerics, of whom the greatest was the king, and who did nothing without first consulting the other two "estates." The second category included the "noblemen," who were the governors of the villages, and the free warriors. The third "estate" is difficult to discern from the text, but it appears to have been the merchants. The commandant added that Bundu had always been well-maintained "since its first founder," and that its citizens had originally come from the land of the "Siratiques," having left because of exorbitant taxation. This is a clear reference to Malik Sy, as there are no other candidates who fit this description. Furthermore, there is the complementary account of Boucard, who journeyed through Bambuk in 1728, and reported that the "Republique de Bondou" was west of Bambuk.[41] It was the custom of the French at this time to label African theocratic states as "republiques." Therefore, based upon reports in 1725 and 1728, Bundu had reconstituted its central authority by these dates, and was once again under the control of the descendants of the founder of the state, Malik Sy.[42]

There is an obvious conflict in the sources. Ayuba Sulayman Diallo does not mention the Sissibe, yet there are clear, independent sources which state that Bundu was thriving some three to six years before Ayuba Sulayman Diallo's capture and exportation to the western hemisphere. The probable key to the disparity lies in the political orientation of Ayuba Sulayman and the Diallo family. According to his own account, the Diallo family was allied to the Denyanke dynasty. His failure to mention Malik Sy and Bubu Malik is therefore in keeping with his family's refusal to acknowledge Sissibe sovereignty. His omissions must have been deliberate, for Bundu was definitely under Sissibe control in 1725.

In light of the foregoing, this study proposes that the interregnum lasted only five years, based upon several factors. The first is the likelihood that Bundu was reconstructed by 1725. Secondly, in contrast to Rançon and Roux, the Bundunke rulers' lists do not recognize the interregnum. Instead, they record that Tumane Bubu Malik Sy succeeded Bubu Malik, and that he reigned either four or five years.[43] Rançon simply says that Tumane Bubu Malik died shortly after his father.[44] It is probable that the rulers' lists seek to mask the fact that the Sissibe had lost power during this period, while maintaining accuracy regarding the period's duration. The last factor concerns the consensus among the sources that the reign of Maka Jiba was an extremely long one, with estimates ranging from thirty-one to forty-four years.[45] Since most of the sources agree that his tenure ended in 1764, forty-four years subtracted from this date yields 1720, supporting the assertion that the interregnum ended around this time.

In sum, Bubu Malik had succeeded in restoring order to the microstate of Bundu around the turn of the eighteenth century. Steps were taken to enhance Bundu's productive capacity in conjunction with its need to grow in population. The move to lay the foundation for the domestic economy stimulated expansionist behavior, and was the beginning of the tensions which characterized Bundu's relations with its neighbors for the remainder of its existence. Nascent commercial activity also began to contribute to the state's meager coffers. But the death of Bubu Malik momentarily halted progress towards realization of a prosperous, pragmatic, Muslim-controlled polity. That the interregnum did not result in the permanent dismemberment of Bundu is evidence of the belief by some in the potential of the state. In particular, it is testimony to the abilities of Bundu's next ruler, Maka Jiba.

The emergence of Maka Jiba

Between the ages of thirty and thirty-two, Maka Jiba decided to reestablish the Sissibe in Bundu.[46] Rançon states that he left his asylum in Fissa-Tamba to discuss his intentions with his family in Futa Toro, many of whom had fled Bundu with the death of Bubu Malik and the rise of anti-Sissibe sentiment.[47] The descendants of Malik Sy's uncle, N'Diob-Hamet, are spoken of in the sources as already residing in Futa Toro, so apparently they never left Suyuma.

Ironically, it was the sons and grandsons of N'Diob-Hamet who were receptive to Maka Jiba's plans, and agreed to help him. Maka Jiba's uncles, the brothers of Bubu Malik, refused to return to Bundu, and remained in Futa Toro. Maka Jiba and his small cohort of relatives journeyed back to Bundu, where he arranged for a meeting with the N'Guenar at Bubuya. The choice of Bubuya, the home of Bubu Malik, was clearly intended to lend credibility to Maka Jiba's call for a renewed Bundu under Sissibe rule. In response, certain of the *Torodbe* vehemently disagreed. Maka Jiba, supported by family, the residents of Fissa-Tamba, and probably a contingent of armed slaves from the *tata* at Fena (under Maka Jiba's command during Bubu Malik's reign), enjoyed an advantage in the brief armed struggle which ensued. The vanquished N'Guenar were forced to recognize Maka Jiba's authority, and in time regained their noble rank. With the matter of executive power settled, those villages formerly under Bubu Malik were once again united, and Maka Jiba was named *Eliman*.[48]

It must be underscored that Maka Jiba's initial sphere of control extended to only a few villages. There were a number of communities which, after the dissolution of the state in 1716, refused to acknowledge Sissibe sovereignty. Thus, the primary objective of the Maka Jiba court was to reestablish and consolidate the power of the state over recalcitrant villages. The evidence would suggest that this was a task that was both difficult and fully realized only towards the end of Maka Jiba's reign. One example of the difficulty is the case of "Eliman" Salum, an unidentified Bundunke dignitary who may have been Alium Bubu Malik, Maka Jiba's youngest brother. In 1744 Pierre David, director of the Compagnie des Indes from 1738 to 1746, met with representatives of Maka Jiba's court at Fort Saint James, near Makhana.[49] He then received "Eliman" Salum, who was introduced as the "second most important person in the country."[50] David, interested in the gold of Bambuk, had originally planned to construct a settlement on the Faleme's east bank, but Salum had objected because the area was beyond his control.[51] Kidira, equidistant from Farabana in Bambuk and Fort Saint Joseph, was a compromise solution.[52]

When Maka Jiba arrived later at Fort Saint Joseph, he became incensed at the news that "Eliman" Salum had "cut his own deal."[53] Maka Jiba was described to David as "the master of all Bundu."[54] Whether Salum's actions represented insubordination or competition from an independent source is unclear. In either case, the fact that he was conducting trade talks with the French in the name of Bundu, almost twenty-five years into the reign of Maka Jiba, suggests the problems associated with consolidating Sissibe rule at this time.

A second example of the difficulty of consolidation is much more speculative. According to several sources (cited in the previous chapter), Tumane Bubu Malik Sy, Maka Jiba's eldest brother, succeeded his father Bubu Malik as *Eliman* (as opposed to the interregnum). These sources do not discuss the way in which power was transferred from Tumane Bubu Malik Sy to Maka Jiba, but they agree that such a transfer was made. Given the violence associated with Maka Jiba's assumption of authority, it is not beyond credulity that he contested the control of Bundu with his brother as well as other *Torodbe* opposition following the interregnum.

To facilitate the consolidation process, Maka Jiba selected immediate family members for crucial posts. For example, the important *tata* at Fena was placed under the command of his youngest son Pate Gai, celebrated for his military prowess. Besides Pate Gai, Maka Jiba had six other sons, all of whom were associated with political or military positions of leadership during and after Maka Jiba's reign. In addition to the sons of Maka Jiba, who formed the upper stratum of power, the *Eliman* consulted with the N'Guenar and the Jakhanke in matters of importance. Consultation with this council of notables became an established practice of all Bundunke rulers from Maka Jiba on, although relations between the principals antedate him.

It is under Maka Jiba that Bundu began to maintain a standing army, although the proportion of free persons to slaves would have been small at this junction. The increase in the number of *tatas* during this period from one to three signals the growth of Bundu's military capacity. These *tatas* were staffed with armed slaves, whose primary task was to fight under the direction of Sissibe commanders. Their specific duties will be discussed shortly; suffice it to say here that under Maka Jiba, an armed force capable of responding immediately to a given challenge had grown quickly and relatively significantly.

As a consequence of both administrative and social developments, and in response to regional challenges, Maka Jiba would develop a four-fold strategy. First, he would emphasize the expansion of an agricultural base along the Faleme, a policy inaugurated by Bubu Malik. Second, he would seek to control the goldfields of Bambuk, given rising European interest. Third, the *Eliman* would attempt to control the trade routes in and near Bundu by providing adequate security for traders, and by taxing caravans at certain towns along the routes. Finally, Maka Jiba, in addition to expanding to the east and south, would defend Bundu's northern frontier against the Moors and the Denyanke rulers of Futa Toro. In the end, he would achieve tremendous success in accomplishing the majority of his goals, and is therefore considered by the Bundunkobe themselves as second only to Malik Sy in honor and greatness. If Malik Sy founded the state, it was Maka Jiba who made it truly viable.

The Jakhanke clerisy

Assisting Maka Jiba in his efforts to establish the polity were the Jakhanke, whose role in the development of Bundunke government and society was both unique and substantial. With regard to the life of the court, the earlier relationship between Malik Sy and Muhammad Fudi flourished into a commitment between the Sissibe and the Jakhanke that would extend into the late nineteenth century. The latter continued to accept Sissibe political authority, and served as counselors to the court; in turn, the Jakhanke enjoyed a high level of autonomy in their settlements.[55] The Jakhanke, for example, were never required to serve in the military; however, they were expected to maintain defensive walls around their towns, and they had to pay taxes to the government in the form of food and livestock.[56]

The political union of the Sissibe and the Jakhanke had resulted in the aforementioned Muhammad Fatima of Didecoto. He served as a teacher, counselor, and $q\bar{a}\d{d}\bar{\imath}$ to the Sissibe elite until his death c. 1772, which makes him a contemporary of Maka Jiba.[57] Such was the rapport between Muhammad Fatima and the Sissibe that large numbers of Jakhanke were encouraged to migrate from Diakha Ba in Bambuk to Didecoto, and the town grew rapidly in both population and prestige.[58] All four of the major Jakhanke clans were represented: the Suware, the Jakhite-Kabba, the Silla, and the Jabi-Gassama. It is estimated that 300 compounds of Jakhanke families settled there, together with sixty additional compounds composed of slaves and various caste groups (ironworkers, leatherworkers, etc.).[59] The growth of the town's population, however, led to its ultimate ruin, as the land could not sustain the densification. Exhausted soil, combined with interclan rivalries among the Jakhanke, eventually led to an exodus from Didecoto by the end of the eighteenth century.

Muhammad Fatima's considerable reputation for learning, combined with the support and protection of the Sissibe, were important factors in Didecoto's emergence. But another factor, indirectly alluded to earlier, concerned the relative richness of the soil prior to its exhaustion. Because of its productivity, agriculture and animal husbandry were major activities in Didecoto, and in other Jakhanke settlements as well.[60] With the labor provided by slaves and students, Didecoto and other Jakhanke centers became important sources of farm production. Such a capacity was crucial to the success of Bundu's attempts at territorial expansion and stabilization.

Another factor stimulating Sissibe support for Jakhanke activity, in addition to their clerical services and agriculture, was the fact that the Jakhanke settlements tended to be either identical with or proximate to key entrepots within the trading networks of the region.[61] The precise role of the Jakhanke in commerce is arguable; nevertheless, it is clear that they sought to benefit from trade in some way by locating at important staging points along the various routes.[62] Again, the control of area trade routes constituted a principal focus of Bundu's activities during this period, so that Jakhanke and Sissibe interests were mutually reinforcing.

From the foregoing discussion, it is apparent that the growth of the Jakhanke in Bundu during the eighteenth century was directly related to the concurrent consolidation and expansion of Sissibe authority. The Jakhanke not only played key advisory roles in the government, but they were also important as commercial and productive allies. In this way, the prosperity of the Jakhanke was important to the overall economic welfare of the state.

In addition to their contribution to the court, the Jakhanke's impact upon Bundunke society was considerable. This society-wide influence was clerical in nature, and tended to emanate from their settlements throughout Bundu, including Didecoto, Bani Israila, and Qayrawan.[63] By the second half of the nineteenth century, the Jakhanke had spread to a number of towns to the southwest of Didecoto, in Diakha province.[64] From these centers, the Jakhanke provided both the Sissibe elite and the society as a whole with such services as education, prayer (of all kinds), psychological healing (often through amulets), and divination (usually via dream interpretation).[65] Prayers for the success of military campaigns were especially important, as was divination, a category that included a complex and highly-valued form of prayer (*al-istikhārah*) that sought God's guidance when faced with a set of alternatives. But the Jakhanke were also skilled in Islamic law, and provided the majority of *qāḍīs* for the various towns.[66]

While Muslims utilized the services of the Jakhanke, non-Muslims also sought to benefit from their availability. Non-Muslims frequented the Jakhanke for divination and amulets, and the Jakhanke accepted non-Muslim children into their schools. The Jakhanke educational system was by far the most important in Bundu, attracting students from all ethnic groups. Through the instrumentality of these various means, the Jakhanke constituted the principal forces in the conversion of non-Muslims to Islam. Their active presence was also fundamental to the health of the Muslim community. By giving their full support to the Sissibe regime, the Jakhanke granted the ruling elite enormous legitimacy. The *quid pro quo* was protection and non-interference from the regime. In this way, Bundu gradually became a Muslim land, under Muslim political leadership, but without benefit of an Islamic revolution.

Notwithstanding the tremendous influence of the Jakhanke, there were also other forces in operation within Bundu. It is possible that the first half of the eighteenth century saw significant change in that considerable numbers of immigrants may have settled in Bundu to escape the accelerated pace of the slave trade, especially in the form of the raiding Ormankobe. Paradoxically, as a result of Bundunke raiding of the Malinke along the Faleme, and in conjunction with the rise of Segu and its involvement in producing human captives, it is likely that there was a noticeable increase in domestic slaves in Bundu.

Immigration from the Middle Senegal Valley, along with the rise in prominence of the Jakhanke clerisy, suggests that Islam was making significant strides in becoming the predominant religion of Bundu. The emergence of Islam could only support the struggle of the Bundunkobe against their non-Muslim neighbors, and would be used to justify the confiscation of land and enslavement of various communities. The confiscation of land was critical to the agricultural needs of the state, and was calculated into the first part of Maka Jiba's four-fold strategy; namely, establishing control of the Faleme.

Expansion along the Faleme

Although David's visit to the Upper Senegal indicated increasing French interest in the area, and notwithstanding the reciprocating attitude of the Bundunke rulers, the primary focus of the state during the reign of Maka Jiba was the Faleme and the southern frontier, and as such it represented continuity with the previous orientation of Bubu Malik and Malik Sy. The fertile lands of the Faleme, the proximity to the Bambuk goldfields, the increasingly traveled routes of the slave caravans, and the greater access to British traced commodities constituted ideal circumstances by which Bundu could develop its potential. The *Eliman* naturally gravitated towards such an opportunity.

As evidence of his territorial expansion, Maka Jiba constructed two *tatas* in addition to the one at Fena. Dara (twenty kilometers east of Senoudebou) and Dyunfung (six kilometers west of Farabana), both on the east side of the Faleme River, were designed to provide bases from which Maka Jiba could launch forays into the surrounding country.[67] So important was the eastern Faleme to his plans that Maka Jiba himself moved to Dara, entrusting the *tata* at Fena to his youngest son Pate Gai. Maka Jiba then expanded to the south, attacking the kingdom of "Contou."[68] Those who managed to escape traveled southwest, where they later established the village of Tambacounda in Wuli.[69]

In his push along the Faleme, Maka Jiba engendered a conflict that would survive his own tenure; namely, the struggle with Farabana over the Bambuk goldfields and the slave caravan routes. According to Rançon, Maka Jiba sought revenge for the death of his father by attacking the village of Miramguiku, near Samba N'Gala.[70] The village head, Sambu Amadi Tumane, fled to the other (east) side of the Faleme, where he reportedly founded Farabana. However, Farabana antedates Amadi Tumane, for he became the ruler of Farabana at the death of his father, the former ruler of Farabana, in 1737.[71] These two accounts can be reconciled by assuming that Miramguiku was a satellite of Farabana. It was not unusual for rulers of large towns to also control nearby villages. Maka Jiba, in consolidating Bundunke territory, pushed Amadi Tumane beyond the Faleme, where he assumed leadership of Farabana at his father's death.

The struggle between Maka Jiba and Amadi Tumane was long and uncelebrated. Given Maka Jiba's relocation to the eastern bank of the Faleme, it can be surmised that he was not only interested in controlling the trade routes over which the gold passed, but that he was vying for control of the goldfields themselves. From his *tatas* in Dara and Dyunfung, Maka Jiba could continually challenge Amadi Tumane's authority in Bambuk.[72] The conflict between the two rivals was such that David found it necessary to attempt a mediation between the two in order to successfully operate in the area. He spoke with Bundunke envoys and with Amadi Tumane, who was credited with ruling Seconuduwa, Niamila, and other villages in Bambuk, in addition to Farabana.[73] David went on to establish posts at both Farabana and Kidira, but they never became very significant, due in part to the continuation of hostilities between Bundu and Farabana.

While Bundu was contesting the control of Bambuk, the British along the Gambia were developing a lively interest in Bundu's strategic and commercial potential. This is well illustrated by the account of Ayuba Sulayman Diallo, a Pullo from Bundu who had been captured along the Gambia and sold into the transatlantic slave trade in 1731. After a short stay in Maryland, his literacy in Arabic attracted considerable attention, and upon persuading a British benefactor to purchase his freedom, he returned to West Africa in August of 1734.[74] Arriving on the Gambia, he sent a message to his father in Bundu, and waited until 14 February 1735, when an envoy returned. At that time he was informed that his father had died, and that since he was away, "there has been such a dreadful War, that there is not so much as one Cow left in it, tho' when Job was there, it was a very noted Country for numerous herds of large Cattle."[75] Curtin has suggested that this war was a reference to the civil war between the N'Guenar and the Sissibe.[76] However, as has been discussed, the "civil war" between the *Torodbe* was of a limited nature, and did not include groups or areas which had never acknowledged Sissibe sovereignty. The war that was reported to Ayuba Sulayman Diallo was apparently on a much larger scale; the messenger's account was more than likely a description of the devastation caused by the Ormankobe incursions. It could also have been related to the ouster of Samba Gelaajo Jegi by 1735, concerning whom more will be said later in this chapter.

Ayuba Sulayman Diallo was returning to his native land not solely as a weary repatriate, but also as an agent for British trading interests. On 4 July 1734, the Royal African Company sent a letter to Governor Richard Hull in Gambia regarding the freed slave: "If the person you should send up river with him should be willing to accompany him into his own country, possibly he might by that means be able to do the Company good service by opening and settling a trade and correspondence between the natives of those parts and our highest factories."[77] In addition to slaves and Bambuk gold, the British were also interested in the gum trade. Governor Hull had learned of the gum tree forests southwest of Bundu, not far from Niani-Maro, in the Ferlo.[78] The forests were divided between the people of Niani, the "grands

Jalaofs," and "Futa" (i.e., Bundu), and it was reported that no one actually lived there.[79] Governor Hull therefore determined to accompany Ayuba Sulayman Diallo from Joar (on the Gambia) to Bundu, but was obliged to return to England before he could do so.[80] Instead, the repatriate was accompanied by Thomas Hull, Governor Hull's relative.[81] Thomas Hull would make a second trip to Bundu and Bambuk in 1736.[82]

By 1736, Ayuba Sulayman's activities in Bundu were causing quite a stir among the French. On 15 June 1736, a report from Fort Saint Joseph stated that an English delegation of about sixteen people had visited Bundu, accompanied by fifty Bundunke escorts, bearing merchandise and a few horses.[83] The report went on to advise that steps be taken "to find and apprehend the Negro Job."[84] Later in November of the same year, a report was issued warning that "the affair concerning the Negro Job deserves attention ..."[85] Again, in December, it was reported that "Job had to be chased out of Bundu by any means possible."[86] In fact, "Job" was captured and imprisoned by the French at Fort Saint Joseph sometime in December of 1736 for having been a British agent.[87]

The brief detention did not succeed in stopping Ayuba Sulayman. He was able to send two letters to the Royal African Company, expressing appreciation for their help.[88] One of the letters, composed in Arabic, was translated by Melchoir de Jaspas, "an Armenian, native of Diarbekir, the capital city of Mesopotamia."[89] In 1737, the Royal African Company sent de Jaspas to Fort James along with a "Persian" slave named Joseph. After a brief interlude, he went to Bundu with "Lahamin Jay," who had been captured and enslaved along with Ayuba Sulayman in 1731, and who was being returned at the Bundunke's request.[90] De Jaspas was in Bundu from 1738 to 1740, but there is no account extant.[91] In 1744 de Jaspas journeyed to Portuguese Guinea, where he was killed the next year. As for Ayuba Sulayman Diallo, all mention of him in the Company's records ceases after the 1740s.[92] However, he maintained contact with the British along the Gambia until he died in 1773.[93]

Despite Gray's assertion that "no material advantage was derived by the Company from these visits to Bondu,"[94] it is clear from the flurry of British activity that commercial contact with the Bundunkobe was seen by both parties as important, and was in the process of becoming regularized. Hence, the southern gravitation of Maka Jiba.

Challenge of the north-west

The expedition of David to the Upper Senegal, combined with the preoccupation of the French with Ayuba Sulayman Diallo, indicates the interest of the French in establishing diplomatic and commercial relations in the area. However, the story of Ayuba Sulayman demonstrates how little the French actually knew of Bundu at this time; few Europeans had actually ever visited Bundu. Consequently, while the Bundunkobe were aware of the French

Pragmatism in the age of Jihad

presence, and sought to capitalize on it, they were more inclined to conduct business with agents associated with the southern frontier.

Another factor that contributed to the early Bundunke orientation towards the south and east concerned the Ormankobe incursions, a combination of Moroccan and Hassani forces originally under the control of Sultan Mawlay Isma'il (reigned 1672–1727) of Morocco.[95] The Moroccans were interested in recruiting candidates for their *'abīd*, or slave army. Mawlay Isma'il formed a corps of black troops separate from the regular army, and maintained them in the garrison town of Mashra' al-Rami.[96] At the beginning, Mawlay Isma'il extended his authority into certain areas in the Sahara, apparently during the period of the Shurrbubba.[97] In the 1690s he began sending expeditions into Senegambia on an annual basis. In the 1720s and 1730s, the raids were especially heavy in Futa Toro, Gajaaga, Bambuk, and Bundu.[98] The raids continued well into the 1760s, and were a major factor in the formulation of the 1760s *jihād* in Futa Toro.[99] Towards the conclusion of the Sultan's reign, the ranks of the *'abīd* had reportedly swelled to 150,000.[100]

The Ormankobe excursions produced a significant change in the pattern of the Senegambian slave trade. The policies of such states as Futa Toro, Bundu, Gajaaga, and the microstates of Bambuk were alike in that they forbade the sale of their own citizens in the trade.[101] Even Ayuba Sulayman, technically beyond the authority of the Sy *elimans*, reported that anyone who sought asylum in his town could not be made a slave.[102] Although states such as Bundu and Futa Toro opposed selling their own subjects, they were hardpressed to protect their constituencies from the Ormankobe raids. Widespread insecurity set in; populations living north of the Senegal River crossed to the south, and emigration to Bundu and Futa Jallon was further stimulated.

In addition to raiding for slaves, the Ormankobe began making alliances with certain rulers, arbitrating differences, and making and deposing various *Satigis* in Futa Toro.[103] This indicates that their influence was much stronger in Futa Toro than in Bundu, which did not experience such meddling in their internal affairs, and was sheltered from more serious disruption by Gajaaga's position to the north. An example of the complex relations at the time was the figure of Samba Gelaajo Jegi, reportedly the best known of all Senegambian traditional heroes.[104] Samba Gelaajo Jegi spent time in Bundu as a political refugee, and became the contested *Satigi* of Futa Toro from 1725 to 1735, and again from 1740 to 1743.[105] In 1724, he made an alliance with both the Ormankobe forces and the French at Fort Saint Joseph. Ayuba Sulayman Diallo was part of the faction that recognized Samba Gelaajo Jegi as *Satigi*, and his presence in Bundu during this period is a measure of the difficulty Maka Jiba experienced in implementing his dominion.[106]

Perhaps the most serious challenge to Bundu during the reign of Maka Jiba came not from the Moroccans, nor from Farabana, but from the Denyanke of Futa Toro. Samba Gelaajo Jegi had been removed from office by Konko Bubu Musa, a decided enemy of the French. The *Satigi* Konko reigned from 1743 to 1747, when he turned power over to his brother Sule N'jai. Sule N'jai was immediately run out of office by Sire Sawa Lamu, but retook office in 1749 and remained until 1751.[107] Some time between 1747 and 1751, the emergence of Bundu attracted Sule N'jai's attention.[108] David had just visited the area in 1744, giving Bundu increased status in the eyes of the Denyankobe. The rise and potential of Bundu, in an area probably viewed by Futa Toro as its colony, caused Sule N'jai to attempt to extract tribute. Rançon records a letter from the *Satigi* to substantiate this development, although the form in which he received the correspondence is unclear. While the specifics are therefore susceptible to challenge, the overall tone of the letter suggests the posture of the Denyanke dynasty towards the Sissibe. The themes contained in it are reflective of the historical reality, as they include: the Denyanke contempt for and fear of the *Torodbe*, the existing prosperity and potential wealth of Bundu, the difficulties of the new polity in gaining legitimacy, and the growing importance of the Upper Senegal. Sule N'jai wrote:

> From the glorious, powerful and formidable Sattigui, ruler of all Futa, he who was created in order to be happy here below, and in order to be destined for eternal life in the other world; the proof is that he drinks a full cup of the pleasures of life; he who is so kind and charitable towards his friends, as well as being dreadful, redoubtable and implacable towards his enemies, to his lowly and faithful servant Maka-Guiba, who has the audacity to call himself 'almamy,' and who signs his name as such, whose family is the issue of the Torodos, who were created to be continually miserable and to ask for charity from others. Greetings!
>
> Maka-Guiba, I need the smiths to make some gold ornaments for my wives and my children. I need gold, and that in large supply; you are to therefore send to me five full bars of gold, with the briefest delay.
>
> I have learned that you have an all-white Arabian horse that dances a great deal; you are to send the horse to me, at the same time as the gold, for one of my men who does not have one.
>
> I have learned that, among your wives, you have one who knows how to prepare couscous well; it will be necessary to send her to me also so that she can prepare my food. All of this is to be done immediately, otherwise you will force me to come to Bundu.
>
> I think that you would like to avoid my coming, because if I come to Bundu, there will only be death and ruin, and I swear to smash over your head the lone calabash that your parents left to you in your inheritance, which you still use in obtaining alms from the hands of others, as they themselves obtained alms when they were alive.
>
> You are only Torodo; you were created only for misery and slavery.[109]

Maka Jiba convened a war council, and after lengthy debate, prepared to confront the *Satigi*'s forces. Although Sule N'jai was initially successful in his march through Bundu, his army suffered heavy losses in a subsequent battle and was forced to retreat to Futa Toro. A formal peace was signed later.[110]

The retreat of the Futanke army, combined with the cessation of the Ormankobe incursions in the 1750s, allowed the Bundunke government to entertain thoughts of modest expansion to the north. Some time after the war with Futa Toro, Bundu entered a prolonged period of hostilities with Gajaaga.[111] The conflict saw Bundu allied with Khasso, whereas Gajaaga enlisted the aid of the Bambara. However, the struggle was waged at a relatively low level of intensity; Bundu's primary focus remained the south and east.

Revolution in Futa Jallon

Early in Maka Jiba's reign, forces were gathering in the mountains of Futa Jallon which would have serious political, economic, and social ramifications for Senegambia in particular and West Africa as a whole. Between 1725 and 1728, a "holy war" was launched at Fugumba by a combination of Fulbe and Jallonke elements, under the clerical leadership of Karamoko Alfa.[112] The *jihād* culminated with the victory of the jihadists at Talansan in 1747. With this accomplishment, the forces of militant Islam established the *almaamate* of Futa Jallon.

Maka Jiba enjoyed special ties to the clerical leadership of the Futa Jallonke *jihād*. His mother, Jiba Hammadi, was the sister of Haba Hammadi, the mother of Karamoko Alfa.[113] Karamoke Alfa and Maka Jiba both studied under the renowned Tierno Samba in Fugumba.[114] In view of this, it is very likely that events in Bundu and Futa Jallon were carefully monitored by both leaders.

While the sources speak glowingly of the familial ties between the two men, there is silence on the role of Bundu in the Futa Jallonke *jihād*. This suggests that if the Bundunkobe did participate, the effort was rather minimal. This lack of assistance on the part of the Bundunkobe, especially in view of the earlier support of Bubu Malik by elements within Futa Jallon, can be explained by the fact that Bundu was having tremendous problems of its own between the 1720s and the 1740s – reconstitution, the Ormankobe, Farabana, etc. – and was in no position to give tangible aid.

In addition to this, however, is the matter of policy. Notwithstanding Maka Jiba's training and acquaintance with Futa Jallonke political stirrings, there is absolutely no evidence that he ever entertained militant or reformist views. In fact, he apparently had a "reputation" for drinking alcohol, and was forced upon threat of war to abstain by Karamoko Alfa's successor Ibrahim Sori.[115] Sule N'jai, one of Maka Jiba's most ardent foes, was reputed to have been a devout Muslim and a convert of Ibrahim Sori.[116] Consequently, if it is accurate to portray Maka Jiba as having been an adherent of pragmatism, then it would have been problematic for him to have fought for an ideal that he himself did not embrace. Therefore, in conjunction with pressing domestic problems, the question of the implications for the Bundunke state could have also reduced Maka Jiba's enthusiasm for the *jihād* under Karamoko Alfa.

Maka Jiba died in an unsuccessful siege of Farabana.[117] Forced to retreat under pursuit from his old nemesis Amadi Tumane, Maka Jiba's turban reportedly became lodged in a tree branch; his decision to retrieve it was a fatal one.[118] At his death, executive power passed to Samba Tumane, the son of Maka Jiba's oldest brother, Tumane Bubu Malik Sy. Elected by the *Torodbe* notables, an intrigue was soon formed against him, led by Maka Jiba's son Amadi Gai. Employing the argument that Samba Tumane's father had refused to aid Maka Jiba's reconquest efforts, he was stripped of power and sent into exile in Fute Toro. His tenure lasted only two or three months, although the rulers' lists give him credit for an entire year.[119] It was also decided at that time that all those families who had failed to support Maka Jiba would be prevented from ever becoming *Eliman* of Bundu. Besides Samba Tumane, the families of Mudi Bubu Malik (who lived in N'Dagor and Amaguie) and Alium Bubu Malik were so affected.[120] This reduced the succession to the descendants of Maka Jiba; the claims of the N'Guenar, under the old pact with Malik Sy, had been effectively rejected with the seizure of power by Maka Jiba.

The overthrow of Samba Tumane strengthens the possibility that his father, Tumane Bubu Malik Sy, had been previously opposed by Maka Jiba. Furthermore, the exclusion of Alium Bubu Malik's family from the succession may also indicate that Alium was in fact "Eliman" Salum, who had negotiated with David independently of Maka Jiba, and who was now suffering the consequences of his actions. In any case, the refinement of the succession process clearly demonstrates Maka Jiba's resounding success in having consolidated power by the end of his reign.

It is the scions of Maka Jiba who form the two reigning branches of the Sissibe.[121] By his first wife, Jelia Gai, he had four sons: Amadi Gai, Musa Gai, Sega Gai, and Pate Gai. The first three went on to rule, while Pate Gai died in a raid on Tenda. The children of Jelia Gai would establish Koussan, in southern Bundu. Maka Jiba's second wife, Aissata Bela, was reportedly of Susu rather than Fulbe origin.[122] By her he had three sons: Amadi Aissata, Malik Aissata, and Usuman Tunkara. Amadi Aissata would go on to reign, but the other two died at the Battle of Dara Lamine (*c.* 1800). The Aissata progeny would found the Boulebane branch, and would reside in that northern town.

The children of Jelia Gai were older than those of Aissata Bela, and were conscious of the purity of their Fulbe heritage. These distinctions were important in that they helped to determine the specificity of the succession. In the late eighteenth century, however, these distinctions would translate into an informal division between the two branches, a consequence of the victory of militant Islam in Futa Toro. Bundu will be faced with the claims of reform Islam much more directly than was the case with the reformist victory in Futa Jallon, and will be forced to either accept or reject its social and governmental implications.

4

External reforms and internal consequences: Futa Toro and Bundu

The last quarter of the eighteenth century proved to be a critical test for the pragmatism of Bundu. The victory of militant Islam in the neighboring state of Futa Toro would reverberate throughout the Bundunke court and society. Together with the preceding establishment of a reform government in Futa Jallon, Futa Toro's militancy constituted a powerful alternative to the practicalism of Bundu's leadership. The Bundunke ruling elite was both Muslim and Fulbe, as was true of the two Futas, and the three entities enjoyed important economic, religious, and familial relations. Trade routes, clerical traditions and lineages, Muslim schools and peripatetic scholars, and ongoing migratory activity were the principal vehicles through which these three polities were closely linked within a single region. As a result, Bundu was profoundly affected by the Islamic revolution in Futa Toro.

The moderate orientation of Bundu, initiated by Malik Sy, was maintained by Bubu Malik and Maka Jiba. In spite of the establishment of Futa Jallon as a theocratic paradigm by 1747, to which Maka Jiba had personal and lineage ties, the *Eliman* continued to pursue policies identical to those of his father and grandfather: the development of the productive and commercial sectors of the economy, an acceptance of ethnically diverse immigrants, and a tolerance of non-Muslim communities. The religious leadership originally displayed by Malik Sy (keeping in mind his reputation as an amulet-maker) began to dissipate, and was gradually assumed by the Jakhanke clerisy. But while the Sissibe were becoming more secularized, every evidence indicates that the population was becoming increasingly Islamized. In turn, this increase in the relative Muslim population tended to legitimize Sissibe rule. Together with the growth of Bundu's economy, the flowering of the Muslim religion worked against the emergence of a self-sustaining reform movement within Bundu.

However, the rise of militant Islam in Futa Toro would create pressures for the Bundunke elite to embrace reform. A small portion of Bundunke society would support reform efforts, but it would be dependent fundamentally upon Futanke strength, and would become insignificant in the wake of the latter's diminished influence. Given this reliance upon Futa Toro, it is difficult to establish an independent tradition of reform within Bundu. It would appear, however, based upon the capitulation of Amadi Gai to demands for reform, that those Bundunkobe who were inspired by the Futanke militants also had specific concerns of their own. These included the call for an *eliman* who would lead an exemplary life of piety; the implementation of Islamic law in the structure and function of government; and a definitive rejection of alliances with non-Muslim entities, a response to the growing affinity between Bundu and encroaching Kaarta. The elite's disproportionate share in the state's growing prosperity may also have been a factor in the rise of militancy in Bundu; the disaffected would have found their collective voice in the demand for reform.

The campaign to institute reforms began under the reign of Amadi Gai (1764–86), waned with the installation of Musa Gai (1786–90), and came to full fruitition with the advent of Sega Gai (1790–97). But the forces of militancy within Bundu alone were not strong enough to challenge the government, and their short-lived success was a direct consequence of the intervention of the Futanke jihadist, Abdul Qadir.

Concomitant with these developments was the emergence of another regional power, the non-Muslim Massassi of Kaarta. Having achieved their sovereignty in 1754, by 1777 they had extended their control to Diara. The shadow of Kaarta quickly lengthened to encompass much of commercially strategic eastern Senegambia, and resulted in Kaarta's political and economic domination. From the end of the eighteenth century until the *jihād* of *al-ḥājj* Umar, Bundu would be concerned with maintaining its independence in the face of this challenge and, contrary to the experience of many of its neighbors, was largely successful in so doing.

Materials for this period are more diverse than those previously employed. The endogenous data of Rançon and Lamartiny continues in significance, but just as important are the exogenous accounts of various travelers who passed through the land during this time. In addition, the oral compilations of Kamara and Curtin became much more pertinent. The greater diversity is a consequence of the later time frame, and results in the capability of increased verification of specific detail via corroboration of the various genres.

At the same time, the sources fail to provide a cohesive picture of Bundu's development. The emergence of militancy within Bundu and the related influence of Abdul Qadir, combined with the growing competition between the two branches of the Sissibe, are examples of two major themes into which the sources give little insight. This may be because both developments are sources of embarrassment for the Sissibe, and are consequently understated in the traditions. A third example concerns the end of Sega Gai's tenure, which must be pieced together from very different angles. The challenge, then, is to elucidate the context and content of the period with sufficient clarity.

Internal developments

The last quarter of the eighteenth century, until the involvement of Adul Qadir, saw relatively tranquil, peaceful conditions among the Bundunke peasantry. Proliferation of Bundunke villages along the eastern bank of the Faleme greatly augmented agricultural production, and facilitated the commercial activity of the state. The rise of the eastern Faleme as a commercial focus encouraged successive *elimans* to maintain capitals there. In addition to this general prospering of the state was the growth of the Muslim population vis-a-vis the non-Muslim; not one traveler failed to comment on what appeared to them to be a monolithic religious community.

Within the circle of power, two developments which would affect the polity for the remainder of its existence began to take form. The first concerned the growing resentment of the sons of Aissata Bela towards the domination of political office by Amadi Gai and his full brothers. The tension between the two sets of Maka Jiba's progeny did not become critical, however, until the introduction of a second conflict. In the latter instance, the moderate ruling elite began to experience pressure from Futa Toro's reformists to change the direction of the government.

The victory of the jihadists in Futa Toro created such a climate for reform that the Bundunke court was forced to embrace the movement. *Eliman* Amadi Gai was the first to acquiesce, and he and his full brothers became identified with the reform effort. However, the new militancy did nothing to address the grievances of the sons of Aissata Bela and, in fact, exacerbated them. The latter would eventually marshal sufficient anti-reform forces to take power and return to a more moderate posture.

In spite of the internal conflicts, Bundu managed to pursue coherent economic and political policies within the larger region. In the first place, Bundu sought to solidify its existing territorial authority rather than to expand into new areas. Secondly, there was a greater emphasis on commerce than previously, consisting of exporting agricultural goods to the Gambia and gold to the Moors. In order to realize the former, Bundu focused on controlling the eastern Faleme; three capitals – Dyungfung, Dara, and Fatteconda – were established there to direct this effort. As for the gold trade, Bundu sought to direct the commodity from its place of origin in Bambuk to a principal point of exchange along the Upper Senegal, the town of Bakel. Undergirding all of this activity was the importation of European firearms into Bundu. Ownership of these firearms was limited to the nobility, and was of increasingly critical importance.

Regarding Amadi Gai, his reign was a veritable calm before the storm. In contrast to his father Maka Jiba, Amadi Gai was more interested in solidifying his authority over lands already under nominal Bundunke control. He is described as having inherited great wealth, while his constituents "were able to enjoy a peaceful life, and to devote themselves to agriculture and the raising of cattle."[1] Dara had served as the capital of Bundu under Maka

External reforms and internal consequences: Futa Toro and Bundu

Jiba, having been established along with Dyunfung as *tatas* along the eastern Faleme. Apparently Amadi Gai alternated his residence between both towns early in his reign.[2] But at some later point, he chose for security reasons the town of Koussan as a third capital of Bundu.[3] Koussan is described in 1786 as having consisted of 1,000 to 2,000 residents, and having previously served as a *tata* for Amadi Gai. The ruler's residence was a compound of several houses surrounded by walls of earth: "The sight of this surrounding wall resembles the idea of a citadel."[4] The main entrance to the royal house was guarded, as were all the houses within the complex. The layout was more or less a maze, wherein it was difficult to locate the actual house of the ruler without an escort.

Commerce and firearms

The reputation of Bundu as a exporter of agricultural products continued to develop during the last quarter of the eighteenth century. Late in 1795, Mungo Park traveled through Bundu, and described a tranquil, almost idyllic scene. The "Foulahs" were cultivators and herders, whose livestock was on the whole in better condition than those of the Malinke.[5] They reportedly raised an "excellent breed of horses, but the usual beast of burden in all the Negro territories is the ass."[6] The price of a fowl was a button or a small piece of amber, while goat meat and mutton were "proportionately cheap." The Bundunkobe enjoyed "all the necessaries of life in the greatest profusion," while the states along the Gambia were "also supplied, in considerable quantities, with sweet-smelling gums and frankincense, the produce of Bondu."[7] Just a few years earlier (some time between 1784 and 1787), Goldberry also passed through Bundu, and described it as a center of cotton and indigo production.[8]

With regard to northern commerce, there was a flourishing trade between Bundu and the Moors. Bundu was part of the "desert-edge" system of complementary exchange between the ecologically distinct zones of the southern Sahara and the savannah. From the mines of Ijil and Tawdenni, the caravans of the Moors crisscrossed the desert bearing slabs of salt. The Moors, specifically the Kunta *zwāya* confederation, had taken control of the commodity's production and transport by the last quarter of the eighteenth century. Passing through such oases as Tishit (also a source of salt) in the Tagant and Walata in the Hodh, the Moors would deliver the salt at various termini in the savannah, including Bundu. There, the Moors would trade for cereals, cattle products, slaves, Bundunke cloth, and Bambuk gold. As a cotton-producer, Bundu was a key supplier of the Moorish demand for white and indigo-dyed cloth.[9]

The slave trade was also of significance; Saugnier and Labarthe even traveled to the Upper Senegal with the intent to further stimulate the exchange in Africans.[10] The foregoing suggests the growing importance of the northern trade, in that trade to the south and east had preoccupied the

Bundunke governments through the reign of Maka Jiba. However, the latter trades remained fundamental to Bundu's prosperity. A sizeable proportion of that trade passed through the Bundunke border village of Tillika (or Tallico) to the south. The Frenchman Rubault, commissioned by Durand to travel overland to the Upper Senegal, visited the village in 1786, and characterized it as a merchant village, whose residents made money by selling food and ivory to passing caravans.[11] When Park visited Bundu in 1795, he claims to also have visited Tillika, describing it as a town of Muslim "Foulahs," "who live in considerable affluence."[12]

The visits of Europeans to Bundu sparked the energies of the Bundunkobe to participate even more in every aspect of the region's commerce. These visits, although rare, alerted the leadership to the upper valleys' growing importance within the framework of international exchange. Perhaps more pertinent is the fact that such visits underscored how critical Bundu's need had become for European firearms. A case in point was the 1786 visit of Rubault, for whom an audience with Amadi Gai was held. Rubault was interrogated about his native land and the power of its ruler. He was then asked if he had brought "gifts," to which he replied in the negative. Rubault's account of Amadi Gai's response is a good example of how the Eurocentric perspective can obfuscate the indigenous reality:

> The Compagnie des Indes used to have a settlement in Galam, and my father received from it expensive gifts; I thought that the same thing would happen under my reign and that I would not have to wait. Vain hope! I received nothing. But should I not hope for a white traveler? However, that which had never been came about [the arrival of Rubault]. I left my camp in order to see him, and I did not receive the gift that I had anticipated. It is in vain that you would like to leave without satisfying me. I will never consent to it.[13]

According to Rubault, the "Almamy" changed his mind the following day, and agreed to allow Rubault to continue on to Gajaaga under escort. Upon reaching Gajaaga, he was to send back two pieces of "guinée," a single-barreled firearm, one hundred flints, one hundred balls, four pounds of gunpowder, and a pair of pistols.[14] It is in the request for firearms that we see the real interest of Amadi Gai; his own personal prestige, in addition to the security of the state, was becoming more dependent upon European weaponry. Indeed, the continued supply of such weaponry from both the Gambia and Senegal Rivers would partially explain Bundu's successful expansion in the nineteenth century.

A further illustration of the importance of European firearms comes from the reign of Musa Gai (1786–90). The French had failed to reoccupy their former posts in Gajaaga following their setback in the Seven Years' War, although by 1779 they had returned to Saint Louis. Either just before or after his taking executive power, Musa Gai traveled to Saint Louis to discuss the absence of the French in the Upper Senegal.[15] He was undoubtedly attempting to persuade the French to hasten their return, as the developing regional power of Bundu was becoming dependent upon the procurement of firearms.

Bundu's ability to purchase those arms came through taxing caravans from other lands en route to the various entrepots, as well as levies placed on the sale of gold, gum, cotton, indigo, and other commodities by the Bundunkobe themselves. However, there are no data on the substance of these talks, and no evidence of any tangible results.

Impasse to the south and east

Amadi Gai was generally uninterested in territorial expansion. He began his reign in 1764 by agreeing to a "treaty of alliance" with Wuli, whereby the remaining inhabitants of Contou were required to relocate to Tambacounda.[16] His control of the trade to the Gambia continued to be challenged by the power of Farabana, and the rise of a new adversary, the Malinke kingdom of Tenda.[17] Tenda, together with Farabana, proved to be an unending source of military harassment, preventing Bundu from ever realizing the kind of control it sought over the Faleme and the southlands. While Amadi Gai achieved some success in extending his suzerainty over several Tenda villages, he was simply unattracted to campaigning on the scale of his father Maka Jiba. Before he died, however, Amadi Gai made two attempts to capture Farabana. As has been previously noted, Farabana was a nexus for several caravan routes, and in close proximity to the Bambuk goldfields. As long as Farabana remained autonomous, Bundu could not possibly control all of the trade routes extending from there, routes leading north to Gajaaga and Khasso, east to the centuries-old markets of the Upper Niger, and south to the Gambia and beyond to the highlands of Futa Jallon. In view of Farabana's commercial versatility, Amadi Gai could not completely ignore the potential gain for Bundu. A report filed in 1784 underscores the overall character of the conflict: "This people Mandingis [sic] almost always at war with those of Bundu, who are separated by the Faleme, and in order to go beyond Galam to the land of the mines, one does not go around the land of Bundu."[18]

Farabana's resilience is explained not only by its multiple trade connections, but also by the military cooperation of the Malinke independent towns within Bambuk as a whole. Although politically autonomous, they were able to join forces for purposes of defense.[19] Because of Farabana's formidability, Amadi Gai's two attempts at conquest were unsuccessful and Farabana remained independent.[20] However, it is likely that Bundu won a partial victory in that it was able to wrest control of the trade routes to the Gambia from Farabana. This assertion is based upon the testimony of Major Daniel Houghton, who had been active in Senegambia between 1772 and 1783, and who made a scientific expedition to Bundu in May of 1791, with the intent of going as far inland as the Niger.[21] Houghton reported that Bundu had "won" the recent conflict with Farabana, but he then goes on to talk about his additional visit to the "king" of Bambuk.[22] The "king" complained that although he had previously been able to procure munitions from Fort Saint Joseph, the French had abandoned the site for some time; meanwhile,

Bundu was still able to obtain military goods from the English on the Gambia, putting the "king" at a decided disadvantage.[23] Thus, it would appear that Farabana remained free of Bundunke political control, but lost its access to the Gambia. These circumstances were extremely fluid, and would change several times in the course of the nineteenth century.

Gajaaga

Although Amadi Gai was unable to seize Farabana, his efforts were sufficient to give Bundu greater control over the Faleme River as far south as Tomboura.[24] The advantage temporarily enjoyed by Bundu over Farabana allowed Musa Gai, Amadi Gai's successor, to turn his attention north to Gajaaga. Amadi Gai had experienced peaceful relations with Gajaaga during his reign, but Musa Gai embarked upon a different strategy.[25] Some years prior to Musa Gai's coming to power, the N'Diaye family, under N'Diaye Gauki, had established themselves at Bakel under the protection of the *Eliman* of Bundu.[26] Amadi Gai extended this arrangement to N'Diaye Gauki's successor, Silman Molaju. At some point after 1779, the *Tunka* at Tiyaabu began a dispute with the N'Diaybe over who actually owned the land around Bakel, and who should therefore receive payments from the French. Because of the superior forces of the *Tunka*, Silman Molaju was forced to rely upon the military aid of Bundu, which continued to provide protection in exchange for a fee.

Apparently the cost of Bundu's protection became very steep. The N'Diaybe sought to escape the oppression by soliciting the help of Kounguel, a thriving commercial center near the mouth of the Faleme. Having worked out an arrangement with the merchants of Kounguel, the N'Diaybe stopped payment to Bundu during Musa Gai's tenure. The ruler responded by attacking Bakel; Silman Molaju took flight, and the Bundunkobe temporarily took over the town. Musa Gai then imposed levies on the merchants who conducted business at Bakel and Kounguel.[27]

As is demonstrated in this account, Bakel was an important entrepot in the Upper Senegal, and would become even more important after 1820 and the establishment of a French fort there. Gajaaga and Bundu consequently fought over its control, with the result that Bundu's tight political grip, established over the town under Musa Gai, would weaken in the nineteenth century. Firm political domination over a subject Bakel would change to political influence over an autonomous Bakel, and this influence would vary in intensity from time to time.

The brief dispute with Tiyaabu and Kounguel over the status of Bakel carried portents of Bundu's future. Increasingly, the northern frontier would play a larger role in the development of Bundu. While commercial and political activity to the south and east remained important, nineteenth-century developments in the Upper Senegal would more deeply impact the course of Bundunke history.

Attempts at reform

At some point during his reign, Amadi Gai constructed the *tata* at Koussan, the eventual site of one of his residences. The reason given for this construction was to defend against raiding and the "enemies of his family, who, excited by the clerics, attempted to foment revolts."[28] This vague statement is undoubtedly a reference to the growing influence of the jihadists of Futa Toro. The holy war against the Denyanke dynasty began in the 1760s under the leadership of Sulayman Bal, and culminated in the victory of Abdul Qadir in 1776. Having begun his reign in 1764, Amadi Gai came under the scrutiny of those Bundunkobe who were ideologically in support of the Futanke jihadists. Such supporters questioned the secular character of the leadership, and called for implementation of Islamic law within Bundunke society. As Futanke influence grew, the reformers created sufficient pressures upon Amadi Gai to force his removal to Koussan. The vehicles through which these pressures were brought to bear included: contact between Bundu and Futa Toro at the clerical levels; students from Bundu studying in Futa Toro, and vice-versa; and a number of Bundunkobe who may have fought under Abdul Qadir, and who returned to Bundu. All of these categories would have included individuals who advocated the reformist position in Bundu.

The Futanke jihadists, coupled with the need to effectively govern the state, eventually forced Amadi Gai to abandon the centrist posture of his predecessors. The principal indication of this shift was the adoption of the title *Almaami*, in lieu of *Eliman*. More than simply a Pulaarization of the term *imām*, the Sissibe adoption of this title reflects the influence of the Futanke jihadists, as Abdul Qadir had taken the title *Almaami*.[29] This, in turn, suggests that the title was assumed by Amadi Gai after 1776.

But beyond the mere adoption of a modified title, Amadi Gai began to implement reforms according to Islamic law, such that Rançon describes him as the first sovereign of Bundu "who accomplished something, from the point of view of the administration of the country."[30] He attempted to adhere to *sharīa* in matters of taxation and civil behavior, organizing a police force as well. Bowing to the pressures for reform generated by Abdul Qadir, "he tried to apply the Koran in every circumstance where it was possible."[31] The transformation of Amadi Gai from moderate to reformer was startling; it was also shrewd politics, as the waves of militancy emanating from Futa Toro threatened to overwhelm the ship of the Bundunke state.

Almaami Amadi Gai spent his last years in Dara, and at his death he was survived by seven sons.[32] Amadi Makumba was the only one born of a free woman, and he was killed in Tenda. Tumane Mudi, Malik Kumba, and Amadu Sy went on to reign. The others were Abd al-Rahman Amadi Gai, Sega Amadi Gai (who died at Dara Lamine *c.* 1880), and Salif Amadi Gai. The rulers' lists disagree on the length of Amadi Gai's tenure, ranging anywhere from ten to twenty-one years. Only Curtin has suggested a twenty-one-year span, which is consistent with the current proposal.

Amadi Gai's brother and immediate successor, Musa Gai (1786–90), was the oldest surviving Sy, and therefore the rightful *Almaami*. In addition to what has already been discussed regarding his activity along the frontiers, the tenure of Musa Gai was relatively uneventful. The sources do not address the question of whether he followed the reform policies of Amadi Gai or not. Musa Gai also died at Dara, and was survived by one son, Umar Musa, who established himself at Belpounegui. His other son, Malik Musa, died in infancy.[33] All of the sources agree that he reigned either four or five years.[34]

Sega (or Ishaq) Gai, Musa Gai's younger brother, succeeded him as *Almaami* (1790–97). From his new residence at Fatteconda on the east side of the Faleme, Sega Gai ruled over a land of growing tensions. Park visited Bundu as late as 1795, and described it as inhabited by devout Muslims. Small *madrasas* were sprinkled among the various towns, while most of the Bundunkobe Park encountered possessed a "slight acquaintance" with the Arabic language.[35] Boars ran wild in the woods, "but their flesh was not esteemed."[36] In comparing Bundu with the Malinke states along the Gambia, Park found that the differene was "in this, that they are more immediately under the influence of the Mahomedan laws; for all the chief men (the king excepted) and a large majority of the inhabitants of Bondou, are Mussulmen, and the authority and laws of the prophet are every where looked upon as sacred and decisive."[37] The exception made for the "king" is most revealing. Park was told that the ruler was not a Muslim, but a *kāfir*; that he was a "Soninke, or pagan, like the king of Woolli, but he adopted the Moorish name of Almaami..."[38] Park's informants were clearly disaffected Muslims, so upset with Sega Gai's policies that they considered him an apostate. Unwittingly, Park was painting a striking picture of Bundu in 1795: a surface peace, behind which was developing a mounting resentment.

In fact, it is under Sega Gai that civil, religious, and interstate war erupt simultaneously, largely the consequence of the emergence of militant Islam. Almost as soon as the new *Almaami* took office, he was forced to repress a number of local uprisings, the participants of which had "made common cause with his enemies."[39] It is a distinct possibility that his "enemies" were from several different camps. First of all, there were the militants, who were actually following the leadership of Abdul Qadir, and who were clearly opposed to Sega Gai. Beyond this group, it is likely that his half-brothers, the sons of Aissata Bela, were also beginning to resent the domination of the Gai branch. To this must be added those communities in Bundu which still maintained some ties to Gajaaga, and were adversely affected by the recent Bundunke forays into the north. Indirect evidence suggests that all three camps were operating in opposition to Sega Gai. While there may have been collusion between the latter two factions, it is evident that the militant camp was being "agitated" by influences from Futa Toro.

The beginning of the end for Sega Gai is marked by his sack of the Muslim village of Sangalou in 1797. The casualties were numerous, with many women and children taken captive.[40] The sources differ as to what happened after that. According to Roux, the Sangalou affair was nothing short of an outrage to the Muslim community. When he heard of it, Abdul Qadir decided to punish Sega Gai and expand his reform by marching on Bundu. He arrived at Marsa, where he met Sega Gai, and proceeded to reprimand him severely for his treatment of Sangalou's people, "a harmless village," and asked the clerics to make a judgment of his fate.[41] He was sentenced to die, a verdict which Abdul Qadir carried out in the presence of Bundu's powerless army.

An alternate version has Sega Gai and the Bambara army of Kaarta raiding the village of Njukunturu, reducing the women and children to slavery.[42] Among the inhabitants of the village, one Fudiya Ansura complained to Abdul Qadir, who subsequently led an army to Bundu and put the Bundu *Almaami* to death. Both this story and its predecessor have in common the allegation that Sega Gai attacked and enslaved Muslims, in contravention of *sharī'a*. (Fudiya Ansura was the father of *Shaykh* Musa Makka, who reportedly collected *zakāt* for either *al-ḥājj* Umar or his son Amadu in Guidimakha.)[43]

Gray, Rançon, and Lamartiny introduce several new factors.[44] Agreeing that Sangalou was sacked by Sega Gai, they state that it was the *Tunka* of Tiyaabu who sought the aid of Abdul Qadir, and that the latter was motivated by feelings of revenge to respond. This was because Abdul Qadir was born in Bundu, in the village of Diamwali, and was reportedly chased out of the realm by Musa Gai because of his "religious fanaticism." Therefore, according to this version, Abdul Qadir was eager to aid the *Tunka*, but the Sangalou affair was not sufficient provocation. It was around this time, however, that a group of Kaartans were chased west by forces from Segu, the former seeking refuge in Gajaaga. Abdul Qadir, now supervising Gajaaga's affairs, refused them permission, and sent an army to chase them out. As the Kaartans retreated, they burned several villages in their path. A leader of one of these villages, "Imam," complained to Abdul Qadir that Sega Gai had assisted the Kaartans, taking his wife and daughter for himself. Sega Gai was also accused of destroying a number of important books. Adul Qadir thereupon led 20,000 men (i.e. an uncountable number) to Marsa, where he summoned Sega Gai. He then sentenced the Sy to exile in Futa Toro, but before Sega Gai could leave the Futanke camp he was killed by Abdul Qadir's men.

From the preceding accounts, it would appear that the Kaartans and Sega Gai had united to make common assault upon the villages of Gajaaga, among which Sangalou was one. It would also appear that Abdul Qadir had obtained tremendous influence over the militant factions of Gajaaga and Bundu, and even had some form of agreement with Sega Gai that recognized the Futanke *Almaami* as ascendant.[45] To support this, Kamara writes that Sega Gai has sworn fealty (*bay'a*) to Abdul Qadir, and had become his *khalīfa* (lieutenant).

It does not require long contemplation to recognize the bias of Rançon and Lamartiny in the matter. The French had had their share of problems with African Muslim reformers by the late nineteenth century. The allegation that revenge was Abdul Qadir's motive cannot be taken seriously. Neither can it be denied that the Futanke *Almaami* was a reformer. He was considered erudite, a cleric who scrupulously observed *shari'a*. The move on Bundu was clearly an attempt to expand his reform, if not his authority.[46]

The implication of these events is that the reform measures of Amadi Gai had fallen short of their objectives, and that Sega Gai was anything but a rightly guided *imām*. One view is that after Maka Jiba, the Bundunke *almaamies* became *kāfirs* ("unbelievers," or in this sense, "apostates") and that their constituency reverted to unspecified, pre-Islamic ritual observances.[47] Sega Gai was accused of entering the mosque in Marsa without performing *ghusl* (a total bath), having just been with his wife.[48] Kamara more or less supports this view, stating that Abdul Qadir had made Sega Gai promise to abandon the dance of the Bambara, a pledge he later disregarded.[49] Although this indicates that relations between Kaarta and Bundu had become important, and were a source of discomfort for the militant camp, it is a bit much to contend that the Bundunke *almaamies* were not Muslims. It should be kept in mind that, aside from Demba Sock and Moussa Kamara's comments on Sega Gai, none of the sources imply that syncretism or even dualism characterized the Bundunke *almaamies* or people.

The execution of Sega Gai was most unpopular in both Bundu and Futa Toro. When Abdul Qadir gave the initial order, his troops refused to carry it out.[50] After the execution was finally performed, the resulting collective revulsion was expressed by the Moor Mukhtar-uld-Buna, who reportedly was an eyewitness:

> As for me, I was disgusted with the religion of the whites [Moors], and I came to the land of the blacks in order to be instucted in their religion, and I abandoned the teaching of the people who do not believe. But you, you sent for this man under the protection of Islam ... ' They did not enter into discussion with him, for it had not been a good affair, and Mokhtar-uld-Buna returned to the land of the Moors.[51]

At the news of Sega Gai's death, the notables convened to choose a successor. Bowing to the wishes of Abdul Qadir, Amadi Pate Gai, the son of the deceased Pate Gai, was named *Almaami*. Sega Gai's own son, Bubacar Sega, never became very important. The sources disagree on the length of Sega Gai's reign.[52]

The eighteenth century had witnessed the development of Bundu from a tiny entity into a relatively influential state. Its growth was fundamentally tied to the commerce of the region, over which it sought to strengthen its control. The extent to which Bundu was successful in achieving this was becoming increasingly a function of its ability to access European firearms. The nineteenth-century expansion of the French in the Upper Senegal would only intensify the pattern of Bundu's dependency on such arms, and on trade with French and British merchants in general.

At the same time, the pragmatic orientation of the state came under fire with the rise of Abdul Qadir. The struggle between the Futanke-led militants and the moderates of Bundu would issue into a dynastic war between the two branches of the Sissibe. Ironically, Abdul Qadir's intervention in Bundunke internal affairs sowed the seeds for his own demise, and that at the hands of the Bundunke moderates, who would win the internecine conflict.

5

The reassertion of Sissibe integrity

Abdul Qadir's intrusion into Bundunke affairs galvanized those moderate forces which had steadily lost ground to the proponents of Islamic militancy in both Futa Toro and Bundu. The execution of Sega Gai was the beginning of an informal split between the Boulebane and Koussan branches of the Sissibe dynasty. While the division was never hard and fast, the Boulebane branch, during the ascendency of Abdul Qadir, assumed an anti-militant posture, whereas the Koussan branch represented reform interests. With the defeat of Abdul Qadir, reform ceased to be a viable option in Bundu. Subsequently, Boulebane tended to be associated with pro-French and pro-Kaarta sentiments; the latter connection would vacillate between amity and enmity, and would involve intermarriage between the royal families of Kaarta and Bundu. In contrast, Koussan was hostile to alliances with non-Muslim entities, and maintained a commercial orientation towards the politically non-threatening British along the Gambia. In the final analysis, however, Bundu's pragmatism and centralized character survived these differences until the advent and intervention of *al-ḥājj* Umar in the middle of the nineteenth century. The split between the Sissibe was therefore not as powerful as the common threads linking the two.

The first third of the nineteenth century in Bundu is represented by a blend of endogenous, exogenous, and intermediate sources. Reports from the *comptoirs* are fairly substantial, so that details are more precise, and corroboration more extensive. However, the challenge of developing a clear understanding of the Bundunke perspective persists. The strategy and internal dynamics of the court are by no means apparent, and must be extracted from the data.

Overview of internal affairs

The start of the nineteenth century saw the polity beset with civil strife, only to be followed by a protracted engagement with Kaarta. The economic expansion of Bundu, so well demonstrated by its growth during the second half of the eighteenth century, was temporarily halted by the exigencies of war. But while the realm suffered some agricultural decline, the Faleme remained the breadbasket of the state, and commerce continued to flow, as evidenced by the activity of Segu merchants in Bundu immediately following the Kaartan conflict. At the same time, Bundu began to experience some difficulties with its servile population, who began absconding beyond the Faleme to the east. Their flight, which could very well have been deliberately encouraged by Bambuk and Kaarta, was in any case a direct indication of the free populations' preoccupation with war during this period, to the extent that they had problems maintaining control over their slaves.

Within the court, the period was decidedly marked by the internecine struggle among the Sissibe. This followed the antebellum creation of dual administrative nuclei, reflecting the two ruling factions. The moderate wing would ultimately prevail, but the forceful seizure of power by the moderate candidate, Amadi Aissata, indicates that the fissures within the ruling elite were deep and pervasive. In a procedure reminiscent of Maka Jiba, Amadi Aissata took the *almaamate* against the wishes and to the consternation of the non-Sissibe nobility, who had decided to resolve the internal contretemps by selecting a head of state from outside of the Sissibe. Once in power, the Boulebane branch began to manipulate the succession process to their advantage.

The strategy employed by Bundu during this period was one of shifting alliances based upon expediency as opposed to religion or ethnicity. Bundu would seek to use Kaarta to rid itself of Abdul Qadir, only to turn and form an alliance against Kaarta. Bundu sought nothing less than hegemony over the Upper Senegal, a region characterized by rapid political change and escalating competition over control of regional commerce. In order to prevail, Bundu became very aggressive militarily. The focus was the northern entrepot of Bakel, but the slave and kola nut trades from the south remained very important. In the end, the French would take notice of Bundu's rise, and would actively resist its expansion.

Amadi Aissata (1797–1819) and the First Civil War

According to Moussa Kamara, Amadi Pate Gai, Abdul Qadir's candidate to succeed Sega Gai, proved to be unjust, tyrannical, and wanton.[1] That he was constantly accompanied by "les griots et les flutistes" is further indication that he was not a reformer, and that he was chosen by Abdul Qadir because he could be controlled.

But more important than the question of Amadi Pate Gai's weakness or Abdul Qadir's sense of loyalty to Pate Gai was the fact that Amadi Pate Gai's selection was an attempt on the part of Abdul Qadir to disrupt the legal succession process. By so doing, he was assuming the authority to determine Bundu's leadership and, in essence, reducing Bundu to vassalage. By subordinating the Bundunke elite, Abdul Qadir could then alter the state's moderate posture, as it was viewed as antithetical to the reforms of the Futanke *Almaami*. The demise of Sega Gai therefore represented an opportunity for Abdul Qadir to implement this strategy, but the consequent choice of Amadi Pate Gai proved to be an unmitigated disaster. It was unacceptable in that an outsider had made the determination, and it was illegal in that the rightful successor was Amadi Aissata, another of Maka Jiba's sons.

Amadi Pate Gai's selection would touch off a civil war. As a result of Abdul Qadir's intervention, the Boulebane branch was forced to fight for its privilege and dignity, after which the sons of Maka Jiba found it desirable to create spatial distance between their respective residences. While the two branches would achieve some reconciliation in subsequent years, the consequences of the Futanke *Almaami*'s policies would linger and continue to affect relations between Boulebane and Koussan.[2]

In response to Abdul Qadir's choice of Amadi Pate Gai, the Bundunke nobility, consisting of various *Torodbe* groups, met at Fissa-Daro to ponder their options. The discussions resulted in the selection of the leader of Fissa-Daro as *Almaami*, by invocation of the ancient agreement between Malik Sy and the N'Guenar that the oldest of the two groups should rule. Amadi Aissata, present at the meeting, vehemently took exception to the decision, and ordered his chief slave to assassinate the village head. This being carried out, the meeting hastily adjourned in confusion.[3] Shortly thereafter, Amadi Aissata was proclaimed *Almaami* by the Boulebane branch.

According to Rançon, Boulebane was founded by Amadi Aissata after the death of Amadi Gai in 1786.[4] Moussa Kamara confirms that Amadi Aissata founded Boulebane.[5] However, it is not clear when this branch moved to Boulebane from Dyunfung. Rançon gives the impression that Amadi Aissata was already residing in Boulebane before the war with Amadi Pate Gai, whereas Amadi Bokar Sy, Roux, and Kamara state that he had remained at Dyunfung until later in his reign.[6]

Evidence that the division between the Koussan and Boulebane branches was not absolute can be seen in the kind of support Amadi Aissata received. Two of his chief lieutenants, Tumane Mudi and Malik Kumba, were from the Koussan branch. Without question, self-interest was the important factor in their decision to back Boulebane. Amadi Pate Gai was not only behind Amadi Aissata in the line of succession, he was also behind Tumane Mudi and Malik Kumba. To back Amadi Aissata was to support order and to insure their own opportunity; to side with Amadi Pate Gai was to embrace uncertainty. As it turned out, their loyalty to Boulebane proved sagacious; both would reign as *Almaami*.

For his part, Amadi Aissata had not always been opposed to Abdul Qadir. The former was responsible for the construction of a mosque at Kobillo in Futa Toro, in the province of Bosseya.[7] He had commissioned Bundunke masons to build the structure as a way of honoring Abdul Qadir, easily the most powerful figure in the Upper Senegal. But the reformer's declaration in favor of Amadi Pate Gai angered Amadi Aissata. The rightful heir met with his nephew and reportedly said: "'He names you as ruler to the detriment of your uncles, and you accept. What an odious act you have performed'."[8]

Amadi Aissata understood that to rebel against Abdul Qadir's selection was to rebel against Abdul Qadir. Even with the backing of a substantial number of Sissibe "princes," however, Amadi Aissata needed additional help to overcome the Futanke forces. Kamara records that immediately following his brief meeting with Amadi Pate Gai, Amadi Aissata journeyed to Kaarta and remained there for the next two years. While there, he was given the king's daughter to marry, but he declined because he was much older than she. The king's daughter, Kurubarai Kulubali, was instead given to Amadi Aissata's son, Saada Amadi Aissata.[9] The marriage sealed an alliance between Bundu and Kaarta that would become problematic in the future. For Kaarta, the alliance meant that it would have an agent representing its growing interests in the Upper Senegal. From Amadi Aissata's perspective, the pact with Kaarta was ideal in that Kaarta could provide substantial military aid for Bundu's quest to challenge Abdul Qadir and to exert control over the upper valley's trade and resources. As matters turned out, both partners underestimated the extent of the other's ambition.

Accompanied by Kaartan reinforcements, Amadi Aissata returned to Bundu. He sent Tumane Mudi on a diplomatic mission to Amadi Pate Gai, but the latter refused to participate in any negotiations, having taken residence at the old *tata* at Fena. The forces of Boulebane, reportedly 15,000 to 20,000 strong (i.e. an uncountable number) laid siege to Fena under the command of Tumane Mudi. The assault was successful, and Amadi Pate Gai was forced to seek exile in Futa Toro with Abdul Qadir.

The following year (*c.* 1800), Abdul Qadir led a force of 4,000 Futankobe to Bundu in order to reinstate Amadi Pate Gai. For his part, Amadi Aissata assembled his army at Dara Lamine, about forty-five kilometers southeast of Bakel.[10] The ensuing Battle of Dara Lamine lasted for several days, and has assumed epic proportions as one of the few times in which Sissibe actually killed Sissibe. In all, seven Sissibe lost their lives, including Amadi Aissata's brother Malik Aissata. Abdul Qadir emerged a winner, but at great cost in lives, and was forced to retreat to Futa Toro.[11]

Amadi Aissata lost little time in reorganizing his army, an important contingent of which came from Kaarta. He soon established control over all of Bundu. It was at this time that he also began pushing into Gajaaga. The combined forces of Bundu, Kaarta, and Khasso proved too powerful for Gajaaga, and by the beginning of 1802, Bundu controlled the Senegal River, from the convergence with the Faleme to slightly south of Bakel. These events were being monitored by the French, who were concerned about their effect upon trade. Bundu's ascendency was reassuring: "The Eliman of Bundu has forced the ruler of Galam to divide his kingdom into two sections, of which he [Eliman] has kept one. This ruler [Eliman], being also a friend of the French, is one we are able to rely upon."[12] That Bundu had freed itself of Futanke control is confirmed by a report filed later in 1802, stating that the *Almaami* of Futa Toro was unable to safeguard passage beyond his own borders, since the frontier was occupied by "a formidable army, composed in part of Bambara (soldiers), along with the allied troops of Kasson and Bundu."[13]

In the meantime, Abdul Qadir's support in Futa Toro was eroding. By the turn of the century he was around eighty years old. As a result of his failures, advanced age, and strict adherence to *shari'a* in meting out punishments, the central provinces began to rebel. Abdul Qadir was eventually driven out of the capital at Thiologne in Bosseya province.[14]

The decision to oust Abdul Qadir had a partial basis in *fiqh*. According to the statutes governing the *almaamate*, the office was invalidated through loss of mental or physical fitness, or loss of liberty.[15] Abdul Qadir, having been enslaved for three months by the *Damel* of Cayor following a 1796 military defeat, and now in rapid physical decline, forfeited the position on both counts. Consequently, *Shaykh* Mukhtar Kudaije delivered a *fatwa* (legal opinion) that Abdul Qadir was unfit for the *almaamate*. The ruling was accepted throughout Futa Toro.[16]

Abdul Qadir, abandoned by all except his faithful entourage, eventually sought refuge in the village of Gooriel in Futa Toro.[17] By that time, elements identified specifically with Bosseya province had been soliciting Kaarta for aid in terminating their problem with Abdul Qadir.[18] Their supplications were honored in 1806-7, when the combined forces of Bundu, Kaarta, and Khasso invaded Futa Toro. Abdul Qadir's small force was decimated. It is generally reported that when the old reformer saw his followers being crushed, he dismounted, sat under a tree, and began to pray. Amadi Aissata personally saluted his enemy, and demanded that he give an account for the death of Sega Gai. Receiving no response, he shot the kneeling man "in cold blood."[19] His death signaled the defeat of the forces of militancy within Bundu and the termination of their viability.

Troubles with Kaarta

The end of one problem facing Bundu saw the beginning of another. The ruler of Kaarta, Musa Kurabo (*c.* 1799-1808), fully expected that the defeat of Abdul Qadir would translate into greater influence in the Upper Senegal for Kaarta; further, he now viewed Bundu as a client state.[20] At the same time, Bundu envisioned a reduction in the Kaartan presence with the demise of the Futanke *Almaami*. These conflicting expectations soon issued into a military confrontation.

The Bundunke leaders, in conjunction with the Futanke nobility, met to discuss the Kaartan threat as well as the future of the alliance between Futa Toro, Bundu, Gajaaga and Kaarta.[21] "The people of Foota, fearing that Amadi Isata's connexion with so powerful a pagan chief as Modiba would militate against the advance of the Mahomedan faith in Bondoo, and might ultimately lead the Kartans into their country, called a general assembly, and required the attendance of Amadi Isata and Samba Congole."[22] Samba Kongole was the *Tunka* of Gajaaga, with his residence at Makhana. He had previously concluded an alliance with Kaarta, under which Gajaaga assumed tributary status. Whereas Bundu and Futa Toro agreed to break off the alliance with Kaarta, Gajaaga did not. The latter, continually subject to raiding by Bundu, needed a strong ally to maintain itself in the fiercely contested upper valley. The Kaartans, informed of the *Torodbe* decision, vowed to return as adversaries. This whole process of expunging the Bambara forces apparently took a few years, since Isaaco found the joint armies of Bundu and Kaarta ravaging Wuli in 1810.[23]

Moriba, or Bodian Mori Ba, became ruler of Kaarta in 1815.[24] He immediately demanded tribute of Amadi Aissata. The *Almaami*'s response was to decapitate all of the Kaartan's emissaries except one, sending him back with firearm ammunition, a declaration of war.[25] In the beginning of 1817, Amadi Aissata began a march on Yelimane, capital of Kaarta.[26] Moriba, for his part, simultaneously headed for Boulebane. While the army of Khasso prevented Amadi Aissata from reaching Yelimane, Boulebane was left exposed to the incoming Kaartans.[27] After several attempts to take the town, it was decided to construct a camp nearby and induce starvation upon the town's residents. The siege of Boulebane was of several months duration, and was nearly successful.[28] However, Moriba made the critical mistake of allowing a breakdown in discipline; his men were given permission to attack neighboring villages and collect booty. It was at this point that Amadi Aissata, reinforced with Bambuk recruits, relieved the siege of Boulebane.[29] The Bambara forces were completely disorganized, and retreated with Moriba to Yelimane.[30]

The Bundunke victory was short-lived. In April of 1818, the combined armies of Kaarta, Guidimakha, and Khasso returned to Bundu. Led by Samba Gangioli of Guidimakha, they were opposed by the troops of Bundu, Futa Toro, and Gajaaga. Futa Toro and Bundu had remained allies since the defeat of Abdul Qadir, while Gajaaga, having momentarily sided with Kaarta, returned to the Futa Toro–Bundu alliance in the aftermath of Bundu's victory over Kaarta. This frequent shifting of military partnerships would remain a feature of Upper Senegal politics, as such pacts were made or broken on the basis of expediency as opposed to religion, ethnicity, or any other consideration. In the course of events, the Bundu alliance was soundly defeated, and Amadi Aissata was forced to seek asylum in Futa Toro. Amadi Aissata's allies pressured him to accept the idea of a negotiated settlement; delegates were sent to Samba Gangioli later in the year, who in turn agreed to the peace.[31]

Aftermath of the Kaartan conflict

A year before the 1818 conflict with the Kaartan alliance, Amadi Aissata was described by visitors as the most powerful monarch in the region.[32] This finding came on the heels of the *Almaami*'s victories over Abdul Qadir and Moriba. But just a year later, the Kaartan forces had Bundu reeling. Mollien visited Bundu during this period and, in contrast to Mungo Park's 1795 account, described it as generally poor and unproductive.[33] Bundunke clothes and other manufactured goods were inferior in quality to those of Futa Toro. "All of the Poulas of Bondou dwell in the woods, attending to the culture of small millet and cotton. They have some cows and fowls, but no horses. Their villages are of a wretched description."[34] Mollien failed to appreciate the fact that Bundu had been at war for some time. He did mention, however, that the lands bordering the Faleme were "uncommonly fertile," where large plots of tobacco were grown.

In addition to the French missions, the Englishmen Gray and Dochard also ventured to Bundu just prior to Amadi Aissata's death in 1819. They described Boulebane as being situated in a vast plain surrounded by a range of hills.[35] The ruler made his home there, but "it is by no means so large a town as we expected to see in the capital of so thickly inhabited a country. The number of souls did not exceed fifteen or eighteen hundred; the greater number are either the relatives, slaves, tradesmen, or followers of Almamy, or those of the royal family."[36] The town was surrounded by a clay wall ten feet high and eighteen inches thick, in bad repair since the Bambara siege of 1817. The mosque was "by no means a good one," located in an open space at the southwest end of the town. Boulebane was divided into streets, "or more properly lanes," which were highly irregular. Outside of the town's walls was "nothing but a continuous heap of filth."[37] There was a regular market place, where corn, rice, milk, butter, eggs, fowls, and game were sold. While Boulebane was the principal site of exchange for all of the surrounding villages up to eight miles away, the Englishmen also observed a large number of merchants from Segu.

On the whole. Gray's description of Boulebane was similar to Rubault's concerning Koussan. As was the case in Koussan, the Boulebane royal complex was divided into several courts, housing relatives, wives and concubines, arms, and goods. The exterior walls were thirteen feet high, drawing attention to the location. Elsewhere in Bundu, the valleys where the villages were found were mostly cleared for cultivation, although the proportion under cultivation was small compared to the remaining land.[38] The Englishmen substantiate Rubault's claim that Qur'anic schools were established in most of the villages, but they reveal their own ignorance in stating that "numbers and their uses are unknown."[39]

As a consequence of the wars with Kaarta, it would appear that Bundu experienced a brief period of decline. By the time of Gray and Dochard's visit, the capital at Boulebane had not had sufficient time to recuperate.

However, the bustle of the market place, combined with the presence of merchants from the Upper Niger, is evidence of Bundu's vitality and enduring importance in the Upper Senegal and Gambia Valleys, and that the realm was on the mend.

From the time that Amadi Aissata assumed the *almaamate*, he was engaged in incessant war. The severity of the struggle for Bundu's survival was embodied in the very person of Amadi Aissata, before whom Gray and Dochard had an audience just prior to his death, and from whom was projected the image of the quintessential warrior. At the audience, the aged Amadi Aissata was covered with amulets "to the ankles," a direct indication of the seriousness of his military strategies, given that amulets were used as protective agents by soldiers in battle.[40] To underscore the gravity of the regional competition, the *Almaami* requested arms; to be specific, 120 bottles of gunpowder, twenty "common" guns, and other military goods.[41] He never received them; he died while Gray and Dochard were in Bundu. They record the date as 8 January 1819.[42]

By the time of Amadi Aissata's passing, the two major conflicts facing Bundu had been momentarily resolved: the reformers' aspirations had been checked by the defeat and death of Abdul Qadir, and the dynastic struggle had ended. Amadi Pate Gai's brothers had been allowed to return from Futa Toro.[43] Koussan even came to Boulebane's aid in 1817. But the fact that the two branches maintained separate capitals meant that the potential for civil strife remained.

Although a consensus of rulers' lists credits Amadi Aissata with a seventeen-year reign, independent evidence establishes that his tenure spanned twenty-one years.[44] He was survived by three sons: Saada Amadi Aissata and Umar Sane, who both went on to rule, and Bokar Sane, who apparently accomplished little of note.[45]

Bakel

Three Sissibe contested the succession after Amadi Aissata's death: Tumane Mudi, Amadi Gai's oldest son and representative of the Koussan branch; Musa Yero, Amadi Aissata's nephew and a member of the Boulebane wing; and Malik Samba Tumane, their cousin and the legitimate heir.[46] Beyond these three, a descendant of Tumane Bubu Malik, Amadi Kama, also sought the *almaamate*; Amadi Gai had banned this part of the family from holding office, so that Amadi Kama's candidacy was not even discussed.[47] Despite Malik Samba Tumane's claims, the *Torodbe* elected Musa Yero as the new *Almaami* on 20 January 1819.[48] Gray and Dochard, who had been allowed to proceed to Bakel earlier in January, were soon joined in Bakel by the new *Almaami*. Suspected of supplying Kaarta with goods, they were forced to return to Boulebane.[49] The Englishmen were detained from February to the end of May, being summoned to numerous meetings with Musa Yero. The *Almaami* offered to allow them to go to Segu through Bambuk, or to Saint

Pragmatism in the age of Jihad

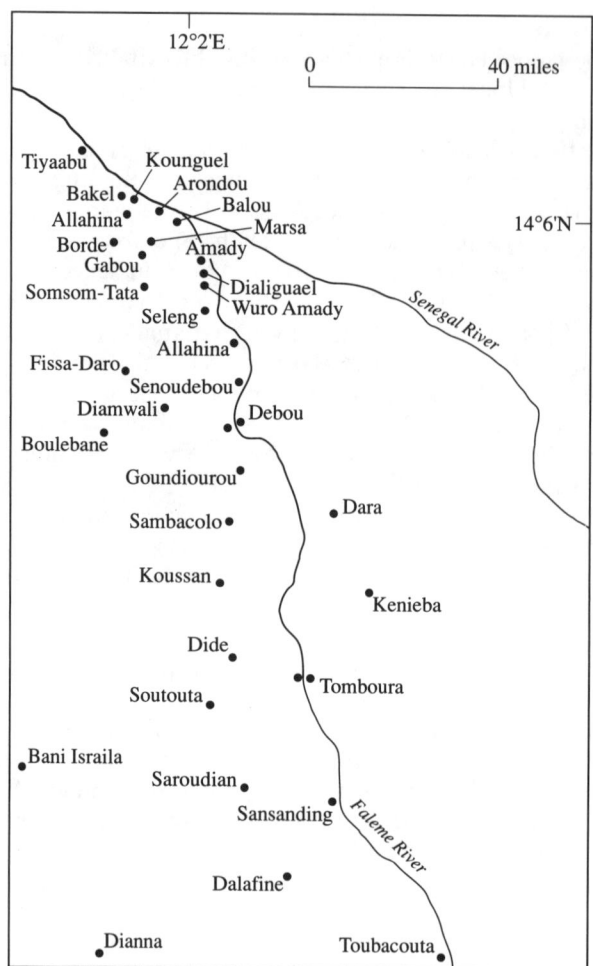

Map 2 Bundunke towns in the nineteenth century

Louis through Futa Toro, but they could not return to Bakel, from where they could easily reach Kaarta.[50] Besides the fear of an English–Bambara alliance, the Bundunkobe were also wary of an English–French domination of the upper valley.[51] Bundu had no objections to trading with the strangers, so long as the latter remained inferior in number and separated by substantial distance. Gray and Dochard wisely elected to go to Saint Louis, and were escorted to Futa Toro to make sure they did not deviate.[52]

The most significant event during the rule of Musa Yero was the establishment of a French post at Bakel. The post would become the most important market in the Upper Senegal, and would spark intense competition among the various upper valley states to procure exclusive trading privileges. In September of 1818, the French sent its first expedition up the Senegal River since reoccupying Saint Louis in 1817. A temporary post was constructed at Bakel, following the approval of Bundu, whose consent and goodwill were indispensable.[53] While Bakel was not actually a part of Bundu, neither was it under the control of Gajaaga, as was demonstrated in the dispute between the N'Diaybe and Tiyaabu during the reign of *Almaami* Musa Gai (1786–90).

Nevertheless, Bundunke influence continued to extend to Bakel in 1817, a fact recognized by the French in that they sought Bundunke approval for their post. Amadi Aissata has agreed to the post for twenty pieces of *guinée*.[54] However, Musa Yero initially displayed misgivings about the new fort; such reticence was probably related to the fact that the post would not be firmly under Bundu's dominion, and would therefore spark increased competition among the regional powers over access to it.[55] He went to Bakel in early 1819 to negotiate the conditions under which he would accept the new fort, conditions which included substantial payments to Bundu in the form of *jizya* (poll tax).[56] However, the negotiations did not go well; the French viewed his demands as exorbitant. Musa Yero's response was to attempt a blockade of the settlement.[57] The staff were able to survive, however, by selling salt to the neighboring villages in exchange for food.

By 1820, Bakel had become a permanent French fort.[58] Precisely because of its success, the *Tunka* of Tiyaabu once again began to press his claims to dominion. Having rebuffed Bundunke demands the previous year, the French now determined that the threat from Tiyaabu was sufficient to warrant new negotiations with Bundu. In preparation for such talks, Hesse, Commandant of Bakel in 1820, led an expedition up the river from Bakel to Felou Falls.[59] He found that Bundu had sufficient centralization to direct its commerce to Bakel, as well as to divert other traffic to the post. In a separate report, a Lieutenant LeBlanc argued that good relations with Bundu were essential because of its commercial influence, and that the Soninke of Gajaaga lived in fear of Bundu.[60] Therefore, Hesse prevailed upon Musa Yero to sign a treaty on 12 November 1820. The provisions of the treaty required the *Almaami* to protect France's commercial interests, while pledging to join the French against any and all enemies. In return, the Bundunkobe would receive annual payments from the French. It was a partnership born of necessity.[61]

The 1820 Bundunke–French treaty was tested the following year, when relations between Bakel and Tiyaabu began to unravel. The *Tunka*, "emboldened by his raids on the cattle of the post, became more and more troublesome and unreasonable ... His demands no longer had any limits; he wanted Hesse to pay him customs for the wood chopped outside of Bakel, for the vessels sitting in the river, for the site of the fort, ..., etc., etc."[62] The discussions continued from the beginning of 1821 until May of the same year, when Tiyaabu attacked the French at Bakel. The initial siege was beaten back with the help of the *Almaami*, who was at the same time fighting the Malinke of Bambuk.[63] The successful defense of Bakel caused Musa Yero to seek realization of a long-standing aspiration: the elimination of Bacili rule in Gajaaga. In June, he wrote to the *Tunka* of Tiyaabu demanding that he give up his designs on Bakel, lest Tiyaabu suffer assault by the Bundunkobe on land and by the French on the river.[64] Meanwhile, Saint Louis wrote to Bakel in June that reinforcements would be arriving in about two months, and would put the *Tunka* "in his place," if Musa Yero had not done so already.[65] Musa Yero, seeking to exploit the potential of his new alliance, proposed to Hesse his plan of replacing the Bacili with people he claimed would be loyal to the French, but who would certainly have owed a greater debt to Bundu. Hesse deferred the matter to LeCoupe, Governor at Saint Louis. It was at this point that the French made a conscious decision to resist the creation of Bundunke hegemony in the upper valley. Wrote LeCoupe:

> As soon as M. Hesse wrote on July 12 and made me aware of this proposal, I feared that he would fall into an evil far greater than the one from which he sought to escape, and I wrote to him immediately that the project made known by Bundu, to become master of all of the left bank, sufficiently indicated to us that we would not be politically astute in destroying Tuabo and its Bakiri (Princes); that the interests of Bundu and these Sarracolet chiefs appear to me to be in so great an opposition, that without question it was to our advantage to keep them in their present position, in order to be able, if the need arises, to be aided by the one against the aggressions of the other.[66]

The French rejection of Bundu's proposal caused great consternation at Boulebane. Musa Yero responded by raiding the villages neighboring Bakel, as well as intercepting the trade to and from the post. "Only the cannon of the fort, and the fear of fighting against us, prevented him from assaulting Bakel."[67] In short, the Bundunke *Almaami* had decided to force Bakel out of its neutrality.

By August, Musa Yero's strategy had worked, and Bakel could no longer maintain its position. Hesse was instructed to tell Musa Yero that the French wanted to punish Tiyaabu, and needed his aid.[68] Musa Yero responded with a brilliant move, sending a large contingent to Bakel in order to jointly attack Tiyaabu.[69] Hesse had no choice but to join the Bundunkobe. This was probably Bundu's greatest opportunity to conclusively defeat Gajaaga, and to seize the lion's share of control over the Upper Senegal's commerce. Instead, the expedition met with utter disaster; the *Almaami*'s troops were thoroughly routed. One can only speculate that this otherwise inexplicable turn of events was the result of half-hearted (or even duplicitous) French aid, and was in keeping with the decision of LeCoupe to prevent Bundu's expansion. In support of this possibility, it is instructive to note that a peace treaty was signed on 21 September 1821, between Bakel and Tiyaabu, without Musa Yero's knowledge. Bundu had been defeated, but Tiyaabu had, in light of the conflict with Bundu, changed its belligerent stance towards the French post. The French, in the end, achieved precisely what they wanted: Tiyaabu's cooperation, combined with the containment of Bundu. Bundu, in turn, decided against engaging in reprisal.

As demonstrated by LeCoupe's correspondence and French policy in the region, the thinking in Saint Louis was that Bundu should be prevented from becoming too powerful. This approach to Bundu was again apparent when in January of 1822, Bundu suffered "a great assault" by the Bambara of Kaarta.[70] The French viewed the Bambara incursions into Bundu, as well as Gajaaga, as advantageous to Bakel: according to this logic, Bundu's preoccupation with the east allowed the French to solidify their position.[71] The French concern over Bundu's potential is understandable, but it was also risky in that a weakened Bundu could spell the disruption of trade to Bakel.

Although relations between Bakel and Bundu were strained, commercial transactions continued. In 1824, one Beaufort was given permission by Musa Yero to station a merchant at Sansanding, on the Faleme.[72] Sansanding was a bustling town, split in two by the river. It was especially noted for the gold that passed through it on its way to the Gambia.[73] In an effort to further demonstrate Sansanding's value, Musa Yero sent to Bakel letters he had received from the English. In 1825, a *comptoir* was reestablished at Sansanding. However, the French lost interest in Sansanding due to the interminable wars in the area, and their *comptoir* never became important.[74]

Notwithstanding his affairs with Gajaaga and Bakel, and in spite of his forays into Wuli, Tenda and Bambuk, Rançon depicts Musa Yero as a "relatively peaceful" man.[75] He is credited, however, with reducing the frequency of border raids from neighboring lands. He died sometime toward the end of 1826.[76] That he reigned eight years is generally agreed upon by all the sources.[77] He was survived by three sons: Demba Musa, Saada Dude, and Bala Setai. They all died fighting under *al-ḥājj* Umar.

At Musa Yero's death, Amadi Aissata's son Saada sought to become *Almaami*, but "his greed was his downfall."[78] This is an apparent reference to his inability to compromise on such matters as appointees to important offices and distribution of revenues. Instead, Tumane Mudi, son of Amadi Gai, became *Almaami* (1827–35). Although he represented the Koussan branch, his support of Amadi Aissata won him the reciprocating approval of Boulebane. However, Saada Amadi Aissata never fully accepted Tumane Mudi, and was busy throughout the *Almaami*'s tenure garnering support for his next bid for power.[79]

In July of 1827, hostilities again erupted between Bundu and Gajaaga. The treaty of 1821 between the French at Bakel and Tiyaabu was abrogated by the latter, and Bundu intervened to support its old allies, the N'Diaybe.[80] Although Bundu's activities against the Bacili were not very intense, they did result in the recovery of some Bundunke prestige after the fiasco of 1821. In recognition of Bundu's improved position, the French at Bakel decided to send the *Almaami* additional gifts to complement the annual *jizya* payments he received in keeping with the 1820 French–Bundunke treaty.[81]

During the reigns of Musa Yero and Tumane Mudi, Bundunke activity along the north-west frontier had been largely focused on the French post at Bakel. The decision to place the post beyond the territorial authority of any regional power was designed to insure the autonomy of the *comptoir*, but it also exacerbated tensions between the various states in the upper valley. Those tensions would only increase in subsequent decades, and invite powers such as Kaarta and the Moors of southern Mauritania to also join the competition, as would be the case in the 1830s, when these powers repeatedly invaded Bundu and the upper valley.[82] In addition to trade goods in general, the Moors were searching for slaves, and would be repelled on several occasions by Bundunke forces.[83]

The south

While the establishment of the French fort at Bakel and related developments commanded most of the attention of the *almaamies* through the reign of Tumane Mudi (1827–35), there was some activity to the south. Earlier, Amadi Aissata had engaged in minor conflicts with Tenda and its principal village of Gamon. This was an effort to reestablish Bundu's control over the southern trade routes, which had atrophied due to the struggles with Abdul Qadir and Kaarta from 1799 to 1818.[84] Amadi Aissata also paid some attention to the perpetual conflict with Bambuk. But in addition to the question of gold and commercial routes, Bundu was also concerned with the problem of absconding slaves. Many of Bundu's slaves were Malinke, and hence escaped when possible into Bambuk, where they formed maroon communities.[85] This matter could become a source of considerable aggravation, as the standing army relied heavily upon the recruitment of slaves. Slave labor was also crucial in the successful pursuit of agriculture, and in any event was important to the productive sector of the economy. Hence, Amadi Aissata's attention to the matter.

Musa Yero also led a few strikes into Tenda and Wuli for the purpose of controlling the kola nut trade, and to possibly replenish servile labor, depleted due to the increase in absconding. However, it was Tumane Mudi who commanded a major expedition into Wuli, probably for the same reasons. By 1829, he had been joined by Awa Demba of Khasso, and together they pillaged the countryside.[86] Although Awa Demba had to return to Khasso to repress a serious rebellion, the Bundunkobe continued their raids into Wuli as late as 1832.[87] Tumane Mudi even ventured beyond Wuli, crossing the Gambia River on several occasions.[88] One of these raids took place during the last year of his reign, when he crossed the Gambia into Kaabu. He suffered a serious wound while retreating from a counterattack, and never recovered.[89]

Tumane Mudi reigned for the most part from Koussan, a fact confirmed by Tourette's visit to Bundu in 1829. However, he spent his last years in Boulebane in order to strengthen support there for his intended successor and brother, Malik Kumba. This was done to counteract the claims of Saada

Amadi Aissata, the "home" representative of Boulebane's interest.[90] At his death, Tumane Mudi had at least twelve sons.[91] Two sons, Abbas and Ibrahim Tenendia, died without reigning. Samba Tumane died in the Civil War of 1852–54, while al-Kusun was assassinated at Somsom-Tata. A fifth son, Salif, was still living in Koussan when Rançon visited there. The seven remaining sons, Umar Bili Kari, Abdul Salum, Eli Gitta, Hamet, Bubacar Sidiq, Sega Tumane, and Suracoto all followed *al-ḥājj* Umar in his eastern *jihād*, where they remained. All of the sources agree that Tumane Mudi reigned eight years.

Malik Kumba, brother of Tumane Mudi and supporter of the late Amadi Aissata, was named the new *Almaami* (1835–37).[92] His selection caused a rebellion by unidentified malcontents within Bundu. The *Almaami* was forced to "repress harmful activities of some of the Sissibe, who sought to turn the people against him, ..."[93] The leader of the rebellion was in all probability Saada Amadi Aissata, whose previous bid for the *almaamate*, in conjunction with the absence of any other viable challenger, qualifies him as the likely ringleader of the sedition.

Malik Kumba's tenure was uniquely uneventful. William Fox, traveling through Bundu in 1838, reported that Malik Kumba had died in 1837.[94] That he was no longer *Almaami* in 1838 is also supported by the Bakel correspondence. Yet, the majority of the sources state that he reigned for four years.[95] The reasons for this slight but uniform discrepancy are not clear. He was survived by five sons, all of whom fought and died under *al-ḥājj* Umar. They were: Samba Gaissiri, Musa Yero Malik, Bubacar Malik, Boila Malik, and Alium Malik.

From the reign of Amadi Aissata to that of Malik Kumba, the *almaamate* of Bundu was directed by men who were essentially concerned with the preservation and commercial expansion of the state. The demise of militant Islam in the person of Abdul Qadir, combined with his interference in the Bundunke succession, worked together to undermine the reformist position. At the same time, the imperialist designs of Kaarta, together with the construction of the French fort at Bakel, further encouraged pragmatic policies on the part of states throughout the upper valley, all of which were concerned with both survival and greater access to the commerce of the region. Bundu was no exception, and was left with little choice except to develop in the same direction as its neighboring states. The ability to access weapons and control trade routes was crucial in Bundu's effort to stay afloat in the increasingly dangerous upper valley.

6
Structure of the Bundunke Almaamate

The end of Malik Kumba's reign provides an appropriate juncture at which the theme of government in Bundu can be addressed. The *almaamate*, having experienced significant instability between 1698 and 1720, had managed to survive and develop within a region characterized by expansionist, competitive states. That Bundu thrived during the eighteenth and first half of the nineteenth centuries can to a large extent be attributed to the increasing efficacy of its statecraft.

From the dawn of the polity until the reign of Amadi Gai (1764–86), the principles of pragmatism guided the Bundunke leadership in matters of state. Expanding the boundaries to appropriate fertile lands; encompassing important trade routes; and accessing sources of primary materials (e.g., gold from Bambuk, gum from the Upper Senegal, kola nut from the Gambia) were the chief determinants in fashioning a regional policy vis-a-vis neighboring states. Islam continued to expand within Bundu throughout the eighteenth century in that the population of Muslims relative to non-Muslims steadily increased. However, the option of militant or reform Islam was viewed by the Bundunke rulers as an unnecessary extreme. Not until the external influence of Abdul Qadir after 1776 did the Bundunke government begin to experiment with reform Islam at the administrative level.[1]

The sovereign

By the end of the eighteenth century, the core area of Bundu had been largely defined. Stretching from the vicinity of Gabou in the north to Didecoto in the south, and from the Faleme River to Boulebane in the west, the Bundunke rulers had succeeded in imposing a centralized government over ethnically diverse communities. With the rise of Amadi Aissata in 1797, the realm was informally divided into two spheres: Boulebane was the focus of the northern sphere, while Koussan controlled the southern half of the state. The *Almaami* ruled all of Bundu, from either Koussan or Boulebane. However, his influence and share of tax revenues would diminish outside of his "home" sphere. No precise boundaries between the two spheres existed before 1887, but with Malik Ture and the virtual takeover of the Bundunke government by the French, the lines between north and south became more definitive. In 1905, those lines were formally demarcated, as Bundu was divided by the French into southern and northern Bundu out of recognition of the *de facto* arrangement.[2]

During the second half of the nineteenth century, the peripheral areas were added to the core, largely through the conquests of Bokar Saada (1857–85). The status of the peripheral communities was subordinate to that of the core, in that the periphery consisted of previously autonomous entities forcibly recruited into the Bundunke orbit. By the 1880s provinces within the two main spheres had been created: Leze-Bundu, Leze-Maio, Ferlo-Baliniama, Ferlo M'Bal, and Ferlo-Nieri were within the jurisdiction of Boulebane; while Koussan directly supervised activities in Nague-Hore Bundu, Do-Maio, Tiali, Nieri, Diakha, and Ferlo Maodo provinces.[3] Sissibe family members governed the provinces, with the more important ones issued to the most influential members.[4] Supporting this three-tier system (the *Almaami*, the two Sissibe branches at Koussan and Boulebane, and the provincial governors) were the local villages.

The sources are unanimous in stating that the Bundunke *Almaami* held absolute authority by the nineteenth century, a considerable development from the days of Bubu Malik and Maka Jiba in the eighteenth.[5] In contrast to Futa Toro, the Bundunke ruler was not required to defer to the advisory council of notables,[6] a fact that has led some to the conclusion that Bundunke absolutism resulted in that ruler being more powerful than his Futanke counterpart.[7] However, in extremely difficult decisions, in times of national emergency, and as a matter of protocol, the *Almaami* was expected to consult with the advisory council of notables.[8] The council's key constituent members were representatives of the Sissibe, the N'Guenar, and the Jakhanke clerisy.[9]

The *Almaami* was both the head of religion and the temporal ruler.[10] As a political sovereign, his responsibilities included the security of the state, the safeguarding of the caravan routes, the conducting of foreign affairs, and the collecting of taxes to finance these endeavors. When the *Almaami* was conscientious about performing his duties, commerce flowed uninterrupted by brigands. Merchants consistently preferred Bundu to Futa Toro or Futa Jallon due to the safety provided along the caravan routes.

The succession process was not formalized until the death of Maka Jiba (1764), at which time certain families were forever excluded from exercising executive power. Quite simply, executive power was to pass through the line of brothers, beginning with the eldest, until it returned to the eldest son of the eldest brother.[11] However, the rightful heir had to enjoy substantial backing among the remaining Sissibe, otherwise he risked forfeiting his birthright. This was a practical matter; rulers who through weakness encouraged rebellion and instability were necessarily rejected. Several legal heirs were denied the executive office as a consequence of some perceived

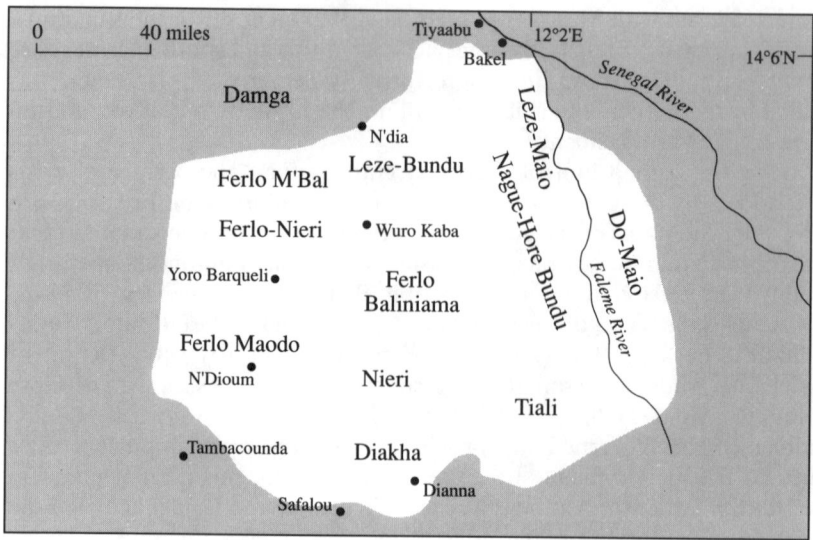

Map 3 Areas inside Bundu in the late nineteenth century

shortcoming: Malik Samba Tumane in 1819, Saada Amadi Aissata in 1827 (although he later succeeded), and Amadu Sy in 1837 (he also subsequently took power).

Although the succession was usually straightforward, it had to be sanctioned by an electoral council, which involved the gathering of advisory council members and additional representatives of the leading families. It was at the death of an *Almaami* that the electoral council exercised its greatest influence; once the succession was ratified, the electoral council disbanded, and had no legal method of reversing its decision. An example of this was Saada Amadi Aissata. Rejected in 1827, he finally took power ten years later, after which he made the extremely unpopular decision of allowing the French to build a fort at Senoudebou. For all of their objections, the Sissibe had no viable recourse, and had to abide by the *Almaami*'s determination.

At the death of an *Almaami*, each village was required to send a delegation to assist in the funeral.[12] Almost immediately, a potential conflict was set in motion: while the brother next-in-line inherited the executive office, the deceased's eldest son was given almost three-fourths of his possessions.[13] Included in this were all of the deceased's amulets, his dwelling, and a large number of his slaves (this is precisely what happened following Bokar Saada's death in 1885: Umar Penda assumed the title, but Usuman Gassi received the lion's share of the inheritance). Once the new *Almaami* was agreed upon, the installation ceremony was held the next day. It was accompanied by a large-scale celebration, which included dancing, shouting, and firearm salutes.[14]

The court usually consisted of the *Almaami*'s advisory council, the royal *griots*, family members, and trusted slaves. Lamartiny remarked that the head advisor was always from outside of the royal family.[15] When Fox traveled through Bundu in 1838, he noted that the *Almaami* was accompanied by about 250 advisors, warriors, and "priests."[16] This was at a time when the *Almaami* was preparing for war. Later in 1843, Raffenel observed that Saada Amadi Aissata's entourage was much more modest.[17] From Gray and Dochard's perspective in 1819, the entire town of Boulebane was a royal "court," since everyone in it was either the sovereign's slave, relative, confidant, or tradesman.[18] As for slaves within the administration, their numbers and influence would dramatically increase under Bokar Saada.[19] This was an entirely logical development, since the hostility he generated left him with few free men in whom he could trust.

Assemblies were generally held in the great court of the *Almaami*'s home, or in the village central meeting place.[20] The sovereign was always seated on sheepskin covered with amulets. The chief advisor stood to his right, and acted as the intermediary between the power and the supplicant.[21] Foreigners were granted special audiences; otherwise, visitors were not allowed to be present during the assemblies of the notables, or to enter the royal court.[22] It was Bokar Saada's habit to receive his advisors, Sissibe "princes," and others from seven to ten in the morning, and from four to six in the evening.[23] When traveling, he usually rode on horseback, followed by other mounted Sissibe; then came his *griots* on foot, followed by the royal slaves.

Beneath the province was the village, the basic component of Bundunke society, over which were the leading lineages.[24] From these lineages the headman was chosen, who ruled local affairs and adjudicated cases in conjunction with the *imām* of the village. The leading families were so because their ancestors were purported to have been the first to make the land productive, either through digging a well or clearing the bush.[25] The successive village heads were always from the same families. The *Almaami* rarely intervened in the local succession process, except in situations where there was no legitimate heir, in which case the *Almaami* chose a council of leading men to govern until the residents themselves elected a headman. If the heir was a minor, the *Almaami* would again select several notables to govern until the heir came of age. The *Almaami* reserved the right to dismiss any headman who displeased him.

Those villages along key caravan routes made money by both trading commodities and selling food to the passing caravans.[26] According to Mungo Park, the village of Tillika had a representative of the *Almaami* who resided there permanently, in addition to the local rulers.[27] His function was to keep track of all incoming caravans from Wuli and points south, and to levy a tax in the name of the *Almaami*. It is probable, based upon this single reference, that Bundu stationed similar agents in all border villages through which there were caravan routes. This agent did not get involved with local affairs. Neither does it appear that he collected taxes from the village.

Critical to the health of the Bundunke state was the maintenance of safe and accessible trade routes. Within Bundu, there was little problem with brigands. It was outside the limits of Bundu that serious disruptions occurred from time to time. The question arises as to how the security of the routes was effected. There is no evidence of Bundunke garrisons being stationed at regular intervals along the roads; the only mention of any Bundunke official operating outside of Bundu concerns Amadi Musa, who is described as a "lieutenant" of Saada Amadi Aissata (1837–51), permanently stationed in Kantora.[28] (What his function was is unclear; he may have actually set up an independent polity in Kantora, over which Bundu claimed suzerainty.) In any event, the only method clearly utilized by Bundu to control the trade routes was that of punitive raiding: once a caravan was attacked, the offending village would be identified. The destruction of the village served as an example to all would-be brigands.[29]

The military

In contrast to Futa Toro, Bundu maintained a standing army. This difference between the two states is largely explained by the fact that throughout much of its history, Bundu was constantly expanding. The army was modest at first, and probably began under Maka Jiba at some point in the mid-eighteenth century.[30] Also unlike the Futanke state, the absolutism of the Bundunke *Almaami* provided for the consistent loyalty of such an army.[31] This body would eventually become responsible for the security of the trade routes, and garrisons were kept at the principal towns of Boulebane and Koussan. The army would be called upon to quell minor border skirmishes, and units were especially concentrated along the southern and eastern frontiers, at *tatas* such as Fena. However, in times of national emergency (war, large raiding expeditions, etc.), it would be necessary to conscript civilians. In such times, the *Almaami* notified the villages of his increased need for troops. The sources mention three ways through which the call to arms was transmitted: through slaves, who went from village to village; via the Sissibe nobility, who would also crisscross the country; and through the use of drums.[32] The villages would be given as many as four days to send men to the pre-arranged meeting place; any village that refused to participate would be pillaged by the *Almaami*'s slaves.[33]

Each free family was reportedly required to send one man to serve in the military during periods of crisis, but the magnitude of the challenge may have demanded even greater enlistments; this certainly seems to have been the case under Amadi Aissata, who assembled an uncountable number for the siege of Fena c. 1799. During stretches of relative peace, however, the number of men comprising the standing army fluctuated from 400 to 1,000, depending upon the ruler. This "peace time" force was composed primarily of slaves, over whom was a command structure of free persons, at the top of which was Sissibe leadership.[34] In this way, the essentially servile standing army of Bundu resembled similar slave forces in seventeenth/eighteenth century Morocco and Egypt from the twelfth through the sixteenth centuries.

As was true of all Sudanic states which achieved significant empire, the strength of Bundu's army was its cavalry.[35] It was the responsibility of the *Almaami* to supply mounts for all his courtiers, his relatives, and his royal slaves.[36] The various subdivisions and units of the army were placed under the command of the *Almaami*'s sons and brothers.[37] The commanding officers were distinguished by their blue colors, and by an ostrich plume extending from their turbans.[38] Whoever functioned as the general wore three such plumes.

Although the Bundunke armies were capable of battlefield maneuvers, how much time they devoted to drilling is unclear. When Rubault was in Bundu, he had an opportunity to review the troops heading for an encounter with Bambuk. The *Almaami* gave several commands, to which the troops did not satisfactorily respond (of course, their failure on this occasion does not preclude their success at other times).[39] The Bundunke armies did exhibit a degree of discipline, however, and usually camped in the open air (except for the *Almaami* and the leading officers, who had tents).[40] Durand, who wrote of Rubault's travels, observed that the army marched without any provision trains or baggage, and that each man had to carry his own arms and food.[41]

Once the battle was engaged, the Bundunkobe usually dispersed and fought hand-to-hand.[42] Faidherbe noted that the "Toucouleurs" fought similarly to the Moors and usually on foot.[43] Music, specifically the drum, was an important ingredient in signaling advance or retreat, and in inspiring the men.[44] Concerning weapons, Rubault in 1786 mentions that the infantry carried firearms, daggers, swords, and either bows and poisoned arrows, or assegais.[45] Each person had to supply his own armament, however. Mollien, some thirty-two years later, commented that firearms were rare, and that most used bows and arrows.[46] Fox noted the same weapons, but failed to comment on proportions.[47] Overall evidence, however, suggests that firearms had become an important component of the Bundunke arsenal during the last quarter of the eighteenth century. By the nineteenth century, most of the army bore firearms of poor quality, and poisoned arrows were almost completely in disuse.[48] In the second half of the nineteenth century much, if not most, of the Bundunke arms were of British manufacture.[49]

The numbers involved in any one expedition fluctuated widely throughout Bundu's history, from the few adherents of Bokar Saada after he initially defected, to the uncountable numbers under Amadi Aissata. Given a maximum population for Bundu of 30,000, the army at no time represented more than one-tenth of the general populace. Of that number, the cavalry comprised anywhere from one-tenth to one-fourth of the army.[50]

The legal treasury

While it is clear that Bundu collected taxes of various kinds from its inception, the precise forms of taxation and the methods of collection are very unclear. There are no extant written records, or evidence that such ever existed. In the absence of the necessary data, one cannot argue with any degree of assurance that Bundu complied with Islamic law in raising revenue; or, conversely, that it failed to do so. It is logical, however, to anticipate that certain categories of taxation would be levied in an Islamic state.[51] What follows is an attempt to discern from the sources those forms of taxes which were collected in Bundu, and the ways in which they may have been assessed.

There are several types of revenue which are discussed to some extent in the Bundunke sources. These types can be divided into two classes: "religious revenue," collected from Muslims, and "secular revenue," provided by non-Muslims.[52] Regarding the first category, all Muslims are required to pay *zakāt*, or obligatory alms. This is fundamental to the religion; *zakāt* is one of the "five pillars" of the faith. Curiously, although Willis consistently mentions *zakāt* as a source of revenue in Bundu, none of the literary sources actually refer to it.[53] However, since *zakāt* is a *farḍ* (obligation), it is unthinkable that the Bundunkobe did not pay *zakāt*.[54] That the Bundunkobe did so can be demonstrated more convincingly by considering the literary evidence in light of the principles of Islamic law.

Zakāt can be divided into three separate kinds of taxes: levies on flocks and herds, on specie and commercial goods, and on harvests.[55] The literary sources are redundant in stating that the Bundunke government collected the "tenth" of the harvest, or *'ushr*.[56] According to Maliki law, *'ushr* is in fact a constituent part of *zakāt* and equated with it.[57] Clearly then, Bundunkobe paid *zakāt*. Interestingly, there are no references to taxation on Fulbe herds. There are references, however, concerning the taxing of merchants. Gray and Dochard report that the *Almaami* received a tenth of all salt arriving from the Atlantic coast.[58] This salt was transported by Bundunke merchants, not foreigners. Since they were Muslims, the duties they paid would have to be considered as *zakāt*.

Concerning the collection of *zakāt* from the various settlements, the sources suggest that the village heads carried their contributions to the town where the *Almaami* resided.[59] This was performed every harvest. Difficulties would arise when Sissibe heads of principal towns and villages began collecting revenue for themselves, in contravention of Islamic law. After Bokar Saada's death, Bundu was more or less partitioned into numerous zones of influence, akin to fiefs, where the individual "princes," based in their home towns, extended their authority into the nearby villages. As a consequence, *zakāt* payments were still collected, but only occasionally reached the *Almaami*.

Although the *Almaami* was to receive *zakāt* revenues, theoretically he was not free to distribute them as he wished. The beneficiaries were clearly specified in the law as follows: the poor (the determination of which was left to the *Almaami*), the indigent (more needy than the poor, in the Maliki view), those appointed by the *Almaami* to collect *zakāt*, slaves seeking manumission, debtors, those unable to perform *jihād*, transients, and the *mu'allafah qulūbuhum* (a complicated category primarily composed of potential converts and those of weak faith).[60] In view of the foregoing, and assuming that the *Almaami* did not misappropriate *zakāt* revenues, he would necessarily need additional sources of income to finance his wars and other pursuits. He could legally meet these needs through "secular revenue," which in turn consisted of three main types: tribute, booty, and the poll tax.

Tribute (*fay'*) and booty (*ganīmah*) were absolutely essential to the strategies of the Bundunke state (or any other expansionist polity, be it Muslim or non-Muslim). Tribute was regularly imposed upon the vanquished by the *Almaami*, and was a source of income that gave him much more discretionary flexibility than did the *zakāt* revenues.[61] However, it would appear that booty was a much more important category of revenue, judging from the frequency and scale of Bundu's raiding activities. A fifth of the booty was to be administered by the *Almaami*, while the remaining four-fifths belonged to his army. Although there are guidelines for how the fifth is to be distributed, the evidence indicates that the *Almaami* benefitted personally, especially in the augmentation of his slaves.[62] Raffenel goes so far as to say that the *Almaami* took one-half of the booty.[63] During the periods of reform activity, the *Almaami*'s violation of the law in this regard would have constituted grounds for opposition to his authority.

The last consideration under secular revenue is that of the poll tax, or *jizya*, and in this category the nature of the tax required collection agents, or *'āshirs*.[64] Based upon information regarding the town of Tillika, there is evidence that the equivalent of this office existed at certain points in Bundunke history, and in certain localities. Included in this category were the payments made by the French for the right to trade and maintain their posts. According to Maliki law, *dhimmi* or "protected" traders were required to pay a duty of ten percent of their goods.[65] Gray and Dochard confirm that merchants were forced to yield ten percent of their merchandise.[66] This usually was carried out by the merchant giving seven bottles of gunpowder and a musket, or their equivalent, for every donkey load of European merchandise.[67] Some twenty-three years earlier, Mungo Park characterized the Bundunke levies as "very heavy," noting that for each donkey load, a merchant paid one Indian baft (blue cloth of East Indian manufacture), or a musket, and six bottles of gunpowder.[68] "By means of these duties, the king of Bondou is well supplied with arms and ammunition; a circumstance which makes him formidable."[69]

In sum, the Bundunke *almaamate* collected both religious and secular revenues. In the absence of written records, however, it is entirely possible that their collection was arbitrary and subject to illegalities.

Justice in Bundu

As was the case with the legal treasury, only a modicum of documentation gives insight into the Bundunke judicial system. What can be said is most applicable to the nineteenth century, as was also true of the data on the treasury. With these constraints in mind, there existed within the Bundunke system of justice a three-tier hierarchy of authority. In the first instance, cases were heard at the local level, over which the village head presided in conjunction with the village *imām*.[70] In this scheme, the *imām* is the functional equivalent of a *qāḍī*. Rançon in fact states that the *qāḍīs* formed the basis of the lower courts; but the term *qāḍī* rarely appears in any of the data, written or oral.[71] The official in question then was most likely the *imām* of the local mosque. If a person was found guilty of an offense at the village level, that individual could appeal his case to the intermediate judge, the *tamsir*. The *tamsir* was usually a Jakhanke cleric and a member of the *Almaami*'s entourage, serving as one of his closest advisors.[72] He handled all appeals that did not carry a death sentence. There may have been several *tamsirs* at the same time, headed by a chief *tamsir*.[73]

The final court of appeal was that of the *Almaami* himself. He handled only the most serious cases.[74] A kind of police force was maintained that answered solely to the *Almaami*; perhaps this force regulated the court procedures in addition to maintaining order within the royal towns.[75] When the *Almaami* was trying a case, it was a grand event open to the public. All of his courtiers would be present; the case would be stated, the appropriate legal texts read by the clerics, and the decision reached.[76]

Bundu, as was true of Futa Toro and Futa Jallon, was known for its severity in meting out punishments. Theft was punishable by amputation of the right hand; a repeat offender suffered death through starvation.[77] Murderers were either shot, strangled, or beheaded.[78] The violation of a virgin saw the confiscation of all the offender's possessions if he were a free man; a slave would be instantly killed.[79] Likewise, the punishment for adultery was either death of the loss of one's goods. Illegitimate children were social outcasts, and literally driven out of their villages when they reached a mature age.[80] In those matters less serious, offenders would often receive a thorough flogging; Bundu was notorious for its severe public chastisements.[81] It was possible to avoid a flogging by payment of some sort; according to Carrère and Holle, a cow was worth ten lashes. Whether one escaped humiliation through payment, or suffered the loss of possessions after being found guilty, all material advantage went to the *Almaami*, to do with it what he pleased.[82] Clearly, many of these punishments went beyond the stipulations of Islamic law.

Under the Bundunke system of government, the state was able to field impressive armies, defend its borders, maintain order among ethnically diverse communities, protect the trade routes, participate in skilled diplomacy with representatives of both African and European powers, dispense justice, and collect revenues. Bundu's leaders also displayed some capacity to change and adapt to novel circumstances. But the essential character of the state remained pragmatic. This moderate tradition was severely tested in the last quarter of the eighteenth century by developments in Futa Toro and the emergence of a second paradigm of militant Islam under the clerical leadership of Abdul Qadir (the first having been Futa Jallon). After a fifty year interim, during which Bundu engaged in a fierce struggle for control of the Upper Senegal, the tradition would be challenged again; this time, in the person of *al-ḥājj* Umar.

7

Struggle for the Upper Senegal Valley

The first half of the nineteenth century witnessed a slow increase in the number of French *comptoirs* in the Senegal Valley. Besides Bakel, the French constructed fortified posts at Dagana (1821), Meringhen (1822), Lampbar (1843), Senoudebou (1845), and Podor (1854).[1] In 1850, these forts and posts were given the name *Sénégal et Dépendances*. Between 1854 and 1855, eight more were built, from Richard Toll to Medine. Such growth, while modest, provided some support for a much more dramatic French expansion in the second half of the century, or what has been described as the French "shift from 'water' to 'land', from a coastal enclave with riverine interests to control of the territory of today's Senegal."[2]

Echoing the French, the British were also increasing their commercial activities along the Upper Gambia, with their principal settlement at McCarthy Island. In the 1820s, the British signed a series of treaties with the kingdom of Wuli for the purpose of facilitating such trade. Bundu, already in contact with British merchants along the Gambia, became even more involved with the latter in the exchange of various commodities, thereby diversifying its trade options.

The response to this gradual increase in the European presence was a rise in hostilities between the various states in the Upper Senegal. The struggle was over control of the region's commerce, considerably enhanced with the growth of French and British entrepots, and made much more deadly by a rise in the availability of European firearms. As the upper valley states intensified their competition, their dependency upon such weaponry concomitantly deepened, which in turn further fueled the hostilities.

Bundu played a major role in the struggle for the Upper Senegal. The government pursued a multifaceted policy which sought to encourage increased trade with the Europeans, while limiting the influence of the Kaartans. The problem with this approach was that, given the proximity of the French, their trading activities also resulted in the augmentation of their influence in upper valley politics. Consequently, Bundu walked a thin line, attempting to curb French political intervention, while continuing to cultivate trade relations. This was especially evident in Gajaaga, where a civil war saw the Bundunkobe adopt a simultaneous anti-Kaartan, anti-French position.

For the period under investigation, exogenous sources provide much more data than do the endogenous and intermediate genres. The number of reports emanating from the trading posts allows for substantial corroboration on events in the upper valley. On the other hand, the sources (from all three genres) are deficient in explaining or interpreting the significance of such events. Once again, it is necessary to deduce from the sources the perspective and strategy of the court, and by the same process speculate on those social conditions which were most likely in existence.

The election of Saada Amadi Aissata

After ten years of rule by individuals who ostensibly belonged to the Koussan branch, but who in fact had been key supporters of Amadi Aissata, the Sissibe formally returned executive power to Boulebane. Amadu Sy of Koussan, son of Amadi Gai and the legal successor to *Almaami* Malik Kumba, was unable to muster the necessary support to succeed; instead, significant *Torodbe* backing, together with the overwhelming support of courtiers and royal slaves who had risen to prominence, combined to elect Saada Amadi Aissata (1837–51) as *Almaami*.[3] The election of the Boulebane candidate produced a considerable ripple in the pond of relations between the two branches, which up to this time had managed to overcome the more pernicious effects of the 1797–1807 Civil War. The following enjoyed by Saada Amadi Aissata in 1837 was in fact the fruit of long and deliberate cultivation, dating back to his bid for power after the death of Musa Yero in 1826. From that time to his eventual election, Saada Amadi made little effort to conceal his ambition, as was the case when he publicly opposed the reign of Tumane Mudi.[4] His disregard for the legal succession was again demonstrated when he fought against Malik Kumba's candidacy in 1835. Consequently, his elevation to power in 1837 caused great consternation to the Sissibe of Koussan, who "lowered their heads, without voicing their discontent."[5]

Under Saada Amadi Aissata, Bundu's economy and morale initially suffered as a result of incessant warfare. The second half of the reign, however, was characterized by economic recovery, which was directly stimulated by a substantial influx of ethnically diverse immigrants, encouraged by the Bundunke government to resettle in order to increase cultivation.

Saada Amadi Aissata's ascendance continued the domination of government by the Boulebane branch. It is of interest that sources for his tenure make reference to the rising influence of royal slaves. This development is probably the end-product of at least two factors: an increase in the number of domestic slaves, and growing tension within the Sissibe clan, necessitating a greater reliance upon those who could be trusted, and who would be the least likely to benefit from various intrigues.

The court under Saada Amadi Aissata encouraged trade with the French and British, while seeking to contain Kaartan expansion in the upper valley. These two aims were directly related, as the Bundunkobe relied upon European firearms, especially those of British manufacture, to achieve the goal of containment. In pursuit of the latter, Bundu led the attempt to forge a middle and upper valley alliance against Kaarta, an attempt that met with some success. However, Kaarta maintained its influence over eastern Senegambia.

The southern strategy employed by Bundu was also related to the upper valley contest, as kola, slaves, and produce were acquired to trade with the Moors in the north in exchange for horses. At the same time, the southern raids helped Bundu to overcome its agricultural woes by accessing both foodstuffs and slaves for cultivation.

While Bundu traded with the French, the polity was suspicious of French intentions in the upper valley. When Saada Amadi Aissata signed the 1845 treaty with the French for the establishment of a French fort at Senoudebou, this distrust was openly expressed most vociferously by the Koussan branch. Šaada Amadi Aissata had his own doubts about the treaty as well, but chose in the end to approve the treaty for political as well as economic reasons. As a result, Senoudebou became a serious source of contention between the two branches.

Civil war in Gajaaga

Saada Amadi's distrust of the French was initially displayed early in his reign, during the civil war in Gajaaga, where the transfer of the office of chief *Tunka* from one town to another was not always problem-free. Since an unspecified time early in its history, Gajaaga had been divided into the provinces of Guey (Lower Gajaaga, with the provincial capital at Tiyaabu) and Kamera (Upper Gajaaga, controlled by Makhana). In 1833 the *Tunka* of Tiyaabu-Guey (and of all Gajaaga at that time) died, and was succeeded by Samba Kumba Diama as *Tunka* of Tiyaabu-Guey only.[6] The other center of power, Makhana-Kamera, was ruled by the *Tunka* Samba Yacine. At the death of the *Tunka* of all Gajaaga in 1833, Samba Yacine began to receive from the French both the customs due to him as ruler of Makhana-Kamera and the customs paid to the overall sovereign of Gajaaga. The French action in fact constituted meddling, as it was a deliberate decision to support the claims of Samba Yacine of Makhana-Kamera against those of Samba Kumba Diama of Tiyaabu-Guey. The repercussions of this policy were serious; Gajaaga soon descended into civil war, resulting in the creation of two politically distinct entities at its conclusion.[7] Hostilities commenced in 1834, when Samba Yacine of Makhana-Kamera attacked Tiyaabu with Bambara assistance, killing all of the Bacili there except for Samba Kumba Diama, who was at Bakel at the time. Samba Kumba Diama was unable to reconstruct the town, and consequently moved to Kounguel.[8]

It was also during this time that the Frenchman Duranton, living in Khasso, began to independently implement his own policies. It was his aim to continue the feud between Samba Yacine and Samba Kumba Diama in order to detract from the influence of Kaarta.[9] Convinced that French policies were ineffective, he took matters into his own hands and tried to form an alliance between Bundu, Khasso, and Bambuk. This alliance, under French authority, would then be able to resist the Kaartans.[10] One of the ways he pursued this was by trying to turn Saada Amadi Aissata against Samba Yacine of Makhana-Kamera. Not much persuasion was necessary, however, for the *Almaami* was already predisposed against Makhana-Kamera, as the latter had received considerable French and Kaartan aid. The Bundunkobe, having concluded that the French were opposed to their hegemony in the upper valley, had assumed a cool posture towards them since the construction of the fort at Bakel in 1818. Saada Amadi's decision to fight Makhana-Kamera, following Duranton's 1837 visit, indicates Bundu's distrust of French intentions, in addition to its hostility towards Kaarta.

Working against the personal diplomacy of Duranton was the Commandant at Bakel, who was instructed to promote good relations between Bundu and Makhana-Kamera in view of the fact that Samba Yacine was a French ally by way of a 28 August 1806 treaty.[11] However, Saint Louis misunderstood Duranton's intentions; as early as 1833, the French suspected Duranton of conspiring with Kaarta.[12] By April of 1837, they were convinced that he was persuading the Bundunkobe to direct commerce away from Bakel to the Gambia.[13] When Duranton visited Bakel in either June or July of 1837, he was arrested on charges of furnishing Samba Kumba Diama of Guey with arms and aiding the English on the Gambia. Sent "downriver" to Saint Louis, he was later freed and allowed to return to Khasso, where he remained.

Samba Yacine of Makhana-Kamera died in the latter part of 1841. At this point, Guey and Kamera became distinct polities, a development at least partially attributable to French involvement. Samba Kumba Diama was officially recognized as the *Tunka* of independent Guey, while the control of Kamera was disputed between Tambu, Samba Yacine's brother, and Barka, the deceased's son. The French began paying half of the usual customs to Samba Kumba of Guey, and the other half to Tambu, the eventual victor of the contest in Kamera.[14] Saint Louis' attempt to establish peace on its own terms was shattered, however, by the 1842 assault of Bundu and Guey on Kamera. Matters became further complicated in 1844, when Bundu attacked Guidimakha. a vassal state to Kaarta.[15]

At this juncture the French found themselves in an interesting position: while they wanted to see Bundu defeat Guidimakha and thereby weaken Kaarta's power in the upper valley, they did not want to encourage any movement by Bundu towards domination of the valley. As a consequence, the Commandant at Bakel was instructed to use all his influence to prevent Samba Kumba Diama of Guey from aiding Saada Amadi Aissata.[16] Officials in Saint Louis wrote of their desire to see Bundu teach Guidimakha "a good lesson," without such an accomplishment issuing into Bundunke hegemony in the area.[17] At the same time, however, the French opposed Kaartan hegemony in the upper valley, and therefore did not interfere in Bundu's organization of an anti-Kaartan alliance, which by early 1846 consisted of itself, Futa Toro, and Bambuk.[18]

The first half of 1846 was one of intense fighting in the upper valley. Despite Bundu's efforts at organizing an anti-Kaartan league, the alliance proved to be less than effective. In March of 1846, the Kaartans defeated the alliance in a major battle, and subsequently began sending forays into Bundu.[19] The conflict extended into January of 1847, at which point the Bundunkobe, extremely weary of the prolonged engagement, finally came to terms with Kaarta and Kamera.[20] In fact, Bundu did a complete about-face in 1849 and raided Guey, its former ally.[21] However, the latter conflict was not a serious one, and the French were able to mediate a peace in March of 1850.

Senoudebou

A major event during Saada Amadi Aissata's reign was the establishment in 1845 of a French fort at Senoudebou, an important village on the caravan route between Farabana and Bakel.[22] This event, in turn, must be seen in the context of the civil war in Gajaaga and the struggle against Kaarta. The affair in Gajaaga began in 1834, so that by 1845, Bundu was experiencing some fatigue. Saada Amadi was also fearful that a competitor, in particular Farabana, would succeed in persuading the French to build the fort within its territory. Given its ailing, wartime economy, Bundu made the decision to accept the French fort.

The decision to allow the construction of a French fort on Bundunke soil, however, resulted in increased tensions between Boulebane and Koussan, still simmering from the assumption of power by Saada Amadi Aissata. In fact, the presence of the French, already acting as a divisive force throughout the upper valley, would provoke further civil strife among the Sissibe of Bundu.

In 1843, a French expedition under Huard-Bessinière, and consisting of Jamin, Raffenel, and Potin-Patterson, set out to both investigate the gold mines of Bambuk and to seek a site for establishing another *comptoir*.[23] They arrived in Senoudebou on 30 December, and proceeded to negotiate with the *Almaami* on ceding the surrounding land to the French.[24] At this point, Bundu faced a dilemma. The French had proven to be treacherous in the past, and therefore unworthy of trust. At the same time, the Bundunkobe found it unacceptable to bypass the opportunity for increased trade with France at a location that was uncontestably on Bundunke soil (in contrast to Bakel). Furthermore, the Bundunkobe were faced with the prospect that if they did not agree to the establishment of a French *comptoir* in Bundu, such an arrangement would be made with an eager Farabana in Bambuk.[25] In view of these alternatives, Saada Amadi acquiesced, and an initial agreement was reached under which the French could settle at Senoudebou.[26]

On 23 August 1845, a final treaty on the French post at Senoudebou was reached.[27] Representing the French were Parent, Menu Dessable, Paul Holle and Potin-Patterson, and it was signed by the then-Governor Thomas. Under its provisions, the land surrounding Senoudebou became French property. The *Almaami* received payment for the land, plus annual customs. The "alcaty" (from *al-qāḍī*) Sapato, apparently the leading official in the advisory council to the *Almaami*, also received an annual payment, as did the *Almaami*'s son Bokar Saada, who was in charge of Senoudebou. Beyond promising to direct caravans to Bakel, Bundu also pledged to prevent any caravans from crossing through to the Gambia. The treaty was drawn up in both French and Arabic.

As would be expected, given the past behavior of the French, the treaty did not meet with the unanimous approval of the Sissibe. In fact, the Koussan branch was vigorously opposed to the treaty.[28] "'If you permit the whites', they said to the Almamy, 'to establish themselves in our land, we will soon no longer be masters of our wives and our slaves; we want to trade with them, but we do not intend for them to be our masters'."[29] The 1845 arrangement went far beyond that of 1820: instead of simply allowing foreigners to establish a few traders in a village, Bundu was now ceding Bundunke land to the non-Muslim French. The Sissibe justifiably feared an eventual loss of sovereignty.

The second aspect to the objection was the promise to shut down all trade to the Gambia. Koussan was oriented towards trading in the south, and was hardly willing to give it up. At the same time, Koussan suspected the French of trying to intervene in Bundu's internal affairs. Consequently, relations between Koussan and Saint Louis were irreparably damaged. Wrote one Frenchman: "Ever since this time, the people of Koussan have continued to regard us with an evil eye ... "[30]

Saada Amadi Aissata overruled the dissenting Sissibe, and signed the treaty. But even he was surprised to see that the French proceeded to install cannon at the site, and protested this development, stating that he "'had given permission for the establishment of a trading post, not an armed fort'."[31] It was not until August of 1847, when the then-Governor deGrammont visited Senoudebou with Paul Holle, that the *Almaami* was persuaded to accept the cannon.[32]

The benefits of trading with the English were, however, too great to resist. In 1844, the Governor of Gambia, Richard Graves MacDonnell, reached Boulebane to discuss the security of the caravan routes to the Gambia.[33] There he learned of the initial agreement with Saint Louis. The Bundunkobe told the French that MacDonnell was sent back empty-handed.[34] What actually transpired was the opposite: "He persuaded the chief to disavow that treaty and to make another, whereby he agreed to keep open the road between Bondou and the river Gambia."[35] In other words, the Bundunkobe engaged in a little duplicity of their own, and went on to sign the final treaty in 1845 in full view of the agreement with MacDonnell. This is the reason why the Koussan branch articulated their objection to the French treaty based upon the land question, and had little to say about the trade to the Gambia. Although the provision made them uncomfortable, there was an understanding that it would not be enforced. And while there is no evidence of any treaty having been signed between MacDonnell and Saada Amadi in 1844, the precise formulation of the Koussan protest is evidence that some sort of agreement had been reached. Beyond this, the subsequent pattern of trade also supports the notion that MacDonnell had been given certain assurances. Notwithstanding such an agreement, the 1845 treaty with the French had the effect of restoring distrust and suspicion between Boulebane and Koussan.

At first, it appeared to the French that Boulebane was keeping its promise to ban the southern trade.[36] However, by July of 1846, it had become clear that commerce between Bundu and the Gambia was very active.[37] When Raffenel visited Bundu for the second time in 1847, he found Saada Amadi Aissata clad in the red jacket of an English officer.[38] He went on to say that the English continually sent delegates to the *Almaami*, and that these solicitations could result in the disruption of the French-Bundunke alliance. His solution was that the French should visit the *Almaami* more frequently, with more gifts. In 1850, however, Bundu was still trading with the English.[39]

The south

By 1847, the incessant fighting on several fronts had succeeded in demoralizing the inhabitants of the Upper Senegal. Agricultural production had been disrupted by the protracted warfare, and complicating matters was the onset of the perennial "hungry season" or summer drought.[40] In response, Saada Amadi Aissata marched on the small-scale Malinke societies to the south to acquire both booty and slaves for agricultural purposes. In particular, the *Almaami* targeted Wuli, often the object of raiding by preceding *almaamies*. Immediately following the peace with Kamera and Kaarta in 1847, the *Almaami* led an expedition to the south.[41] In this first expedition the Bundunkobe, combined with forces from Khasso and Bambuk, clearly crossed into Wuli and Niani, but their primary destination is unclear. There is evidence that they penetrated Kantora, south of the Gambia, and once a part of the larger Kaabu empire.[42] But Rançon, whose account in this instance is unsupported by other sources and therefore questionable, maintains that the primary objective was Salum, which had been pillaging caravans returning to Bundu after having traded there.[43] According to this scenario, Bundu forced the submission of Salum, which pledged to cease interfering with the caravans. Saada Amadi Aissata reportedly returned to Boulebane with an immense amount of booty, including numerous slaves.[44]

By June of 1848, the *Almaami* was again traveling south. After attacking the people of Tenda, he headed for Wuli, his primary target.[45] In fact, because of Bundu's ability to raid Wuli with near impunity, the English began to regard it as a province of Bundu as early as the 1820s.[46] Although the English were interested in Bundunke trade, they also realized that Wuli acted as a buffer to the potentially disruptive forces of Bundu and Futa Toro. And while Bundu greatly influenced Wuli, it left no administrative apparatus there, nor is there evidence that it ever sought to do so. It would appear, then, that rather than seeking to expand the boundaries of Bundu to include Wuli, Bundu perceived the non-Muslim land primarily as a "hunting" ground, an almost inexhaustible source of goods and slaves.

It should be noted that a general uprising of Muslims was taking place against the states of Niani and Wuli during the 1840s; and that Bundu, Futa Jallon, the *alkali* of Walia, and the head cleric in Niani combined forces to overthrow the non-Muslim dynasties.[47] By 1850, Kantora was paying tribute to Bundu.[48] In contrast to Wuli, however, Bundu maintained a military presence in Kantora: "Almost all the chiefs of Kantora thus had in their pay some men of Diawara (a province of Bundu) who, in case of war or the expeditions of pillagers, obeyed Amadi Musa, lieutenant in this country of the Almamy Sada, chief of Bundu."[49] The involvement of a moderately oriented Bundu in what would appear to be a movement of militant Islam deserves comment. First of all, Bundu had regularly, almost since its inception, raided the south. There is no indication that Bundu was ever interested in spreading Islam beyond its borders – these raids were purely economic in purpose. That is, Bundu's southern strategy antedates that of Islam's growth in the area. Secondly, the involvement of other Muslim entities, and the justification of such expeditions as constituting *jihād*, was not inconsistent with the self-image of the Bundunkobe as Muslims, albeit moderates. Finally, given the rise of Muslim communities in the south and their subsequent struggle with non-Muslims, Bundu really had little choice other than to support the aspirations of the former.

Termination of the reign

During his 1847 visit, Raffenel went to Senoudebou, where he estimated the population to be 500 people.[50] In this sense Senoudebou was not much different from the average town, which usually contained about 400 to 600 residents.[51] In contrast, he estimated Boulebane's population to be as great as 2,000.[52] On his second trip in 1847, he expanded the maximum possible number to 3,000.[53] In addition to the entrenched Fulbe, Malinke, Wolof, and Soninke groups long established in Bundu, Raffenel found that other communities had settled there more recently: the Dianicunda from Tenda; the Kulet from Salum; the Sandarabe from Niani, a Fulbe group; the Toronke-Niani, a Mande-speaking people from Niani; the Anann from Toronke; the Kamana, Fulbe from Futa Jallon; a shadowy group called the

Pragmatism in the age of Jihad

"Balbade"; and several more Sarakolle, or Soninke groups.[54] The influx of new groups into Bundu suggests that Saada Amadi Aissata's efforts at returning stability and prosperity to Bundu were succeeding to some extent. Since most of these groups were from the south, it is possible that they were brought to Bundu for agricultural purposes; some of them may have been enslaved.

By the end of Saada Amadi Aissata's reign, Bundu was experiencing relatively peaceful relations with Kamera and Guey, and was increasingly more powerful vis-a-vis its neighbors to the south.[55] At his death, the *Almaami* left six sons; Amadi Saada, who died at Gabou without ruling; Bokar Saada, who went on to become *Almaami*; Cire Suma and Usuman Saada, who both died without reigning; Koli Mudi, who followed the Umarians to Maasina; and Umar Penda, who reigned and was killed by Mamadu Lamine in 1886.[56] The sources differ as to the length of Saada Amadi Aissata's tenure.[57]

Saada Amadi Aissata died near the end of 1851. As the oldest of the Sissibe, Amadu Sy of the Koussan branch became *Almaami* (1852–53). According to the sources, he was always accompanied by a pet lizard that he claimed as his brother, and with which he had frequent conversations.[58] It is very possible that he was either senile or quite mad. It is also possible that such a description is meant to somehow symbolize the nature of the Sissibe reign at this time. If the latter is intended, then perhaps the demented behavior of Amadu Sy reflects the view that the Sissibe had made a tragic mistake in agreeing to the French post at Senoudebou, thereby insuring increased French pressures and interference. In this sense, the economic imperative of the Bundunke state, so fundamental to its character, was proving to be its undoing.

Amadu Sy was opposed by the Boulebane branch because of his inability, and civil disorder prevailed during his rule.[59] The leader of the Boulebane branch, Amadi Saada, moved his residence to Gabou in protest.[60] During the early part of 1853, both the French and the Bundunkobe tried to persuade Amadi Saada to return to Boulebane, but he refused.[61] Amadu Sy died in September of 1853 at ninety years of age, having participated in a few conflicts with Kamera and Bambuk.[62] Three of his sons, Amadi Amadu, Tumane Amadu, and Musa Yero, died at Segu under *al-ḥājj* Umar. A fourth son, Sega Amadu, was living in Senoudebou while Rançon was there.[63] Most of the sources agree his was a short tenure.[64]

By the middle of the nineteenth century, Bundu was perched on a precipice. Relative to the other states in the region, it was still strong, with none to match it in military capability save Kaarta. The incessant wars and raiding suffered by the Bundunkobe were being experienced by the surrounding entities as well. That Bundu could send expeditions into Gajaaga, Guidimakha, and Kaarta, sustain invasions itself, and yet mount major campaigns into Wuli, Niani, Kantora and possibly Salum is a testimony to its organizational capacity and resilience. It is also evidence of a very serious struggle over control of trade in the area. The growing presence of the French and British gradually introduced a new element into the equation, as the Europeans emerged as much more than merchants; they were now political players who were becoming increasingly involved in the internal affairs of the upper valley states. The apparent attempt by the French to influence the dynastic struggle in Bundu had the effect of renewing animosities between the two Sissibe branches. The timing of the French initiative was most ironic in that it coincided with the reemergence of militant Islam under *al-ḥājj* Umar. The conjunction of these two forces within Bundu would have profound consequences for the future of the state.

8

Al-hajj Umar in Bundu

The return of *al-ḥājj* Umar to Senegambia from the east, his involvement in Bundunke political decisions, and his subsequent *jihāds*, proved an important turning point in the fortunes of the Bundunkobe. Their homeland became a principal theater for the struggle between the French and the followers of *al-ḥājj* Umar over control of the upper valley. With the advent of the *Shaykh*, the forces of militancy fought both within Bundu and the Upper Niger. By the end of the contest, however, these forces had moved permanently to the Upper Niger, leaving behind a Bundu largely devastated by war, and under the French-imposed leadership of Bokar Saada.

Materials for the Umarian period are relatively abundant, and are a blend of exogenous, intermediate, and secondary varieties. The first two types are heavily biased against Umar, as is to be expected. The major difficulty with all of the sources, as has been true up to this point in Bundu's development, is their inability to provide significant insight into Bundu's internal dynamics. This deficiency can be addressed, however, by deductive reasoning based upon the following: the assumption that the pre-existing rivalry between the Sissibe branches would continue to have an impact upon developments at the court; the probability that the Ṣissibe would be apprehensive about a loss of sovereignty to Umar; the idea that by considering various military engagements in conjunction with prevailing geopolitical circumstances, overall military strategies and objectives can be discerned and given a coherent meaning; and the likelihood that pivotal events will influence and to some extent explain unexpected changes in the behavior of key individuals.

At the beginning of this period, the dynamic struggle within Bundu witnessed a relatively weak Koussan against the leadership of Amadi Saada, the Boulebane leader who had moved his residence to Gabou. However, he too had suffered some diminution of influence as a result of his failure to support the crazed Amadu Sy, a decision that angered many of the Sissibe. The result was that neither branch had sufficient power to control the *almaamate*.

The ensuing civil war saw significant emigratory activity from Bundu. The

Al-hajj Umar in Bundu

Umarian campaign would result in a further decline in the Fulbe population, as many participated in the *fergo* or migration to the Upper Niger. This would leave proportionately larger Soninke and Malinke communities, an important development for the succeeding, post-war reign of Bokar Saada. Of course, the removal of such large numbers of people would also adversely impact both agriculture and commerce.

The Second Civil War and the coming of al-ḥājj Umar

Saada Amadi Aissata's illegal seizure of power had already driven a wedge between Koussan and Boulebane. The 1845 treaty with the French concerning Senoudebou exacerbated the tensions, as Koussan interpreted the development as the beginning of direct French intervention in Bundunke affairs. The bizarre career of Amadu Sy succeeded in creating greater distance between the two Sissibe branches, resulting in Amadi Saada's removal to Gabou to essentially function autonomously. That civil disorder reportedly ensued indicates that the two branches were entering a state of crisis. This is confirmed by the fact that both branches developed independent leadership in the persons of Amadi Saada (Boulebane) and Sega Tumane (Koussan), the late *Almaami* Tumane Mudi's son. That is, the perception that the branches possessed conflicting agendas congealed to the extent that leaders emerged based upon their abilities to represent the interests of their respective constituencies, as opposed to their relationship to the legal succession. At the same time, it was not unusual for members of the Koussan branch to support Boulebane candidates for executive office, and vice-versa. The decision, therefore, to back the candidates of the opposing branch was informed by considerations other than foreign policy and familial ties; the matter of personal gain also weighed heavily. Even so, views on external affairs and descent were sufficient criteria by which the branches maintained their separation.

The death of Amadu Sy in September of 1853 resulted in a succession crisis even more serious than that of 1797. Umar Sane, a Boulebane member, was viewed by Koussan as the rightful heir to Amadu Sy, as he was son of Amadi Aissata and the *Almaami* Saada Amadi Aissata's brother.[1] Such support indicates the weakness of Koussan, as it could not advance a member of its own branch. However, Boulebane rejected his claims, even though he himself belonged to that branch. Notwithstanding this rejection, he was embraced by Koussan and proclaimed *Almaami*. He subsequently returned to Boulebane, but was in fact a Koussan candidate.

Umar Sane's election was not well-received in the north. The Boulebane leader out of Gabou, Amadi Saada, rejected the proclamation of Umar Sane as fraudulent, as did his brother Bokar Saada of Senoudebou. Instead, he presented his own candidate, Amadi Gai, the son of Usuman Kumba Tunkara (who perished at Dara Lamine c. 1800).[2] It was Amadi Saada's contention that his father Saada Amadi Aissata had designated Amadi Gai as his successor on his deathbed; in point of fact, Amadi Gai was older than Umar Sane.[3] With Umar Sane residing in Boulebane, Amadi Gai was forced to take up quarters in Gabou with Amadi Saada.

The proclamation of Amadi Gai was of course unacceptable to Koussan. It was also fraught with danger, since it constituted a second, rival claim for the post of *Almaami*. Under the Koussan leader Sega Tumane, the southern Sissibe repeatedly sought to convince Amadi Saada of Umar Sane's rights, but the latter proved intractable. Consequently, Bundu had two *almaamies*, who each tried to function in a sovereign manner. The friction between the Sissibe grew, and it was not long before a military solution was sought.[4]

Although there is little detail on the war, both Rançon and Kamara agreed that it devastated the countryside and resulted in substantial migrations to Futa Jallon, Futa Toro, Wuli, and other surrounding states.[5] While Kamara contends that the Second Civil War lasted for three years, it actually persisted for only one.[6] There is some evidence of an unsuccessful attack on Senoudebou by Koussan.[7] The only battle consistently mentioned by the various sources was at Fissa-Daro, where one Tumane Samba led the Koussan army in an attack upon the Gabou forces under Amadi Saada.[8] Amadi Saada, with reinforcements from Kaarta, was able to withstand the assault. The war went on, however, with neither side gaining a significant advantage over the other.

According to Roux and Rançon, the Sissibe all agreed to negotiate a settlement to the struggle.[9] They go on to say that at a meeting in Diamwali, in the middle of Bundu, both sides were on the verge of agreeing on a single sovereign, when the process was interrupted by the arrival of Umar. Of course, it would be in the interests of the French to portray the *Shaykh* as preempting the peace process. Kamara's version is probably more accurate in recording that Koussan requested *al-ḥājj* Umār's mediation of the dispute, which would be consistent with its earlier efforts at diplomacy. However, the *Shaykh*'s involvement in Bundunke affairs began the process by which Bundu eventually lost its sovereignty.

Al-ḥājj Umar Tal al-Futi was born *c.* 1796 in the village of Aloar (Halwar) in Futa Toro.[10] His father, Eliman Saidu, had participated in the *Torodbe* revolt against the Denyanke dynasty, and was probably the leading Muslim in the village. The seventh of ten children, Umar was precocious and greatly influenced by the piety of his mother, Adama. His family, as was true of the *Torodbe* in general, belonged to the Qadiriyya brotherhood (*ṭarīqa*). It was during Umar's youth that the Tijaniyya penetrated Senegambia. Around 1815, Umar began traveling, studying first in eastern Futa, then going on to study in Futa Jallon from 1820 to 1825.[11] At some point within the next three years, he may have journeyed to Saint Louis and obtained financial assistance.[12] His subsequent travels brought him to Hamdullahi and Sokoto, then north to Air, the Fezzan, and on to Cairo. He spent two-and-a-half years in the Hijaz, where he studied Tijani sufism and was appointed lieutenant (*khalīfa*) of the order in the western Sudan.

He returned to West Africa sometime in 1831, and spent six more years in Sokoto.[13] A visit to Bornu resulted in a temporary conflict with al-Kanemi, but a reconciliation was later effected and a Bornuese woman was given to Umar for a wife. After 1835, his acclaim was heightened to Sokoto as a result of his participation in Muhammad Bello's fight against Gobir, Katsina, and the Tuareg. In return, the Sokoto ruler gave his daughter Mariam in marriage to *al-ḥājj* Umar, who also began actively recruiting for the Tijaniyya brotherhood. In 1839, a return visit to Hamdullahi brought the fierce opposition of al-Bekkai of Timbuktu to the growing Tijaniyya movement.[14] Finally, Umar returned to Futa Jallon in 1840, and developed his community of followers at Jagunko between 1841 and 1845. After touring Futa Toro, Bundu, Gajaaga and Khasso, he relocated his community at Dingiray in 1849. In 1852, he launched his first *jihād* against Tamba. By 1853, he was formulating plans to assault Kaarta, and he began recruiting in the upper and middle valleys.

It was Umar's intention to secure the upper valley before attacking Kaarta.[15] He therefore first marched from Dingiray to Farabana in Bambuk, from which most of the residents had fled to Makhana. It was from his temporary headquarters at Farabana that *al-ḥājj* Umar summoned the feuding Sissibe. It is no surprise that he declared for the Koussan candidate, Umar Sane, given Koussan's distrust of non-Muslims and Boulebane's reliance upon the Kaartans during the Second Civil War. However, he required that both contestants follow him in his eastern campaigns.[16] Kamara reports that *Shaykh* Umar reprimanded both leaders for engaging in the internecine war; but there is no evidence, as Oloruntimehin suggests, that he "attacked" Bundu.[17] While at Farabana, the *Shaykh* also met with the leaders of Futa Toro, Guey, Khasso and Guidimakha, and assembled his forces for the struggle with the Bambara. Umar Sane would die at the Battle of Medine in 1857, while Amadi Gai perished at Yelimane in 1855.[18]

As it turned out, the Bundunke civil war proved fortuitous for Umar. Both ruling branches looked to him to resolve their differences, as neither had the means to do so. Not only was the *Shaykh* able to mediate the conflict, but he was also in a position to demand the participation of the Sissibe in his own agenda. Had Bundu been united under Boulebane's control, it is conceivable that Umar would have met with a hostile response, at least from the ruling elite. As matters stood, the Sissibe yielded to the *Shaykh*'s wishes.

Beyond the relative weakness of the Sissibe, Umar's success in the upper valley is directly attributable to his considerable prestige. A renowned teacher, holy man (*walī*), and worker of miracles, Umar was seen by many as an answer to the repetitive wars and strife in the region. His popular following, a factor much more significant than the response of the various local leaders, was phenomenal. The Bundunkobe made up an important part of the Umarian army, which by 1855 was divided into three sections: the N'Guenar, the Yirlabe, and the Toro, after the three provinces of Futa. The

Bundunkobe served in the Toro division, and were supportive of the Umarian effort throughout its existence. By the end of 1854, the jihadists had swelled to 10,000 men. The Umarian reform was in fact a grand social movement.[19]

The response to the jihadist call

The Boulebane branch did not respond positively to the news of Umar Sane's election. Amadi Saada returned to Gabou, where he died shortly afterwards.[20] He was succeeded by his brother Usuman Saada as the head of the Boulebane party.[21] The proposed assault on the "infidels" of Kaarta was filled with risks for the Boulebane branch; beyond the possibility of Umar failing, there was the potentially more dangerous threat of his succeeding. The establishment of an Umarian empire would have two sure consequences: the strict enforcement of *shari'a*, and the loss of autonomy by the Bundunke ruling elite. In fact, Umar Sane had already experienced a diminution in power, becoming "un simple alfa (lieutenant du Cheikh)" while retaining the prestigious title of *Almaami*.[22]

After settling the affairs of Bundu, the *Shaykh* turned his immediate attention to the destruction of Kaartan influence in Kamera. In November of 1854, the *Shaykh* utterly destroyed Makhana and Tamboucane, killing all of Samba Yacine's sons and enslaving the women.[23] This resulted in Kamera becoming more "sympathique" toward the French.[24] The survivors of Makhana were eventually transferred to Arondou in 1857.[25] In place of the Bacili *Tunkas*, Umar elevated a number of clerics to temporal positions, over whom was placed an *almaami*. Not all of Gajaaga submitted to the *Shaykh*, and his departure for the east resulted in the French regaining their leverage.

Towards the end of 1854, Umar began making preparations for the *jihād* against Kaarta itself. The attack was launched in January of 1855, with the Umarians defeating a Kaartan army at Kholu.[26] The next major event, in February, was the Battle of Yelimane, a provincial capital of Kaarta and almost completely Soninke.[27] On the eve of the battle, the *Shaykh* reminded the jihadists of the promise of Paradise. The Umarians were victorious, and by April the main capital of Nioro had also fallen. The *Shaykh* established his new headquarters at Nioro, and there began accumulating the goods he had been previously sending to Dingiray. He immediately set into motion a number of reforms, such as restricting the number of wives to four, the shaving of the head, and the construction of mosques and Qur'anic schools. Of course, the Tijaniyya brotherhood was promoted.[28]

At the same time that the *jihād* was proceeding in the east, the contest for the upper valley was taking shape. Earlier in June of 1854, the French had announced an arms embargo, mainly directed against the Moors and Futa Toro, but affecting Umar as well.[29] For Umar's part, it is not at all clear that he desired hostile relations with Saint Louis. When he met the French in 1847, first at the Coq *escale* and then at Bakel, the *Shaykh* sued for peaceful relations.³⁰ In the summer of 1854, he sent an envoy to Saint Louis requesting a formal alliance, to which he received a noncommittal response. As far as the French were concerned, the *Shaykh* was a primary threat to their aspiration of controlling eastern Senegal.

The decision by the French to pursue a policy of upper valley domination was the result of merchant lobbying in France. The increased French trading presence in the upper valley by the mid-nineteenth century had touched off an acute struggle among the area's powers, in which Bundu played a principal role. But the consequence of the intensified warfare was a reduction in French trading revenues.³¹ French merchants began clamoring for the appointment of a governor in Senegal who would restore order. Barrows has examined this development, and in particular the relationship between the Bordeaux trading and shipping firm of Maurel and Prom and French colonial policy makers.³² It is his argument that colonial policy was directly influenced by such firms, so that governors such as Faidherbe simply implemented plans conceived by Bordeaux merchants: "virtually none of these ideas were his."³³ "These ideas," beyond seeking to relieve the hostilities in the region, called for the elimination of customs payments to Futa Toro, the fortification of French positions along the Senegal River, and the abolition of the privileged role of the mixed race *traitants* at Saint Louis.³⁴ The effect of such changes would be the conducting of trade on the terms of the Bordeaux wholesalers, rather than the prevailing system where commerce was regulated by the Africans themselves and the *traitants*.

In 1854 Faidherbe was appointed Governor of Senegal to pursue these objectives. Having previously served for several years in Algeria, Faidherbe is usually credited with having transformed the role of the French in Senegal from that of traders to soldiers and administrators.³⁵ Under his supervision, about one-third of modern Senegal was brought under French rule. He was responsible for organizing the famous *Tirailleurs sénégalais* ("Senegalese Riflemen"), as well as the publications of *Le Moniteur* and *L'Annuaire du Sénégal*. Faidherbe also founded a school for the "sons of chiefs and interpreters" for the purpose of staffing an expanded bureaucracy. He would be a key figure in the "pacification" of the upper valley.

In November of 1854, tensions between the French and the Umarians increased over the French decision to grant asylum to a Sissibe dissident, and their ill-treatment of the *Shaykh*'s son at Senoudebou. Concerning the former, a "princess and her daughter" from the Boulebane branch of the Sissibe had taken refuge in Bakel.³⁶ The French took them into the fort, while the Umarians demanded their return. Later, when the Shaykh sent one of his sons to Senoudebou (under Commandant Girardot's command), he was rejected as a spy by the French.³⁷

In February of 1855, the *Shaykh*, in need of war materials in his assault on Kaarta, raided the trade entrepots of Khasso and Gajaaga for the purpose of confiscating stored French arms. Relations with the French soured precipitously, as evidenced in the *Shaykh*'s famous correspondence of March, 1855, in which he lodged several complaints against the French, and threatened to disrupt their commercial activities. The real issue, however, was the control of eastern Senegal, to which both the French and the Umarians held claim.

Upon his appointment as Governor, Faidherbe launched a campaign to overturn Umarian control of the Middle and Upper Senegal. His strategy was to both wage war and to effect key alliances with indigenous powers opposed to the *Shaykh*. In the end, Faidherbe's plans would succeed because of the French advantage in three critical areas: their control of the area's trade, the efficacy of their gunboats, and their exclusive control of cannon power.

In April of 1855, Faidherbe began his campaign by ordering the fort at Bakel to level the surrounding town because of its support of the Umarians.[38] From April through August, the French pummeled villages in Gajaaga in order to weaken Umarian influence.[39] The Umarians responded by destroying French commerce east of Bakel.[40] However, the *Shaykh* was in a delicate position. Far from trying to rid the area of the Europeans, he was rather attempting to force the French to trade on his terms, two of which called for increased *jizya* payments and the removal of French forts.

By the fall of 1855, Faidherbe had succeeded in weakening the Umarians in Gajaaga, having sent six gunboats and 1,000 men into the upper valley.[41] He then turned to forming an anti-Umarian league among the upper valley states, signing treaties with Khasso, Kamera, and Guidimakha.[42] In September of the same year, construction of a new fort at Medine began, made possible by an agreement with the town's ruler, Sambala.[43] Faidherbe even attempted to contact Segu to form an alliance against the *Shaykh*.[44] However, he lacked the key ingredient to the strategy: control over Bundu, through which ran routes to the Gambia and hence access by the jihadists to English arms. Furthermore, an alliance with Bundu would enable the French to cripple the important ties the *Shaykh* maintained with the Fulbe to the west, along which flowed men and sustenance. Bundu was critical to Faidherbe's designs.

In October of 1855, Faidherbe met the man through whom he would challenge Umar's ascendancy in Bundu. Bokar Saada, the son of the late *Almaami* Saada Amadi Aissata and the Bambara princess Kurubarai Kulubali, approached the French camp at Medine accompanied by a group of Bambara soldiers.[45] The background to this startling development was the *Shaykh*'s initial victory over Nioro, and the Bambara revolts of 1855 and 1856.[46] The focus of the rebellion was the limitation on wives, but the underlying cause was the Bambara loss of power. When the *tuburu*, those indigenous groups which had submitted to the *Shaykh*'s authority, were required to give half of their booty to the *Shaykh*, they refused (and rightfully so). The uprising was cruelly repressed by the end of June, especially at Yelimane, where many notables were executed by the *Shaykh*.[47] Before this time, Bokar Saada had followed Umar, but he had undoubtedly become uneasy over the dimunition in power of the Bundunke *Almaami*, who had been assigned to combat in the Upper Niger. Such a loss of status and, along with it, state autonomy was a disturbing development. In addition to this, Bokar Saada had inherited the ambition of his father, Saada Amadi Aissata, and had grown accustomed to both power and the French, having governed Senoudebou at least since 1845. He had probably concluded that his loyalty to the *Shaykh* would not be rewarded by a position of prominence, as his brothers Koli Mudi and Usuman Saada, as well as cousin Malik Samba Tumane, had already been placed in posts of importance and high visibility.[48] With these considerations as background, the sight of his relatives' slaughter was the proverbial straw that broke the camel's back. He defected from the Umarian ranks, taking refuge in various places throughout Kaarta. Faidherbe's arrival at Medine gave him the opportunity to come out of hiding.[49]

Not only did Faidherbe extend his protection to Bokar Saada, but he also proposed that the latter cooperate with the French in exchange for French support of his candidacy for the *almaamate*. Bokar Saada accepted, "and all our efforts were directed, from then on, to have him recognized as Almamy of Bundu, ..."[50] Those efforts would take the form of destroying villages which remained loyal to Umar. For the most part, Bokar Saada's claims were rejected by the Muslim community. According to Mavidal, he was the only Sissibe who was not in submission to the *Shaykh* in 1855.[51]

The fight for Bundu

Umar's resounding victory over Kaarta only served to increase his popularity in Bundu, while strengthening the conviction that his was a divinely inspired mission. In contrast, Bokar Saada had no base of support beyond the French: "Enemy of Al-Hajji, Bubakar Saada did not have at that time a single follower in all of Bundu, and even found himself without a slave who could serve him. It was under these conditions that he was recognized by us as Almamy."[52] In Umar Sane's absence, Usuman Saada, Bokar Saada's brother, enjoyed a significant following in Bundu. Politically astute, he had supported *al-ḥājj* Umar since the death of Amadi Saada, his brother and leader of the Boulebane branch. It was he, in fact, who had led an attack on Senoudebou in June of 1855.[53] Bokar Saada's early strategy, therefore, was to remove this obstacle to his control of Bundu. Living under French protection at Senoudebou, Bokar Saada was able to muster a small force from Bakel, which he then led in an attack on Usuman Saada at Gabou.[54] The latter was forced to flee to Somsom-Tata, near Marsa, where he was again assaulted by Bokar Saada. By March of 1856, Usuman Saada had been driven out of Somsom-Tata to Debou, at which point he was confronted by a combined force led by Bokar Saada and Girardot of Senoudebou. Usuman Saada was able to escape to N'Dioum, in the Ferlo (southwestern Bundu), where he would remain until 1857.[55]

With the retreat of Usuman Saada, Bokar Saada was able to fashion a small, anti-Umarian following among the remaining Sissibe in Bundu. His efforts were also assisted by the preoccupation of the Umarians with the Bambara revolts of 1855 and 1856. In turn, the French exploited the opportunity to pressure the Bundunkobe to renounce their allegiance to the *Shaykh* and acknowledge Bokar Saada as *Almaami*. A French-backed Moorish raid into Bundu was conducted to help persuade the recalcitrants; it was successful in that a number of Sissibe submitted to Bokar Saada in a formal ceremony in Bakel on 18 February 1856.

Eight days after this ceremony, the Umarians responded by sending a large detachment from Kaarta under the leadership of two important clerics from Futa Toro, "Belli" and Tierno Alium.[56] They proceeded to remind the Bundunkobe of the *Shaykh*'s claims, and of their obligation to support the *jihād*, and succeeded in stirring up a revolt against Bokar Saada and the French. The Umarians successfully took the village of Borde, near Bakel, which had failed to sever ties to the French. Encouraged by their success, they attempted to seize Bakel's livestock. The French pursued them to Borde, where they killed about fifty of the Umarians.[57] The two clerics who had led the expedition remained on the field of battle.

However, the more substantive Umarian response to Bokar Saada and the French in Bundu early in the war was in the form of an attack on Senoudebou.[58] Beginning in April of 1856, the Umarians repeatedly sought to take the fort. These attacks involved impressive numbers of soldiers; in May, for example, some 4,000 men from Bundu, the Futas, and Kamera attacked the French position. However, the siege of Senoudebou was in the end lifted.

The failure to seize Senoudebou demonstrates a major deficiency in the Umarian military effort: the inability to capture an important French stronghold. All attempts to seize the fort were discontinued at the end of May, allowing the French and Bokar Saada to expand their control. The following month saw the Commandant at Bakel commission Bokar Saada to invest the village of Alana, between Guey and Futa Toro.[59] Prospects for a viable government began to improve for Bokar Saada, and the volume of trade began to increase.[60] By August, all of the previously hostile Sissibe who remained in Bundu had pledged their allegiance to Bokar Saada at Senoudebou; four children of the leading families were sent to Saint Louis as evidence of their loyalty.[61]

Those Sissibe who transferred their allegiance to Bokar Saada were not necessarily compelled to do so by his magnetic character. Rather, it was the open display of French power that succeeded in intimidating Bokar Saada's opposition. As an example, the September voyage of Flize on the steamboat *Le Serpent* left a lasting impression on the Bundunkobe.[62] Traveling up the Senegal with Bokar Saada on board, the war vessel symbolized the Europeans' mastery of the water, and their support of Bokar Saada: "All the residents of the riverside villages, seeing this chief carried in the midst of the water by a steam boat, something that they did not believe possible, came and prostrated themselves on the banks of the river, crying out that they no longer recognized masters other than the whites and Bubakar Saada, their protégé."[63] Following this "show the flag" strategy, Bokar Saada led a successful expedition against Kenieba in southern Bambuk, in conjunction with Bugul, the ruler of Farabana. Kenieba was in a gold-bearing region, and was turned over to the French in 1858. The French were very much interested in the potential of the area, and Bokar Saada's assault of Kenieba helped to facilitate French exploitative designs. After Bokar Saada's victory, Faidherbe placed a garrison and a mining engineer there, but withdrew the crew in 1860 after an intolerable mortality rate and low specie yield.[64]

By the end of 1856, the Umarian position in Bundu was relatively weak. Bokar Saada had been "introduced" to the Bundunke people, and had begun to expand his power beyond Senoudebou. But the Umarians' basic problem was not a defection by the common people from the *Shaykh*; quite simply, they had failed to take the fortified positions of the French. As the Commandant of Senoudebou phrased it, the "people of Bundu do not like Bubacar, they only fear him because he is our protégé."[65] There was strong residual support for the *Shaykh*, and a deep resentment towards the imposition of Bokar Saada: "Bubakar Saada is not well supported by the people of Bundu, who only tolerate him because of their fear of us, and they did not want to openly declare against al-Hadji."[66] The "softness" in Bokar Saada's support would become apparent in the months to come.

The watershed of 1857

The year 1857 saw the defeat of the forces of the *Shaykh* in the upper valley. The victory of the French was a cumulative one, in that it involved four major confrontations, all won by the forces of Europe and collaboration. These four battles were fought at N'Dioum, Amadhie, Medine, and Somsom-Tata. At their conclusion, the Umarian bid for control of eastern Senegal effectively ended.

In January of 1857, Bokar Saada finally put together the forces to defeat his brother Usuman Saada at N'Dioum, in the Ferlo.[67] The latter was forced to pledge his loyalty to Bokar Saada, whose victory was important in that it removed the focal point of local resistance. However, most of Bundu remained loyal to *al-ḥājj* Umar, and news of his imminent return encouraged the expression of anti-French sentiment. Substantial numbers continued to migrate to the east, a movement over which Bokar Saada had little control.[68]

With the loss of Usuman Saada, the Umarians needed another Sy who could lead and organize those loyal to the *Shaykh*. The need was met in the person of Eli Amadi Kaba, who by March had succeeded in emptying several villages into a single fortified town named Amadhie (or Amaguie), near Boulebane. An estimated 6,000 men were housed in the fortification.[69] Bokar Saada responded by attacking Amadhie, aided by 260 Malinke infantrymen, 600 to 700 Douaich Moors on horseback, and some of Girardot's troops from Senoudebou. After an initial failure, Bokar Saada's men were joined by Cornu, Commandant of Bakel, and together they defeated the *tata*.[70] Thus, by early March, the Umarians had lost two key leaders and their fortified posts.

While Bokar Saada was engaged at Amadhie, *al-ḥājj* Umar returned to the upper valley from Kaarta. He needed to replenish his forces for his eastern campaign, but was not yet willing to concede Senegambia to the French. He therefore decided to take the French fort at Medine in Khasso. By the beginning of 1857, most of Khasso had resumed its allegiance to the *Shaykh*.[71] However, Medine remained an important symbol of the French presence. Of the estimated 10,000 people inside of the fort, only 1,000 could be classified as soldiers. Of that number, only sixty-four had received artillery and small arms training, including the eight Europeans who were present. The remaining 9,000 or so were refugees from the surrounding war-torn area, the majority of whom were women, children, and the aged. Notwithstanding these weaknesses, Medine enjoyed certain crucial advantages over the Umarians: its location commanded the surrounding area; its walls had been fortified; and it contained the superior firepower of four cannon. In the end, these advantages proved decisive.

In April, the *Shaykh* began the siege of Medine with an estimated 15,000 troops.[72] The siege lasted until late July, when the Senegal River's rising waters allowed Faidherbe to send relief in the form of two gunboats and 800 men.[73] By the time the siege was finally lifted, the *Shaykh* had lost 2,000 of his elite troops. By August, death and desertion had reduced his army to 7,000; *Almaami* Umar Sane of Bundu was among the casualties. The *Shaykh* retreated up the Bafing River to Kunjan, where he convalesced for five months and planned the *jihād* against Segu. The failure to take Medine carried serious consequences for the Umarians throughout the upper valley.

While the fate of Medine was still in the balance, Bokar Saada was busy trying to contain pro-Umarian sentiment in Bundu. The *Shaykh*'s return to Khasso had ignited a flurry of activity in the west. A significant number of villages in Kamera and Guey, along with "half of Bundu," had crossed the Senegal River into Guidimakha on orders of the *Shaykh*.[74] Numerous trains of "Toucouleurs" from Futa Toro were crossing Bundu for Khasso as late as July.[75] These were entire families who were being moved for resettlement in Kaarta, not just soldiers. Bokar Sada harassed the fleeing caravans, and in one instance forced a group to return to Futa Toro. However, his efforts did little to stop the massive hemorrhage of people from the middle and upper valleys.

During the period of this migration and the fight for Medine, Bokar Saada turned his attention to the fortress of Somsom-Tata, midway between Bakel and Senoudebou. Somsom-Tata had been constructed by *Almaami* Tumane Mudi for the purpose of defending against Bambara raids.[76] The strongest fortress in Bundu, it was staffed almost completely by slaves loyal to the former *almaamies*. The ruler of the village was Malik Samba Tumane, *Almaami* Tumane Mudi's grandson, who had imprisoned a Sy named al-Kusun in 1856 on charges that the latter was a supporter of Bokar Saada. The French finally felt capable of challenging the stronghold.

Both Bokar Saada and Girardot led the siege of Somsom-Tata, which began on the first of August.[77] Commandant Cornu of Bakel also joined the attack, but the French forces were initially turned back. For twelve consecutive days the assault was repulsed. A decision was reached to induce starvation upon the *tata*, when Faidherbe arrived from his succesful defense of Medine. The General demanded that Malik Samba Tumane release al-Kusun; the latter responded by executing his prisoner. But Faidherbe's arrival, combined with news of Medine's defense, weakened the resolve of the Umarian leader, and he managed to escape on the night of the fifteenth, after which he went on to settle in Kingui in Kaarta. The *tata* was forced to surrender, and the French took 400 captives, mostly women and children. In the morning, the village was incinerated.

The French alliance remained on the offensive for the remainder of August. On the twenty-eighth, Brossard de Corbigny commanded the gunboats *Le Serpent* and *Le Grand-Bassam* up the Faleme River to the village of N'Dangan, which had served as a way station for the jihadists coming from Futa Toro and heading for Kaarta.[78] In concert with 800 to 1,000 infantry and 100 cavalry under Bokar Saada, along with troops from Bugul of Farabana, Brossard de Corbigny destroyed the village and took twenty-five captives. Later in the same day, the alliance sacked the village of Sansanding, recovering sixty-four prisoners, 250 heads of cattle, and a large quantity of goats. The dual operation came at a time when a party of Koussan Sissibe, established at Sambacolo near Senoudcbou, was close to an agreement with Bokar Saada.[79] The expedition caused the Umarians to break off negotiations.

The cumulative effect of French victories at N'Dioum, Amadhie, and Somsom-Tata was to greatly enhance the stature of Bokar Saada. Combined with the failure to capture the fort at Medine, these circumstances forced Umar to rethink his overall strategy. It had become clear that the "west," including Bundu, would be lost to the "infidels."

Umarian reaction: the hijra of 1858

Umar realized that his combined losses at N'Dioum, Amadhie, Medine, and Somsom-Tata were tantamount to losing the contest for the upper valley. His response was to empty the upper valley of its Muslim population by calling for a massive *fergo*, or *hijra*, to the Umarian east. His summons was extremely effective.

At the beginning of 1858, Umar needed both a new agricultural base and control of commercial routes free from French domination.[80] His inability to control the Upper Senegal, and the loss of Futa Toro to pro-French rulers, necessitated this reformulation. He therefore saw Segu as this new base, and returned to Bambuk and the upper valley for the purpose of recruiting for a new *jihād* and subsequent establishment of Muslim communities.

One of the *Shaykh*'s lieutenants, Mamadu Diallo, entered southern (or Upper) Bundu and began preaching the *jihād*.[81] He announced that the Sissibe dynasty was no longer legitimate, that their dependance on Saint Louis and opposition to the *jihād* qualified them as infidels. By February, he had succeeded in organizing more than 10,000 soldiers, and proceeded to occupy the old stronghold of N'Dioum. Bokar Saada responded by leading 2,000 men on the *tata*. Commandant Cornu of Bakel came to his aid later in February, attacking the stronghold with the added firepower of two cannon.[82] N'Dioum was partially destroyed, but withstood the assault. Bokar Saada's men retreated in disarray. With the critical confiscation of the French cannon, N'Dioum began seizing caravans heading for the Gambia, and served as an entrepot from which the *Shaykh* could obtain supplies denied by the French.[83]

Bokar Saada did not have the opportunity to recoup and attack again. The news that Umar had come to Tomboura and was heading for central Bundu caused Bokar Saada and Bugul to retreat hastily to Senoudebou.[84] Some time in March, the *Shaykh* arrived in Goundiourou, near Senoudebou. Bokar Saada rarely challenged him throughout his stay in Bundu, "for almost all of Bundu had again abandoned him."[85] Accompanying the *Shaykh* to Goundiourou were two Sissibe representing both branches. They carried with them letters written by those Sissibe who had remained in Kaarta, the contents of which called upon the Bundunkobe to relocate to Kaarta.[86] "The announcement of this order in the towns produced a profound astonishment."[87] The notables of Bundu for the most part responded favorably, and whole families began prepering to move to Kaarta, along with their livestock.

The *Shaykh* moved on from Goundiourou to occupy Boulebane at the beginning of April. He reportedly had thoughts of attacking Senoudebou at that time, but "his army refused."[88] The *Shaykh* wanted to invest Senoudebou, but having already decided to concentrate on Segu, deemed it too risky. Instead, in an effort to "encourage" the Bundunkobe to emigrate, he began incinerating villages, causing great devastation.[89] There developed a steady stream of caravans leaving Bundu and heading for the intermediate point of Goucila, near Makhana, where Bokar Saada's brother Koli Mudi would send them on to Nioro. That many left their homes involuntarily is substantiated by their return upon learning that the *Shaykh* had departed from Bundu. Those who did come back flocked to the posts of Senoudebou and Bakel, while others went to Medine.[90]

Umar remained at Boulebane until 13 May, when he took 2,000 people with him to Futa Toro to continue his recruiting process. The French now realized his intentions of establishing an empire in the east, and reported that he had completely abandoned Bundu and Bambuk.[91] Bugul returned to Farabana, and Senoudebou relaxed.[92] The *Shaykh* passed through Sambacolo, Somsom-Tata, and Borde before entering Futa Toro, where he remained until April of 1859.⁹³ He returned to Nioro in June of that year with some 40,000 people.⁹⁴

In the aftermath of Umar's activities in 1858 widespread famine set in. Cultivation had been abandoned in many areas, and the *Shaykh* had destroyed large quantities of stored millet.⁹⁵ In a letter from a Moor to a friend in Cayor, the situation was briefly described: "Know that the country is no longer such as you would recognize, it is completely destroyed. Al-Hajji Omar ordered everyone to leave and to follow him, and all obeyed."⁹⁶ A more graphic description concerns those who defected and returned from Kaarta: "They are in a great state of misery. The roads are covered with their dead bodies. A ghastly dearth rules in all the upper valley."⁹⁷ This same report estimated that half of southern Bundu's population had perished. By 1859 the suffering had grown worse, and although the state was slowly repopulating, there was little to which to return.⁹⁸ The Commandant of Senoudebou reported in 1859 that the country was peaceful, but that was largely due to its abandonment.⁹⁹ Boulebane and Koussan had both been completely deserted.

Bokar Saada and Senoudebou were not much better off. There reportedly was not a single cow in the village.¹⁰⁰ In order to produce millet, Bokar Saada traded slaves, which he had in abundance, to Wuli, Kantora, and Futa Toro. The millet was head-mounted to be transported back, since the beasts of burden had been taken to Kaarta. Faidherbe tried to transport food from time to time, but the need far exceeded the supply. These meager circumstances obtained until 1860, when hostilities essentially came to an end.

In August of 1858, Bokar Saada signed two treaties with Faidherbe. One had to do with the goldfields of Kenieba, and was jointly signed by Bugul of Farabana. The other involved the status of Senoudebou. According to its terms, the village of Senoudebou became the property of the French, as opposed to the land near it as specified by the treaty of 1845. Bokar Saada was obliged to leave as soon as it was feasible. He would no longer receive customs payments, nor could he tax caravans coming from the east directly to Senoudebou (the French had actually stopped paying customs to Senoudebou in 1854).¹⁰¹ In return, the "autonomy" of Bundu would be respected.

The reasons for the French decision to demand Bokar Saada's removal from Senoudebou are not clear. Among the possible explanations is the inappropriateness of Bundu's capital remaining on what had essentially become French soil. Also, from Senoudebou the French could more effectively curb the flow of trade to the Gambia. Finally, the French viewed Senoudebou as a staging area for its expansion into Bambuk and even beyond to the Upper Niger, and possibly did not want Bokar Saada so close to such projected operations. In any event, Bokar Saada complied by moving to Ambdallaye, some twenty-five kilometers south of the fort.

However, the French quickly lost interest in the post, after the disastrous experience of Kenieba, and abandoned it by 1862.[102] The *Almaami* obtained permission from Saint Louis to reoccupy Senoudebou, with the understanding that he would vacate whenever the French so requested.

Resolution

The last major battle between the Umarians and Bokar Saada took place at Guemou in Guidimakha. En route to the east from Futa Toro, Umar had built a *tata* there in 1859, and placed it under the command of his nephew, Cire Adama.[103] Cire Adama's primary responsibility was to turn back any who sought to return to Futa Toro or Bundu from the east.[104] The French called Cire Adama's men "marauders," and complained that many were being prevented from returning to Bundu.[105] Although progress was reported in checking the Umarians, it would appear that Guemou was causing quite a problem.[106] With the crisis mounting, Bokar Saada sent an urgent plea to Faidherbe for help.[107] The Governor responded by sending a column of the Senegalese Riflemen under a Lieutenant-Colonel Faron in September. On 25 October, aided by Bokar Saada and his army of 400, Faron annihilated the *tata* at Guemou. The French suffered thirty-nine casualties and ninety-seven injured, while the Umarians lost 250 men.[108] Some 1,500 prisoners were taken. Cire Adama remained on the field of battle.

From 1855 to 1858, Umar and Faidherbe fought over the Upper Senegal. By the latter year, the *Shaykh* had come to the conclusion that he would not be able to dislodge the French from the valley. This conclusion was consistent with the earlier decision to concentrate on the east, a decision that antedated the military engagements of 1858 and 1859, and which featured a massive exodus from the Middle and Upper Senegal Valleys. It is not surprising then, that in August of 1860, Umar and Faidherbe reached an understanding whereby *de facto* French control in Senegambia and Umarian hegemony over what is modern Mali were mutually recognized.[109] Bokar Saada became the uncontested *Almaami* over what remained of Bundu. As for the *Shaykh*, he went on to defeat Segu between 1859 and 1861. Between 1862 and 1864, Hamdullahi and the rest of Maasina fell to the Umarians after a bitter polemical as well as military campaign. Al-Bekkai of Timbuktu would label the *Shaykh* as "'the imposter who does evil and against whom God has ordained *jihād*.'"[110] After Umar was killed in February of 1864, his empire was effectively split into three parts: Maasina, Segu, and Kaarta. His nephew Tijani became the uncontested ruler of Maasina in 1854, while his son Amadu Sheku ruled Segu. Kaarta, based upon Hanson's argument, constituted a third autonomous region, whose control was contested in 1870 by two sons of the *Shaykh*, Habib and Mukhtar, and again in 1885 by others of Amadu Sheku's brothers. These bids for autonomy would be defeated, as would Amadu Sheku in the eventual conquest of the region by the French by 1893.[111]

The *Shaykh*'s failure to subdue the French in the upper valley was a direct consequence of his inability to defeat the key posts of Bakel, Senoudebou, and Medine. A principal reason for this inability, in turn, was the French domination of the Senegal and Faleme Rivers by way of gunboats. It was the Umarians' pattern to attack these posts just prior to the rainy season; not having succeeded by July, their prospects of victory diminished considerably due to rising waters and Saint Louis' ability to dispatch gunboats along the rivers. Had the attacks begun sooner, the Umarians might have succeeded in taking these posts.

But a second and just as critical reason for the Umarian failure was their lack of cannon power. Indeed, the French strongholds were able to hold on until the arrival of the gunboats precisely because of their exclusive possession of cannon. When the Umarians managed to acquire a cannon, as was the case with N'Dioum in 1858, they were successful in attaining their objectives. In short, the technological disadvantages experienced by the Umarians, combined with the ill-timing of their assaults, were factors too great to overcome.

Finally, it must be noted that the *Shaykh* placed his primary emphasis on Kaarta and Segu. Had he chosen to really concentrate on Senegambia instead of the Upper Niger, the French forts may yet have fallen. These observations must be balanced, however, by the *Shaykh*'s own sense of priorities. If the east was simply more important to him, the costs of fighting in the west would have to be kept to a minimum. Clearly, the investment was deemed too costly.

But beyond factors of naval superiority and strategic weakness is the role of Bokar Saada. Having begun as a follower of the *Shaykh* and a participant in his *jihād*, he soon determined that his interests would be better served by assuming an antithetical role. He is therefore unique in that, of all the Bundunke nobility, he stood virtually alone against the *Shaykh*. Of the Sissibe leadership who were active during this period (from the sons of Musa Yero to those of Amadu Sy), sixty-seven percent enlisted in the Umarian ranks; fifty-six percent were from the Boulebane branch, while seventy-one percent represented Koussan. If Bokar Saada is included, the percentage of Sissibe following the *Shaykh* rises to seventy percent. Of the remaining thirty percent, few actually opposed Umar. Most did not join the jihadists due to other causes (early deaths, casualties in other conflicts, etc.)[112]

Given that the overwhelming support of Umar by the Bundunke nobility was seconded by the majority of the population, one could surmise that Bokar Saada was not initially much of a factor in the Umarian *jihād*. But as the war dragged on, and the Umarian failures mounted, his stature began to improve. When the Bundunkobe returned from the eastern wars, or revolted against involuntary relocation, they came to Bokar Saada. When widespread famine set in, and villages were razed by the Umarians in an attempt to promote the *fergo*, the suffering turned to Bokar Saada. With the abandonment of the upper valley by the Umarians, there was no one left to contest the claims of Bokar Saada. He became *Almaami* by default.

With the establishment of French hegemony in the upper valley, and the consolidation of Bokar Saada's authority, the concept of pragmatism would come to an end, as it ceased to have any relative meaning. Reform Islam had been defeated in dramatic and conclusive fashion. Bokar Saada would be free to practice the politics of expediency, in his own interests as well as those of the state, outside of the context of reformist pressures from regional militant regimes. Militant Islam would again impact Bundu later in the century under the direction of Mamadu Lamine, but this subsequent movement would be qualitatively different from those led by *al-ḥājj* Umar and Abdul Qadir. First of all, Mamadu Lamine was profoundly ambitious; there were other considerations which informed his thinking besides religion. Secondly, his movement did not emerge out of the same tradition of militancy that produced the revolutions of the two Futas and the Umarians; it would not be Fulbe-led, nor would it engender a significant following among the Fulbe. Finally, whereas *al-ḥājj* Umar and Abdul Qadir sought to implement their policies through a subordinate but preserved Sissibe dynasty, Mamadu Lamine would seek to completely redefine privilege and power in Bundu by eliminating the dynasty altogether. In sum, there are fundamental discontinuities between the earlier reformers and Mamadu Lamine; the latter represents a clear break with the Bundunke past.

9

The age of Bokar Saada

With the peace established between *ah-ḥājj* Umar and Faidherbe in 1860, Bokar Saada became the undisputed sovereign over all of Bundu. He would rule until 1885, longer than any previous *Almaami*, save Maka Jiba. His immediate challenge was to rebuild the state's economy. The French-Umarian struggle had devastated the upper valley, resulting in the disruption of trade and neglect of agriculture. Further exacerbating Bundu's suffering was a cholera epidemic that impacted the whole of the Senegal Valley during the 1860s. In an effort to remedy these problems, and in a manner reminiscent of his father Saada Amadi Aissata, Bokar Saada developed a policy of perennial raiding in the neighboring territories, particularly to the south, to realize several objectives: first, the repopulation of Bundu and the revitalization of its agriculture via the importation of servile labor; second, direct access to British trade along the Gambia, and in particular the cultivation of groundnuts, the latter the result of European promotion during the second half of the nineteenth century; and last, the acquisition of foodstuffs and cattle to offset their scarcity in Bundu. Bambuk gold continued to be a lure as well. This rebuilding of Bundu via repopulation and exploitation of regional trade resulted in approximately ten years of modest economic recovery. But by the 1870s, and partially as a consequence of the previously mentioned cholera epidemic, the *Almaami* resorted to exacting greater revenue from the Bundunkobe to compensate for the failure of the economy to sustain satisfactory growth, a policy that caused even more emigratory activity. In turn, the rise in taxation took on ethnically directed connotations, as most of the burden was borne by the Soninke and Malinke. These communities greatly outnumbered those of the Fulbe, a significant proportion of which had resettled in the Umarian east. As a result, resentment against both Bokar Saada and the Fulbe ruling elite became both pervasive and deep-seated.

Regarding the sources for the reign of Bokar Saada, there is a heavy reliance upon correspondence with both the French and the British, who are more concerned with events transpiring along Bundu's periphery than its center. However, the data are sufficient to allow for insight into the internal affairs of the polity. Concerning domestic matters, the exogenous and intermediate sources are very consistent, and contradict 1984/1987–88 oral data which cast a very different light on the *Almaami*. To be specific, the suffering of the period, and the intense unpopularity of Bokar Saada are nowhere admitted in the most recent interviews. Given that the *Almaami* was a French protégé, the latter had little to gain by fabricating reports that he was greatly disliked by his constituency. Consensus among the exogenous and intermediate genres, combined with a careful analysis of conditions during this time, result in the assignment of greater credibility to the characterization of Bokar Saada's reign as despotic.

The decision by the French to emphasize peanut cultivation along the west coast in Wolof areas, coupled with their withdrawal from Kenieba in 1860 and Senoudebou in 1862, left Bokar Saada as the only stationary representative of French interests east of Bakel, besides Sambala of Khasso. He quickly moved to fill the vacuum, consolidating his base and projecting influence beyond Bundu's borders. He soon emerged as the most powerful figure in either the middle or upper valley. The military prowess of the Bundunke army became a celebrated accomplishment, and Bokar Saada's friendship was eagerly sought by surrounding potentates, more out of fear than anything else. But the *Almaami*, while maintaining the alliance with Saint Louis, also pursued his own agenda, often against the wishes of the French. In effect, the French had unleased a force that they could not completely control. But the emphasis on west coast cultivation, combined with the lack of a suitable replacement for Bokar Saada, left Saint Louis with little choice other than to work with the *Almaami*.

The campaigns

Throughout his reign, Bokar Saada was continually marching on the states to the south. This was an entirely logical strategy in view of the fact that the French controlled the trade to Bakel and points further west. In addition, the Bundunkobe were expressly prohibited from taxing caravans arriving in Senoudebou, and the French had discontinued paying customs to the *Almaami*. Bokar Saada's solution was to initiate raids, and those raids, whether punitive in design or expressly intended to collect booty, soon assumed a cyclical nature: successful campaigns led to large armies, which in turn led to more campaigns. Ironically, Bokar Saada would consistently maintain that his military ventures were in fact *jihāds*.

Bambuk. In September of 1860, the *Almaami* turned a hostile eye towards his former friend, Bugul of Farabana, ruler of the most important town in Bambuk. Prior to the wars of *al-ḥājj* Umar, Bundu and Farabana had experienced strained relations; previous *almaamies* had failed to subdue the town. With the Umarians out of the way, old animosities were rekindled. Together with Sambala of Khasso, Bokar Saada razed the town.[1]

Between 1861 and 1877, Bokar Saada led at least fourteen raids into

The age of Bokar Saada

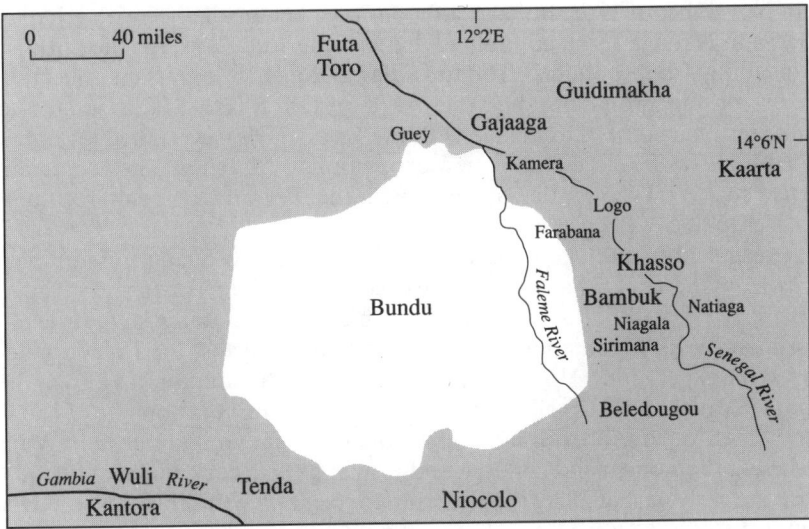

Map 4 Regional perspective in the nineteenth century

Bambuk, attacking the villages of Kakadian and Diangounte (above Medine, in the province of Niagala), Marougou (southwest Bambuk, in the province of Sirimana), Sandicounda (near Tenda), Kenieba (in Beledougou, south of Farabana and the Kenieba goldfields), Mamakono (also in Beledougou), and Saboucire.[2] Not all of these ventures were successful. The battle of Mamakono (1868) was more significant than the others in that an alliance of Malinke warriors from Niagala, central Bambuk, and Dentilia (south of Bundu) united against the Bundunkobe. The Malinke forces were routed, and all of the defeated lands agreed to pay tribute to Bokar Saada. The *Almaami* returned to Senoudebou with a rich booty of gold and slaves, and control over a substantial portion of Bambuk.

Wuli. Far more important than the Bambuk raids were Bokar Saada's wars with the Upper Gambia state of Wuli. From the time when Pate Gai chased the Malinke of Contou into Wuli (under the reign of Maka Jiba), relations between that country and Bundu had been adversarial. Wuli served as a refuge for the Kamara, Damfa, Nanki, Neri, Diata and the N'Dao, groups which had similarly been driven out of the Faleme Valley by the Bundunkobe. Wolof from Salum had also settled there to escape war.[3] The first large migration into Wuli from Bundu and Bambuk took place under Maka Jiba; Bokar Saada's policy of exorbitant taxation within Bundu, and the constant pillaging of Bambuk, would force the second significant departure. This flight from Bundu into Wuli, in turn, was one of the causes of the *Almaami*'s heightened interest in the Upper Gambia. A second cause was the presence of English trading posts and the expansion of groundnut production.

139

In November of 1863, Bokar Saada put together an alliance with Khasso, Logo and Natiaga (both adjoining Khasso), and Futa Toro for the purpose of invading Tambacounda.[4] The town had become an important collection center for the groundnut harvest. As a result, Bokar Saada sought to command this point of exchange with the English. However, the November expedition was unsuccessful. A new expedition in March of 1864 was again turned back, and was particularly costly for the *Almaami* as he suffered numerous casualties.

Determined to subjugate the Upper Gambia, Bokar Saada raised a new army from the same alliance (with the exception of Futa Toro), and invaded Wuli in April of 1865.[5] He told the French that he was doing so in order to reprimand Wuli for interfering with Bundunke caravans; the French sanctioned the expedition.[6] However, there is evidence that Bundu was also in the region in order to help quell a revolt by jihadists against the Soninke of Katabar.[7] Later in November, Bundu seized the village of Goundiourou in Wuli, enslaving the women and children and bringing them back to Senoudebou.[8]

By the early part of 1866, the French were beginning to show concern over Bundu's southern campaigns. The Commandant at Bakel was instructed to try to dissuade Bokar Saada from undertaking his annual assaults.[9] Such advice fell on deaf ears, for the *Almaami* was preparing to invade Wuli again. By April, the news of the Bundunke invasion reached Governor LaPrade at Saint Louis; not from Bokar Saada, but from Governor D'Arcy of Gambia: "With much concern I have the honor to inform you that the King of Bondoo at the head of 12,000 warriors, has broken the kingdom of Wooloo, burning in his course the British factories at Fatuh-Tenda destroying property belonging to British Merchants to the account of 7000 pounds."[10] D'Arcy went on to remind LaPrade of the English alliance with Wuli, and called upon the French to restrain the *Almaami*, while requiring him to make restitution for Fattetenda. LaPrade responded by saying that France had a lone treaty with Bundu regarding boundaries between French and Bundunke land, and that Bundu was an independent power.[11] While he could not make Bokar Saada desist, the French Governor would attempt to influence him. This he did, warning the *Almaami* that he must stop the ravages, adding: "You ignore, no doubt, that France and England are allied at all points of the globe."[12] For his part, Bokar Saada refused to either stop the expeditions or pay the English for damages.[13] The burning of Fattetenda was important to his overall strategy for exploiting Upper Gambian trade: such a policy would reduce the number of entrepots available to the traders of groundnuts, forcing them to go to those over which Bundu exercised control. LaPrade, in view of Bundunke resolve, warned Bakel to be wary of the *Almaami*, and wrote to Paris for further instructions.[14] Paris simply seconded the policy already adopted by the Governor.[15]

The Wuli campaign of 1866 made a deep impression upon the English. A report by McCarthy Island Manager B. Tanner summed up Wuli's predicament after the raid:

The next country is Woolie (a Sonninke Country) the inhabitants for the most part are Pagans and it also has suffered from pillage, war and the attendant consequences – mainly brought on by the obstinancy of the Chiefs who in 1864–65 refused to allow the King of Bundoo to pass through to give assistance to the Catabar people and his friends who were at war with Koonting – great destruction of property and loss of the merchants resulted – this occurred in 1866.

Since this period the Woolie people have sued for peace – the kingdom is at an end – and the Chiefs who were instrumental in preventing the King and his people from submitting to the rule of Bundoo ... have recently died ... Being free from the influence of these chiefs the King (with the consent of his people) has sent to Bundoo promising submission and desiring peace.[16]

Bokar Saada's conquest of Wuli was so complete that D'Arcy suspected "collusion between the Kings of Wooli and Bondoo, otherwise the former would have fought."[17] He warned the British agent David Brown to take refuge at McCarthy Island in the event of a renewed attack. Brown, however, viewed the Bundunke conquest differently, stating that Wuli was not to be blamed; it was simply unable to protect the British merchants "against a superior force."[18]

In January of 1867, Bokar Saada launched an effort to subdue all of Wuli. His army passed through much of that country without the slightest resistance until it reached the capital of Medina. The ruler, or *Mansa* of Wuli immediately surrendered, asking for clemency. Bokar Saada was content to grant the *Mansa* his wish, on condition that the latter agree to pay a hefty tribute. That settled, the *Almaami* returned to Senoudebou. It had taken eight years to conquer Bambuk, and seven to do the same to Wuli. With the acquisition of these two entities, rich in slaves, gold, and foodstuffs, Bundu was able to partially offset the difficulties caused by the French–Umarian wars. Beyond that, Bokar Saada now had direct access to both British goods and the rich markets of the Niger. Segu had apparently reconciled itself to the fact that Bokar Saada ruled Bundu; the Englishman Cooper spoke of the free flow of commerce coming from Segu and Timbuktu to the Gambia through Bundu.[19] An independent French source also referred to the "active" commercial relations between Segu and Bundu.[20] Wuli remained a favorite target for Bokar Saada through much of his reign. He was there almost annually from 1868 to 1879. Much of this "jihadist" activity was no more than slave-raiding.[21]

Niani. In 1879, Bokar Saada entered into an important alliance with *Alfa* Mulu, sovereign of Fouladougou (south of the Gambia), and *Alfa* Ibrahima, ruler of Labe province in Futa Jallon.[22] They each had separate objectives. *Alfa* Mulu was interested in conquering Kantora (along the Gambia), *Alfa* Ibrahima needed help in subduing the village of Kouttang in Kade (in Kaabu, in the Upper Rivières-du-Sud), while Bokar Saada had set his sights on Niani, adjacent to Wuli. Both *Alfa* Mulu and *Alfa* Ibrahima achieved their objectives that same year.[23] After a period of inactivity, the allies resumed the campaign in March of 1880. Confident of victory, the allies were deeply humiliated when they were turned back at Koussalan, Niani's most powerful village. Celebrated as a tremendous victory in the traditions of the Wolof and Malinke, the failure at Koussalan effectively ended Bokar Saada's activities in Wuli and in areas further west along the Gambia.[24]

Niocolo. Closer to Bundu, but still to the south, was the territory of Niocolo, an important source of kola nuts. Officially a tributary of Futa Jallon and largely inhabited by Fulbe, it failed to escape Bokar Saada's attention. In 1869, 1873 and 1875, the *Almaami* attacked the territory. The first two expeditions were successful, resulting in large numbers of captives. But the third proved disastrous, and ended Bundu's interest in Niocolo.[25]

Tenda. East of Niocolo lay the territory of Tenda. The villages of Talicori, Guenou-Dialla and Tingueto were subjected to Bundunke raids in 1862, 1864, 1870 and 1874. Most of these campaigns were led by Bokar Saada's son Usuman Gassi.[26] While Guenou-Dialla suffered the loss of its men to death, and its women and children to captivity, the other villages were not seriously disrupted.

The conflict between Bundu and Tenda intensified in 1881, and concerned the village of Gamon. This *tata* had the same origins as Tambacounda; that is, Malinke who had been driven from the Faleme by Bundunke expansionists. According to traditions collected by Rançon, Gamon was actually founded by a Malinke slave named Samba Takuru, who absconded from Bundu.[27] Over a period of time, Gamon came to be known as a "slave village," in that a large number of slaves from Bundu settled there. By the late nineteenth century, it had grown to 1200 residents.[28]

In 1881, 1883, and 1884, Bokar Saada made successive attempts to seize Gamon. The 1883 campaign involved a six-month siege, and was unsuccessful. The final assault culminated in the loss of 300 Bundunke men; Bokar Saada himself was forced to flee to Senoudebou. Nearly 200 Bundunke captives were later sold into slavery in Niani.[29]

Bundu and the English

Clearly related to Bokar Saada's southern campaigns were his connections to the English along the Gambia River. With or without a formal agreement, trade between the English and Bundu had been vigorous, and was the main source of external revenue for Koussan. In turn, the English had been just as eager to trade with Bundu. As early as May of 1827, a treaty between "King Quia" of Wuli and the Governor of Gambia, Major-General Sir Neil Campbell, called upon Wuli to "open the paths to Bundoo and other directions to the east and south of Wooli."[30] The outbreak of hostilities between *Almaami* Tumane Mudi and Wuli in 1827 was a source of grave concern for the English. Captain A. M. Fraser, stationed in Gambia at the time, tried to halt the conflict by sending a letter to "his majesty the Almamy and King of Bondou," expressing a desire to bypass Wuli as an intermediate and establish direct relations.[31] In an 1829 treaty with the *Mansa* of Wuli and

William Hutton, the Acting-Governor of Gambia, the *Mansa* agreed to "exert his influence with his ally the King of Bondoo" to promote trade with the English.[32] The correspondence demonstrates that relations with Bundu were important to the English, and that the latter took pains to improve relations between Wuli and Bundu to facilitate trade. However, the effort to establish peace between Wuli and Bundu was wholly unsuccessful.

As a result of Faidherbe's policies, Bundu's alliance with France was no longer as financially profitable as it once was. Bokar Saada violated no understanding by maintaining commercial relations with England; the Treaty of 1858 did not call for exclusive commercial dealings with France, as did the Treaty of 1845, which in any event was abrogated. Nevertheless, the French tried to prevent any formal alliance between Bundu and England. In 1867, the Commandant at Bakel was instructed to make every effort to frustrate such a development.[33] In the preceding year, the French had sought to stop Bokar Saada from attacking Wuli as a favor to the British. It may be that Saint Louis had its own reasons for seeking to dissuade the *Almaami*; the destruction of Wuli would have led to a more intensified interaction between Senoudebou and Banjul (Bathhurst).

Saint Louis' attempts were less than successful. After Bokar Saada's ravaging of Wuli in 1866, it became clear to the English that Bundu had emerged as the premier power in the area, and that a treaty was necessary to safeguard English interests. As a result, the *Almaami* was approached and subsequently signed a treaty with Colonel Samuel Wensley Blackall, Governor of Gambia, on 12 November 1869. Concluded at McCarthy Island, the agreement called for peace between the English and the Bundunkobe. Bokar Saada was to respect the property rights of the English, and was to resist the temptation to war against any of the states bordering the Gambia. The most important provision, however, regarded commerce:

> The said King of Bondoo does hereby acknowledge the rights which the subjects of the Queen of England have heretofore and at all times enjoyed of free and uninterrupted intercourse for trade and commerce, and for all other legitimate purpose in and throughout the countries adjacent to and bordering on both banks of the River Gambia and its branches, ...[34]

Bokar Saada signed the documents in Arabic, the English having agreed to pay him fifty pounds annually. That accomplished, Bokar Saada promptly went out and invaded Niocolo the following month. By 1870, he was back in Wuli.

Bokar Saada held the upper hand in his dealings with the English; they were powerless to resist his incursions. More important than what Bundu itself had to offer was the fact that it lay between the Gambia and the Niger. English merchants had been in contact with Segu, and were trying to develop a route that would go around Bundunke territory.[35] However, Bundu remained important to the English. In April of 1875 it was reported that Bokar Saada had returned to McCarthy Island, where the English had offered him an annual payment worth 7,000 francs to steer caravans from Kaarta and Segu to the Gambia.[36] The *Almaami* accepted the payment for 1875, as well as gifts of arms and munitions.[37] The English were described as "wooing" Bundu by its generous gifts; when Bokar Saada visited Bakel earlier in the year, he was described as possessing British arms "of superior quality to those usually furnished through trade."[38]

Since Bathurst was helpless to halt the Bundunke ravages, it followed that the only available option was to continue courting the *Almaami*'s favor. To have cut off commerce with Bundu would have ensured even greater hostilities in the Gambia, and would have retarded trade with the Niger Valley states. Therefore, after Bokar Saada had directed no less than seven expeditions into the Gambia between 1870 and 1876, the English stopped complaining to Saint Louis and simply continued contributing to the *Almaami*'s coffers. In May of 1876, H. J. Cooper, the "Acting Administrator of the British Settlement of the Gambia," wrote to Bokar Saada and informed him of British plans to connect with Segu and Timbuktu. He planned to visit Senoudebou personally, and from there he would "pass to Khasso and visit your father-in-law, King Sambala, and from thence through Guemakoro, Marcoaia, Yamina, and on to Segou to visit King Amade Syhou."[39] Relations with the English grew to the point that by 1879, all of the arms in Bundu, as was the case in Wuli, were of English manufacture.[40] The shilling was being used as part of the currency, and numerous products made in England were visible. Briere de l'Isle, Governor of Senegal, went on to complain in 1877 that Bokar Saada was being paid by the English, and that Bundu was paying (and trading) for goods in Kamera and Guey with English currency.[41] Such currency was showing up in substantial amounts, and was circulating in Bakel as well.

Bokar Saada's statements on maintaining good relations with both Saint Louis and Bathurst reveal the calculations of a very shrewd leader. As early as 1863 he wrote to the Governor at Saint Louis: "I love all those whom you love, and I detest those whom you detest, all the orders that you give me I will execute, if it pleases God, ... I will say to you that since Bakel and Senoudebou have existed, our goods have always been directed toward these settlements."[42] The reality, however, was that French policies partially dictated the *Almaami*'s southern activities. Even the French admitted that their "neglect" of the *Almaami* led the latter to direct commerce towards the Gambia.[43] The *Almaami*, on the other hand, sought to minimize his English connections to the French: "'The English are simply my friends, but I will never permit them to come and establish themselves in Bundu, which is French'."[44] But on the other hand, it was never to Bundu's advantage to completely conceal good relations with the English. Indeed, those relations were an important bargaining tool in obtaining greater concessions from the French. Saint Louis was concerned about those relations, that they could eventually undermine the French position in the Upper Senegal. They were also concerned that the more direct caravan route of Bathurst–Gambia–

Bundu–Saboucire–Koniakari–Segu would rival and eclipse the older route of Saint Louis–Bakel–Medine–Segu.[45] However, their concern was tempered by their involvement along the Wolof coast, and by Bokar Saada's professed loyalty.

Bundu's relations with the English have led Barrows to argue that Bokar Saada and Sambala were in fact "more than mere puppets."[46] He further contends that while Faidherbe succeeded in creating an anti-Umarian league, it did not in turn become pro-French once the Umarian threat was removed.[47] While it is largely true that Bokar Saada followed a strategy independent of Saint Louis, it is also true that he never lost sight of the fact that it was the French who initially put him in power; he was careful not to exceed certain limits in his relations with them. Indeed, in contrast to his dealings with the English, Bokar Saada never attacked a French post, interfered with their commerce, or threatened to pull out of the alliance. In all that he did, he never violated the letter of the 1858 treaty. As the *Almaami* himself put it: "'Je suis noir, et je suis français'."[48]

Role in the north

With the French–Umarian understanding of 1860, the Upper Senegal grew relatively quiet. The depopulation of the area, combined with the French emphasis upon groundnut cultivation along the Wolof coast, resulted in a diminution of the upper valley's importance. Consequently, Bokar Saada was primarily concerned with controlling lands to the south. With regard to the north, he basically sought to limit Bundunke involvement, unless he believed success was assured. His efforts in the Upper Senegal were therefore largely confined to assisting the struggle of Abdul Bokar Kan, effective head of Futa Toro.

Besides Sambala of Khasso, Bokar Saada maintained a strong relationship with Abdul Bokar Kan. The Futanke grand elector was from Bosseya province, and was noted for his anti-Umarian activity.[49] In 1861 he established his base of power in eastern Futa, as Futa Toro had disintegrated into its three basic components of western, central, and eastern Futa.[50] He soon rose to become the most powerful figure in Futa Toro, and exercised power over the traditional offices.

In 1862, the elector skirmished with French forces over control of the middle valley. Interestingly enough, he now called upon pro-Umarian sentiment to mobilise his anti-French movement, and named Amadu Thierno Demba Ly as *Almaami*, originally designated as such by the *Shaykh*.[51] After a series of battles and political maneuvers, the French conceded Abdul Bokar's control over eastern Futa by 1864.[52] The elector found himself in the enviable position of enjoying the anti-French, the anti-Umarian, and the pro-Umarian sentiment concurrently. More than embodying a religious ideal, he had emerged as the consummate politician.

Formal relations between Bokar Saada and Abdul Bokar date back to at least 1859, when the latter contracted a marriage with the *Almaami*'s niece Jiba.[53] During the difficulties with the French in 1862–63, Bokar Saada was enlisted by the French to mediate.[54] However, the Futanke rejected the *Almaami*'s efforts, insulting him in the process. Bokar Saada responded by preventing his niece from going to Futa Toro to be with her husband. Abdul Bokar, afraid that his alliance with Bundu was in jeopardy, sought to make amends.[55] In 1866, a reconciliation was reached after the Futanke presented Bokar Saada with cattle and slaves. Abdul Bokar went on to accompany Bokar Saada in his expedition to Wuli, and returned to Futa Toro some time in May with substantial booty. Saint Louis viewed the developing alliance as potentially helpful; after giving Bokar Saada a cannon, it asked him to use his influence to get Abdul Bokar involved in more of his expeditions. Said the French Governor of Abdul Bokar: "We can only benefit from this troublemaker and his followers being away from Futa as long as possible."[56]

The emergence of Tierno Brahim in eastern Futa was the first test of the Bokar Saada–Abdul Bokar alliance. Tierno Brahim was a reformer who had studied with Sidiya al-Kabir, the famous *shaykh* and leader of the Sidiyya brotherhood who lived in Mauritania, and who had in turn studied under the Kunta *shaykhs* near Timbuktu.[57] Tierno Brahim, having established his headquarters at Magama, began encouraging migration to Magama as well as launching raids into the river valley. In May of 1868, Abdul Bokar achieved a major victory over Tierno Brahim's forces with the help of Guey and Khasso, but by the fall of 1868, the reformer had rebuilt Magama. Later, with the aid of Guey and Khasso, Abdul Bokar again defeated Magama in April of 1869, and Tierno Brahim was hanged.[58]

In the campaign against Tierno Brahim, Bokar Saada was extremely reticent about fighting the reformer, and provided little assistance. In fact, Tierno Brahim had established contacts of his own with Bokar Saada, and was trying to convince the latter to renounce ties to Saint Louis.[59] The *Almaami*'s position was informed by two factors: the preeminence of the Sidiyya in the region, and Bokar Saada's interest in maintaining as much power as possible in the middle and upper valleys. Given the strain in relations with Abdul Bokar as late as 1866, the struggle with Tierno Brahim, in demonstrating Abdul Bokar's need for external assistance, was an opportunity to prevent the grand elector from becoming too powerful by withholding such aid.[60] However, with the demise of Tierno Brahim, and Bokar Saada's own need for aid in subsequent ventures, relations between the two men became more cooperative.

The utilization of troops from Khasso and Guey was particularly unsettling for the other Futankobe.[61] They feared that such large infusions of foreigners would sooner or later result in pillaging and possibly even occupation. Their anxieties were exacerbated in 1871, when Abdul Bokar contracted to marry Sambala of Khasso's daughter. In order to complete the arrangement, Abdul Bokar needed to give a substantial gift to Sambala in cattle and slaves. He tried to obtain cattle in eastern Futa, but his constituents resisted his appeals. His decision to confiscate their property led to widespread disaffection. When the elector returned from Khasso in May of 1871, he was met with organized hostility. An important battle at Mbumba in March of 1872 was disastrous for Abdul Bokar.[62] In order to redress his fortunes, he traveled to various Upper Senegal states to obtain assistance.

Although Abdul Bokar spent some time in Guey and Khasso, the focus of his attention was Bokar Saada. Easily the most powerful ruler in the Senegal Valley, the *Almaami* could prove to be the decisive factor in the struggle back in Futa Toro. But Bundunke forces were busy in Wuli, Niocolo, and Bambuk that year, and the *Almaami* was consequently short of manpower. A meeting was held in Tiyaabu between the representatives of Bundu and Guey to discuss Abdul Bokar's request for auxiliaries.[63] It was decided that Guey would supply the infantry and some cavalry, while Bokar Saada would take the command.

Eastern Futa, or Damga, repeatedly sent envoys to Bokar Saada, pleading with him to remain neutral.[64] Their appeals were futile; Bokar Saada replied by asking Damga to restore relations with Abdul Bokar.[65] When, in turn, the *Almaami*'s request was refused, he and Abdul Bokar decided to head for Damga on 15 April. They led about 2,000 infantry and 1,000 cavalry, half the number used to defeat Tierno Brahim.[66] Facing them were the smaller forces of Bubu Cire and Malik Hamet, both from eastern Futa. On 19 April, the battle was joined at Bofel; at its conclusion Bokar Saada tasted bitter defeat, and returned to Senoudebou in utter humiliation.[67] Abdul Bokar was able to recover later, however, by convincing Malik Hamet's followers to remain neutral. The following month, he won two key battles, and went on to restore his authority in eastern Futa.

Despite Bokar Saada's defeat at Bofel, his relations with Abdul Bokar remained cordial. After Abdul Bokar regained his Damga base, Saada recovered sufficiently to intervene in matters affecting the upper valley. In 1875, the towns of Lanel and Kotere in Kamera were unable to resolve their differences.[68] Bokar Saada sent his son Usuman Gassi against Kotere, but the Bundunkobe were turned back. Again, in 1876 the *Almaami* tried to take the village and, again, the Bundunke forces were turned away, with great loss of life. It was not until 1877, when Abdul Bokar came to Bokar Saada's aid, that Lanel and Kotere agreed to peace.[69] Abdul Bokar would continue to maintain some form of control over eastern Futa until his death in 1891, when he was assassinated at the instigation of the French.[70]

Barrows makes the point that Bokar Saada's friendship with Abdul Bokar is further indication that the *Almaami* functioned independently of Saint Louis.[71] While it is true that the French were concerned about this relationship, they also expressed optimism that Bokar Saada would influence Abdul Bokar to become less anti-French. If nothing more, he could keep the Futanke elector occupied in some campaign along the Gambia. In fact, it can be argued that there was some gravitation on the part of Abdul Bokar towards the French as his career continued, an indication of various influences, including those of the *Almaami* and his niece Jiba.

Conditions within Bundu

Up to this point, the discussion of Bokar Saada has focused upon his activities outside of Bundu. One of his major concerns within Bundu was the fort at Senoudebou. The fort was never in very good condition. Raffenel complained about it as early as 1847. Five years after Bokar Saada moved back into the fort (1862), he wrote to the Commandant at Bakel complaining of its deplorable state.[72] Ten years later, Governor Briere de l'Isle responded that he would finally repair Senoudebou, but he did not follow through.[73] When Laude visited Bundu in 1879, one of the first subjects Bokar Saada raised was the condition of Senoudebou.[74] He feared that the French had no intention of making repairs, and that he would have to move his court to Boulebane if aid was not forthcoming. As it turned out, his fears were justified: Senoudebou was never repaired.

Another domestic issue was the influx of Bambara immigrants from the eastern *jihād*. *Al-ḥajj* Umar's harsh treatment of the Bambara nobility was a factor in Bokar Saada's defection and subsequent opposition. He never denied his origins, and with the defeat of Kaarta by the *Shaykh*, he permitted Bambara survivors to settle in Bundu.[75] Many took refuge near Senoudebou and Bakel, while others sought protection at Medine in Khasso.[76] Within Bundu, the Bambara constructed two villages: Allahina and Kidira.[77] Others settled in Fouladougou near the Gambia River.

It should be noted that some Sissibe had given their daughters in marriage to the Bambara nobility. The blood ties between Kaarta and Bundu were extensive in some instances. It is not clear, however, that Bokar Saada wanted the Bambara immigrants to become absorbed into Bundunke society, or even if the immigrants desired as much. Regarding those who settled in areas adjoining Bundu, Bokar Saada tried to force them into a tributary status.[78] Many rejected this arrangement, and moved beyond the *Almaami*'s reach. With the fall of Amadu Sheku by 1893, substantial numbers returned to Kaarta.[79]

Based upon the previous discussion, Bokar Saada appeared to have been a successful ruler; projecting power throughout Senegambia, the object of numerous petitions to form alliances, and so on. But an examination of what was transpiring inside of Bundu reveals something quite different. For all of his external success, the *Almaami* was a tragic figure, a marginal man on several levels. He was Bundunke, yet he retained an affinity to Kaarta; a Muslim, yet the enemy of one of the most important Muslims in West African history; an African, yet loyal to France; a descendant of Malik Sy, but the first to achieve executive power in Bundu via the instrumentality of non-Muslim foreigners. In some instances he was forced to identify with one extreme or the other, but in most cases he chose to maintain the dualities, having little care to address the inherent contradictions. In a sense he was the victim of circumstances beyond his control, a consequence of the policies of *Almaami* Amadi Aissata, who forged a short-lived alliance with the Bambara towards the turn of the nineteenth century, the seal of which was the marriage of Bokar Saada's mother to Saada Amadi Aissata. As a result, Bokar Saada literally embodied the Bundu–Kaarta, Muslim–traditionalist alliance.

However Bokar Saada chose to reconcile the conflicting subsets of his personality, the Bundunke people were making choices of their own. Before 1859, many had already made the journey to Kaarta and Segu, where the "true Muslims" now lived. The 1860s saw some economic recovery in Bundu with the cessation of warfare and the raids of Bokar Saada, but this was mitigated by the cholera epidemic of the decade. By the 1870s, the *Almaami* was frustrated over his inability to command sufficient revenues, and he therefore decided to increase exactions upon the Bundunkobe themselves. The Bundunke cultivators, having never fully recovered from the devastation caused by the French–Umarian conflict, were hardly able to support the *Almaami*'s desired standard of living.

> The despotic government of Bubakar Saada was not designed to repeople Bundu, and to restore it such as it was before the invasion of Al-Hajj Omar ...
> The populations, pillaged and ruined by the arbitrary exactions with which they were struck by the Almamy, turn their eyes toward a country more hospitable. A general emigration takes place every year from the prosperous villages of the Ferlo. The banks of the Faleme, at other times lined with numerous villages, today exhibit completely deserted forests without end.[80]

The result of Bokar Saada's oppression was in fact the further depopulation of Bundu.[81] Its richest area, the banks of the Faleme, received the *Almaami*'s heaviest demands. Those villages which resisted were pillaged. It soon became a cyclical decline: economic oppression led to emigration, which led to increased oppression. Most emigrants moved further south.[82] By 1879, long after the cholera epidemic had run its course, Bundu was still characterized as a poor country, "sadly populated."[83] Gone were the days of its fabled productivity and abundance. In 1881, Bundu was calm and peaceful, but also largely abandoned.[84]

The oppression shouldered by the Bundunke people was not completely the function of Bokar Saada's singular greed. Those Sissibe who remained with him also sought out their own advantage.[85] In addition to the nobility, the royal slaves enjoyed influential positions within the court, and pressured the *Almaami* to increase levies on Bundunke subjects.[86] In other words, the *Almaami*'s entourage was as committed to plunder and self-advancement as it was to the *Almaami*, and probably more so. The chief incentive for supporting Bokar Saada, other than the fear of reprisal, was the spoils of war and oppression.

It is very likely that relations between the Sissibe and the Jakhanke also became strained under Bokar Saada, based upon future Jakhanke support of

Mamadu Lamine, whose movement was in part a reaction to Bokar Saada's oppression. In addition, the French suspected the Jakhanke of maintaining links to Samori, and therefore asked Bokar Saada to monitor relations between the two. The *Almaami* reportedly even seized a group of slaves given by Samori to one Bakari Jabi, who had visited Samori.[87] However, it is not clear that in confiscating the slaves Bokar Saada was following a French directive; he may have simply been exploiting the fears of the French as an excuse to personally benefit from the Jakhanke's growing number of slaves taken captive in Samori's wars.

The sense of public trust in the Bundunke *almaamate*, to the extent that it existed, was destroyed under Bokar Saada. Bundu, and more specifically Senoudebou, was no more than his base of operations. Never very popular in the first place, his domestic policies succeeded in reducing the few adherents he once had. "Boubakar is no longer well-loved by his people; he has domestic difficulties and oppressed subjects who only seek to throw off the yoke."[88] Whenever he traveled, he was always accompanied by a large retinue and cavalry, the latter sometimes reaching 600 men.[89] Beyond this indirect evidence of unpopularity was the behavior of a few members of the Sy family. As early as 1866, his nephew Saada Amadi, fresh from defeat at Kenieba in Bambuk, abandoned the *Almaami*. His reason was his disgust at the ruler's policies, a reference to Bokar Saada's incessant raiding of neighboring states and apparent greed in the distribution of booty.[90] He sought refuge with Abdul Bokar Kan. By 1879, several more Sissibe had gone to Abdul Bokar Kan, including some of the *Almaami*'s sons, who were concerned with the harmful effects of overtaxation on the peasantry. According to Laude, there was even a plan under consideration to recruit Futanke soldiers, return to Bundu, and force the *Almaami* to change his destructive ways.[91] Umar Penda was Bokar Saada's brother and in charge of Boulebane, but even he refused entrance to the *Almaami*, a further indication of a fundamental disagreement with the destructive policies of the *Almaami*. Facing this kind of dissension, Bokar Saada told Laude: "'Everyone has forsakened me now; I am going to go to Gambia'."[92]

The combination of the defeat by Gamon in 1884, and the depopulation of the Ferlo, served to greatly discourage the warrior-ruler.[93] An old man by now, he eventually took ill. Negotiations with Gamon in May and June of 1885 were fruitless.[94] Shortly before his death, he sent Usuman Gassi into Bambuk in a punitive raid against Farabana.[95] He died after this last success on 10 December 1885. He was survived by seven sons: Usuman Gassi, Saada Bokar, Wopa Bokar, Cire Ture, Musa Yero, Sulayman Bokar, and Sega Bokar. An eighth son, Amadi Bokar, had died earlier.[96] There is general agreement about the length of his reign.[97]

Bokar Saada's personal prestige eclipsed the actual condition of Bundu, which suffered greatly under his tenure. His incredible indifference to his constituency left him a man without a "country," a lonely figure when all was said and done. Awarded the cross of the French Legion of Honor in

1860, he was noted for his love of alcohol, "esteeming the Bordeaux wines above all."⁹⁸ Married to five women, he obviously lived beyond the boundaries of *sharī'a*.⁹⁹

10

Mamadu Lamine and the demise of Bundu

Bundu in the second half of the nineteenth century is a study in pathos. From the Civil War of 1853–54, to the *jihāds* of *al-ḥājj* Umar, to the ravenous policies of Bokar Saada, the Bundunkobe endured crisis after crisis. Any hope for relief was quickly dashed with the "invasion" of the cleric Mamadu Lamine in the early part of 1886. The combined effect of these incessant wars was a dramatic decline in Bundu's population. In the late 1850s, during the wars of Umar, Faidherbe estimated Bundu's population to have been around 100,000.[1] This is surely exaggerated; a more credible figure would have been about 15,000, given the period. By 1887, in the midst of Mamadu Lamine's campaign, estimates on the population range from 9,350 to 10,000.[2] While the method of estimation is not clear, nor is it certain that the various estimators were working within the same parameters, the qualitative evidence is consistent with the implications of the quantitative efforts that Bundu's population declined significantly within a span of thirty-five years. As a result of Mamadu Lamine's *jihād*, Bundu ceased to be a power of any substance or importance.

Bokar Saada's death was a major turning point in the fortunes of the Bundunke people. The French had lost an ally, the Bundunkobe a tyrant. Umar Penda, Bokar Saada's brother, became *Almaami*. Around fifty years old, he had fought alongside Bokar Saada, but he was not as loyal to the French. Actually Bokar Saada's first son Amadi Bokar was being groomed as his heir at the "School of Chiefs" in Saint Louis. His death in November of 1875 was a sore disappointment.[3] Under the circumstances, the French chose to abide by the legal succession process.

The period from the advent of Mamadu Lamine to 1905 is chiefly informed by intermediate and exogenous materials, with the same consequences as previously encountered – a preoccupation with external developments and de-emphasis on events within the Bundunke court and society. The sources must be approached with due caution, as the French assumed an adversarial relationship to Mamadu Lamine. The account of Henri Frey is particularly suspect; he consistently portrays the cleric as the aggressor who was opposed to the French from early in his career. In view of these difficulties, records such as Frey's can be employed to reconstruct basic chronologies, but cannot be relied upon for interpretive purposes. The analysis of events must be arrived at via independent evaluation of the sources and the circumstances they seek to describe.

Scholarship concerning Mamadu Lamine himself suggests the difficulty in assessing his place and purpose in West African history. From the perspective of people such as Bathily and Oloruntimehin, Mamadu Lamine was a leader in the anti-colonial resistance. Fisher begs to differ, arguing that the cleric's activities were much more of a response to local political conditions, and were in essence a religious movement. Hrbek approximates Fisher's position by placing Mamadu Lamine "in the ranks of the Western Sudan revivalists of Islam," where he seeks (unsuccessfully) the friendship of the French against the *Torodbe* of Segu and, to a lesser extent, Bundu.[4]

In contrast to all of the foregoing interpretations, it would appear that, upon closer scrutiny of Mamadu Lamine, he was neither a leader *par excellence* of the resistance to colonialism, nor was he the quintessential reformer. Rather, Mamadu Lamine should be viewed as a cleric who greatly aspired to assume theopolitical leadership of a Muslim state. His desire to undertake such a responsibility was conditioned by his having lived for many years in various lands under Muslim rule, where he was afforded the opportunity to observe the machinery of Islamic government, and to which he grew accustomed. In particular, he became associated with the ruling elite in Maasina and Segu, where he clearly demonstrated leadership potential. Such was his promise that he was eventually perceived as a threat in Segu, and consequently detained. This development essentially crushed his hopes of succeeding (or perhaps replacing) Amadu Sheku, and upon his release, forced him to look elsewhere in order to realize his ambition. The bitter experience in Segu was never forgotten.

Upon returning to the Upper Senegal, Mamadu Lamine would call for the launching of *jihād* against Gamon, in Tenda. He would receive tremendous support because of his reputation as a scholar, a holy man (*walī*), and a miracle-worker. At the same time, all of the evidence indicates that Lamine was also extremely prudent; he understood the commercial and political entrenchment of the French, and sought to avoid any hostilities with them. Rather than a confrontation, Mamadu Lamine sought a *modus vivendi* with Saint Louis, particularly in view of his designs on Segu. As matters turned out, confrontation did occur, to the irreversible misfortune of the cleric, but such a development does not qualify him as an anticolonial figure. He fought the French out of necessity, in self-defense. The eradication of the French was not his primary objective.

Notwithstanding the religious content of Mamadu Lamine's appeal, his movement was also assisted by certain adverse conditions operating in the upper valley. First of all, he benefitted from resentment to French military encroachment into the area and its economic consequences. Briere de l'Isle, who had become Governor of Senegal in 1876, adopted an imperialistic policy towards the upper valleys, and viewed the Umarian territories as an impediment to French interests. He and former Governor Jean Jaureguiberry persuaded the Colonial Office to adopt the "Niger Plan," part of which provided for the creation of an Upper River Command in 1880, which was staffed by a large number of troops (*Tirailleurs sénégalais*). Concentrations of soldiers were kept stationed at Kita and Bamako, which were supplied by the commercial posts of Bakel and Medine, over which was the administrative center at Kayes. Most of these troops were recruited from the Senegal Valley, which involved some social disruption. Perhaps more disturbing, however, was that portion of the Niger Plan that required the use of forced labor for the purpose of constructing telegraph and railway lines, beginning in 1879. The French "freedom villages" for absconded slaves proved to be little more than involuntary labor pools, and they unwittingly paved the way for the start of Archinard's conquest in 1890. In fact, the French presence tended to exacerbate the plight of slaves, as the food demands of the expanded military meant that the need for agricultural slave labor kept apace.[5]

A second factor contributing to the growth of Mamadu Lamine's following was the disaffection of the people of Jombokho-Jafunu and Guidimakha, who had launched a rebellion against Amadu Sheku's brothers in Kaarta in 1876 and were brutally repressed. These subject populations were receptive to Mamadu Lamine's call for a more just society. Finally, a third factor which aided the development of the cleric's community was centered in Bundu, where the people were still reeling from the oppression of Bokar Saada.

An important constituency in Lamine's following were the Mande-speaking communities of the upper valley, and in particular the Soninke. By the second half of the nineteenth century, the Mande-speakers outnumbered the Fulbe in Bundu.[6] Up until the wars of *al-ḥājj* Umar, they had been willing to adhere to the Bundunke formulation of power. But the ensuing *fergo*, or emigration, resulted in an even greater population imbalance in their favor. In addition, the Soninke had to a great extent rallied behind the *Shaykh*. That they suffered disproportionately under Bokar Saada is possibly explained by this earlier support of the Umarians. In any event, the policies of Bokar Saada resulted in the alienation of the Soninke, and provided a critical base for Mamadu Lamine's early efforts at organization.

In view of the foregoing, Mamadu Lamine, propelled by personal ambition, promoted the possibility of a more equitable society under the laws of religion. In response, considerable numbers in the upper valley gravitated to his camp, as they were both inspired by his vision, and disgruntled by economic and social conditions already operative.

Mamadu Lamine's background

Mamadu Lamine was born Ma Lamine Demba Dibassi some time between 1830 and 1840.[7] His birthplace was Safalou, in Diakha (in southern Bundu), and he is therefore considered to have been Jakhanke by Smith and Sanneh.[8] On the other hand, Rançon argues that his ethnicity is in doubt, and was possibly a mixture of Fulbe and Bambara.[9] His father was named *Alfa* Mamadu, the son of *Alfa* Mamadu Salif, the latter originally from the Jakhanke center of Goundiourou in Khasso.[10] Lamine's clear association with both Goundiourou and Diakha province, combined with his strong subsequent identification with the Soninke, suggests that he was probably either Jakhanke or Soninke.

It was *Alfa* Mamadu Salif who emigrated to Safalou; his son married a woman from Diafounou (northeast of Guidimakha), who became Mamadu Lamine's mother. Mamadu Lamine's father, as can be deduced from his title, was a teacher of the Qur'an and a *qāḍī* in the village.[11] Mamadu Lamine attended Qur'anic school under his father's instruction, after which he went to Bakel to further his studies. His *shaykh* was Fudi Muhammad Salum, renowned throughout the upper valley.[12] Lamine was in Bakel when *al-ḥājj* Umar passed through in 1847.[13] According to Mahammadou Aliou Tyam, Mamadu Lamine fought under the *Shaykh*, but Bathily disputes this.[14] At some point after 1855, he made the *ḥajj*; however, the precise itinerary of his travels is shrouded in uncertainty.[15] On his return to West Africa in 1879, he went to Timbuktu and Maasina, where al-Tijani received him with valuable gifts. From there he journeyed to Segu, where he was apparently placed under house arrest by a suspicious Amadu Sheku.[16] In 1885, Mamadu Lamine departed from Segu, after reportedly performing numerous miracles, and arrived in Goundiourou in July of that year.[17] He had spent some thirty years away from Senegambia.[18]

When Mamadu Lamine returned to Khasso, he found a very different set of circumstances. Before he left, *al-ḥājj* Umar had created a sensation in the west, and was marching on Kaarta in 1854; by 1885, the *Shaykh* was dead, his empire split, and his heir unalterably opposed to the celebrated traveler. In the early 1850s, Khasso and Guidimakha were strongholds of Umarian sentiment; by 1885, the anti-Umarian Sambala ruled Khasso and its environs. Before he made the *ḥajj*, Bundu had been an important supplier of recruits for the *jihād*; in 1885, Bokar Saada was wielding power. Above all, the French had become the dominant power in the upper valley.

A reappraisal of Mamadu Lamine's initial objective constitutes the focus of the remainder of this section and the beginning of the next. In anticipation of that discussion, and within the context of the preceding paragraphs, it is possible to summarize Mamadu Lamine's plans for establishing his leadership in the upper valley. First of all, he was from the area. He had extensive ties throughout the upper valley, as evidenced by the backgrounds of his parents and grandfather. He had been educated there. Consequently, rather than seizing control of an existing Muslim state, he targeted non-Muslim Gamon for a *jihād*. Gamon had maintained poor relations with the upper valley states, particularly Bundu. Lamine reasoned that this historical enmity would help to persuade Bundu and others to join his campaign. But in addition to its religious nonconformity and political isolation, Gamon was also targeted because of its proximity to the Gambia and the groundnut trade. From Gamon, Lamine would be able to access the commerce of the region, including that of the French and the British.

By calling for *jihād*, Lamine had in mind something beyond the raids of Bokar Saada. Rather, he was advocating a prescriptive holy war for the purpose of planting a Muslim state on the soil of the vanquished. He would then be in position to fashion either a confederation (in which existing states would enjoy autonomy, except in cases of war and in matters involving foreign policy, and would probably pay tribute); or an empire (in which existing states would become provinces in a centralized and integrated administrative structure). The "existing states" consisted of Bundu, Khasso, Guidimakha, Kamera, and Guey, which by 1885 constituted the heartland of the Soninke diaspora. With the creation of either option, Lamine could then determine whether or not his vendetta against Amadu Sheku remained desirable.

While Lamine may have been moved by principle and ambition, his followers were motivated by other factors. Suffering under French domination, many saw the *jihād* as a means of escaping the forced labor requisitions and the attendant disruption of the social order. Under Muslim rule in Gamon, they would have an opportunity to renew their communities and way of life. This hope would be particularly true of disaffected Bundunkobe, who were fed up with both the Fulbe and the French. For the Soninke, the call to *jihād* was in many ways an invitation to self-determination.

Between July and December of 1885, Mamadu Lamine began promoting his vision of a new Muslim empire by sending letters throughout Senegambia calling for *jihād* against Gamon.[19] He was well-received by Sambala of Khasso, who was either unaware of or unthreatened by the cleric's plans.[20] Mamadu Lamine also contacted the French. In August, he wrote a letter to the Governor, expressing an interest in establishing cordial relations:

> I have the honor of bringing to your attention that I have arrived from a pilgrimage to Mecca, after an absence from my native land of thirty-six years ...
> I am the friend of the French and will only follow their orders wherever I am.
> I come therefore to ask you in good faith, M. Governor, to allow me to pursue my activities in integrity and in wisdom, and to teach all of my people who will be under my authority to walk in the same path.[21]

The following month, Mamadu Lamine reiterated his peaceful intentions toward the French:

> The infidels are very numerous. I am not even able to make war against them all, all the more reason to make war against the French [*sic*, should be: *not* to make war ...], because they are able to improve my situation; for the powder,

the balls, the firearms, and munitions of war, as well as the paper, are all French articles, which we are only able to obtain from you and with your approval; because of that, it is necessary to be in peace.[22]

Nyambarza argues that Mamadu Lamine really desired friendship with Saint Louis.[23] In contrast, Bathily maintains that, based upon his volatile personality and the fact that he was already stockpiling arms, Mamadu Lamine was only engaging in "dissimulation" with the French, that he was only deceiving them into believing he wanted peaceful relations.[24] Rançon also maintains that the reformer was involved in subterfuge, based upon Frey's contention that the Soninke would not follow him if he had a hostile relationship with Saint Louis.[25] In other words, Mamadu Lamine was deceiving both the French and his own followers. However, the logic of the situation would suggest that Mamadu Lamine did not desire a confrontation with the French. Instead, he sought to exploit a good relationship with Saint Louis to achieve his objective. It was his hope that he could realize the latter without antagonizing the former. In the end, he could not.

While articulating the need for the Gamon *jihād*, Lamine also probed the French on the question of attacking Segu.[26] In November of 1885, Colonel Frey went to Kayes and met with Mamadu Lamine, who proposed that the French join him in his plan to defeat Amadu Sheku.[27] Frey refused. The cleric then asked permission to go through Guidimakha and Guey; Frey approved as long as Lamine did not take a large entourage with him. Sambala was present, and vouched for the cleric's sincerity.[28] At this point, Mamadu Lamine began exhorting the various Muslim communities to join him in his *jihād* against the unbelievers. According to Frey, he actually sought to stir up sentiment against the French; the Soninke in particular became extremely hostile, and refused to even help transport the French correspondence.[29] However, Frey's official position makes his contention dubious. At the same time, given the forced labor requisitions of the French, Soninke resentment towards them would be neither surprising nor contingent upon Mamadu Lamine's agitation.[30]

Around the beginning of December, Mamadu Lamine paid a visit to Dramane, near Makhana, a town known for its religious zeal.[31] From there he visited Bakel, continuing to proclaim his loyalty to the French. As evidence of his good faith, he left his family and slaves behind in Goundiourou, something he had agreed to do in his talks with Frey in November.[32] Since Goundiourou was between Kayes and Medine, it was relatively helpless and subject to reprisal if Mamadu Lamine reneged on his agreement with Frey. From Bakel he went to Balou, near the mouth of the Faleme, and from there invited Bundu's participation in the *jihād* against Gamon.[33]

War against the Sissibe

When Mamadu Lamine re-entered Senegambia in 1885, the French were not terribly concerned about what his return might mean. They were busy with

Lat Dior, Abdul Bokar Kan, Amadu Sheku in Nioro, and the emergence of the Malinke under Samori. Mamadu Lamine's activities in Goundiourou had caused some discomfort, hence Frey's visit to Kayes; but his continued pledges of loyalty went a long way to disarm the French. They watched his activities at Balou with interest, not alarm.

From Balou, Mamadu Lamine wrote to Bokar Saada, asking him to join in the *jihād* against Gamon.[34] Since Bundu had recently been defeated by Gamon, it was possible that the Bundunke ruler would seize another opportunity to take the village. Instead, the old, sickly *Almaami* refused either to participate in such a venture, or to allow Mamadu Lamine to cross Bundunke territory en route to Tenda. His reason for the denial was that he only marched with "the friends of France."[35] However, the unstated reasons for Bokar Saada's denial included his fear of a potentially hostile theocracy on his southern border, and his apprehension of Lamine's appeal to the disgruntled within Bundu. Neither was he interested in Bundu's incorporation into a larger political arrangement; he had opposed Bundu's subordination under *al-ḥājj* Umar, and was no more disposed towards the idea now than he was then. Finally, Bokar Saada did not exactly relish the thought of a possible impediment to his relatively free access to the trade and spoils of the Gambia.

In the course of a developing situation in which Lamine's forces were massing at Balou, Bokar Saada died, just fifteen days after the cleric's original request to cross Bundu.[36] Suddenly, the executive office of the most strategically placed power in the upper valley was vacant. At this point, Bundu was very vulnerable, and Lamine understood this. He knew that the Bundunkobe were extremely dissatisfied with Sissibe rule. He also anticipated a succession struggle, as Umar Penda was sickly and nearly blind, while Usuman Gassi had every intention of becoming *Almaami*, having inherited his father's wealth and influence.[37] Umar Penda, in contrast, did not inspire confidence, and "was without authority over his subjects." He remained at Boulebane, where he had become a recluse some time prior to Bokar Saada's death. In short, Bundu was fully enveloped by the crisis, and the cleric was well aware of it.

It is difficult to believe, then, that the thought of shifting his focus from Gamon to Bundu did not enter Lamine's mind with Bokar Saada's death. Given Bundu's problems, it probably would have been easier to defeat the Sissibe than to have taken on Gamon. However, it is not at all clear that the cleric changed his original objective at this time. Besides, he did not want to engender a conflict with the French, a likely consequence of such an alteration in plans. Therefore, it is more probable than not that he resisted the temptation to seize Bundu at this point.

While Mamadu Lamine was sensitive to the difficulties that could ensue if he crossed into Bundu without authorization, he had another problem: his burgeoning forces at Balou. He therefore requested permission from Umar Penda to enter Bundu as soon as Penda was named *Almaami*.[38] The latter declined, as he was under instructions from the French.[39] He really had little choice except to depend on the French for help and direction, as Usuman Gassi, the real power in Bundu, was refusing to cooperate with the new ruler.[40]

Mamadu Lamine, with his forces growing in number, enthusiasm, and restlessness, also began to grow impatient. He again implored Penda for permission to enter Bundu, and appealed to their common religion, insisting that his intention was to wage *jihād* against Gamon.[41] Meanwhile, the camp of the cleric continued to swell with the Soninke and other Mande-speakers from Bambuk, Khasso, Kamera, and Bundu.[42] He also drew support from the young and idealistic, and from those who had been conscripted into the involuntary labor details of the French: laborers, soldiers, those who handled watercraft, etc.[43] All of the foregoing were joined to the core of his support, his *ṭālibs* or original circle of followers.[44]

In addition to the Soninke populations, Mamadu Lamine also recruited from the Jakhanke, somewhat surprising in view of their pacifist ideology. In fact, it would appear that he received significant Jakhanke support, an indication of their disapproval of the policies of Bokar Saada. However, the Jakhanke, while distancing themselves from Bokar Saada, still valued their extensive and historical ties to the Sissibe family. When it became clear to them that Lamine intended to wage war against the Sissibe as a whole, and to create a new political order in Bundu, they withdrew their prayers, sustenance, and token military support from the cleric. The consequences of the Jakhanke's decision would be disastrous for them, as will be subsequently explained.[45]

With Mamadu Lamine's forces steadily growing at Balou, Umar Penda decided to move from Boulebane to Gabou, where he would be closer to Bakel. Upon receiving his final denial from the *Almaami*, Mamadu Lamine felt he could no longer wait, and announced that he was going up the Faleme River to Senoudebou, where he would visit Bokar Saada's grave.[46] However, he insisted that Gamon remained his objective, not Bundu.

Hrbek has forwarded the very plausible suggestion that Usuman Gassi may have given the cleric permission to enter Bundu, hoping that the probable conflict between Lamine and Umar Penda would topple the *Almaami*, and thus leave Usuman Gassi in charge of all Bundu.[47] Indeed, Rançon does record that after entering Bundu, Mamadu Lamine sent two envoys to Usuman Gassi at Diamwali (between Senoudebou and Boulebane).[48] Usuman Gassi refused to receive the envoys, but he kept the horses. It is not clear whether the horses were gifts, or simply confiscated. The context does reveal, however, that Usuman Gassi was not with Umar Penda during this moment of crisis, and that he did nothing to impede the cleric's progress into Bundu. Indirect evidence would therefore support Hrbek's proposal, but this cannot be confirmed.

From Balou, Mamadu Lamine went to Allahina, then on to Senoudebou. He did not try to enter the fort, but proceeded to Debou and camped there.[49]

He remained only one day, before he headed north back to Diamwali. There is some evidence that he was invited to Diamwali by Usuman Gassi for the purpose of agreeing to a treaty.[50] Whether Usuman Gassi called for this meeting or not, it is clear that Mamadu Lamine was interested in negotiations, possibly to persuade the Sissibe to join the *jihād*, or, to effect a post-victory alliance. This speculation is consistent with the cleric's treatment of Senoudebou. The town had fully expected an assault; the cleric's about-face to Diamwali suggests that he wanted to avoid a confrontation with Umar Penda. Rançon's contention that the reformer planned to convene the Sissibe in order to assassinate them is unlikely.[51]

When Mamadu Lamine arrived at Diamwali, he sent word to Umar Penda. The *Almaami*, frightened and convinced that conflict was inevitable, personally led a troop of men against the cleric.[52] By Rançon's own admission, Umar Penda fired the first shot.[53] His troops were quickly overwhelmed by the Soninke, forcing him to retreat to Boulebane. He left his son Bokar Umar (or Boubakar Saada) to fend for himself with a company of thirty men; twenty of that party perished, and Bokar Umar was made a captive. The next day, Diamwali was pillaged and burned. Usuman Gassi had apparently escaped unnoticed, perhaps before the cleric's army had even arrived.[54] Umar Penda, after leaving Boulebane under the care of a small force, went to Bakel to request aid. Bakel was unable, however, to accomodate its ally; most of the French forces were in the Upper Niger fighting Samori.[55] It is also possible that the French were not convinced that Lamine threatened their interests at this time. The *Almaami* hastened to Futa Damga, and appealed to Abdul Bokar Kan for help, but the grand elector was unable to oblige.

Umar Penda's attack on Mamadu Lamine, after the latter had sought a diplomatic exchange, greatly facilitated the shift in the cleric's focus from Gamon to Bundu. This change in strategy is evidenced by Lamine's subsequent activities, and represents a fateful decision on his part. The choice to remain in Bundu and fight the Sissibe would ultimately lead to war with the French. However, such a fate must have appeared avoidable at the time.

While Umar Penda was away trying to procure additional men and arms, the cleric appeared before Boulebane at the head of three columns. Abdul Amadi Gai, a Sy "prince," was in charge of defending the capital, as Umar Penda's wives and daughters were still there. The small garrison was able to hold off the assault for a brief time, but was short of ammunition, firearms, and men. Among the twenty-five Bundunkobe who perished behind the walls, three were members of the Sy family. Although most of the residents were able to escape, all of the surviving Sissibe, their royal slaves, and their court officials were taken captive. Only Abdul Amadi Gai managed to elude the cleric, thanks to a few sympathetic Soninke who feared he would be executed.

Following these two victories, the ranks of the cleric swelled with Soninke volunteers, and further encouraged him to continue on in Bundu.[56] Mamadu Lamine remained in Boulebane for four days.[57] On the fifth day, his forces marched on Senoudebou, the seat of the late Bokar Saada's power. To his surprise, the cleric entered a deserted town.[58] Upon learning of the twin debacles of Diamwali and Boulebane, the population of Senoudebou had quickly dispersed to all points on the map. Included in this group was Bokar Saada's widow, Lallya, the daughter of Sambala, who returned to Khasso.[59] Usuman Gassi, from wherever he had disappeared, arrived in Bakel and asked for asylum. If he had anticipated a mutually destructive conflict between Umar Penda and Mamadu Lamine, from which he would benefit, he now realized that his projections had gone awry, and that Mamadu Lamine had emerged as the preeminent power in Bundu. Of the multi-faceted Bundunke army, with its fabled cavalry and fearsome reputation, none remained to face the cleric.

Mamadu Lamine occupied Senoudebou for no less than three weeks; Frey states he was proclaimed "king" of Bundu, and announced that he was the "Mahdi of the west."[60] Whatever else the cleric might accomplish, the taking of Senoudebou was his crowning achievement. The amount of support following the victories over Diamwali and Boulebane grew with the cleric's third and most resounding accomplishment. Joining the cleric, in addition to those from Khasso, Guidimakha, and Gajaaga, were recruits from Niani, Niocolo and Bambuk, who had also suffered under Bokar Saada.[61] The Soninke of Gajaaga were given permission to take over villages in northern Bundu (Leze-Bundu and Leze-Maio). They soon entered western Bundu (Ferlo Baliniama and Ferlo M'Bal), extending the cleric's control all the way to N'Dia and Wuro-Kaba (the westernmost reaches of Bundu). Mamadu Lamine showed himself politically astute, and offered his friendship and amnesty to the remaining Bundunke villages. He even sent to Umar Penda, asking him and all the "chiefs of the land" to come to Senoudebou and talk with him.[62] However, the *Almaami* responded negatively. By 15 February 1886, the forces of the Soninke leader had taken control of most of Bundu, including villages neighboring Bakel.[63] In just two weeks, he had become the new master of Bundu, and had assembled some 6,000 to 7,000 armed men at Senoudebou.[64]

As with any social movement, it would be erroneous to suggest that Mamadu Lamine enjoyed unanimous support among the Soninke. Not even *al-ḥājj* Umar, who probably had the largest popular following in Senegambia's history, met with universal approval; indeed, even he resorted to forcibly moving the reticent into his camp. Mamadu Lamine was no different. Those villages which resisted his advances were incinerated; the village heads were killed, the women and children taken captive, and the men sometimes forced to serve in the army.[65]

Pragmatism in the age of Jihad

Engaging the French

In an attempt to consolidate his authority over Bundu, Mamadu Lamine made the tactical decision of attacking Borde village, near Bakel, where Usuman Gassi had taken refuge.[66] The operation was risky due to Borde's proximity to Bakel and the French. However, Lamine gambled that the French would not interpret the attack as a move against them. After all, the cleric's family remained at Goundiourou. Hence, the cleric sent an unsuccessful expedition against Borde in March of 1886. Following the failure to dislodge Usuman Gassi, the cleric ordered his men to remove to Kounguel.

Unfortunately for Mamadu Lamine, the Borde assault was indeed interpreted by the French as an attack on Bakel and French interests. The French had chosen to avoid involvement up to this point, but the Borde affair was unnerving. Lamine had all along claimed that Gamon was his goal, but he was actually concentrating on targets in the opposite direction. The French determined that they could no longer afford to remain idle.

On 14 March, the French took two actions against the cleric. First, they sent a troop of Senegalese Riflemen against the cleric's men at Kounguel. Although the latter were victorious, the attack clearly signaled that Lamine was now considered an enemy of France.[67] Secondly, the French seized the cleric's wives, children, and slaves in Goundiourou.[68] They were all transported to Medine and kept under house arrest. That they had remained at Goundiourou until this late date demonstrates that Mamadu Lamine did not desire a conflict with the French, even after entering Bundunke territory.

Mamadu Lamine was stung by the swift and coordinated attack on Goundiourou and seizure of his family. Perhaps without considering the full implications of his actions, he responded angrily by striking at the very heart of French power in the upper valley: Bakel itself. By 1886, Bakel consisted of the French fort, the village itself, and several other villages all clustered together.[69] There were some 4,000 refugees in Bakel at that time, including the Bundunke royal family. At least 250 soldiers were defending the position; Colonel Frey, whose official designation was "Commandant Supérieur de Haut-Sénégal," had sent reinforcements to Bakel as early as February.[70] By attacking Bakel, the cleric committed himself to a struggle that he had consistently sought to avoid.

Mamadu Lamine began the Bakel assault on 1 April, personally commanding some 10,000 to 12,000 men (a possible exaggeration).[71] For the next four days, the reformer's forces attacked, only to be repulsed. Following their failure to storm the fort, the Soninke army attempted a siege, but the effort was largely finished by 12 April.[72] For all practical purposes, the inability to take Bakel was the turning point in this war, though it would drag on for two more years. The fact that some of the surrounding villages were torched, that casualties were inflicted, and that the cleric's men desecrated the European cemetery were small consolations indeed.[73]

Frey lost no time in taking the offensive, and marched into Kamera and

Guidimakha to punish those communities which had aided the cleric. This strategy was adopted because the Colonel was not yet in a position to attack Mamadu Lamine directly; he could not afford to remove the column at Kayes.[74] Attacking villages in Guidimakha would be less risky because of the proximity to Kayes, and it would also cause the cleric's men to abandon the army in order to help in the recovery of their home villages. Bangassi, Samankidy, Salancounda, Gagny, Bokhoro, Goumbe, Guemou-Bambella, Manahel, and Diougountouron were all taken by 30 April, and a small garrison left at each village. On 19 April, Mamadu Lamine attacked the French column at Tamboucane, but was thoroughly defeated.[75]

Retreat to the south

In view of his sudden reversal, Mamadu Lamine retreated to the south, where he would attempt to reorganize his followers and establish a network of Muslim and Soninke support throughout the upper valley. By moving to the southern extremes of Diakha, and consequently just beyond the limits of Bundu's control of the area, Lamine was in effect conceding northern Bundu to the French. However, there was strong anti-Sissibe sentiment in southern Bundu, so that Lamine retained his control over this area. He reasoned that an accommodation with the French was still possible, and that a good military showing might persuade the French to grant him authority over at least a portion of southern Bundu. However, the French were unwilling, and continued to push for the cleric's total annihilation.

While Lamine regrouped in Diakha, the Sissibe, rescued from certain destruction by the French, were able to regain their composure and contribute to the struggle against the cleric. Usuman Gassi was ordered to pursue the cleric, with 400 cavalry under his command. By 25 April, Gassi reached Senoudebou, only to find that the cleric had burned it to the ground in his retreat.[76] Umar Penda, commanding a force of 300 cavalry, also pursued the cleric, but was unable to catch up with him before he entered Diakha.[77] Perhaps neither was fully prepared to engage Mamadu Lamine at this time.

The month of May saw the French in an effort to pacify the upper valley.[78] During this period the three most important villages of western Guidimakha, which had been among the first to support the cleric, were subdued.[79] Guey and Kamera were also brought under control. *Almaami* Umar Penda, meanwhile, had received a large contingent of Futanke soldiers from Abdul Bokar Kan. Numbering around 2,000 now, the Bundunke loyalists set out to reclaim Bundu, attacking villages which had turned against the Sissibe.[80] The forces of the cleric fought back, however, and sent expeditions from Diakha against Dalafine and Goulongo (both in Tiali), Nionsonko, and Sansanding, pillaging and burning all four.[81] Mamadu Lamine continued to wield considerable influence over most of the realm's southern portion. Frey commented: "The great fatigue of the troops did not allow me to pursue the cleric into Diakha, ... "[82] Neither did Mamadu Abdul, Abdul Bokar Kan's son and commander of the Futanke forces, feel comfortable about going into Diakha, more or less unified in its support of Mamadu Lamine.[83]

Lamine established himself at the town of Dianna, in Diakha.[84] From there he maintained contact with the various Soninke communities.[85] He continued to exhort the populations of Guidimakha and Gajaaga to remain faithful:

> In the name of God ... Oh! resident of Gajaaga and Guidimakha, ... unite completely under the true religion, that is to say, the one of the beneficient God, unite as well in order to make war against the Christians. Note well that the Christians are mothers of lies and demons. Oh! residents of Gajaaga and Guidimakha; I swear to you by God [that] if you do not unite to make war against the Christians, you will never have proper religion in our times, that is, the one [religion] of God. The religion of Christians is the one of *satan*, know that *satan* is your enemy, ...[86]

Several insignificant skirmishes took place between the Sissibe and the forces of Lamine until July, when the cleric sent 1,500 men into Bundu.[87] Umar Penda, believing that Lamine's forces would take the usual route and pass near Boulebane, sent all of the troops with him to intercept Lamine from the ancient capital. Blind and ailing, the *Almaami* remained at Fissa-Daro with the women and children. The cleric's forces, however, took an alternate route, passing between Koussan and Boggal, and came upon a defenseless Fissa-Daro. Umar Penda was killed, his body mutilated and decapitated, and his family and slaves taken captive.[88] Usuman Gassi, consistent with his previous pattern, arrived too late to prevent the *Almaami*'s death. Umar Penda had reigned only seven months.[89] He was survived by six sons: Bokar Umar, Usuman Umar, Tumane, Cire Bokar, Sega Umar, and Musa Yero.[90]

Saada Amadi, the son of Amadi Saada who had led the Boulebane branch for a short period during the wars of *al-ḥājj* Umar, succeeded Umar Penda as *Almaami* of Bundu.[91] He was the legal heir, and was grudgingly recognized by the Sissibe and the French, even though he had exhibited little interest in fighting for Bundu's security.[92] When word spread that Umar Penda had been killed, many Bundunkobe began emigrating to the Ferlo area beyond Bundu's southwestern border. Saada Amadi was able to send his nephew Amadi Cire against Dalafine in Tiali, a stronghold for the followers of the cleric. The village was defeated, with significant loss of life and freedom.

In response to the loss at Dalafine, Mamadu Lamine personally led a force of 2,000 into Bundu to retake Senoudebou. The cleric attempted to capture the crumbling fort by stealth, but a heavy rain on the night preceding the attack forced his men to create fires in order to dry their munitions. The fires lit up the night sky, and the jihadists lost the element of surprise. On 23 September 1886, the cleric proceeded to launch an all-out assault on the fort. His forces walked into a cross-fire under the direction of the Bundunke *Tirailleur* Yoro Kumba, and were forced to beat a retreat.

According to French estimates, Mamadu Lamine lost at least 170 men through death, and another 150 to 200 through capture.[93] Only the heavy rains prevented the Bundunkobe from inflicting greater losses.

The cleric retreated in haste to Dianna, his men gradually returning in groups of eight to ten. The major losses were beginning to accumulate; first Bakel, then Dalafine, now Senoudebou. The clerical camp began to diminish, and Lamine faced the considerable challenge of convincing his remaining adherents that matters were under control. In particular, his early support among the Jakhanke had largely dissipated in view of the fact that not only was he at war with the Sissibe, the Jakhanke's long-time allies, but he was now suffering successive defeats at the hands of the French. Lamine responded to the Jakhanke about-face by attacking their villages in Bundu, which resulted in significant Jakhanke emigration from Bundu towards the Gambia. In fact, the Jakhanke community in Bundu never recovered from the overall effects of this war, and would remain dispersed throughout Senegambia.[94]

The correspondence emanating from both Mamadu Lamine and the French is quite illuminating in that it reveals a full-scale propaganda war being waged by both sides for the allegiance of the people. For example, on 24 September the day after his defeat at Senoudebou, the cleric sent a letter to the Governor, suing for peace between his forces and the French.[95] He repeated that he never wanted a war with the French, that the whole affair began with Umar Penda's refusal to permit his followers to cross Bundu. It was the *Almaami* who fired first, ignoring the cleric's demonstrations of peaceful intentions. He went on to say that it was the French who made a belligerent move by seizing his family, and attacking his forces at Kounguel. He then added:

> I make known to you, to your governor, ... and I swear to you two times before God, that I never wanted to fight with you, for I would like to live in peace with the French ... Know that I have many enemies, other than the French. The infidels are very numerous ...
> How would I be able to declare war, I who know all that [that the French supply necessary goods] and understand it well. No! No! This is that which God has decided between us:
> I have forgotten all that which you have done to me ... Accept and forget also; this is what I fervently ask and it is my great desire. If I am able to receive that from God and from you, I will give thanks to God.[96]

Earlier in 1886, Colonel Gallieni had taken over from Frey as Commandant Supérieur. He had three objectives in mind: to destroy Mamadu Lamine, to establish good relations with Amadu Sheku to Saint Louis' advantage, and to drive Samori from the Upper Niger.[97] With the latest attack at Senoudebou, Gallieni could not afford to allow Mamadu Lamine to simply recover at Dianna, as Frey had done. He ordered one Lieutenant Bonacorsi to go to Bundu in October, and to determine the cleric's level of popular support.[98] He was also to find out if *Almaami* Saada Amadi was capable of leading

Bundu. The Commandant Supérieur then launched his own campaign of intimidation, sending a circular to the communities of the Upper Faleme, along with those in Wuli, Tenda, and even Dianna:

> An evil man, an impostor, a liar, a man who seeks to enrich himself at your expense, came into your lands to ask for forces to combat the French. Some of you had the weakness to follow him, and you know what has happened. As soon as they were before the French, they were killed or forced to flee.
>
> If you are reasonable, listen to my advice. This is what I say to you. Chase far from you Mamadu Lamine, refuse to give him access to your country and the cooperation of your arms.
>
> If you do not do that, if you continue to help Mamadu Lamine, there will be great unhappiness, the columns of my soldiers will come to find him in your land, and then there will be disaster for all.[99]

Besides Lamine, the French were also unhappy with Saada Amadi, and looked more and more to Usuman Gassi. They viewed Saada Amadi as lacking the will to prosecute the war. "With uncaring attitude and without authority, he allowed the partition of Bundu into a series of appanages, where each of the Sissibe princes, operating on a small scale, continued the traditions of Bu Bakar Sada."[100] That is to say, the oppressive tactics of the late *Almaami* were continued by the "princes." At the same time, what Saada Amadi did not rule, the other Sissibe controlled. When Gallieni met Saada Amadi in December of 1886, he described him as "a sovereign without a kingdom."[101] He had about fifty cavalry with him, and a number of untrained, inexperienced "civilians" who were likely to disrupt the discipline of the *Tirailleurs*.[102] The *Almaami* controlled only Senoudebou, and was apparently not very enthusiastic about extending his authority. It must be remembered, however, that this was the same Saada Amadi who abandoned Bokar Saada in 1866 in protest against his fiscal oppression. It is therefore possible that, rather than simply being lethargic by nature, Saada Amadi understood only too well the basis for Mamadu Lamine's popular following.

At the same time that Gallieni was writing his circulars, he came to Arondou and began preparing to march on Dianna. Since Mamadu Lamine was being furnished with volunteers from both sides of the Faleme, the Lieutenant-Colonel decided to form two columns. He would lead the first column from Arondou.[103] The second column, under Captain Vallière, was to proceed southwest from Diamou, located fifty-four kilometers east of Kayes, the actual terminal point for the Upper Senegal railroad.[104] The two columns, totalling 975 men, began marching on 12 December, with Gallieni stopping at Senoudebou.[105] He took the opportunity to persuade the *Almaami* to place Bundu under the exclusive protectorate of France.[106] He then placed the Bundunke contingent under the command of one Guerrin.[107] Usuman Gassi also marched with the French forces.

By the end of 1886, after a series of skirmishes which forced Mamadu Lamine's steady retreat, the cleric was finished in Bundu. The Soninke communities which remained, including those in Diakha, had all submitted to French authority.[108] Bambuk was also under their control, and negotiations were opened with Wuli, Tenda, Badon, Niocolo, and the communities bordering the Faleme. "Bundu, with all of its dependences being returned to their old masters, became from then on the docile subjects of the authority of the French."[109] As for Usuman Gassi, he was nominated for, and later received in 1888, the cross of the French Legion of Honor, in recognition of his military leadership against Mamadu Lamine.[110]

Toubacouta

Having escaped to Wuli, Mamadu Lamine eventually found refuge in nearby Toubacouta. Founded in 1869, this village had a history of conflicts with the Sissibe of Bundu.[111] It was therefore disposed to receive the beleaguered cleric. According to Rançon, the town quickly became the headquarters of marginal elements from the neighboring states of Niani, Sandugu, Salum, and other sections of the Gambia Valley. While at Toubacouta, Mamadu Lamine experienced great success in reconstructing his army. Apparently the Malinke population of the Gambia, especially those of Niani, were as receptive to the cleric's message as were the Soninke of the Upper Senegal. In the course of a few months, the cleric's strength had grown to an estimated 4,000 to 5,000 men, a possible exaggeration to justify the French pursuit of a man who was clearly finished in Bundu.[112]

During this lull before the final storm, northern and central Bundu were described as peaceful, with most of the population involved in cultivation.[113] They were also depicted as evincing little interest in taking up the war with Mamadu Lamine. The ravages of the preceding year, followed by yet another famine, and aggravated by unchecked raiding on the part of the people of Gamon, were debilitating to say the least.[114]

On 28 November 1887, the French forces departed for Toubacouta from Bani Israila, having passed the previous seven months at the ancient site.[115] The *Tirailleurs* totaled 250 men, of which there was a "Torodo" contingent of 120, a unit from Wuli of 200, and auxiliaries from Fouladougou numbering 2,000.[116] Bundu could only muster 300 infantry and thirty cavalry, the latter led by Usuman Gassi. The French estimated that Mamadu Lamine's 4,000 man force was composed of the following groups: 700 Soninke, who represented the remainder of his earliest following; 800 residents of Toubacouta; 200 Wolof from Salum; 300 led by Mamadu Fatuma, an ally of the cleric and characterized by Rançon as a "rogue"; and 2,000 supplied by Niani.[117]

On 8 December the French finally reached Toubacouta. The attack began at seven in the morning, and Usuman Gassi once again distinguished himself on the field of battle. Toubacouta was destroyed; many lost their lives.[118] Among the casualties were some of the key figures in Mamadu Lamine's inner circle, including Amadi Bure, his *qāḍī*; Sura Kate Jawara, his advisor, and the *ṭālibs* who had been with him since Bakel. As for the

French forces, all fifty casualties were from among the Bundu and Wuli soldiers.[119] No European casualties were reported; three or four *Tirailleurs* were wounded.

Although Mamadu Lamine escaped the Toubacouta debacle, his following had been irreversibly dismembered. Pursued by the ruler of Fouladougou and Bundunke soldiers, the cleric made his way west along the Gambia until he reached the tiny village of N'Goga-Soukota, two or three kilometers south of the river.[120] No sooner did he reach the sanctuary than the Fouladougou–Bundu forces surrounded him. He was fatally wounded, and expired before he could be brought to the French camp. The hour of his death occurred sometime between 9 and 11 December.[121] The *griot* of Fouladougou's ruler decapitated the body, satisfied with bringing the grisly trophy back to the French camp.[122]

Commentary

Mamadu Lamine and *al-ḥājj* Umar are more similar than not in that they were both driven by ambition and operated out of a vision to establish theocratic empires. Notwithstanding their appeals to a universal religion, both men had followings which were dominated by particular ethnic groups: the Fulbe under Umar, and the Soninke under Mamadu Lamine. Likewise, as Umar began his *jihād* from Futa Jallon against nearby Tamba, so Mamadu Lamine identified non-Muslim Gamon as the initial target of his campaign. However, the plans of the clerics diverge after this point. Umar would go on to concentrate his efforts in the "pagan" east, and transported his vision of Muslim domination to the Upper Niger. In contrast, Mamadu Lamine sought to create a confederation or empire in his native Upper Senegal. To a large extent, Umar's decision to focus on the east was determined by the French conquest of the Upper Senegal; the *Shaykh* had the option of going elsewhere. By the time of Mamadu Lamine's activities, however, he had very few options: the French were in the Upper Senegal, and the Umarians in the Upper Niger. His more accommodating posture towards the French, therefore, was chiefly informed by the political realities in which he found himself. Even so, it must be recalled that Umar also sought some degree of accommodation with the French before their struggle for the Upper Senegal.

While both leaders were motivated by religious ideals and personal agendas, this was not necessarily the case for their constituencies. In particular, the followers of Mamadu Lamine were reacting to the expansion of French military and economic control in the Upper Senegal, as evidenced by military conscription, involuntary labor, and the intensification of agricultural slavery. They were also responding to Sissibe domination; they were therefore not so much agitating for a new theocracy as they were fighting against the status quo. In this way, Mamadu Lamine was the beneficiary of factors which he himself did not help to create. In contrast, *al-ḥājj* Umar's

Mamadu Lamine and the demise of Bundu

following was largely composed of those inspired by his vision, who were not necessarily distruntled over socioeconomic conditions in the Middle and Upper Senegal. To the extent that this is true is testimony to the extraordinary abilities of the *Shaykh*.

Finally, both Umar and Mamadu Lamine fought the French, but the former did so on a much larger scale, for a longer period of time, and with much more resolve. During the period of the struggle for the Upper Senegal, the Umarians were quite earnest in their bid to drive the French out. In contrast, Mamadu Lamine, with the exception of his initial attack on Bakel, was forever on the defensive, and fought reluctantly. While he engaged the French, it was not out of a clear conviction that the European presence had to be expunged. The view of him as an anticolonial figure is therefore not altogether justified.

Though the duration of his activities was brief, Mamadu Lamine's accomplishments were impressive. In less than two months, he had defeated the preeminent power of the region. But his "success" in Bundu can be directly attributed to the destructive policies of Bokar Saada. In the midst of an economic crunch, the *Almaami* had resorted to exorbitant taxation of his subjects. Trying to minimize the political fallout of his measures, the Soninke were selected to carry a disproportionate share of the burden. Bundu unraveled into its constituent ethnicities, to all of which Mamadu Lamine appealed. But the deep and unique despair of the Soninke community in particular, along with the fractured loyalties of the Sissibe, were both functions of Bokar Saada's policies, and suffice to explain Bundu's rapid submission to Mamadu Lamine.

The "French Almaami"

With the defeat of Mamadu Lamine at the close of 1887, the French decided to end once and for all any threat to its continued domination of Senegal. By the latter part of 1888, most of western Senegal was under their control, with the exception of Jolof.[123] It fell two years later, with the help of Bundunke forces among others. From 1890 to 1893, the new Commandant Supérieur, Louis Archinard, defeated Amadu Sheku and the east. That old nemesis Abdul Bokar Kan was assassinated in 1891, leaving the French as the uncontested rulers of all Futa Toro. It should be remembered that both Abdul Bokar Kan and, to a lesser extent, Amadu Sheku had been supportive of the French in their efforts to overcome Mamadu Lamine. Given the overall French thrust since Faidherbe, no independent power could have survived.

As far as Bundu was concerned, the French began to control the succession by selecting and placing into power their own candidates from among the Sissibe contestants. There was no need to send the *Tirailleurs* to gain control of the area; the French were already in command, and now assumed the authority to dictate the terms of the *almaamate*. In a move that presaged subsequent events in Futa Damga and Segu, the French removed the Bundunke ruler in 1888. Having backed Usuman Gassi all along, they had been disturbed about *Almaami* Saada Amadi's lackluster performance in the struggle with Mamadu Lamine. Therefore Gallieni, at that time still the Commandant Supérieur, deposed Saada Amadi in May of 1888. He was replaced by Usuman Gassi.[124]

Usuman Gassi (1888–91) was not a passive participant in his own ascension. He was one of the first to malign the conduct of Saada Amadi during the last war, and his charges were the most serious.[125] Already suspicious of Saada Amadi, the French installed Usuman Gassi in Senoudebou. Saada Amadi, fearing for his life, fled to Futa Damga and took refuge with Abdul Bokar Kan.[126] From his asylum in Futa Damga, Saada Amadi wrote to the Commandant of Bakel, protesting his ouster.[127]

The selection of Usuman Gassi was not well-received in Bundu; at least three groups opposed him, differentiated on the basis of their distinct grievances. One group was simply opposed to the French intervening in Bundunke affairs, and continued to pay taxes to Saada Amadi in Futa Damga.[128] A second, more numerous faction was against Usuman Gassi because of Usuman Gassi, not because of their reverence for Bundunke succession law. For them, the new *Almaami* represented life under Bokar Saada; Usuman Gassi had been one of the principal vehicles, if not an architect, through which Bokar Saada carried out his policies. The military prowess he displayed in fighting Mamadu Lamine was derivative of his activities under his father, so that his rise was ominous.

A third group consisted primarily of Sissibe. Their opposition to Usuman Gassi is most revealing. The basic problem was not Saada Amadi's ouster. Rather, the installation of Usuman Gassi disrupted the succession process that *followed* Saada Amadi. There were four Sy "princes" who were ahead of Usuman Gassi, in the following order: Amadi Cire, a nephew of Bokar Saada; Saada Bokar, Bokar Saada's son; Amadi Usuman, another nephew of Bokar Saada; and Umar Sane, Amadi Usuman's brother.[129] Amadi Cire and Saada Bokar resided at Senoudebou, while Amadi Usuman and Umar Sane lived in Boulebane. The key to understanding the nature of the third group's resistance is the fact that they all declared for Amadi Cire, not the deposed Saada Amadi.[130]

The French responded to this potential difficulty by sending two separate missions to Bundu in order to emphasize Saint Louis' support of Usuman Gassi. Dorr went to Senoudebou in 1888, and reported that the new *Almaami*'s brothers, courtiers, and notables all pledged their allegiance to the French candidate.[131] However, the resistance continued to manifest itself, and in the spring of 1889, Briquelot was sent to Bundu by Archinard to affirm the French position.[132] He was instructed to visit all the important villages, where he was to assemble the leaders and make it clear that Usuman Gassi was the only *Almaami* recognized by the French. Anyone who did not pledge to Usuman Gassi would be an enemy of France. In a report filed in

May, Briquelot related that he had been successful in persuading Amadi Usuman and Malik Ture (who followed Usuman Gassi in the order of succession) to acknowledge the new *Almaami*.[133]

That Briquelot was only able to influence two principals indicates the depth of resentment towards the French nomination. However, the resentment was of a quality that did not require a military solution. In the face of this passive resistance (by ignoring the ruler's imperatives and refusing to pay taxes), Usuman Gassi showed himself an astute politician. "Usuman was eager to declare that if he was the Almamy for the French, Amady Cire will always be the true ruler of Bundu."[134] From 1888 to 1889, Amadi Cire was the effective ruler of Bundu, recognized by a majority of the popular as well as the ruling strata.[135] In response to Usuman Gassi's diplomacy, the Bundunke elite ceased to resist, for the most part, his claim to be the "French *Almaami*."[136]

Given the rapprochement between Usuman Gassi and Amadi Cire, the French turned their attention to Saada Amadi in Futa Damga. When Briquelot was in Bundu, his primary objective was to extinguish the fires caused by Saada Amadi's deposition. He was instructed to ignore any correspondence the ex-*Almaami* might send.[137] If the Bundunkobe brought up his ouster, Briquelot was to remind them of Saada Amadi's supposed cowardice in the wars against Mamadu Lamine. For his part, Saada Amadi continued to remonstrate. He repeatedly reminded the Bundunkobe of his forced exile, and of the illegality of Usuman Gassi's selection.[138] His agitation created concern; Saint Louis feared both the possibility of an internal uprising and the invasion of Bundu by Abdul Bokar Kan and Saada Amadi. To protect Usuman Gassi, the French sent a small company of soldiers to Senoudebou, who remained throughout 1888.[139] The Futanke grand elector was repeatedly warned not to intervene on behalf of Saada Amadi.[140] Archinard in fact reports that a Futanke invasion on behalf of Saada Amadi was under way in the spring of 1888, but that reinforcements from Kayes and Bambuk convinced Abdul Bokar Kan to recall the mission before any fighting actually occurred.[141] Saada Amadi remained in Futa Damga until Abdul Bokar Kan's death in 1891.[142]

French expectations concerning Usuman Gassi ran very high when he first took office. Having performed so valiantly against Mamadu Lamine, he was thought to be the ideal choice to lead Bundu into "prosperity." It was believed that he could offset the considerable influence and prestige of Abdul Bokar Kan; Archinard was convinced that he would defend Bundunke territory against any encroachment from Futa Damga with the utmost vigor. Archinard, in devising his grandiose schemes, envisioned a unitary Fulbe state. In referring to Futa Toro and Futa Jallon, the "father of French imperialism" observed that "these contingents are capable of being a great help to us once they are united under the control of a single chief, the Almamy of Bundu."[143] That is, the Commandant Supérieur intended to build his upper valley policies around the stable, reliable cornerstone that was Bundu.

Usuman Gassi proved to be a major disappointment to the French. "Surrounded by his wives and his griots, he became apathetic and absolutely incapable of energy."[144] Reflective of his primary concerns was his correspondence with the French, a substantial proportion of which discusses at length such matters as the death of his horse and the need for its replacement.[145] A disciple of Bokar Saada as well as a son, the *Almaami* soon reverted to the policies of his father: exorbitant taxation and the illegal confiscation of goods.[146] As a result, Bundu remained underpopulated, with even more emigratory activity towards Niani and Niocolo.

The highlight of his brief tenure was his voyage to Paris in 1889. Archinard planned the trip in order to acquaint the *Almaami* with "some ideas on the order of work and on organization."[147] According to Rançon, Usuman Gassi's visit caused a considerable stir among the Parisians, who were quite taken with his tall stature, exotic dress, and numerous entourage.[148] However, Roux reports that he went back to Bundu "without one new idea, happy to return to his cohort of griots, the privation of which had been very painful for him."[149] Archinard's vision of a single Fulbe entity under Bundu's hegemony would have to await another *Almaami*. He never materialized.

Usuman Gassi participated in Archinard's campaign against Nioro. In the course of this operation, the *Almaami* succumbed to a fever, and died 31 January 1891.[150] He was survived by a single son, Amadi Usuman, having reigned one year and eight months.[151]

At the death of Usuman Gassi, the French chose Malik Ture as *Almaami* (1891–1902), as he had been one of the few Sissibe who had supported the deceased ruler from the beginning. The decision, like that concerning Usuman Gassi, was ill-received. Malik Ture was sixth in the order of succession, behind Usuman Gassi.[152] As a consequence, the new *Almaami* was "abandoned" by the Sissibe and everyone else.[153] The opposition to Malik Ture was led by Amadi Cire and Amadi Usuman, who had led the resistance to Usuman Gassi.[154] This was the second time that the French had bypassed the legal process, the second time that these two had been overlooked. By this point in the history of Senegambia, however, it is clear that the last concern on the part of the French was the offending of indigenous sensibilities.

In addition to his problems with the Sissibe nobility, Malik Ture faced a potentially disastrous challenge from Saada Amadi. Abdul Bokar Kan's death in 1891 removed Saada Amadi's source of asylum; he returned to Bundu, where he was embraced by many Sissibe and the royal *awlube*.[155] He immediately began agitating for his own empowerment, emphasizing the illegality of Malik Ture's selection.[156] Roux, Commandant at Bakel at the time, finally put an end to the difficulty by arresting Saada Amadi in March of 1892. He remained confined at Bakel until January of 1893, when he was released. He again took refuge, this time in Futa Jallon, at which point the sources cease to discuss him.[157]

Malik Ture's reign was quiet, but not entirely uneventful. In 1893, he and the French officer Hostains conducted campaigns against the Jakhanke centers of Sillacounda, Samecounta, and Laminia, all in Niocolo. These settlements had received considerable numbers of slaves from Samori in payment for their prayers of support for the latter's military success, and were therefore viewed by the French as allies of Samori. The result was further Jakhanke emigration towards the Gambia, where they enjoyed greater autonomy under the British.[158]

Bundu under Malik Ture also experienced the impact of some 20,000 people returning to the Senegal Valley from Kaarta between 1891 and 1893, following the French conquest of the area. This repatriation was to some degree mitigated by another outbreak of cholera at Bakel, Podor and Dagana in August of 1893.[159] At the same time, the influx of such a large number of Fulbe repatriates and (in all probability) their slaves, combined with the previous emigration of substantial numbers of Soninke during the wars of Mamadu Lamine, resulted in a more ethnically balanced, albeit smaller population. However, the Bundu to which they returned was very different from the one they had left. Fields had been left unattended, and cultivation languished. In response to the crisis, the repatriates focused their energies on resuscitating the agricultural sector.

Abandoned by most of the important Sissibe, Malik Ture lived out his tenure at Gabou, where the population was estimated at 500, most of whom had come from Boulebane.[160] Malik Ture had resided in Gabou as early as 1888, and chose to remain there to be in closer proximity to Bakel, given Sissibe hostility. They never forgave his acceptance of the *Almaami* position.[161] Toward the latter end of his reign, he was reported to have been surrounded by worthless *griots* and incompetent advisors.[162] He died in 1902, having reigned fourteen years.[163] He was the last of the Bundunke *almaamies*.

Termination

On 4 February 1905, France officially ended the Bundunke *almaamate*. On that day, Bundu was divided into two sections. The southern half (Bundu *meridional*) was placed under *chef de canton* Abdul Sega, a resident of Koussan and a former assistant to Bokar Saada.[164] Northern Bundu (Bundu *septentrional*) was given to *chef du canton* Wopa Bokar, who lived at Senoudebou. Abdul Sega is registered as an *Almaami* in the *Fonds Curtin*, and "reigned" for twelve years, having died in 1917.[165] He was succeeded by his son, Saada Abdul Sy, who was *chef du canton* from 1918 to 1954.[166] Saada Abdul Sy's widow, Maimouna Mamadu Sy, was among those interviewed by Curtin in 1966.

Although both Abdul Sega and Wopa Bokar were Sissibe, they were far removed from the *almaamate* according to the legal order. Their selection by the French, and designation as *chefs*, was consistent with French policy since the removal of Saada Amadi in 1888, and indicates the view in Saint Louis that the most effective way of ending the *almaamate* was through weakening its ties to those most closely associated with it. Bundu had proved a loyal friend and ally, but its insignificance relative to the general scheme of things allowed the French to set it aside. In a real sense, the Bundunke *almaamies* had been *chefs du canton* since Bokar Saada.

11

Conclusion

Malik Sy, as portrayed by the Bundunke traditions, is not presented as a scholar, but rather as a fashioner of amulets, a practitioner of the *bāṭin* sciences. Consequently, while not necessarily erudite, he nevertheless performed the services of a cleric, and was considered to be a member of the *Torodbe*. In view of this, the critical issue for the establishment of Bundu in the late seventeenth century was the transformation of Malik Sy from an advisor to the court to actually constituting the court. That is, the real question facing Malik Sy was whether or not his leadership could be extended from the domain of spirituality to that of political governance. That the answer to this question was affirmative, notwithstanding Bundu's inauspicious beginnings, is all the more remarkable in light of the available paradigms. To be quite specific, there were no existing examples of successful, clerically led polities anywhere in West Africa. The *tubenan* experience had been nothing short of an unmitigated disaster; stability had been re-introduced into the region via traditional forms of government. The followers of Nasır al-Dın had failed to sustain his reform movement, thus casting considerable doubt upon any such subsequent attempts within Senegambia. But at the same time, the policies of the Denyanke dynasty of Futa Toro, Malik Sy's homeland, proved to be increasingly incompatible with the needs of Muslims to pursue their faith in a secure environment, free of harassment from officials fearful of lingering *tubenan* sentiments, and protected from the ravages of the transsaharan and transatlantic slave trades.

Given such conditions, Malik Sy founded a polity that was to be ruled by clerics, but not necessarily governed by a strict adherence to Islamic law (although it is possible that elements of *sharī'a* were implemented; the data simply do not allow for a conclusive finding on this matter). As evidence of this approach, non-Muslim communities would also be encouraged to reside in Bundu, as it was very practical and beneficial to the new micro-state. This was because southern Gajaaga, historically a land of asylum for political refugees, was sparsely populated. Malik Sy and the early *Torodbe* leadership sought to increase the population by various means, including the acceptance of non-Muslims. The need for increasing the population, combined

Conclusion

with both the egalitarian ideals of the *Torodbe* and the identification of southern Gajaaga with refuge, explains Bundu's early and abiding reception of a variety of groups. Immigrants who were productive, and who could contribute to the economy of the state, were highly valued; the fact that they failed to embrace Islam, or that they were the political or social outcasts of other societies, was immaterial. In Bundu they all found asylum, and consented to live under an Islamic but tolerant political leadership.

From the foregoing, it is clear that Bundu adopted a pragmatic posture from its inception. As the polity matured, its leadership emphasized the state's commercial and agricultural growth, and tended to resist attempts at reformation via the rigid application of *shari'a* to either the structure of government or the related social order. Within the context of the preceding *tubenan* failure, and in conjunction with the ongoing danger emanating from the slave trades, such an arrangement was most acceptable to the Muslim community in Bundu. If anything, they sought to avoid further political upheaval and uncertainty; indeed, this is why they came to southern Gajaaga, the land historically associated with apolitical existence. This pragmatic approach was further strengthened by the examples of governing dynasties in the region, from some of which Malik Sy had learned aspects of statecraft. The movement towards a moderate, anti-militant approach to government was accelerated by the presence of the pacifist Jakhanke clerisy, whose prestige quickly eclipsed that of the Sissibe in the realm of religion. In turn, the spiritual ascendance of the Jakhanke, together with the pressures of governing a temporal entity, encouraged the Sissibe to move away from scholarly endeavors and piety, to which they had never made significant pretense. As a result, the Sissibe leadership of Bundu began to function more and more as a secular dynasty; that is, their foreign and domestic policies were influenced more by considerations of expendiency than by religion. At the same time, however, the Sissibe remained Muslim in the area of their personal lives, and restricted positions of political and commercial influence to other Muslims. In other words, Bundu began to function very early on as a moderate Muslim power.

After a period of instability, the state was reconstituted by Maka Jiba, at which time it can be considered a successful experiment. As such, it is within the context of eighteenth and nineteenth century West Africa that the characterization of Bundu as a pragmatic polity takes on greater meaning. For it is during these centuries that West Africa became a veritable hotbed of Islamic reformist activity, often assuming the proportions of social revolutions via military campaigns; i.e., militancy. By the late nineteenth century, there were few areas within West Africa which remained fundamentally unchanged by the rise of militant Islam; Senegambia had certainly been thoroughly affected by several successive waves of militant movements. It is in light of the onset of militant Islam that Bundu becomes even more unique, in that it struggled to remain distinctive from both non-Muslim powers and militant entities.

Conclusion

Under Maka Jiba, the gravitation of the Sissibe towards secular rule intensified as a result of the area's commercial growth. Bundu greatly expanded in the course of the eighteenth century, as it sought to exploit its strategic position between the Upper Senegal and Gambia Rivers. The productive and commercial sectors of the economy became intertwined, and the success of these sectors undergirded the prosperity of Bundu itself. By virtue of its location, Bundu rapidly grew from a collection of a few humble villages into a state of some importance, with aspirations of becoming a regional power. The emphasis within the ruling elite on agriculture, artisanry, and trade was such that any question of comprehensive Islamization became positively unacceptable, as it was perceived as antithetical to the welfare of the state. That is, in a climate of growing prosperity and economic expansion, the disruption to the productive capacity of the Bundunkobe that would accompany substantial social change was seen as undesirable and dangerous. Hence, the economic growth of the realm served to reinforce pragmatism among the ruling elite.

It is an observation of no small irony that the very success of the Bundunke experiment was to some extent related to the development in Senegambia of domestic, political, and social fissures of lethal potential. To be more direct, the demonstration that the clerical community could in fact wield temporal power did not go unnoticed among the Muslims of Futa Jallon and Futa Toro. Indeed, the struggles of Bubu Malik and Maka Jiba were greatly aided by elements from both territories, so that the eventual consolidation of Muslim clerical power in Bundu necessarily reached the hearing of those who would lead the *jihāds* in the two Futas. This is not at all to argue that the eighteenth-century social transformations experienced by the two Futas were directly inspired by the example of Bundu; however, it is to say that, whatever the actual factors of causation, the militant camps of the Futas were cognizant of the Bundunke experiment. From the militant perspective, the *jihāds* and consequent implementation of *sharī'a* within their respective societies was in a very real sense the pursuit of the Bundunke experiment to its logical end; i.e., the social implementation of religious prescription by clerical leaders. Armed with the sure knowledge that clerical temporal leadership was feasible in West Africa, the adherents of militant Islam successfully prosecuted the *jihād* in the mountains of present day Guinea and in the Middle Senegal.

The victory of militancy in the Futas proved to be an ominous development for the Sissibe of Bundu, as it would result in external pressures for Bundu to conform to the more complete ideal of Islamic theocratic rule as expressed in the Futas. The creation of *almaamates* which embraced *sharī'a* clearly illuminated the contrasting secular proclivities of the Bundunke ruling elite, and found some support within Bundu to embrace comprehensive reform, as can be seen in Amadi Gai's attempt to structural change in response to external stimuli. The Bundunke elite, however, remained preoccupied with the economic health and political viability of the state within

Conclusion

the context of intense regional competition. The pragmatists remained convinced of the sagacity of their approach, and felt their authority threatened by those who argued for thoroughgoing reform. Indeed, the moderate Bundunke view of the social upheavals of the Futas was very different from that of the militants; for the former, the very duration of the *jihāds* (1720s to 1740s in Futa Jallon, 1760s to 1770s in Futa Toro) was sufficient cause for recoil, as disruption over such prolonged periods would surely spell the decline of Bundu in the region. Armed with the approbation of the esteemed Jakhanke clerisy, the Sissibe resisted the protestations of the reformers. That the moderate order was maintained in the face of Islamic militancy is testimony to both the efficacy of Sissibe pragmatism, and the dependence of the Bundunke reformers upon the leadership and success of external militancy. With the removal of such support, the reform movement within Bundu quickly withered away.

To be more specific, the division of the Sissibe into two branches was eventually exploited by the *Almaami* Abdul Qadir of Futa Toro, whose popularity and commitment to the expansion of the Islamic revolution overwhelmed the position of Bundunke pragmatism in the last decade of the eighteenth century. But the way in which Abdul Qadir orchestrated the succession process was perceived by most Bundunkobe as a violation of their sovereignty, so that the controversy over Islamic law became secondary to that of legitimacy. The position of the Koussan branch, backed by Abdul Qadir, was effectively undermined by the latter's lack of political sensitivity. That position became even weaker with the summary execution of Sega Gai. The entire political arrangement was greatly supported by the prestige of Abdul Qadir; combined with the callousness he demonstrated towards the Bundunkobe, his misfortunes in Cayor eventually led to his demise. With his decline, the Koussan branch's position became untenable, and Amadi Aissata was able to seize power in the name of Boulebane. His ascension marked the reassertion of pragmatism in Bundu, without the state ever having had an opportunity to experience the full implementation of *sharī'a*.

Under the leadership of the Boulebane branch in the mid-nineteenth century, Bundu experienced its greatest territorial expansion. The principal motivation was the growth of regional trade, accelerated by the establishment of the French fort at Bakel. As the competition increased, Bundu's prominence became more and more pronounced, as it was able to exploit its strategic location to its advantage vis-a-vis other neighboring states. By virtue of its successful development, the forces of pragmatism became even more entrenched, convinced that theirs was the appropriate method of governance. However, French resistance to Bundunke hegemony in the Upper Senegal was a major factor in preventing the former from realizing its full potential.

The 1845 treaty with the French would again divide the Bundunke ruling elite. For the Koussan branch in particular, the relinquishing of Bundunke soil at Senoudebou was completely unacceptable. The French were neither

Muslims nor Bundunke. Furthermore, from Senoudebou the French would be able to monitor the agreement to halt trade with the British along the Gambia. Finally, the French presence represented interference in Bundu's internal affairs. This portentous development resulted in the degeneration of relations between the two royal branches, as the ensuing controversy came to preoccupy the attention of the Sissibe. In short order, other matters of state became hostage to the debate between the branches.

The culmination of the controversy was armed conflict, into which entered the luminary of the age, *al-ḥājj* Umar. His advent once again raised the issue of reform within Bundu. Once again, militancy was championed by someone from outside Bundu. But the magnitude of this particular movement far exceeded that led by Abdul Qadir. And, in contrast to Abdul Qadir's emphasis upon administrative change, reform under Umar meant the submission of Bundu to his authority and its enlistment in his campaigns against a "pagan" east. Bundu was literally swept away with the swelling tide of the Umarian movement, along with the rest of Senegambia. So charged became the atmosphere with religious and political expectancy that virtually the whole of the Sissibe nobility embraced the vision of the *Shaykh*. Many would pay the ultimate price in a foreign land, the Umarian east. Few dared to swim against the powerful current of the Futanke's *jihād*.

The rise of the Umarians coincided with the heightened interest of the French in the Senegal Valley. The simultaneous development of both powers in the region, followed by the acrimonious turn in their relations, spelled disaster for the Bundunkobe, who were either relocated in Kaarta and the Upper Niger, or forced to witness the gradual destruction of their land. Because Bundu assumed such a role, the viability of the central government was essentially destroyed, preventing the militants from ever having an opportunity to govern the state.

In the contest for the Upper Senegal, Bundu was a major arena for the conflicting forces of the Umarians and the French. The latter, while enjoying superior firepower, needed someone to whom indigenous, anti-Umarian elements could rally, and to whom political power could be entrusted. The need was met in the person of Bokar Saada, who displayed all of the characteristics of an opportunist in his rejection of the Umarian movement. The French victory in the Upper Senegal, together with the 1860 "understanding" between Faidherbe and the *Shaykh*, left Bundu in the hands of this descendant of Fulbe and Bambara nobility. With his ascendance, the pragmatic–versus–militant dichotomy within Bundunke society effectively came to an end; the vast majority of reformers relocated to the east, leaving the west to the "infidels" and Bokar Saada.

Having initially begun his tenure as a French agent, Bokar Saada eventually fashioned commercial and diplomatic policies at variance with those of Saint Louis. Such autonomy became possible through French preoccupation with groundnut cultivation along the Wolof coast. But Bokar Saada inherited a land seared by war and great hardship. He immediately embarked

Conclusion

upon a series of campaigns into the Malinke states to the south, from which he extracted slaves and others for purposes of population augmentation and agriculture. But after a period of reconstruction, the *Almaami* began to exact exorbitant taxation from the Mande-speaking populations. The Malinke and Soninke components of Bundu now surpassed that of the Fulbe, many of whom had resettled in the east. Bokar Saada's economic oppression resulted in growing hostility and renewed emigration. His policies represented a refutation of the early established principle of toleration within a heterogeneous state, and greatly exacerbated the problems of the Bundunkobe, begun earlier during the French-Umarian wars. Feared and despised, Bokar Saada was the epitome of unrestrained power gone awry.

The *Almaami*'s policies created such depth of despair and discontent that, immediately after his death, the state once more entered a period of war. In this instance, the cleric Mamadu Lamine was able to seize control of the state, having benefitted from anti-Sissibe and anti-French sentiment throughout the Upper Senegal. The Bundunkobe, now largely Mande-speaking, responded with enthusiasm to the cleric's call for the expulsion of the Sissibe. Eventually, though reluctantly, the cleric would have to issue the same call with regard to the French. This call represents, once again, an external bid to direct internal change, and was eagerly received because of Bokar Saada's oppression and French conscription policies. In the end, however, Mamadu Lamine's efforts were frustrated and nullified by the French, who were resolute in their determination to control the Upper Senegal. With the defeat of this last clerically led movement, Bundu accepted a much more insignificant role in the area, as the upper valley itself became peripheral to the periphery of groundnut production along the Wolof coast and astride the Gambia River.

In sum, the experiment in Islamic pragmatism begun by Malik Sy was, with the exception of Bokar Saada's reign, a remarkable success. The polity not only survived for approximately 200 years, but it expanded its territorial control over the course of the eighteenth and nineteenth centuries. The policies of the pragmatists resulted in prosperity for many of the Bundunkobe; fidelity to the original vision of a multiethnic state assured its steady growth. While remaining opposed to the claims of the reformers, Bundu was able to influence the development of Islamic government in the Futas. By restricting administrative posts and commercial opportunities to Muslims, and by supporting the activities of the Jakhanke clerisy, Bundunke leaders encouraged the gradual Islamization of the society, so that by the end of the eighteenth century, Bundu was declared by inhabitant and visitor alike as a Muslim land.

The Sissibe of Bundu sought to maintain a balance between the demands of religious law and the politico-economic realities of their time. Their approach to the Islamization of their society was in sharp contrast to the pattern of militancy in the Futas and under the Umarians. In many ways, the contrast points to the fundamental question of what it means to be a Muslim in an environment characterized by rapid change and under the increasing control of non-Muslim, foreign powers. As such, the contrast anticipates the contemporary Muslim world's struggle to reconcile the words of the Prophet with the challenges of post-modernity.

Appendices

Appendix A

Ruler list

	Rançon	*Curtin*	*Corrected*
Malik Sy	1693-99		1698–99
Bubu Malik	1699–1718	(1700–2)–(1719–27)	1699–1715
Tumane Bubu (in other traditions, a four or five year reign)	not mentioned		
Interregnum	1718–28	ended 1731–35	1716–20
Maka Jiba	1728–64	(1731–35)–64	1720–64
Samba Tumane	1764	not mentioned	1764
Amadi Gai	1764–85	1764–86	1764–86
Musa Gai	1785–90	1786–90	1786–90
Sega Gai	1790–94	1790–97	1790–97
Amadi Aissata	1794–1819	1797–1/1819	1797–1/1819
Musa Yero	1819–27	1819–26	1819–26
Tumane Mudi	1827–35		
Malik Kumba	1835–39	1835–37	1835–37
Saada Amadi Aissata	1839–51	1837–51	1837–51
Amadu Sy	1852–53		
Second Civil War	1852–54		1853–54
Umar Sane	1854–56		1854–4/1857
Bokar Saada	1856–85		1857–85
Umar Penda	1885–86		
Saada Amadi	1886–88		1886–5/1888
Usuman Gassi	1889–91		1888–91
Amadi Cire	not mentioned		1888–91
Malik Ture	1891–1905		1891–1902

Appendix B

Major events in Bundu

1699	Battle of Arondou
1699	Reconquest by Bubu Malik
1720–64	Invasion of "Ormankube"
1725–35	Samba Gelaajo Jegi is *Satigi* in Futa Toro
1740–43	Samba Gelaajo Jegi is *Satigi* in Futa Toro
8/1734	Ayuba Sulayman Diallo arrives at James Fort
1735	Thomas Hull visits
1744	Pierre David visits
1747–51	War with Sule N'jai of Futa Toro
1773	Death of Ayuba Sulayman Diallo
1786	Rubault visits
1791	Houghton visits
1795	Mungo Park visits
1797	First Civil War begins
1800	Battle of Dara Lamine
1806–7	Death of Abdul Qādir
1817–18	War with Kaarta
1817	Brédif and Chastelus visit
1818	Mollien visits
1818–19	Gray and Dochard visit
11/1820	Treaty with the French
1820	French fort at Bakel permanently established
8/1821	Musa Yero unsuccessfully attacks Tiyaabu
1829–32	Tuane Mudi campaigning in Wuli
1830s	Incursions by the Moors and Kaarta
1838	Fox visits
1842	Assault by Bundu against Makhana, Tambucane
1843	Expedition by Huard-Bessinière, Jamin, Raffenel, and Potin-Patterson
1844–46	War with Guidimakha
8/1845	Treaty with the French
1846	Incursions by Guidimakha, Kaarta
1847	Raffenel's second visit
1847–50	Raids into Wuli, Niani, Kantora
1849–50	Raids into Guey
1853–54	Second Civil War
6/1854	French arms embargo
1/1855	Umarian victory over Kaartans at Kholu

2/1855	Umarian victory at Yelimane
4/1855	Fall of Nioro
4/1855	Bakel, Senoudebou defended
6/1855	Senoudebou defended
7/1855	French destroy Tiyaabu, Kounguel
10/1855	Faidherbe meets Bokar Saada
2/1856	Formal submission of remaining Sissibe to Bokar Saada
2/1856	Umarians defeated at Borde (near Bakel)
3/1856	Umarians defeated at Debou
4–5/1856	Senoudebou defeated
1/1857	Usuman Saada defeated at N'Dioum
3/1857	Umarians defeated at Amadhie
4/1857	Invasions by Guidimakha
4/1857	Battle of Medine
8/1857	Battle of Somsom-Tata
1858	Umarian *hijra*
3/1858	*al-ḥājj* Umar arrives in Goundiourou
4–5/1858	*al-ḥājj* Umar occupies Boulebane
5/1858	Beginning of widespread famine
10/1859	Battle of Guemou
8/1860	Faidherbe and *al-ḥājj* Umar recognize separate spheres
1861–85	Raids by Bokar Saada into Bambuk, Wuli, Niocolo, Tenda, Niani, Kantora, Kada
4/1872	Bokar Saada defeated at Bofel
1/1886	Mamadu Lamine invades Bundu
2/1886	Mamadu Lamine controls most of Bundu
4/1886	Bakel defended
6/1886	Umar Penda killed at Fissa-Daro
9/1886	Senoudebou defended
12/1886	French arrive at Dianna
12/1887	Bundu becomes French protectorate
12/1887	Toubacouta falls
12/1887	Death of Mamadu Lamine
5/1888	Saada Amadi deposed by Gallieni; replaced by Usuman Gassi
5/1888	Amadi Cire becomes "*Almaami* of Bundunkobe"
2/1905	Bundunke *Almaamate* officially ended by the French

Appendix C

Descendants of Malik Sy

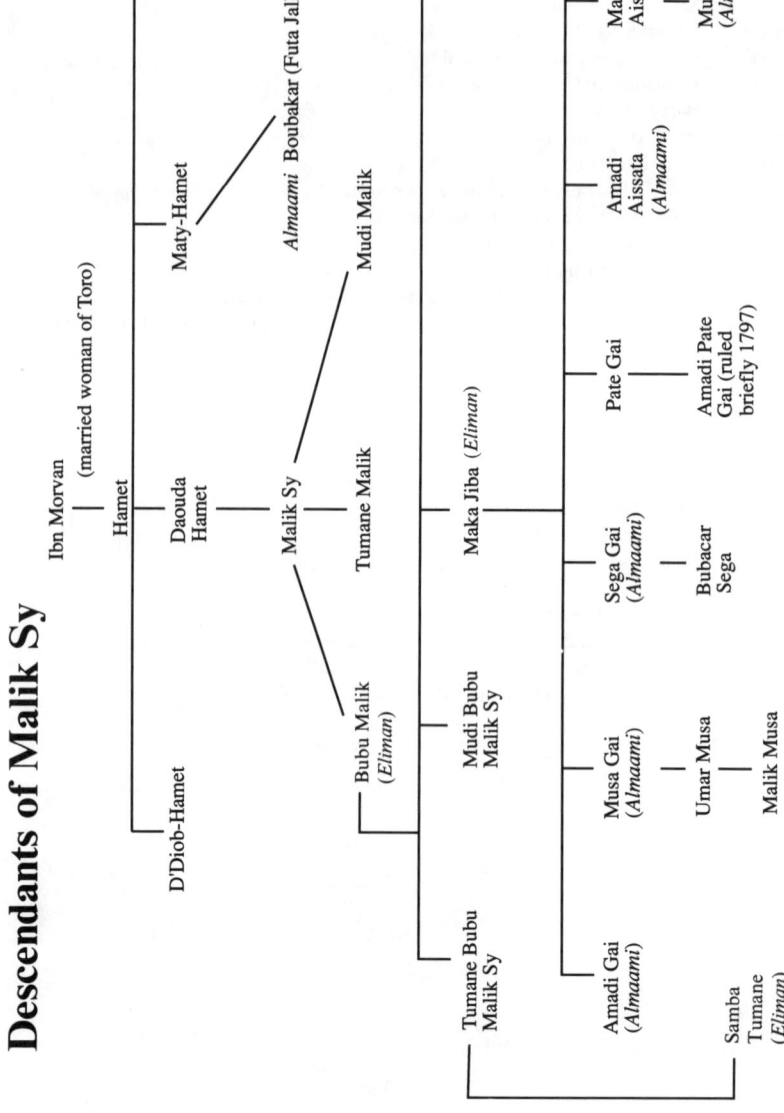

Appendix C Descendants of Malik Sy

Appendix D

Descendants of Amadi Gai and Amadi Aissata

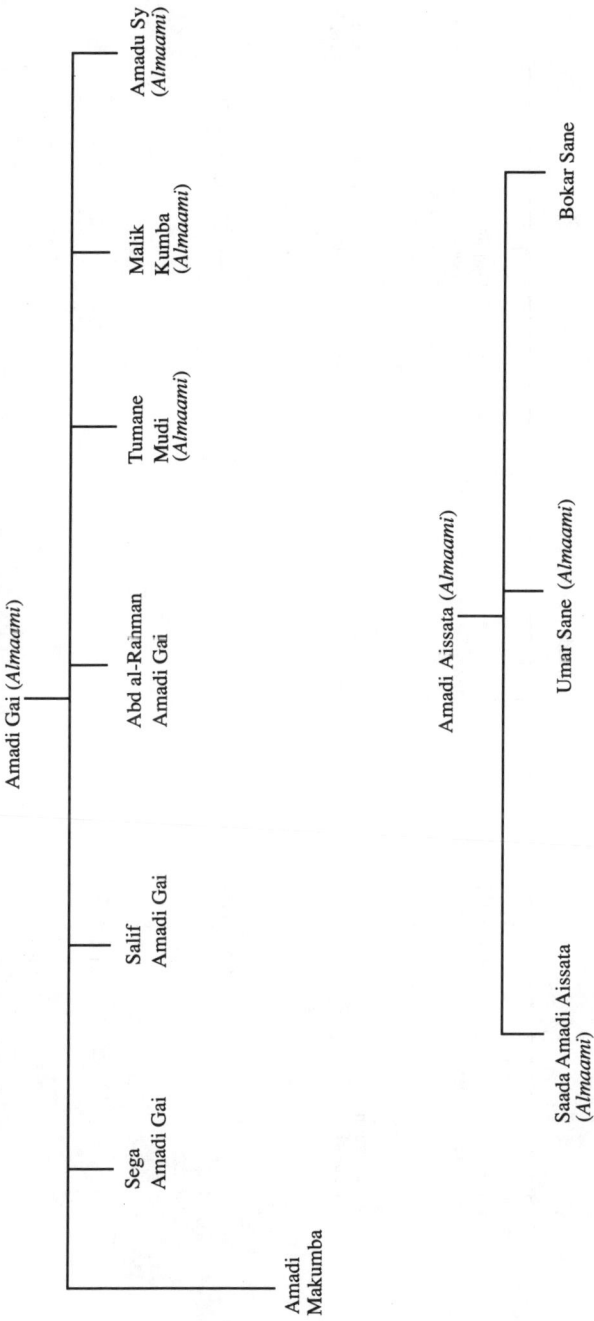

Appendix D Descendants of Amadi Gai and Amadi Aissata

Appendix E

Descendants of Saada Amadi Aissata and the line of succession (1886)

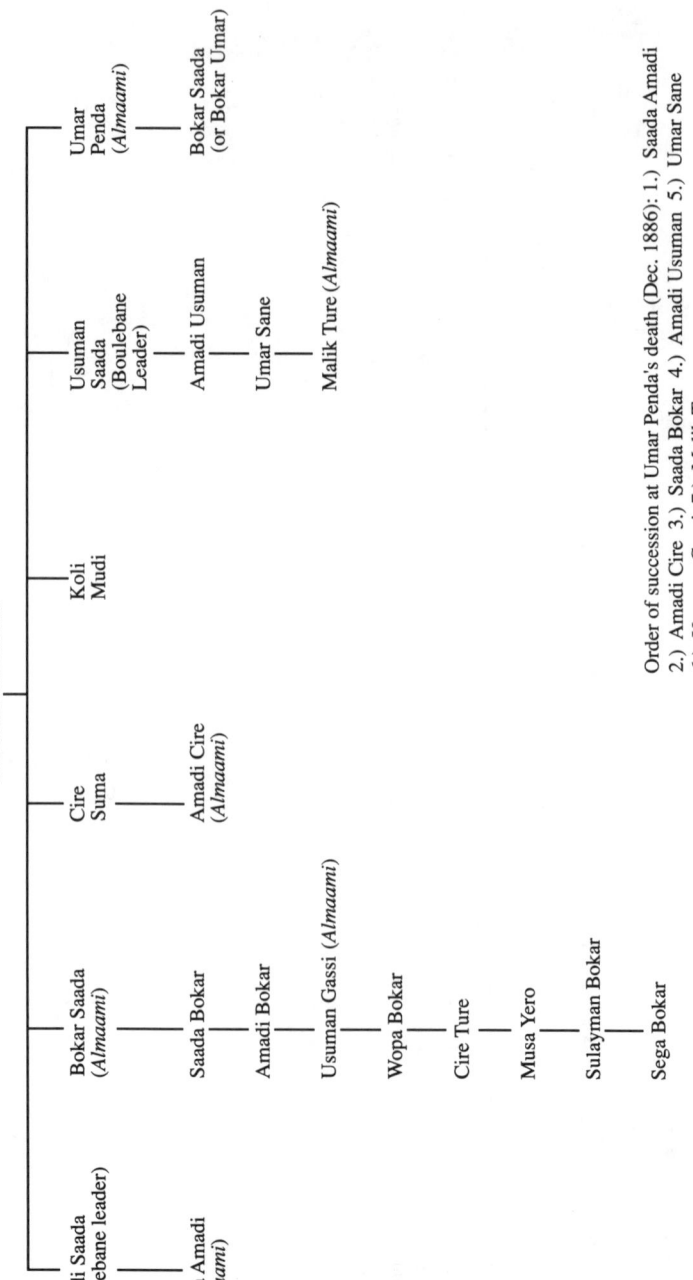

Appendix E Descendants of Saada Amadi Aissata and the line of succession (1886)

Appendix F

The Sissibe Umarians

This is a list of the sons of the *almaamies*, indicating those who followed *al-ḥajj* Umar. It must be remembered that the Sissibe included many members beyond the *almaamies*' immediate families, and it may be assumed that the remaining Sissibe followed the *Shaykh* in proportions similar to the group under consideration.

Musa Yero

Demba Musa
Saada Dude   -*Umarians*
Bala Setai

Malik Kumba

Samba Gaissiri
Musa Yero Malik
Bubacar Malik   -*Umarians*
Boila Malik
Alium Malik

Sada Amadi Aissata

Koli Mudi   -*Umarian*
Usuman Saada   -*Umarian*
Bokar Saada
Amadi Saada
Cire Suma
Umar Penda

Tumane Mudi

Umar Bili Kari
Abdul Salum
Ali Gitta
Hamet
Bubacar Sidiq   -*Umarians*
Sega Tumane
Suracoto
Samba Tumane
al-Kusun
Abbas
Ibrahim Tenendia
Salif

Amadu Sy

Amadi Amadu
Tumane Amadu   -*Umarians*
Musa Yero
Sega Amadu

Umar Sane   -*Umarian*

Appendix G

Treaty of 1820

Conditions aux quelles les Français s'engagents[1]
1. Les Français s'engagent à accorder à tous les habitans de Bondou, qui viendraient au poste.
2. Les Français s'engagent à protéger le commerce entre eux et les gens de Bondou et à les faciliter de tous les moyens.
3. Les Français ne prendront aucune part aux guerres qui pourraient avoir lieu dans le pays.

Conditions aux quelles Almaamy s'engage
1. L'Almamy de Bondou s'engage à protéger tous les Européens ou leurs envoyés dans le pays, sous sa domination, à empecher qu'il ne leur fait aucun tort, ni dommage.
2. L'Almamy promet de faciliter le commerce avec les Européens, de protéger tous ceux des contrées environnantes, qui viendraient à Baquel dans ce but.
3. L'Almamy promet enfin de ne se joindre d'aucune manière à ceux qui seraient ennemis des Français.

Fait et clos à Baquel, le 12 Novembre, 1820.
Signé: Hesse

---

[1] ANF-OM, Senegal IV–15; ANS 136, 242.

Appendix H

Treaty of 1845

Traité avec l'Almamy du Boundou pour la concession d'un terrain devant servir à établir un comptoir commercial à Senoudebou.[1] (Août 23, 1845).

A la Gloire du tout puissant Créateur du ciel, de la terre et des mers, père Éternel et unique de tous les Etres vivants.

Entre Saada Almamy du Boundou et la comission nommé par M. Thomas Gouverneur du Sénégal et Dependances; composée de

> M.A. Parent, Directeur du Génie, President.
> Menn Dessable Chirurgien, 2e Classe de marine.
> Paulholle, Commandant le poste de Bakel.
> Potin-Patterson, Gérant de la Compagnie de Galam, à Sénoudébou.

Article 1er. Il a été convenu ce qui suit: L'Almamy du Boundou cede à la France en toute propriété un terrain situé près du tata de l'Almamy, ayant pour longeur six cents pas d'un grand homme à partir de la Rivière allant dans l'intérieur à cinq cents pas d'un grand homme pour largeur à partir du tata allant plus bas pour y établir un comptoir commercial près d'un village de Sénoudébou pour le montant de:

100 pièces de Guinée bleue
100 fusils dont 10 à 2 coups et 90 simples
100 grains d'Ambre
100 grains de Corail
100 bagateller

Qui leur ont été remis entre les mains "aussitôt" après la Signature du traité.

Article 2. Independamment du Prix d'achat du terrain le Gouvernement français s'engage de payer annuellement et aux principaux chefs désignés ci après les coutumes suivantes.

> A l'Almamy
> 40 Objets dont 30 pièces de Guinée bleue.
> 20 fusils (10 a deux coups et 10 de munitions).
> A ceux qui le remplaceront
> á Amady son fils (après la
> mort de Saada) sur les quarante
> objets précités, 20 à chacun;
> 10 fusils et 10 pièces de
> Guinée.
> A Alcaty Chiapato.

Appendices

        Un fusil a deux coups
        1 pièce de Guinée bleue.

        Un fusil a deux coups.

1 pièce de coton blanc.
1 pièce de mousseline.
A son fils Boubakar à Sénoudébou.
5 pièces de Guinée bleue.

Article 3. L'Almamy du Boundou prend l'engagement par ce traité de protéger notre commerce et de faire arriver au Comptoir tous les produits de leur pays et d'empêcher les caravanes de se diriger vers la Gambie.

Article 4. Au moyen des coutumes annuelles, l'Almamy du Boundou donne droit au comptoir de couper des arbres pour les constructions, 2.) de couper du bois à bruler et à faire des briques, 3.) de prendre de la terre des pièrres ou du sable partout ou il n'existera pas de culture, 4.) de pêcher et de ramasser des coquilles dans la rivière de Falémé.

Article 5. Les coutumes annuelles de 1845 à 1846 ont remisés au Roi et aux chefs en presence de la comission.

Fait double à Sénoudébou écrit en Arabe et en français le toute arrête et convenu en notre présence le 23 Août–1845.

                Approuvé: Le Gouverneur
                    Signé: Thomas

            Signé: Parent, Menn Dessable, Paulholle, et Patterson.

[1] ANS 13G, 242.

Appendix I

Treaty of 18 August 1858

Article 1. En reconnaissance des services qui lui ont été rendus, l'Almamy du Boundou, Boubakar Saada, déclare en son nom et au nom de ses successeurs, que, outre le cours de la Falémé, les territoires suivent appartiennent à la France en toute propriété.[1]

    1.) Le territoire de Sénoudébou, dont Boubakar évacuera la partie qu'il occupe dès que les circonstances le lui permettront.
    2.) Une route de 30 mètres de largeur de Sénoudébou à Bakel.
    3.) Le territoire du village de Ndangan.
    4.) Une route de 20 mètres de largeur de Ndangan à Kénieba.
    5.) Une route de 20 mètres de largeur conduisant directement de Sénoudébou, rive droite, à Kénieba.

    Le tracé de ces routes est au Choix du Gouvernement français.

Article 2. L'Almamy ne percevra aucun droit sur les caravanes qui viennent de l'Est directement à Sénoudébou.

Article 3. Quand Boubakar aura quitté Sénoudébou, il ne mettra aucun obstacle à que des gens du Bondou, libres de leurs personnes, viennent grossir les populations de nos villages.

Article 4. Les Français auront la facilité de fonder un établissement sur la haut Falémé, lorsqu'ils le jugeront à propos, en dédommageant les proprietaires du terrain s'il est occupé.

Article 5. Les Français sont complétement maîtres et indépendants dans leurs établissements. Ils laisseront le gouvernement du pays à ses Chefs naturels Boubakar Saada et ses successeurs.

Article 6. Tous les traités ou Conventions anterieures sont abrogés.

                                          Signé: L. Faidherbe
                                                      Boubakar Saada

Ont signé comme témoins:
Coquet, capitaine, commandant de Sénoudébou
Bonnet, capitaine d'artillerie, chef d'état major.

---

[1] ANF-OM, Senegal IV, 44d.

Appendix J

Treaty of 15 August 1858

Article 1. Pour mettre fin aux discussions entre Bougoul, chef de Farabanna et du Niagalla, et Boubakar Saada, almamy du Bondou, le Gouverner décide que le marigot de Lally séparera le territoire dont les habitants obéissent à Bougoul.[1]

Article 2. Les sujets de l'Almamy, comme les Malinkés du Bambouck, exploiteront les mines d'or de Cotily concurrement avec les Français.

Article 3. Pendant les deux premières années, pour que le gouvernement français puisse se rendre compte de la richesse des mines de Cotily, tout l'or extrait par les indigènes sur ce point sera vendu à l'administration des mines au prix moyen de deux gros pour une pièce de guinée, ou pour d'autres marchandises au prix courant débattu entre les parties.

L'administration des mines sera pourvue de toutes les marchandises dont les indigènes ont besoin, elle aura soin de ne pas faire monter le prix de l'or dans leur pays.

Signé: L. Faidherbe
Bougoul
Boubakar Saada

Ont signé comme témoins:
Le Directeur des mines: Maritz
Le capitaine d'artillerie, chef d'état major: Bonnet.

---

[1] Lamartiny, *Etudes*, p. 55.

Appendix K

Treaty of 12 November 1869

Between His Excellency Colonel Samuel Wensley Blackall, Governor-in-Chief of the West African Settlements, on behalf of Her most Gracious Majesty, Victoria, by the grace of God Queen of Great-Britain and Ireland, and Barcary Sardho, King of Bondou, concluded, ratified, and confirmed by Benjamin Tanner, esquire, specially appointed by his Excellency the said Governor-in-Chief for that purpose.[1]

1. There shall be peace and friendship between the subjects of the Queen of England and the people, subjects of the said Barcary Sardho, King of Bondou.

2. The lives and properties of the subjects of the Queen of England, and of all other persons living under Her Majesty's protection in the British Settlements on the River Gambia, shall be inviolate, and no country law, or customs is to be put in force against them, nor are any of the Queen's subjects or other persons living under Her Majesty's protection to break through any country law, or customs, or to commit any illegal act within the territory or upon any of the subjects of the said Barcary Barcary [sic] Sardho, King of Bondou.

3. The said King of Bondou does hereby acknowledge the rights which the subjects of the Queen of England have heretofore and at all times enjoyed, of free and uninterrupted intercourse for trade and commerce, and for all other legitimate purposes in and throughout the countries adjacent to and bordering on both banks of the River Gambia and its branches, and Barcary Sardho, King of Bondou, does hereby on his own part confirm, guarantee, and assure the same to the subjects of the Queen of England this right of free and unrestricted intercourse, so far as his own country and his power and influence extends, and further engages that the subjects of the Queen of England shall be allowed to remain in peaceable possession of the lands and houses or factories which they have purchased or hired in the countries [and] territories adjacent to and bordering on the said River Gambia, nor shall the goods of the Queen's subjects be seized nor their persons harmed, and if the subjects of the Queen of England are wronged or ill-treated by the subjects of the said Barcary Sardho, King of Bondou, he will punish those who wrong and ill-treat Her Majesty's subjects.

4. The aforesaid Barcary Sardho, King of Bondou, engages not to enter into any war or commit any act of aggression on any of the Chiefs bordering on the banks of the said River Gambia by which the trade of the country with the British settlement on the River Gambia shall be interrupted, and the safety of the persons and property of the subjects of the Queen of England shall be lost, compromised, or endangered.

5. The paths shall be kept open through the kingdom of Bondou to other countries and down to the banks of the said River Gambia, so that English traders may carry goods through the said country to sell or barter them elsewhere, and the traders of other countries may bring their goods or produce through the said country to trade with the English people freely and without molestation.

Appendices

6. If the people or subjects of the King of Bondou take away the property of an English person, or should not pay their just debts to any English person, the aforesaid King engages to do all he can to make the people restore the property taken away and pay their debts, and if English people should take away the property of the people or subjects of the said King of Bondou, or should not pay just debts due to the said people, the said King shall make known the circumstances to the Officer for the time being Administering the Government of the Gambia, who will do all in his power to make the English person restore the property and pay their debts.

7. For the purposes of this Treaty all French subjects resident in the British Settlement on the River Gambia shall be considered to enjoy the same rights and privileges and be subject to the same stipulations as British subjects.

8. In consideration of the foregoing stipulations of this Treaty being agreed upon and strictly adhered to on the part of the said Barcary Sardho, King of Bondou, aforesaid, and of his successors, his Excellency Colonel Samuel Wensley Blackall, Governor-in-Chief of the West Africa Settlements, agrees for himself and successors in the said office on the part of Her Majesty the Queen of England to pay or cause to be paid annually on the first day of July in each year at M'Carthy's Island the sum of two hundred and fifty dollars to any person duly authorized by the said King of Bondou to receive the same.

9. The said King of Bondou shall within forty and eight hours of the ratification of this Treaty proceed to proclaim the same throughout his territory.

Done in duplicate and signed by both parties at M'Carthy's Island on the twelfth day of November in the year of our Lord one thousand eight hundred and sixty-nine (1869).

For the King of Bondou:

(Signed) B. Tanner
(Arabic) Sangary Signarty for the King of Bondou.

Witnesses to signature –
(Signed) Edward Duxeault.
(Signed) Edward Hughes.

Translation of Barcary Sardho's Endorsement on this Treaty

Barcary Sardho sends his compliments to the King of M'Carthy's Island.
   Since the time we agreed there is fifty pounds between us every year.
   (He then sends his compliments to all the merchants).
   Malamin Jammy is to take the customs and the arrears that are due.
   Read by Moree Sao and translated by Thomas B. Moore in the presence of Edward Duxeault.

---

[1] NAG, Class 54, Piece no. 9.

Notes

1: Introduction

1 John H. Hanson, "Umarian Karta (Mali, West Africa) during the Late Nineteenth Century: Dissent and Revolt among the Futanke after Umar Tal's Holy War" (Ph.D. thesis, Michigan State University, 1989), pp. 2, 96–97, 135–39, 222–23; John Yoder, "Fly and Elephant Parties: Political Polarization in Dahomey, 1840–1870," *JAH* 15 (1974): 417–32; Richard W. Bulliet, *The Patricians of Nishapur; A Study in Medieval Islamic Social History* (Cambridge, Mass., 1972).
2 David Robinson, *The Holy War of Umar Tal: The Western Sudan in the mid-Nineteenth Century* (Oxford, 1985), pp. 16–46.
3 See Jan Vansina, *Oral Tradition as History* (Madison, 1985).
4 For further discussion, see Jack Goody, "The Impact of Islamic Writing on the Oral Cultures of West Africa," *CEA* 11 (1971): 455–66; Goody, ed., *Literacy in Traditional Societies* (Cambridge, 1968).
5 Philip D. Curtin, "The Uses of Oral Tradition in Senegambia: Malik Sii and the Foundation of Bundu," *CEA* 15 (1975): 189.
6 Mamadou Aissa Kaba Diakité, "Livre renfermant la généalogie des diverses tribus noires du Soudan et l'histoire des rois après Mahomet, suivant les reseignments fournis par certaines personnes et ceux recueillis dans les anciens livres," *Annales de l'académie des sciences coloniales* 3 (1929): 189–225.
7 Diakité, "Livre," p. 189; M. G. Adam, *Legendes historiques du pays de Nioro* (Paris, 1904).
8 Djibril Ly, "Coutumes et contes des Toucouleurs du Fouta-Toro," *BCEHSAOF* 21 (1938): 316–17.
9 Felix Brigaud, *Etudes Sénégalaises, No. 9: Histoire traditionelle du Sénégal* (St. Louis, 1962), pp. 218–19.
10 See David Robinson, "Un historien et anthropologue sénégalais: Shaikh Musa Kamara," *CEA* 28 (1988): 89–116.
11 André Rançon, *Le Bondou* (Bordeaux, 1894), p. 5. Also in *Bulletin de la société de géographie de Bordeaux* 7 (1894): 433–63, 465–84, 497–548, 561–91, 593–647. By Rançon's own admission, these measurements are not precise. He actually gives the coordinates 14° 20' and 15° 50' longitude; but Paris serves as the prime meridian. Since Paris' longitudinal coordinates are 2° 20', I simply subtracted 2° 20' to return to the Greenwich standard. Lamartiny, also using Paris as the prime, gives Bundu's location at 14° to 15° longitude west, and 13° to 15° latitude north. J. J. Lamartiny, *Etudes africaines: le Bondou et le Bambouck* (Paris, 1884), p. 5.
12 A. Sabatié, *Le Sénégal: sa conquête et son organisation (1364–1925)* (St. Louis du Sénégal, 1925), p. 305; Anne Raffenel, *Voyage dans l'Afrique occidentale* (Paris, 1846), pp. 268–69.
13 Robin Hallet, *Proceedings of the Association for the Discovery of the Interior Parts of Africa* (London, 1967), pp. 334–39.

14 Gaspard T. Mollien, *Travels in Africa to the Sources of the Senegal and Gambia in 1818*, trans. (London, 1825), pp. 77–78; C. A. Walckenaer, *Collection des relations de voyages par mer et par terre, en differentes parties de l'Afrique*, 21 vols. (Paris, 1842), 6: 215–16.
15 Compare this with Rançon, *Bondou*, pp. 6–7; Philip D. Curtin, *Economic Change in Precolonial Africa* (Madison, 1975), p. 23. Lamartiny also divided Bundu into four sections: Upper Bundu, Lower Bundu, the Ferlo, and Wuli, the latter region having been conquered by Bokar Saada (Lamartiny, *Etudes*, p. 5).
16 Rançon, *Bondou*, p. 7.
17 S. L. Pascal, "Voyage d'exploration dans le Bambouck, Haut-Sénégal," *Revue algerienne et coloniale* 3 (1860): 141.
18 Curtin, *Economic Change*, pp. 24–29. For a more complete discussion of the various air masses, see W. B. Morgan and J. C. Pugh, *West Africa* (London, 1969), pp. 176–249.
19 Rançon, *Bondou*, pp. 33–34. Lamartiny, *Etudes*, p. 50.
20 Curtin, *Economic Change*; also Robinson, *Holy War*, pp. 59–60.
21 Curtin, *Economic Change*.
22 Ibid. *Le Moniteur* 25 (16 September 1856): 1.
23 Curtin, *Economic Change*, p. 31; *Le Moniteur* 18 (29 July 1856): 4–5.
24 Mollien, *Travels*, pp. 77–78; Walckenaer, *Collection*, 6: 215–16; 7: 161–62; Major William Gray and Surgeon Dochard, *Travels in Western Africa in the Years 1818, 1819, 1820, and 1821* (London, 1825), pp. 179–80; J. Mavidal, *Le Sénégal* (Paris, 1863), p. 21.
25 This is confirmed by Curtin: out of the total amount of land, only 5.6 percent was considered suitable for cultivation, and only 1.6 percent had ever been cultivated in the past (Curtin, *Economic Change*, p. 25).
26 Curtin, *Economic Change*, pp. 22–29.
27 Hallet, *Proceedings*, pp. 334, 341; *ANF*, C6–9, no. 16; Mungo Park, *Travels in the Interior Districts of Africa, 1795–1797, 1805* (London, 1817), pp. 90–92; Francis Moore, *Travels into the Inland Parts of Africa* (London, 1738), pp. 223–24. Mollien does not agree that cattle and horses were plentiful; his opinion is in the minority (Mollien, *Travels*, pp. 77–78; Walckenaer, *Collection*, 6: 215–16). See also Robin Law, *The Horse in West African History* (New York, 1980).
28 Raffenel, *Voyage*, pp. 105–6. However, one will see as many pastoralists in Bundu today as in the Middle Senegal Valley.
29 Lamartiny, *Etudes*, p. 50.
30 Gray, *Travels*, p. 185. Walckenaer, *Collection*, 6: 163–65.
31 Curtin, *Economic Change*, p. 6. On the other hand, given the similarities between these several cultures, one could argue that Bundu was more homogeneous than not.
32 Curtin, *Economic Change*, pp. 29–37. See Hubert Deschamps, *Le Sénégal et la Gambie* (Paris, 1964), esp. p. 35; Yaya Wane, *Les Toucouleurs du Fouta Toro* (Dakar, 1969), p. 9.
33 See L. J. B. Bérenger-Feraud, *Les peuplades de la Sénégambie* (Paris, 1879). Concerning slavery and useful theoretical frameworks, see Suzanne Miers and Igor Kopytoff, eds., *Slavery in Africa: Historical and Anthropological Perspectives* (Madison, 1977) and Orlando Patterson, *Slavery and Social Death: A Comparative Study* (Cambridge, 1982).
34 The following discussion of ethnicity and social organization in Senegambia is derived from Boubacar Barry, *La Sénégambie du XVe au XIXe siècle: traite negrière, Islam et conquête coloniale* (Paris, 1988), pp. 41–44, 52–53, 62; and Curtin, *Economic Change*, pp. 29–47. See also Nicholas Hopkins, "Maninka Social Organization," in Carleton T. Hodge, ed., *Papers on the Manding* (Bloomington, 1971).
35 *Résultats provisoires du recensement général de la population d'avril 1976* (Dakar: Bureau National du Recensement, 1976). The *département de Bakel* is part of the larger *région du Sénégal-Oriental*. By 1979, the population of the Sénégal-Oriental region had increased from 286,148 to 300,980, representing an annual rate of increase of 2 percent. Therefore, the *département de Bakel* also probably increased. See *La Sénégal en chiffres* (Dakar, 1983).

36 Park, *Travels*, pp. 88–89.
37 Raffenel, *Voyage*, p. 269.
38 Mollien, *Travels*, p. 79; Park, *Travels*, p. 89; Lamartiny, *Etudes*, pp. 45–46.
39 Lamartiny, *Etudes*, pp. 44–45; Raffenel, *Voyage*, pp. 276–77. Rançon (*Bondou*, pp. 166–67) adds a fourth class, the *qāḍīs*. It is my opinion that Rançon confuses Bundu's legal system with its educational and purely religious institutions.
40 Lamin Sanneh, *The Jakhanke* (London, 1979), pp. 150–51.
41 Lamartiny, *Etudes*, pp. 44–45; Rançon, *Bondou*, p. 167.
42 Raffenel, *Voyage*, pp. 275–76; Sanneh, *Jakhanke*, pp. 150–55.
43 Raffenel, *Voyage*, pp. 275–76.
44 See Paul Marty, *L'Islam en Guinée* (Paris, 1921), pp. 108–47; Jean Suret-Canale, "Touba in Guinea: Holy Place of Islam," in *African Perspectives*, ed. Christopher Allen and R. W. Johnson (Cambridge, 1970); Sanneh, *Jakhanke*, pp. 94–106; Thomas Hunter, "The Development of an Islamic Tradition of Learning Among the Jahanka of West Africa" (Ph.D. thesis, University of Chicago, 1977), pp. 250–59.
45 FC, no. 1.
46 The term Fudi meant a "man of learning" to the Malinke and Fulbe, but to the Jakhanke it meant someone who had successfully studied the *Tafsīr al-Jalalayn* of al-Mahalli (d. 1459), and al-Suyuti (d. 1505) (Hunter, "Jahanka," p. 149).
47 FC, no. 1.
48 Ibid.
49 David Robinson, *Chiefs and Clerics: Abdul Bokar Kan and Futa Toro (1853–1891)* (Oxford, 1975), pp. 7–8.
50 FC, no. 1.
51 Park, *Travels*, p. 71. He says that one book was called "Al Shara," and was a work of *tafsīr*, an apparent misnomer.
52 Description of Galaam by Commandant at Fort Saint Joseph, 1 April 1725, ANF C6-9.
53 Paul Marty, *Etudes sénégalaises (1785–1826)* (Paris, [1926]), p. 175.
54 Curtin, *Economic Change*, p. 76.
55 Ibid. Other traditions claim the Jakhanke came to Bundu after Malik Sy, and that Bubu Malik was the first to encounter them. See Maimouna Mamadou Sy, Grand Dakar, 2 February 1966, trans. H. A. Sy; and Kadealy Diakité, Dakar, 23 February 1966, trans. H. A. Sy, CC T1, side 2.
56 Curtin, *Economic Change*, p. 76.
57 Hunter, "Jahanka," p. 195.
58 Sanneh (*Jakhanke*, p. 46) says Malik Sy actually gave his daughter to Abdallah, Muhammad Fudi's grandfather, who then gave her to his grandson.
59 Hunter, "Jahanka," pp. 203–7.
60 FC, nos. 1, 27, 29.
61 Kadealy Diakité, Dakar, 23 February 1966, trans. H. A. Sy, CC T1, side 2; Pierre Smith, "Les Diakhanke: histoire d'une dispersion," *Bulletin et memoire de la société d'anthropologie de Paris* 8 (1965). The Jakhite-Kabba clan had become the favored clerics of the Sissibe by the reign of Bokar Saada (Hunter, "Jahanka," pp. 238–39).
62 Hunter, "Jahanka," pp. 218–20.
63 Ibid., pp. 196–97; Raffenel, *Voyage*, pp. 91–94.
64 Hunter, "Jahanka," pp. 218–20.
65 The exceptions to this rule are the "wars in the public interest" (*hurūb al-masālih*), involving the fighting of marauders, rebels, and apostates. See Rudolph Peters, *Jihad in Medieval and Modern Islam* (Leiden, 1977).
66 William Fox, *A Brief History of the Wesleyan Missions on the Western Coast of Africa* (London, 1851), p. 468.
67 Ibid.

68 Ibid., pp. 466–67.
69 Rançon, *Dans la Haut-Gambie, 1891–1892* (Paris, 1894), pp. 378–9.
70 Bakel to Governor, 16 October 1865, ANF 13G 169 (200Mi 926).

2: Malik Sy and the origins of a pragmatic polity

1 Raffenel, *Voyage*, was published in 1846. The other is Frederic Carrère and Paul Holle, *De la sénégambie française* (Paris, 1855).
2 Curtin, "Uses of Oral Tradition," p. 191.
3 Ibid. I am including the collection of Alfa Ibrahim Sow, *Chroniques et récits du Fouta Djalon* (Paris, 1968), pp. 55–83.
4 Amadou Abdoul Sy, Tambacounda, 12 June 1988; Lamartiny, *Etudes*, p. 6; Rançon, *Bondou*, p. 40; Roux, *Notice*, p. 2; M. G. Adam, *Légendes Historiques du Pays de Nioro (Sahel)* (Paris, 1904), p. 47; Kamara, "Histoire," p. 788; Diakité, "Livre," p. 210; Saki Olal N'Diaye, "The Story of Malik Sy," trans. and ed. Philip Curtin, Neil Skinner, and Hammady Amadou Sy, *CEA* 11 (1971): 471–73. Ly reports that Malik Sy lived in Podor, while Issaga Opa Sy maintains that he was born there (Goudiry, 8 June 1988).
5 L. J. B. Bérenger-Feraud, *Recueil de contes populaires de la Sénégambie* (Paris, 1885), p. 179.
6 Rançon states that Malik Sy "definitely" arrived Bundu c. 1681. His first son was born when he was thirty years old. He subsequently spent at least fourteen years travelling before he arrived in Bundu. I simply subtracted 44 from 1681 (Rançon, *Bondou*, pp. 40–46). Curtin estimates he was born in the 1640s ("Jihad in West Africa: Early Phases and Interrelations in Mauritania and Senegal," *JAH* 12 (1971): 11–24, p. 18.
7 N'Diaye, "Malik Sy," pp. 471–87.
8 Rançon, *Bondou*, p. 41.
9 Kamara, "Histoire," p. 788.
10 Rançon, *Bondou*, pp. 40–41.
11 Kamara, "Histoire," p. 788.
12 Rançon, *Bondou*, p. 41.
13 N'Diaye, "Malik Sy," pp. 471–73; Kamara, "Histoire," p. 788; Adam, *Légendes*, pp. 47–48; Diakité, "Livre," p. 210.
14 Adam, *Légendes*, pp. 47–48; Diakité, "Livre," p. 210.
15 Diakité, "Livre," p. 210; Adam, *Légendes*, p. 47.
16 Ly, "Coutumes," p. 316.
17 Deschamps, *Le Sénégal*, p. 35.
18 Kamara, "Histoire," p. 792; also see J. R. Willis, "The Torodbe Clerisy: A Social View," *JAH* 19 (1978): 195–212.
19 David Robinson, "Abdul Qadir and Shaykh Umar: A Continuing Tradition of Islamic Scholarship in Futa Toro," *IJAHS* 6 (1973): 289; J. R. Willis, "Reflections on the Differences of Islam in West Africa," in *Studies in West Africa Islamic History: The Cultivators of Islam*, ed. J. R. Willis (London, 1979), pp. 21–22.
20 Robinson, "Abdul Qadir," p. 289.
21 Rançon, *Bondou*, p. 39.
22 Kamara, "Histoire," pp. 789–97; Willis, "Reflections," pp. 21–22; Rançon, *Bondou*, p. 39.
23 Rançon, *Bondou*, p. 185.
24 Ibid., pp. 184–85.
25 Hammadi Koulibali, Naye, 8 September 1987, trans. Baba Traore; Rançon, *Bondou*, p. 41; N'Diaye, "Malik Sy," pp. 471–73; Wilks, "Transmission."
26 Stewart, *Islam*, p. 29; Wilks, "Transmission."
27 Rançon, *Bondou*, p. 41.
28 N'Diaye, "Malik Sy," pp. 471–73. *Tierno* was the lowest in the hierarchy of clerical titles.

29 Amadi Bokar Sy, Tambacounda, 13 June 1988. Some sources contend that he went to study in Pir (Rançon, *Bondou*, p. 42; Roux, *Notice*, p. 2; Brigaud, *Etudes*, pp. 218–19), but this is probably a reflection of Pir's prominence in subsequent centuries. Kamara writes that Malik Sy studied with "certain Moorish scholars" (Kamara, "Histoire," p. 797), but he fails to cite a locality. Because of Suyuma's location, southern Mauritania is a distinct possibility.
30 Stewart, *Islam*, p. 29.
31 Rançon, *Bondou*, pp. 41–42; see also Roux, *Notice*, pp. 2–3.
32 Lamartiny, *Etudes*, p. 6; Rançon, *Bondou*, pp. 42–43; Roux, *Notice*, pp. 3–4; Diakité, "Livre," p. 210; Brigaud, *Etudes*, pp. 218–19; Kamara, "Histoire," p. 798; Adam, *Légendes*, pp. 48–54.
33 Levtzion, "The Early States of the Western Sudan to 1500," in Ajayi and Crowder, *History of West Africa*, pp. 130–31
34 Rançon, *Bondou*, p. 42.
35 Bérenger-Feraud. *Recueil*, p. 179; Bérenger-Feraud, *Les peuplades de la Sénégambie*, pp. 219–23.
36 Roux, *Notice*, p. 2.
37 Adam (*Légendes*, pp. 47–54) and Diakité ("Livre," p. 210) both recount an anecdote in which Malik Sy kills a slave of the *Satigi* (title of the Denyanke ruler) over the disposal of a sheep. The point of the story is that there was hostility between the Denyanke and the *Torodbe*.
38 Rançon, *Bondou*, p. 42–43.
39 Ly, "Coutumes," p. 316; Amadi Bokar Sy concurs with this profile (Tambacounda, 13 June 1988).
40 Ibid.
41 N'Diaye, "Malik Sy," pp. 471–87.
42 Carrère and Holle, *Sénégambie*, p. 159.
43 Bérenger-Feraud, *Recueil*, p. 159.
44 Rançon, *Bondou*, p. 42.
45 Ibid.
46 Lamartiny, *Etudes*, p. 6; Rançon, *Bondou*, p. 43.
47 Diakité, "Livre," p. 210; Roux, *Notice*, p. 3; Rançon, *Bondou*, p. 43; Adam, *Légendes*, pp. 48–54; Gaston Boyer, *Un peuple de l'Ouest soudanais: les Diawara* (Dakar, 1953), pp. 28–30.
48 Diakité, "Livre," p. 210; Boyer, *Les Diawara*, pp. 28–30.
49 Adam, *Légendes*, pp. 47–54.
50 Rançon, *Bondou*, pp. 43–45; Roux, *Notice*, p. 210.
51 Louis Tauxier, *Histoire des Bambara* (Paris, 1942), pp. 112–25; Charles Monteil, *Les Bambara du Segou et du Kaarta* (Paris, 1924), p. 104; J. R. Willis, "The Western Sudan from the Moroccan Invasion (1591) to the Death of al-Mukhtar al-Kunti (1811)," in Ajayi and Crowder, *History of West Africa*, pp. 530–31.
52 Amadi Bokar Sy, Tambacounda, 13 June 1988. Malik Sy is described as having unsuccessfully tried to convert the *Tunka* (Brigaud, *Etudes*, pp. 218–19).
53 Bérenger-Feraud, *Recueil*, p. 179.
54 Ibid.; Carrère and Holle, *Sénégambie*, pp. 159–61; Lamartiny, *Etudes*, p. 6.
55 Carrère and Holle, *Sénégambie*, p. 160. Ly does not mention the *Tunka*'s problem; instead, he records that Malik Sy cured the madness of the *Tunka*'s daughter (Ly, "Coutumes," pp. 316–17).
56 Bérenger-Feraud, *Recueil*, pp. 180–84; Lamartiny, *Etudes*, p. 6; Adam, *Légendes*, pp. 47–54; Amadou Abdoul Sy, Tambacounda, 12 June 1988; Amadi Bokar Sy, Tambacounda, 13 June 1988.
57 Rançon, *Bondou*, p. 46. Bérenger-Feraud, *Recueil*, pp. 180–84.
58 Doudou, in Brigaud, *Etudes*, pp. 289–90; Adam, *Légendes*, pp. 48–54; Lamartiny, *Etudes*, p. 6.

59 Walckenaer, *Collection*, 3: 174.
60 Carrère and Holle, *Sénégambie*, p. 159.
61 Lamartiny, *Etudes*, p. 6.
62 Hammadi Koulibali, Naye, 8 September 1988, trans. Baba Traore; Amadou Abdoul Sy, Tambacounda, 12 June 1988; Rançon, *Bondou*, p. 42–44; Brigaud, *Etudes*, pp. 218–19; Willis, "Reflections," p. 24; Willis, "The Torodbe Clerisy," p. 201. Lamartiny says there were four companions (*Etudes*, p. 6).
63 Kamara, "Histoire," p. 798.
64 Adam, *Légendes*, pp. 48–54; Diakité, "Livre," p. 211; Carrère and Holle, *Sénégambie*, p. 159.
65 Rançon, *Bondou*, p. 47; Brigaud, *Etudes*, pp. 218–19; Doudou, in Brigaud, *Etudes*, pp. 289–90; Rançon (p. 38) says Guirobe was eight kilometers from Senoudebou, whereas Roux (p. 1) says twenty kilometers.
66 Rançon, *Bondou*, pp. 37–40; Roux, *Notice*, pp. 1–2.
67 Rançon, *Bondou*, p. 38; Curtin, "Jihad," p. 18; Brigaud, *Etudes*, pp. 218–19; Roux, *Notice*, p. 1.
68 Rançon, *Bondou*, p. 38.
69 Adam, *Légendes*, pp. 53–54.
70 Ibid.
71 N'Diaye, "Malik Sy," pp. 473–87.
72 Ibid; Amadi Bokar Sy, Tambacounda, 13 June 1988.
73 Rançon, *Bondou*, p. 38.
74 Roux, *Notice*, p. 4.
75 Ibid., p. 1. Rançon lifts this passage almost verbatim (*Bondou*, p. 39).
76 Rançon, *Bondou*, p. 39.
77 Ibid.; Roux, *Notice*, p. 2.
78 Rançon, *Bondou*, p. 39.
79 Ibid, pp. 39–40; Roux, *Notice*, p. 2.
80 Rançon, *Bondou*, p. 38; Demba Simbalou Sock, Senoudebou 1966, CC T3, side 2.
81 Rançon, *Bondou*, p. 39; Roux, *Notice*, pp. 1–2. Kamara mentions a group called the "Dyiggobe"; what their role was is unclear ("Histoire," p. 798).
82 Sanneh, *Jakhanke*, p. 54; Hunter, "Jahanka," pp. 195–202; Smith, "Les Diakhanke."
83 Carrère and Holle, *Sénégambie*, pp. 160–62.
84 Bérenger-Feraud, *Recueil*, pp. 179–83.
85 Lamartiny, *Etudes*, p. 6; see also Doudou, in Brigaud, *Etudes*, pp. 289–90; Bérenger-Feraud, *Recueil*, pp. 179–83; repeated in interview with Amadi Bokar Sy, Tambacounda, 13 June 1988.
86 Adam, *Légendes*, p. 54.
87 Rançon, *Bondou*, p. 46.
88 Carrère and Holle, *Sénégambie*, pp. 159–60; Lamartiny, *Etudes*, p. 6, Bérenger-Feraud, *Recueil*, pp. 179–83; Roux, *Notice*, p. 3; Raffenel, *Voyage*, pp. 269–71.
89 Bérenger-Feraud, *Recueil*, pp. 179–83.
90 Ibid.
91 Carrère and Holle, *Sénégambie*, p. 160.
92 Lamartiny, *Etudes*, p. 6; Roux, *Notice*, p. 3; Rançon, *Bondou*, pp. 46–47; Doudou, in Brigaud, *Etudes*, pp. 289–90; Adam, *Légendes*, p. 54; Ly, "Coutumes," p. 316–17; N'Diaye, "Malik Sy," pp. 473–87.
93 Roux, *Notice*, p. 3; Rançon, *Bondou*, p. 46.
94 Rançon, *Bondou*, p. 46.
95 Curtin, "Uses of Oral Tradition," p. 192.
96 Carrère and Holle, Bérenger-Feraud, Dieng Doudou, Adam, Diakité, and Ly all fail to mention Malik Sy's death.
97 Roux, *Notice*, p. 4.

98 Lamartiny, *Etudes*, p. 6.
99 Rançon, *Bondou*, p. 47.
100 Ibid.
101 Hammadi Koulibali, Naye, 7 September 1988, trans. Baba Traore; Lamartiny, *Etudes*, p. 6.
102 Rançon, *Bondou*, pp. 47–48.
103 Sow, *Chronicles*, pp. 59–61.
104 Ibid.; Roux, *Notice*, pp. 6–7. Issaga Opa Sy is adamant that the *Tunka* was responsible for Malik Sy's death (Goudiry, 8 June 1988).
105 See David Robinson, "The Islamic Revolution of Futa Toro," *IJAHS* 8 (1975): 185–221, for a discussion of the meaning of *al-Imām*.
106 On Ayuba Sulayman Diallo, see Thomas Bluett, *Some Memoirs on the Life of Job* (London, 1734) Douglas Grant, *The Fortunate Slave* (London, 1968); Philip D. Curtin, ed., *Africa Remembered* (Madison, 1967), pp. 23–44; Moore, *Travels*. On southern Gajaaga in the late seventeenth century see Cornelius Hodges, in Thora Stone, "The Journey of Cornelius Hodges in Senegambia," *English Historical Review* 39 (1924): 89–95; Le Pere Jean-Baptiste Labat, *Nouvelle relation de l'Afrique occidentale*, 4 vols. (Paris, 1728), 3: 294–371.
107 Rançon, *Bondou*, p. 47.
108 Michael A. Gomez, "The Problem with Malik Sy and the Foundation of Bundu," *CEA* 25 (1985): 537–53. Contrast this with Curtin, "Jihad," 11–14. In contrast, Amadi Bokar Sy characterizes the war with Tiyaabu as *jihād* (Tambacounda, 13 June 1988).
109 For a discussion of this conflict, see Boubacar Barry, "La guerre des marabouts dans la région du fleuve Sénégal de 1673 à 1677," *BIFAN* 33 (1971): 564–89; H. T. Norris, "Znāga Islam during the Seventeenth and Eighteenth Centuries," *BSOAS* 32 (1969): 496–98; Norris, *The Tuaregs: Their Islamic Legacy and its Diffusion in the Sahel* (Wilts, England: 1975); Charles C. Stewart, "Southern Saharan Scholarship and the Bilad al-Sudan," *JAH* 17 (1976): 90–91; Willis, "Reflections," pp. 5–12; Nehemia Levtzion, "North-West Africa," in *Cambridge History of Africa* (Cambridge, 1975), 4: 199–200; Paul Marty, *L'emirat des Trarzas* (Paris, 1919), pp. 38–59; Rene Basset, *Mission au Sénégal* (Paris, 1909), pp. 463–74. For primary sources, review Ismael Hamet, *Chroniques de la Mauritanie sénégalaises* (Paris, 1911); Carson I. A. Ritchie, "Deux textes sur le Sénégal," *BIFAN* 30 (1968): 289–353; P. Cultru, *Premier voyage du Sier de La Courbe fait à la coste d'Afrique en 1685* (Paris, 1913); John Barbot, *A Description of the Coasts of North and South Guinea* (n.p., 1732), p. 62.
110 Abdel Wedoud Ould Cheikh, "Nomadisme, Islam et pouvoir politique dans la société Maure precoloniale (XIème siècle – XIXème siècle)," 3 vols. (Paris: Doctorat d'Etat, 1985), 3: 830–964.
111 Boubacar Barry, *Le royaume de Waalo* (Paris, 1972); Charles C. Stewart, "Political Authority and Social Stratification in Mauritania," in Gellner and Micaud, eds., *Arabs and Berbers* (London, 1973), pp. 375–93. In refocusing attention on the theme of Islam, Ould Cheikh takes issue with both the economic determinism of Barry and the legitimizing mythological interpretation of Stewart.
112 Walckenaer, *Collection*, 3: 174; Ritchie "Deux textes," p. 340.
113 Barbot, *Description*, p. 62; Cultru, *Premier voyage*, p. 133; Walckenaer, *Collection*, 3: 175.
114 Adam, *Légendes*, pp. 48–54. The account of Denyanke oppression of the Sy family is told in anecdotal form.
115 For a more theoretical discussion of the frontier in Africa, see Igor Kopytoff, ed., *The African Frontier: the Reproduction of Traditional African Societies* (Bloomington, 1987).

3: Consolidation and expansion in the eighteenth century

1 Rançon, *Bondou*, p. 48.
2 Ibid.; Lamartiny, *Etudes*, p. 6; Roux, *Notice*, p. 4; Issaga Opa Sy (Goudiry, 8 June 1988)

Notes to pages 55–60

  states that Bubu Malik Sy's mother was from Futa Jallon, a claim unsupported by other sources.
3 Rançon, *Bondou*, pp. 48–49.
4 Roux, *Notice*, p. 4.
5 Rançon, *Bondou*, p. 49; Lamartiny, *Etudes*, p. 6; Roux, *Notice*, p. 4; Issaga Opa Sy, Goudiry, 8 June 1988.
6 Rançon, *Bondou*, p. 48. Lamartiny and Roux do not support this.
7 Since Maka Jiba found refuge at Fissa-Tiambe, this *Torodbe* village had probably recognized his father as ruler (Rançon, *Bondou*, p. 51).
8 Lamartiny, *Etudes*, p. 7. See also Kamara, "Histoire," p. 800.
9 Labat, *Nouvelle relation*, 4: 1–6; *Supplement*, p. 22.
10 Lamartiny, *Etudes*, pp. 6–7.
11 Rançon, *Bondou*, pp. 49–50; Roux, *Notice*, pp. 4–5; Rançon lifts this verbatim from Roux.
12 Ibid. (again, Rançon simply repeats Roux); Amadou Abdoul Sy, Tambacounda, 12 June 1988.
13 Curtin, "Uses of Oral Tradition," p. 195.
14 Amadi Bokar Sy, 13 June 1988, Tambacounda; N'Diaye, "Malik Sy," pp. 473–81, n. See also Hunter, "Jahanka," pp. 340–402, for a discussion of *baṭin* learning. Amadi Bokar Sy reiterates the account (Tambacounda, 13 June 1988).
15 N'Diaye, "Malik Sy," pp. 473–81.
16 Ibid.
17 Rançon, *Bondou*, p. 49.
18 Rançon (*Bondou*, p. 49) says that Bubu Malik had become more confident in his relations with the Bacili, "certain that the claims of his father were respected by the Tunka, ... "
19 Rançon, *Bondou*, p. 50; Lamartiny, *Etudes*, p. 7.
20 Rançon, *Bondou*, p. 50; Lamartiny, *Etudes*, p. 7; Roux, *Notice*, p. 4.
21 See K. G. Davies, *The Royal African Company* (London, 1957), pp. 24, 109–13, 170–82, 216–17, 232–33, 344.
22 Gum was necessary for the European textile industry, and was also used in candy and papermaking. Curtin, *Africa Remembered*, p. 18. See also Robin Hallet, *The Penetration of Africa* (London, 1965).
23 Curtin, *Economic Change*, pp. 216–17.
24 Prosper Cultru, *Histoire du Sénégal, du XVe siècle à 1870* (Paris, 1910), p. 245.
25 Curtin, *Economic Change*, pp. 216–17.
26 André Delcourt, *La France et les établissements français au Sénégal, entre 1713 et 1763* (Dakar, 1952), p. 44.
27 See Abdoulaye Bathily, *Les portes de l'or: le royaume de Galam (Sénégal), de l'ère musulmane au temps des negriers (VIIIe – XVIIIe siècle)* (Paris, 1989), for a discussion of the slave trade in the Upper Senegal Valley.
28 Curtin, *Africa Remembered*, pp. 18–20.
29 Curtin, "Lure of Bambuk Gold," p. 624. In light of Bathily, gold was not the major reason, but an important one.
30 Ibid. See also Delcourt, *La France*, pp. 107–8; Labat, *Nouvelle relation*, 2: 113; Hallet, *Penetration of Africa*, pp. 88–90; Curtin, "Lure of Bambuk Gold," pp. 624–26.
31 W. Raymond Wood, "An Archeological Appraisal of Early European Settlements in the Senegambia," *JAH* 8 (1967): 50–51; *Supplement*, p. 1, ff.
32 Rançon, *Bondou*, p. 50; Lamartiny, *Etudes*, p. 7; Roux, *Notice*, p. 4. Kamara says he was killed at Gumbay ("Histoire," p. 799).
33 The dating for Bubu Malik is confused, to say the least. Roux (*Notice*, p. 4) says that he reigned three years, and offers no chronology. Lamartiny (*Etudes*, p. 6) gives the years 1720 to 1747 as his tenure, and Paul Marty (*Etudes sénégalaises [1785–1826]* [Paris, 1926], pp. 103–4) simply repeats these dates. Adam (*Légendes*, p. 54) claims he reigned thirteen

years, the same as Malik Sy. Based upon Rançon's material, the dates are from 1699 to 1718, or nineteen years (*Bondou*, p. 48). Curtin (*Supplement*, pp. 30–31) places Bubu Malik's tenure between 1700/1702 to 1719/1727, a maximum of twenty-seven years.
The current study argues that all of the above are inaccurate. Diakité ("Livre," p. 211) and Kamara ("Histoire," p. 816) in concurrence with Curtin's own Arabic material (FC nos. 4, 18 and 30) agree that Bubu Malik reigned seventeen years. This figure is essentially confirmed by Rançon (*Bondou*, p. 50), who writes that the decentralized interregnum lasted from 1718 to 1728, during which time most of the Sissibe were run out of Bundu. The independent report of Compagnon (Labat, *Nouvelle relation*, 4: 1–6; Walckenaer, *Collection*, 3: 257–58), who traveled through the region in 1716 and who failed to mention Bundu or any other centralized state in the area of Bundu, confirms that the interregnum had commenced by 1716. If Bubu Malik began reigning in 1699, a seventeen-year tenure, consistent with certain of the aforementioned sources, would have ended in 1715, one year before Compagnon's arrival, and thus explain his failure to mention a centralized Bundu. Hence, a reign of seventeen years, from 1699 to 1715, is quite plausible, but should be viewed as an approximation.
34 Rançon, *Bondou*, p. 51; Roux, *Notice*, p. 5.
35 Ibid.
36 Ibid.
37 Rançon, *Bondou*, p. 50.
38 *Supplement*, pp. 30–31.
39 Ibid. I have made a thorough search for Thomas Hull's "Voyage to Bundo." The manuscript is supposed to be in the library of the Duke of Buccleuch. However, the Scottish Record Office cannot locate the document (personal correspondence, 9/84). I have corresponded with Philip D. Curtin on several occasions; so far he has been unable to find his personal copy of the manuscript. The search continues.
40 Report by Commander of Fort Saint Joseph, 1 April 1725, ANF, C6 9.
41 Claude Boucard, "Relation de Bambouc (1729)," *BIFAN* 36 (1974): 246–75, p. 250.
42 Curtin and Boulegue, in Boucard, "Relation de Bambouc," p. 250, n.
43 FC, nos. 4, 18, and 30; *Supplement*, p. 30; Kamara, "Histoire," p. 816 (Kamara has Maka Jiba and Tumane Bubu reversed); Diakité, "Livre," p. 211 (lists Tumane Bubu as *Eliman* Bakar Sy).
44 Rançon, *Bondou*, p. 50.
45 Lamartiny, *Etudes*, p. 7; Roux, *Notice*, p. 5; Rançon, *Bondou*, p. 52; *Supplement*, p. 30; Kamara, "Histoire," p. 816; FC nos. 4, 18, 30; Diakité, "Livre." Diakité refers to him as *Elimam* Manza.
46 Rançon, *Bondou*, Lamartiny, *Etudes*, p. 7; Issaga Opa Sy, Goudiry, 8 June 1988.
47 Rançon, *Bondou*, pp. 51–52.
48 Ibid., p. 52; Roux, *Notice*, p. 5.
49 Pierre David, *Journal d'un voyage fait en Bambouc en 1744* (Paris, 1974).
50 Ibid., p. 83.
51 Ibid., p. 151.
52 Ibid., pp. 83–84.
53 Ibid., p. 157. According to a report filed in 1784, however, a *comptoir* was established at Kidira some time after 1744 ("Observation sur l'importance de la colonie du Sénégal," 1784, ANF C6 17).
54 Ibid., pp. 151–52.
55 Sanneh, *Jakhanke*, pp. 54–57.
56 Hunter, "Jahanka," p. 217; Rançon, *Bondou*, pp. 180–81.
57 Sanneh, *Jakhanke*, pp. 46–47; Hunter, "Jahanka," pp. 203–207.
58 Sanneh, *Jakhanke*, pp. 46–48; Hunter, "Jahanka," pp. 207–209.
59 Sanneh, *Jakhanke*, pp. 46–48. Sanneh estimates that up to sixty people were in the single compound.

60 Hunter, "Jahanka," pp. 209–17; Sanneh, *Jakhanke*, pp. 56–58.
61 Sanneh, *Jakhanke*, pp. 53–57.
62 Sanneh, for example, repeatedly makes the point that the Jakhanke were not traders, and that their involvement in trade was minimal (*Jakhanke*, pp. 53–54). Hunter concurs ("Jahanka," pp. 209–17). In contrast, Curtin maintains that the Jakhanke were fully engaged in commerce (*Economic Change*, pp. 75–83).
63 Sanneh, *Jakhanke*, pp. 56–58. Sanneh also includes Goundiourou, or Gunjur, as a Bundunke town. There was such a town in Bundu, but the one Sanneh describes is the Goundiourou of Khasso, of greater antiquity and far greater renown as an intellectual and spiritual center than its Bundunke namesake.
64 Hunter, "Jahanka," pp. 209–11.
65 Sanneh, *Jakhanke*, pp. 143–203.
66 Amadi Bokar Sy (Tambacounda, 13 June 1988) claims that the N'Guenar were the wisest men in Bundu; Maimouna Mamadou Sy, Grand Dakar, 20 February 1966, trans. Hamady Amadou Sy, CC T1, side 2.
67 Amadi Bokar Sy, Tambacounda, 13 June 1988; Lamartiny, *Etudes*, p. 7; Roux, *Notice*, p. 6.
68 Rançon, *Bondou*, pp. 52–53; Lamartiny, *Etudes*, pp. 7–8. According to Issaga Opa Sy, Maka Jiba actually lived in Koussan (Goudiry, 8 June 1988).
69 Rançon, *Bondou*, pp. 52–53.
70 Ibid.
71 *Supplement*, p. 23.
72 Rançon, *Bondou*, p. 52.
73 David, *Journal*, pp. 151–52.
74 Moore, *Travels*, pp. 202–7.
75 Ibid., pp. 223–24.
76 Curtin, *Africa Remembered*, p. 28.
77 J. M. Gray, *A History of the Gambia* (Cambridge, 1940), p. 210.
78 Niani-Maro was twenty-five miles upstream from Joar (Curtin, *Africa Remembered*, p. 57, n.). The area west of Bundu was also called Ferlo.
79 Moore, *Travels*, p. 225, ff.; Walckenaer, *Collection*, 3: 476–77; Grant, *Fortunate Slave*, p. 162.
80 Moore, *Travels*, p. 230; Walckenaer, *Collection*, 3: 476–77.
81 Gray, *History of the Gambia*, p. 210.
82 *Supplement*, p. 32.
83 Report by Lawrore (or Lauvore), 25 June 1736, ANF C6 11.
84 Ibid.
85 Unsigned report, 6 November 1736, ANF C6 11.
86 Unsigned report, 6 December 1736, ANF C6 11.
87 J. Machat, *Document sur les établissements français et l'Afrique occidentale au XVIIIe siècle* (Paris, 1906), p. 46. In *Supplement*, Curtin claims that Ayuba was actually imprisoned from June of 1736 to early 1737 (p. 12).
88 Gray, *History of the Gambia*, p. 211.
89 Ibid.
90 Ibid., p. 212.
91 Curtin, *Africa Remembered*, p. 33.
92 Gray, *History of the Gambia*, p. 212; Curtin, *Africa Remembered*, p. 33.
93 John Nicholas, *Literary Anecdotes of the Eighteenth Century*, 6 vols. (London, 1812), 6: 90–91.
94 Gray, *History of the Gambia*, p. 212.
95 Hamet, *Chroniques*, p. 9; Robinson, *Chiefs and Clerics*, p. 12; Curtin, *Economic Changes*, pp. 51–54.
96 Levtzion, "North-West Africa," pp. 149–50.

97 Curtin, *Economic Changes*, p. 51.
98 Ibid.; Robinson, *Chiefs and Clerics*, p. 12; *Supplement*, p. 11, ff.
99 Robinson, *Chiefs and Clerics*, p. 12.
100 Levtzion, "North-West Africa," pp. 149–50. The figure of 150,000 is difficult to believe.
101 Curtin, *Economic Change*, pp. 182–83.
102 Bluett, *Memoirs*, pp. 10–15.
103 Curtin, *Economic Change*, p. 53.
104 Ibid., pp. 88–89, n. I would say that Koli Tenguella ranks very high as well. For more information on Samba Gelaajo Jegi, see Raffenel, *Nouveau voyage au pays des nègres*, 2 vols. (Paris 1856), 2: 320–47; Oumar Kane, "Samba Gelajo Jegi," *BIFAN* 32 (1970): 911–26; Bérenger-Feraud, *Recueil*, pp. 39–49; F. V. Equilbecq, *Contes populaires d'Afrique occidentale* (Paris, 1972), pp. 145–61; Frantz de Zeltner, *Contes du Sénégal et du Niger* (Paris, 1913), pp. 151–57; Lanrezac, "Legendes soudanaises," *Revue économique française* 5 (1907): 615–19; Sire Abbas Soh, *Chroniques du Fouta sénégalais*, trans. M. Delafosse and H. Gaden (Paris, 1913), pp. 31–32; CC T13 and T14.
105 Suret-Canale and Barry, "Western Atlantic Coast to 1800," pp. 482–83; also see Soh, *Chroniques du Fouta sénégalais*, and Oumar Kane, "Chronologie des Satigis de XVIIIème siècle," *BIFAN* 32 (1970): 755–65, for a chronology of the Satigis.
106 Bluett, *Memoirs*, pp. 10–15.
107 Suret-Canale and Barry, "Western Atlantic Coast to 1800," pp. 482–83; Soh, *Chroniques du Fouta sénégalais*, pp. 31–34, 151–66; Kane, "Chronologie," pp. 755–65.
108 Issaga Opa Sy, Goudiry, 9 June 1988; Rançon, *Bondou*, p. 53; Lamartiny, *Etudes*, p. 8.
109 Rançon, *Bondou*, pp. 53–54.
110 Issaga Opa Sy, Goudiry, 9 June 1988; Rançon, *Bondou*, pp. 53–55; Lamartiny, *Etudes*, p. 8.
111 Conseil du Sénégal to Compagnie des Indes, 25 July 1752, ANF C6 13; Conseil du Sénégal to CI, 2 March 1747, ANF C6 14; *Supplement*, pp. 12–13.
112 See Marty, *L'Islam en Guinée*, p. 4; Victor Azarya, *Aristocrats Facing Change: The Fulbe in Guinea, Nigeria, and Cameroon* (Chicago, 1978), pp. 18–19; Barry and Suret-Canale, "The Western Atlantic Coast," p. 491; Mervyn Hiskett, *The Development of Islam in West Africa* (New York, 1984), p. 142.
113 Jean Bayol, *Voyage en Sénégambie* (Paris, 1888), pp. 98–104; Sow, *Chroniques*, pp. 45–53; Paul Marty, *L'Islam en Guinée: Fouta-Diallon* (Paris, 1921), pp. 3–8.
114 Bayol, *Voyage*, p. 100. Tierno Samba was a celebrated *shaykh* from Fugumba (Marty, *l'Islam en Guinée*, pp. 3–4). Amadou Abdoul Sy (Tambacounda, 12 June 1988) makes the point that many Sissibe studied in Futa Jallon, but he offers no specific names of individuals.
115 Sow, *Chroniques*, pp. 66–67.
116 Ibid.; also Soh, *Chroniques du Fouta sénégalais*, pp. 35–36.
117 Rançon, *Bondou*, pp. 55–56; Lamartiny *Etudes*, p. 8.
118 Roux, *Notice*, p. 6.
119 Rançon, *Bondou*, pp. 56–57; Roux, *Notice*, p. 6; FC, nos. 4, 18, and 30; Kamara says he reigned four to six years ("Histoire," p. 816).
120 Rançon, *Bondou*, pp. 56–57.
121 Ibid., Lamartiny, *Etudes*, pp. 8–9; Amadou Abdoul Sy, Tambacounda, 12 June 1988.
122 Kamara, "Histoire," p. 800.

4: External reforms and internal consequences: Futa Toro and Bundu

1 Rançon, *Bondou*, p. 57.
2 Ibid., cf. pp. 58, 161; Kamara, "Histoire,'" pp. 800–801; Roux, *Notice*, p. 6.
3 Issaga Opa Sy, Goudiry, 9 June 1988; J. B. L. Durand, *Voyage au Sénégal* (Paris, 1807), p. 318. Durand, *A Voyage to Senegal*, trans. (London 1810); Durand "Voyage du Senegal à

Galam par terre," ANF C6 19; "Voyage de Rubault,'" in Walckenaer, *Collection*, 5: 276. Also see J. Ancelle, *Les explorations au Sénégal et dans les contrées voisines* (Paris, 1900), pp. 39–40, ff.
4 Walckenaer, *Collection*, 5: 283–84.
5 Park, *Travels*, p. 90.
6 Hallet, *Proceedings*, p. 341.
7 Ibid., pp. 342–43; Park, *Travels*, pp. 90–92.
8 Goldberry, in Walckenaer, *Collection*, 5: 443–51.
9 Ibid; E. Ann McDougall, "The Ijil Salt Industry: Its Role in the Precolonial Economy of the Western Sudan," (Ph.D thesis, University of Birmingham, 1980), p. 33, ff.
10 Saugnier and Brisson, *Voyages to the Coast of Africa*, trans., (London, 1792), pp. 216–19. P. Labarthe, *Voyage au Sénégal, pendant les années 1784 et 1785* (Paris, 1802).
11 Walckenaer, *Collection*, 5: 274.
12 Park, *Travels*, p. 66.
13 Walckenaer, *Collection*, 5: 277.
14 Ibid., 5: 277–78.
15 Rançon, *Bondou*, p. 59: Roux, *Notice*, p. 7.
16 Lamartiny, *Etudes*, p. 9; Rançon, *Bondou*, p. 57.
17 Rançon, *Bondou*, p. 57.
18 "Observation sur l'importance de la colonie du Sénégal," 1784, ANF C6 27.
19 Durand, "Etablissemens (*sic*) à Galam," ANF C6 27; Labat, *Nouvelle relation*, 4: 3.
20 Rançon, *Bondou*, p. 58.
21 Robin Hallet, *Records of the African Association, 1788–1831* (New York, 1964), p. 120; Hallet, *Proceedings*, pp. 239–41.
22 Hallet, *Records*, pp. 134–35.
23 Ibid., p. 136.
24 Ibid., pp. 134–35; Hallet, *Proceedings*, p. 247, ff.
25 Rançon, *Bondou*, p. 57; Lamartiny, *Etudes*, p. 9.
26 Rançon, *Bondou*, p. 58; Samani Sy, "Genealogy and History of the N'Diaye Family of Bakel," Bakel, 15 April 1966, trans. Abdoulaye Bathily, CC T4, side 1; Sy, "History of Bakel and the N'Diaybe," Bakel, 15 April 1966, trans. A. Bathily, CC T4, side 1; Saki N'Diaye, 11 May 1966, trans. Hamady Amadou Sy, CC T11, side 1.
27 Rançon, *Bondou*, p. 59.
28 Ibid., p. 57. This passage is lifted from Lamartiny, *Etudes*, p. 9. Issaga Opa Sy maintains that Amadi Gai moved to Koussan to avoid the *razzias* of the Moors (Goudiry, 9 June 1988).
29 Levtzion suggests as much ("North-West Africa," pp. 214–15).
30 Rançon, *Bondou*, p. 58.
31 Ibid. Also see Robinson, *Chiefs and Clerics*, pp. 13–16; Demba Simbalou Sock, "The Story of Abdoul Kader, Almamy of Futa Toro, and Almamy Amady Aissata of Bondou," Senoudebou, 13 March 1966; trans. Hamady Amadou Sy, CC T3, side 2.
32 Roux, *Notice*, p. 6; Kamara, "Histoire," p. 801; Rançon, *Bondou*, p. 58.
33 Rançon, *Bondou*, pp. 59–60.
34 Ibid., p. 58; Kamara, "Histoire," p. 816; Diakité, "Livre," p. 212; Roux, *Notice*, p. 6; Lamartiny, *Etudes*, p. 9; FC, nos. 4, 18, and 30.
35 Park, *Travels*, p. 90.
36 Hallet, *Proceedings*, p. 340.
37 Park, *Travels*, pp. 88–89.
38 Ibid., p. 78; Hallet, *Proccedings*, p. 334.
39 Rançon, *Bondou*, p. 60, lifted from Lamartiny, *Etudes*, p. 10.
40 Rançon, *Bondou*, p. 60.
41 Roux, *Notice*, p. 7. Marsa is fifteen miles southeast of Bakel.

42 Kamara, "Histoire," p. 802. The context implies Njukunturu was in Gajaaga.
43 Ibid.
44 Rançon, *Bondou*, pp. 60–61; Lamartiny, *Etudes*, p. 10; Gray and Dochard, *Travels*, pp. 194–95.
45 Kamara, "Histoire," p. 802; Robinson writes that Sega Gai was Abdul Qadir's "vassal." See "Islamic Revolution," pp. 211–12; Robinson, "Almamy Abdul Kader," *Les Africaines* 10 (1978).
46 D. S. Sock, "Story of Abdoul Kader," CC T3, side 2.
47 Ibid.
48 Ibid.
49 Kamara, "Histoire," pp. 801–802.
50 Soh, *Chroniques de Fouta sénégalais*, p. 46. Soh's account confuses two separate episodes, the execution of Sega Gai and the Battle of Dara Lamine. According to Diakité, Sega Gai was given a choice of either one year in prison or death; he chose the latter (Diakité, "Livre,'" p. 216).
51 Ibid., pp. 46–47.
52 1790 to 1797 is the most accurate. See D. Robinson, P. Curtin, and J. Johnson, "A Tentative Chronology of Futa Toro from the Sixteenth through the Nineteenth Centuries," *CEA* 12 (1972): 580–88; also *Supplement*, pp. 30–31.

5: The reassertion of Sissibe integrity

1 Kamara, "Histoire," pp. 803–804.
2 Amadou Abdoul Sy, Tambacounda, 12 June 1988.
3 Roux, *Notice*, p. 7.
4 Rançon, *Bondou*, p. 161.
5 Kamara, "Histoire," p. 801.
6 Ibid.; Amadi Bokar Sy, Tambacounda, 13 June 1988, Roux, *Notice*, pp. 7–8.
7 Kamara, "Histoire," pp. 802–803.
8 Ibid., p. 803.
9 Ibid.
10 Roux, *Notice*, p. 9.
11 Ibid., pp. 8–9; Rançon, *Bondou*, p. 62; Lamartiny, *Etudes*, pp. 10–11.
12 "Eliman Boundou a forcé le roi de Galam à diviser son royaume en deux portions, dont il a gardé une. Ce roi étant aussi ami des français nous pouvons compter sur lui." Laserre to Citoyen Ministère de la Marine, 16 February 1802, ANF C6 21.
13 "... une armée formidable, composée d'une partie du Bambara, et des troupes du Kasson et du Bondou réunier." Lunio (or Sunio) to Citoyen Ministère de la Marine, 20 June 1802, ANF C6 21.
14 Robinson, *Chiefs and Clerics*, pp. 16–17; Soh, *Chroniques du Fouta sénégalais*, pp. 55–59; Diakité, "Livre," p. 217.
15 "Imama," 'in *EI*.
16 Soh, *Chroniques du Fouta sénégalais*, pp. 50–57.
17 Ibid. Rançon gives the village's name as Goorick (*Bondou*, p. 62); Roux names it Toubel (*Notice*, p. 8).
18 Soh, *Chroniques du Fouta sénégalais*, p. 55.
19 Rançon, *Bondou*, pp. 62–63; Roux, *Notice*, pp. 8–9; Lamartiny, *Etudes*, p. 11; Gray and Dochard, *Travels*, pp. 198–99.
20 Rançon, *Bondou*, p. 63; Lamartiny, *Etudes*, p. 12.
21 Gray and Dochard, *Travels*, p. 200.
22 Ibid.
23 "Isaaco's Journal," in Park, *Travels*, pp. 240–42.

24 Tauxier, *Histoire des Bambara*, (Paris, 1942), p. 137. He lasted until 1832.
25 Rançon, *Bondou*, p. 63; Gray and Dochard, *Travels*, pp. 201–205.
26 Roux, *Notice*, pp. 9–10; Rançon, *Bondou*, pp. 64–65; Gray and Dochard, *Travels*, pp. 204–5.
27 Roux, *Notice*, pp. 9–10.
28 Rançon, *Bondou*, p. 64; Gray and Dochard, *Travels*, pp. 204–205; Lamartiny, *Etudes*, p. 12; Kamara, "Histoire," p. 805.
29 Rançon, *Bondou*, p. 64; Gray and Dochard, *Travels*, pp. 204–5.
30 Rançon, *Bondou*, p. 64. Rançon claims that the Kaartan army was decimated, which is very improbable.
31 Ibid., pp. 64–65; Gray and Dochard, *Travels*, pp. 206–207; Lamartiny, *Etudes*, p. 12.
32 Paul Marty, "L'Etablissement des Français dans le Haut Sénégal (1817–1822)," *Etudes sénégalaises*; also in *RHCF* (1925): 51–118, 210–68, especially p. 96.
33 Mollien, *Travels*, p. 78.
34 Ibid., p. 73.
35 Gray and Dochard, *Travels*, p. 124; also Walckenaer, *Collection*, 7: 125–62.
36 Gray and Dochard, *Travels*, p. 125.
37 Ibid., pp. 125–26.
38 Ibid., pp. 179–80.
39 Ibid., pp. 184–85.
40 Réné Caillié, *Travels Through Central Africa to Timbuctoo and Across the Great Desert, to Morocco, 1824–1828*, 2 vols., trans. (London, 1968), p. 10.
41 Gray and Dochard, *Travels*, p. 116.
42 Ibid., p. 175; Issaga Opa Sy, 9 June 1988.
43 Roux, (*Notice*, p. 9), claims that Amadi Pate Gai's brothers returned from Futa Toro on conditions that they renounce all political pretensions, a claim unsupported by the other souces.
44 Diakité, "Livre," pp. 211–12; FC, nos. 4 and 30. FC, no. 30 states Amadi Aissata reigned seven years, as does Kamara ("Histoire,'" p. 816), while Rançon maintains he ruled twenty-five years (*Bondou*, p. 61). Lamartiny says eight years (*Etudes*, p. 10), while Roux fourteen years (*Notice*, p. 10).
45 Rançon, *Bondou*, p. 66; Kamara names this third son Sire Jibi ("Histoire," p. 805).
46 Rançon, *Bondou*, p. 66; Lamartiny, *Etudes*, p. 13; Gray and Dochard, *Travels*, pp. 175–76.
47 Rançon, *Bondou*, pp. 65–66.
48 Ibid. Malik Samba Rumane must have been the son of Samba Tumane (r. 1764); therefore, he also would have been prohibited from the *almaamate* by Amadi Gai's injunction. Also, Kamara states that Malik Kumba succeeded Amadi Aissata, a claim unsupported by any other souce ("Histoire," p. 805). Since FC, no. 30 gives Musa Yero's name as Malik Musa Yero, it is possible that Kamara heard the name Malik and associated it with Amadi Gai by mistake.
49 Gray and Dochard, *Travels*, p. 176, ff.; Walckenaer, *Collection* 7: 132–33; Eugene Saulnier, *La companie de Galam au Sénégal*, (Paris, 1921), p. 32.
50 Ibid.
51 Caillié, *Travels*, pp. 10–11.
52 Saulnier, *Compagnie de Galam*, p. 33.
53 Marty, "L'Etablissement," *Etudes sénégalaises* pp. 108–21.
54 Saulnier, *Compagnie de Galam*, p. 30.
55 Ibid., pp. 30–32.
56 Ibid.
57 Ibid., p. 340.
58 Commission report, ANS 1G 3.
59 Hesse, 20 September 1820, ANF-OM, Senegal IV–15.
60 LeBlanc, 20 September 1820, ANF-OM, Senegal IV–15.

61 Copy of the treaty of 12 November 1820, ANF-OM, Senegal IV-15; also ANF 3B 92 (200 Mi 241).
62 Marty, "L'Etablissement," *RHCF*, pp. 216–17.
63 Saint Louis to Hesse, Commandant at Bakel, 18 May 1821, ANF 3B 22 (200 Mi 178).
64 Marty, "L'Etablissement," *RHCF*, p. 218.
65 Saint Louis to Bakel, 20 June 1821, ANF 3B 22 (200 Mi 178).
66 Marty, "L'Etablissement," *RHCF*, p. 219.
67 Ibid., p. 220.
68 Marty, "L'Etablissement," *RHCF*, pp. 220–21.
69 Ibid., Saulnier, pp. 40–41. Bundu concluded a separate, temporary peace with Gajaaga in July of 1823, and negotiations were undertaken again in June of 1824. ANF 13G 164 (200 Mi 923).
70 Saint Louis to Bakel, 31 January 1822, ANF 3B 22.
71 Saint Louis to Bakel, 12 February 1822, ANF 3B 22 (200 Mi 178).
72 Saulnier, *Compagnie de Galam*, p. 101.
73 A. W. Mitchinson, *The Expiring Continent: A Narrative of Travel in Senegambia* (London, 1881), pp. 360–61.
74 Ibid.
75 Rançon, *Bondou*, p. 67; Lamartiny, *Etudes*, p. 13.
76 *Supplement*, pp. 30–31.
77 Roux says three years (*Notice*, p. 10).
78 Rançon, *Bondou*, p. 67; Lamartiny, *Etudes*, p. 13. Amadi Kama unsuccessfully tried a second time to become *Almaami* at this time as well.
79 Saint Louis to M. Louis Alain, Bakel, 9 September 1830, ANF 3B (200 Mi 179).
80 *Supplement*, p. 14.
81 Saint Louis to LaRouche, Commandant at Bakel, 16 July 1827, ANF 3B 27 (200 Mi 179).
82 Curtin, *Economic Change*, p. 149.
83 Rançon, *Bondou*, p. 68.
84 Ibid., p. 66.
85 Mollien, *Travels*, pp. 79–83.
86 *Supplement*, p. 28.
87 Ibid., p. 33.
88 Lamartiny, *Etudes*, p. 13.
89 Rançon, *Bondou*, p. 68.
90 Ibid., Tourette, "Voyage dans le Bondou et le Bambouck," ANF 1G 12 (200 Mi 649).
91 Rançon, *Bondou*, p. 68; Lamartiny says he had fourteen children (*Etudes*, p. 13).
92 Amadi Kamba made his last attempt to become *Almaami* at this time. Rançon, *Bondou*, p. 68.
93 Rançon, *Bondou*, p. 68; Lamartiny, *Etudes*, p. 14.
94 Fox, *A Brief History*, p. 477.
95 FC, nos, 4, 18 and 30; Rançon *Bondou*, p. 69; Lamartiny, *Etudes*, pp. 13–14; Roux, *Notice*, p. 10; Kamara says Malik Kumba reigned three or four years ("Histoire," 'p. 816), whereas Diakité says three years ("Livre," pp. 211–12).

6: Structure of the Bundunke Almaamate

1 On Abdul Qadir, see David Robinson, "The Islamic Revolution of Fute Toro," *IJAHS* 8 (1975): 185–221.
2 Sabatié, *Le Sénégal*, pp. 333–34.
3 Issaga Opa Sy, Goudiry, 8 and 9 June 1988; Rançon, *Bondou*, pp. 161–62; Rançon bases his comments on Lamartiny, *Etudes*, p. 50.
4 Hammadi Koulibali, Naye, 8 September 1987, trans. Bubu Traore. Issaga Opa Sy, Goudiry, 8 and 9 June 1988. Sy maintains that Tiali and Nieri were not administered by any official. He also says that each provincial governor took the title *eliman*.

5 Raffenel, *Voyage*, p. 272; Gray and Dochard, *Travels*, pp. 181–82; Lamartiny, *Etudes*, p. 43; Rançon, *Bondou*, p. 164.
6 Rançon, *Bondou*, p. 164; Suret-Canale and Barry, "The Western Atlantic Coast to 1800," p. 504.
7 Paul Gaffarel, *Le Sénégal* (Paris, n.d.), p. 55; Marty, *Etudes sénégalaises*, p. 175.
8 Lamartiny, *Etudes*, p. 44; Rançon, *Bondou*, p. 164.
9 Briquelot, "Mission du Boundou," ANF 1G 107 (200 Mi 668).
10 Bérenger-Feraud, *Peuplades de la Sénégambie*, p. 138.
11 Rançon, *Bondou*, p. 163; Raffenel, *Voyage*, p. 272; Mollien, *Travels*, pp. 77–78; Walckenaer, *Collection*, 6: 215–16; Lamartiny, *Etudes*, p. 43; Curtin, *Economic Change*, p. 43.
12 Raffenel, *Voyage*, p. 273.
13 Ibid.
14 Ibid.; Lamartiny, *Etudes*, p. 43; Rançon (*Bondou*, p. 163) lifts this matter of the succession, as well as most of his comments on the government, from Lamartiny. In many instances it is verbatim.
15 Lamartiny, *Etudes*, p. 44.
16 Fox, *A Brief History*, p. 466.
17 Raffenel, *Voyage*, p. 140.
18 Gray and Dochard, *Travels*, p. 125.
19 Rançon, *Bondou*, pp. 97, 102, 123.
20 Rançon (*Bondou*, p. 164) lifts this from Lamartiny, *Etudes*, p. 44.
21 Walckenaer, *Collection*, 5: 279.
22 Rançon, *Bondou*, p. 164.
23 Lamartiny, *Etudes*, p. 52.
24 Robinson, *Chiefs and Clerics*, pp. 9–10; Raffenel, *Voyage*, p. 275.
25 Rançon, *Bondou*, p. 165.
26 Park, *Travels*, pp. 67–68; Walckenaer, *Collection*, 5: 274.
27 Park, *Travels*, p. 68.
28 Hyacinte Hecquard, *Voyage sur la côte et dans l'intérieur de l'Afrique occidentale* (Paris, 1855), p. 191.
29 Bokar Saada to Governor, 28 October 1863, ANS 13G 242.
30 Robinson, *Chiefs and Clerics*, p. 21; Roux, *Notice*, p. 6; Rançon, *Bondou*, pp. 164, 166.
31 Issaga Opa Sy, Goudiry, 9 June 1988; Robinson, "Islamic Revolution."
32 Hammadi Koulibali, Naye, 8 September 1987, trans. Baba Traore; Gray and Dochard, *Travels*, p. 190; Raffenel, *Voyage*, p. 274. Rançon (*Bondou*, p. 166) maintains, in keeping with his overall scheme, that the provincial rulers organized the villages.
33 Raffenel, *Voyage*, p. 274; P.-D. Boilat, *Esquisses sénégalaises* (Paris, 1853), p. 265.
34 Kadealy Diakité, Dakar, 23 February 1966, trans. H. A. Sy, CC T2, side 1; Saada Denbele, Gabou, 7 September 1987, trans. Sire Sy; Hammadi Koulibali, Naye, 8 September 1987, trans. Baba Traore; Issaga Opa Sy, Goudiry, 8 and 9 June 1988; Amadou Abdou Sy, Tambacounda, 11 June 1988; Amadi Bokar Sy, Tambacounda, 13 June 1988.
35 Hammadi Koulibali, Naye, 8 September 1987, trans. Baba Traore. See Robin Law, *The Horse in West African History* (New York, 1980).
36 Saada Denbele, Gabou, 7 September 1987, trans. Sire Sy; Lamartiny, *Etudes*, p. 44; Rançon, *Bondou*, p. 164.
37 Rançon, *Bondou*, p. 166; Raffenel, *Voyage*, p. 274; Mollien, *Travels*, p. 78; Gray and Dochard, *Travels*, p. 191.
38 Durand, *Voyage*, p. 321. The word translated here as "pants" is actually "pagnes."
39 Ibid.; Walckenaer, *Collection*, 5: 282. The integration of pastoral and sedentary soldiers would also cause coordination problems (Issaga Opa Sy, Goudiry, 9 June 1988).
40 Ibid.
41 Durand to Blanchot, notes on war with Futa Toro and Bundu in 1805, ANF C6 22.

42 Mollien, *Travels*, p. 78; Walckenaer, *Collection*, 6: 216.
43 Faidherbe, *Le Sénégal* (Paris, 1889), p. 165.
44 Mollien, *Travels*, p. 78; Walckenaer, *Collection*, 5: 282, 6: 216; Durand, *Voyage*; pp. 320–21.
45 Durand, *Voyage*, p. 321; Walckenaer, *Collection*, 5: 282.
46 Mollien, *Travels*, p. 78; Walckenaer, *Collection*, 6: 216.
47 Fox, *A Brief History*, p. 467.
48 Ministère de la Marine et des Colonies, *Sénégal et Niger: La France dans l'Afrique occidentale, 1879–1883* (Paris, 1884), p. 85; Faidherbe, *Le Sénégal*, p. 165.
49 "Mission Laude," ANF 1G 44 (200 Mi 651).
50 These observations are based on figures already cited throughout this study, including data from Gray and Dochard, *Travels*, p. 189; Durand, *Voyage*, p. 321; and Raffenel, *Voyage*, p. 274. It must be remembered that Amadi Aissata's army included Kaartans; the Kaartan contingent could have been very numerous.
51 For a full discussion of Islamic taxation, see Usuman dan Fodio, "Kitab al-Farq," trans. M. Hiskett, in *BSOAS* 23 (1960): 558–79; and Nicolas P. Aghnides, *Mohammedan Theories of Finance* (New York, 1916), p. 199.
52 Aghnides, *Mohammedan Theories*, p. 200.
53 Willis, "Reflections on the Differences of Islam in West Africa," pp. 27–28; Willis, "The Torodbe Clerisy," pp. 202–206.
54 Qur'an 9: 2; Aghnides, *Mohammedan Theories*, p. 204.
55 Aghnides, *Mohammedan Theories*, p. 200.
56 Raffenel, *Voyage*, pp. 148–49; Gray and Dochard, *Travels*, pp. 181–82; Walckenaer, *Collection*, 7: 162; Lamartiny, *Etudes*, p. 43; Rançon, *Bondou*, pp. 163–64.
57 Aghnides, *Mohammedan Theories*, p. 284.
58 Gray and Dochard, *Travels*, pp. 182–83; Walckenaer, *Collection*, 7: 162.
59 Rançon, *Bondou*, pp. 109, 166. Rançon states that the "chefs de provinces" gathered the tithe and brought it to the *Almaami*, accompanied by the village heads. In contrast, Hammadi Koulibali states that slaves collected and transported taxes (Naye, 8 September 1987, trans. Baba Traore). Finally, Issaga Opa Sy insists that the family heads were responsible for bringing *zakāt* to the *Almaami* (Goudiry, 8 June 1988).
60 Aghnides, *Mohammedan Theories*, p. 439.
61 Ibid., pp. 470–77.
62 Ibid., pp. 465–70.
63 Raffenel, *Voyage*, p. 149.
64 Aghnides, *Mohammedan Theories*, pp. 314–23.
65 Ibid., p. 315.
66 Gray and Dochard, *Travels*, pp. 181–82; see also "Extract from Governor MacDonnell's Despatch Number 41," 16 June 1849, PRO CO87 116 (1880).
67 Ibid.
68 Park, *Travels*, p. 87.
69 Ibid.
70 Robinson, *Chiefs and Clerics*, p. 9.
71 Rançon, *Bondou*, pp. 166–67.
72 Raffenel, *Voyage*, pp. 140, 275.
73 Ibid., pp. 276–77; Bérenger-Feraud, *Peuplades de la Sénégambie*, p. 137.
74 Rançon, *Bondou*, pp. 166–67; Raffenel, *Voyage*, p. 272.
75 Usuman dan Fodio, *Bayān wujūb al-hijra 'alā al-'ibād*, trans. and ed. by Fathi Hassan El-Masri (Oxford and Khartoum, 1978), pp. 34–35/ tr. 67–68; Carrère and Holle, *Sénégambie*, p. 162; Rançon, *Bondou*, p. 58.
76 Fox, *A Brief History*, pp. 477–78.
77 Raffenel, *Voyage*, pp. 303–304; Fox, *A Brief History*, pp. 478–79.
78 Mollien, *Travels*, p. 79; Fox, *A Brief History*, pp. 478–79.

79 Rançon, *Bondou*, p. 167; Lamartiny, *Etudes*, p. 45.
80 Ibid.
81 Carrère and Holle, *Sénégambie*, p. 162.
82 Ibid.; Rançon, *Bondou*, p. 167.

7: Struggle for the Upper Senegal Valley

1 Oloruntimehin, *Segu Tukulor Empire*, p. 30.
2 Robinson, *Chiefs and Clerics*, p. 168.
3 Rançon, *Bondou*, p. 69; Lamartiny, *Etudes*, p. 14.
4 Rançon, *Bondou*, p. 67.
5 Ibid., p. 69; Lamartiny, *Etudes*, p. 14.
6 *Supplement*, pp. 14–15. See also Samani Sy, "Samba Yacine and Samba Kumba Diame," 15, 16 April 1966, trans. Abdoulaye Bathily, CC T4, side 1.
7 Saint Louis to LaCheusie, 5 August 1838, ANF 3B 52 (200 Mi 182); the French believed the Sambas were brothers; Saint Louis to Bakel, 2 August 1837, ANF 3B 52 (200 Mi 182); Barry, *Sénégambie*, pp. 40–41.
8 Saint Louis to LaCheusie.
9 Claude Faure, "Un politique méconnu: Duranton dans le Haut-Sénégal," *RHCF* 7 (1919): 293–99.
10 Ibid.
11 Saint Louis to Bakel, 2 August 1837, ANF 3B 52 (200 Mi 182). It is unlikely Samba Yacine was a principal in this treaty.
12 Governor to Bakel, 23 August 1833, ANF 13G 164 (200 Mi 923).
13 Governor to Bakel, 7 April 1837, ANF 13G 164 (200 Mi 923).
14 *Supplement*, p. 15.
15 General Faidherbe, "Notice sur la colonie du Sénégal et sur les pays qui sont en relation avec elle," in *Nouvelles annales des voyages*, ed. v. A. Malte-Brun (Paris, 1859), pp. 71–72.
16 Saint Louis to Bakel, 27 July 1844, ANF 3B 53 (200 Mi 182).
17 Saint Louis to Bakel, 7 April 1845, ANF 3B 53 (200 Mi 182).
18 Senoudebou to Saint Louis, 31 January 1846, ANS 13G 247; *Supplement*, p. 33; Saint Louis to Bakel, 6 February 1846, ANF 3B 53 (200 Mi 182).
19 Bakel to Saint Louis, 19 January 1846, ANF 13G 165 (200 Mi 923); Bakel to Saint Louis, 6 March 1846, ANF 13G 165 (200 Mi 923); Senoudebou to Saint Louis, 1 April 1846, ANF 13G 165 (200 Mi 923).
20 Bakel to Saint Louis, 4, 11 April 1846, ANF 13G 165 (200 Mi 923); Senoudebou to Saint Louis, 1 May 1846, ANS 13G 247; Bakel to Saint Louis, 19 May and 5 June 1846, ANF 13G 165 (200 Mi 923); Senoudebou to Saint Louis, 30 May 1846, ANS 13G 247; Bakel to Saint Louis, 21 June 1846, ANF 13G 165 (200 Mi 923); Saint Louis to Bakel, 17 August 1846, ANF 3B 53 (200 Mi 182); Bakel to Saint Louis, 31 January 1847, ANF 13G 165 (200 Mi 924).
21 *Supplement*, pp. 16, 33; Senoudebou to Saint Louis, 15 January 1849, ANF 13G 165 (200 Mi 924).
22 Mitchinson, *Expiring Continent*, p. 371.
23 Report by Huart, Jamin, Raffenel, Patterson, ANF–OM, Senegal III–6.
24 Ibid., Saulnier, *Compagnie de Galam*, p. 146.
25 L. Flize, "Le Bambouck," *Le Moniteur*, 52 (24 March 1857).
26 It should be noted that Saulnier disagrees with the notion that Bundu was forced to acquiesce to the French; that it had built a *tata* at Senoudebou in anticipation of the French settling there (Saulnier, *Compagnie de Galam*, p. 145).
27 Treaty, ANS 13G 242.
28 Senoudebou to Saint Louis, 1 July 1854, ANF 13G 166 (200 Mi 924).
29 Rançon, *Bondou*, p. 71.

30 Senoudebou to Saint Louis, 1 July 1854.
31 Rançon, *Bondou*, p. 72.
32 Ibid.
33 Philip D. Curtin, *Image of Africa* (Madison, 1964), pp. 309–10.
34 Saint Louis to Bakel, 20 August 1844, ANF 3B 53 (200 Mi 182).
35 Gray, *History of the Gambia*, p. 373.
36 Bakel to Saint Louis, 19 January, ANF 13G 165 (200 Mi 923); Saint Louis to Senoudebou, 6 February 1846, ANF 3B 53 (200 Mi 182); Bakel to Saint Louis, 22 January 1845, ANF–OM, Senegal IV–18.
37 Saint Louis to Senoudebou, 26 July 1846, ANF 3B 53 (200 Mi 182).
38 Raffenel to Ministère de la Marine et des colonies, 8 March 1847, ANF–OM, Senegal IV–18.
39 Hecquard, *Voyage*, p. 178.
40 Senoudebou to Citoyen Directeur chargées des affaires extérieures, 3 July 1848, ANS 13G 246; Rançon, *Bondou*, p. 69.
41 Bakel to Saint Louis, 15 February 1847, ANF 13G 165 (200 Mi 924).
42 *Supplement*, p. 33; Bakel to Saint Louis, 4 April 1847, ANF 13G 165 (200 Mi 924). See Charlotte A. Quinn, *Mandingo Kingdoms of the Senegambia* (Evanston, 1972), for more discussion.
43 Rançon, *Bondou*, p. 69.
44 Ibid., pp. 69–70.
45 Senoudebou to Citoyen Gouverneur de Sénégal, 15 June 1848 and 15 January 1849, ANS 13G 246.
46 Quinn, *Mandingo Kingdoms*, p. 32–33.
47 Ibid.
48 Ibid.
49 Hecquard, *Voyage*, p. 191.
50 Raffenel, *Voyage*, pp. 123–31.
51 Raffenel, *Nouveau voyage*, pp. 52–68.
52 Raffenel, *Voyage*, p. 147.
53 Raffenel, *Nouveau voyage*, p. 52. This is up from his 1843–44 estimate of 2,000–2,300 (see Raffenel, *Voyage*, p. 147).
54 Raffenel, *Voyage*, p. 105.
55 Towards the end of his reign, Bundu was once again besieged with annual raids by the Moors. Senoudebou to Directeur des affaires extérieures, 16 May 1848, ANS 13G 246; Bakel to Saint Louis, 16 December 1849, ANF 13G 165 (200 Mi 942); Senoudebou to Saint Louis, 1850, ANF 13G 165 (200 Mi 924); Rançon, *Bondou*, p. 72–73.
56 Rançon, *Bondou*, p. 73; Kamara, "Histoire," p. 806.
57 Kamara ("Histoire," p. 816), Diakité ("Livre," pp. 211–12), and FC, no. 5 all agree that Saada Amadi Aissata reigned fourteen years, which is accurate. The other sources' estimates range from four to thirteen years.
58 Kamara, "Histoire," pp. 806–807; Equilbecq, *Contes indigenes*, pp. 450–51.
59 Rançon, *Bondou*, p. 73. Gabou is twenty-five km. from Bakel.
60 Senoudebou to Saint Louis, 1 July 1854, ANF 13G 166 (200 Mi 924). The correspondence confuses *Almaami* Sy with Amadi Saada.
61 Senoudebou to Saint Louis, 5 January, 8 February, 6 March 1853, ANS 13G 246.
62 Senoudebou to Saint Louis, 1 July 1854, ANF 13G 166 (200 Mi 924); Rançon, *Bondou*, p. 73; Lamartiny, *Etudes*, p. 16.
63 Rançon, *Bondou*, p. 73.
64 Rançon, *Bondou*, p. 73, (*Etudes*, p. 16), and FC, no. 18 state that Amadu Sy reigned one year, while FC, no. 5 does not even mention him. Diakité ("Livre," pp. 211–12), Roux (*Notice*, p. 11), and FC, no. 30 gives him two years. Kamara says he ruled from two to five years ("Histoire," p. 816).

8: Al-Hajj Umar in Bundu

1. Robinson, *Chiefs and Clerics*, p. 74; Roux, *Notice*, p. 11.
2. Rançon, *Bondou*, p. 74; Kamara says that Amadi Gai was in fact the former *Almaami* Sega Gai's son ("Histoire," p. 808).
3. Senoudebou to Governor, 1 July 1854, ANF 13G 166 (200 Mi 924).
4. Senoudebou to Governor, 18 March 1854, ANF 13G 166 (200 Mi 924). Kamara says it is likely that the alliances were reversed: Amadi Gai was supported by Sega Tumane (Sawatumane), whereas Amadi Saada probably backed Umar Sane ("Histoire," pp. 808–9). Lamartiny also presents a variation, stating that Koussan backed Amadi Gai, whereas Umar Sane was the Boulbebane choice (*Etudes*, p. 16).
5. Rançon, *Bondou*, p. 74; Kamara, "Histoire," p. 809. This is supported by correspondence: Senoudebou to Governor, 1 July 1854, ANF 13G 166 (200 Mi 924).
6. Kamara, "Histoire," p. 809. Umar brought the war to a close in September of 1854.
7. Senoudebou to Governor, 12 June 1854, ANF 13G 166 (200 Mi 924).
8. Rançon, *Bondou*, pp. 74–75; Roux, *Notice* p. 11. It is very likely that this Tumane Samba is none other than Malik Samba Tumane, the Sy leader who later emerged as a key lieutenant under Umar. According to Kamara, "Sega Tumane" led the assault, and was subsequently killed ("Histoire," pp. 808–9).
9. Rançon, *Bondou*, p. 75; Roux, *Notice*, pp. 11–12.
10. Sources differ as to his precise date of birth. Robinson, *Holy War*, pp. 65–69; Oloruntimehin, *Segu Tukulor Empire*, p. 36.
11. Robinson, *Holy War*, pp. 70–71.
12. Ibid., p. 95.
13. Robinson, *Holy War*, pp. 99–137.
14. While in Hamdullahi, some of the local leaders, concerned with Umar's growing influence, attempted to assassinate him. William Brown, "The Caliphate of Hamdullahi ca. 1818–1864: A Study in African History and Tradition" (Ph.D thesis: University of Wisconsin, 1969), pp. 150–51.
15. Robinson, *Holy War*, pp. 123–37, 152–55; *Supplement*, pp. 24, 33–34.
16. Rançon, *Bondou*, p. 77; Senoudebou to Governor, 11 and 27 November 1854, ANF 13G 166 (200 Mi 924). See also FC, no. 7, pp. 35 and 2: 3 for this account.
17. Kamara, "Histoire," p. 809; Oloruntimehin, *Segu Tukulor Empire*, p. 57.
18. Rançon, *Bondou*, pp. 77–78; *Supplement*, pp. 33–34. Curtin maintains Amadi Gai died in December of 1854. Another account reports that he was poisoned by Umar Sane's partisans (L. Flize, "Le Bondou," *Le Moniteur* 37 [9 December 1856]).
19. Robinson, *Holy War*, pp. 182–83.
20. Rançon, *Bondou*, p. 77.
21. Kamara, "Histoire," pp. 809–810.
22. Cultru, *Histoire de Sénégal*, p. 335.
23. *Supplement*, p. 17.
24. Faidherbe, "Notice sur la colonie," p. 50.
25. Ibid., p. 51.
26. Robinson, *Holy War*, pp. 160, 180.
27. Paul Marty, *Etudes sur l'Islam et les tribus du Soudan*, 4 vols. (Paris, 1920), 4: 242.
28. Robinson, *Holy War*, pp. 182–84.
29. Leland C. Barrows, "General Faidherbe, the Maurel and Prom Company, and French Expansion in Senegal" (Ph.D. thesis, UCLA: 1974), p. 350. It was this embargo that Umar credits with forcing his hand against the French (Carrère and Holle, *Sénégambie*, pp. 205–206).
30. Ibid., pp. 254–55.
31. Robinson, *Chiefs and Clerics*, p. 30.

32 Leland C. Barrows, "The Merchants and General Faidherbe: Aspects of French Expansion Senegal in the 1850's," *RHCF*, (1974): 236–83; Barrows "General Faidherbe."
33 Barrows, "Merchants and General Faidherbe," p. 243.
34 Leland C. Barrows, "Faidherbe and Senegal: A Critical Discussion," *African Studies Review* 19 (1976): 95–117.
35 Robinson, *Chiefs and Clerics*, pp. 32, ff.; Michael Crowder, *Senegal: A Study of French Assimilation Policy* (London, 1967), pp. 15–16.
36 Faidherbe, *Le Sénégal*, p. 162.
37 Ibid., p. 165.
38 *Supplement*, p. 17.
39 Senoudebou to Governor, 6 June 1855, ANF 13G 167 (200 Mi 924).
40 Faidherbe, *Le Sénégal*, pp. 167–70.
41 Barrows, "General Faidherbe," p. 370.
42 Robinson, *Holy War*, pp. 165–71; Bargone to Governor, 16 April 1855; Parent to Governor, 24 July and 9 August 1855, ANS 13G 167; see also *Annuaire du Sénégal*, 1882, pp. 3–85, p. 95 for Gajaaga treaties.
43 *Supplement*, p. 28.
44 Faidherbe to Commandants of Upper Senegal, 3 October 1855, ANF–OM, Senegal IV–44a.
45 Faidherbe, *Le Sénégal*, p. 175. Saada Amadi Aissata had married the Bambara princess to seal an alliance with Kaarta (Kamara, "Histoire," p. 809).
46 Robinson, *Holy War*, pp. 186–90.
47 Marty, *Etudes sur l'Islam et les tribus du Soudan*, 4: 242; Rançon, *Bondou*, p. 78.
48 See Robinson, *Holy War*, p. 170; Senoudebou to Governor, 1 July 1855, ANF 13G 167 (200 Mi 924). Rançon and Roux maintain Bokar Saada himself was on the verge of being put to death (Rançon, *Bondou*, p. 78; Roux, *Notice*, p. 12). As for Malik Samba Tumane, he apparently continued to exercise some influence in Bundu, and would lead 300 cavaliers from Bundu to Kaarta in 1883, at which point he became embroiled in an internecine struggle for power among the Tal family. He and his following eventually settled in Faradugu (Hanson, "Umarian Karta," p. 224).
49 Kamara's account of how Bokar Saada came to power is at variance with the other sources ("Histoire," pp. 809–10).
50 Faidherbe, *Le Sénégal*, p. 175; FC, no. 7, 2: 7 also records Bokar Saada's defection and subsequent alliance with the French.
51 Mavidal, *Le Sénégal*, p. 88.
52 L. Flize, "Le Bondou," *Le Moniteur* 37 (9 December 1856).
53 Senoudebou to Governor, 6 June 1855, ANF 13G 167 (200 Mi 924).
54 Demba Simbalou Sock, "General History of the Sissibe," and "The Reign of Bokar Saada," 12 March 1966, trans. Hamady Amadou Sy, CC T3, side 2; Kamara, "Histoire," pp. 809–10, substantiates that a battle between the two brothers occurred. See also *Le Moniteur* 1 (16 March 1856).
55 Ibid.; Senoudebou to Governor, March 1856, ANF 13G 167 (200 Mi 924); Rançon, *Bondou*, p. 79.
56 Faidherbe, *Le Sénégal*, pp. 175–76.
57 *Le Moniteur*, Bakel, 3 (16 April 1856); Rançon, *Bondou*, pp. 78–79.
58 *Le Moniteur*, Senoudebou, 12 (17 June 1856); Rançon, *Bondou*, p. 79.
59 *Le Moniteur*, Bakel, 17 (22 July 1856).
60 Ibid.; also 19 (5 August 1856).
61 Ibid., 21 (19 August 1856); Rançon, *Bondou*, p. 80. According to Sock, Bokar Saada decreed that he would execute all who joined the Tijaniyya. (D. S. Sock, 14 March 1966, trans. H. A. Sy, CC T4, side 1.)
62 *Le Moniteur* 29 (14 October 1856); Rançon, *Bondou*, p. 80.
63 *Le Moniteur* 29 (14 October 1856).

64 Curtin, *Economic Change*, pp. 199–202.
65 Senoudebou to Governor, 12 October 1856, ANF 13G 167.
66 *Le Moniteur*, Senoudebou, 45 (15 January 1857).
67 Ibid., Senoudebou, 45 (5 February 1857); Rançon, *Bondou*, p. 80. Both sources mention a "cousin Ousman," a probable reference to Bokar Saada's brother.
68 *Le Moniteur*, Senoudebou, 59 (12 May 1857).
69 Ibid., Bakel, 59 (12 May 1857); Rançon, *Bondou*, p. 80; Lamartiny, *Etudes*, p. 21. There is an obvious similarity in the name Eli Amadi Kaba and Amadi Kama, who unsuccessfully competed for the executive office in 1819. The former may have been Amadi Kama's son.
70 Rançon, *Bondou*, pp. 80–81.
71 Robinson, *Holy War*, pp. 205–11.
72 Robinson, *Chiefs and Clerics*, p. 43.
73 Robinson, *Holy War*, pp. 205–11.
74 *Le Moniteur* 75 (1 September 1857).
75 Ibid., Bakel, 71 (4 August 1857).
76 Rançon, *Bondou*, pp. 81–82. Issaga Opa Sy states that the Kane family controlled Somsom-Tata (Goudiry, 9 June 1988).
77 Ibid., pp. 81–83; *Le Moniteur* 72 (11 August 1857) and 75 (1 September 1857).
78 P. Brossard de Corbigny, "Exploration hydrographique de la Falémé jusqu'à Sansanding. Prise de Ndangan et de Sansanding," *Le Moniteur* 77 (15 September 1857); Rançon, *Bondou*, p. 83; Lamartiny, *Etudes*, pp. 22–23.
79 Ibid.
80 Robinson, *Holy War*, p. 217.
81 Rançon, *Bondou*, pp. 83–84; Lamartiny, *Etudes*, pp. 23–24.
82 Ibid., *Le Moniteur* 109 (27 April 1858).
83 *Le Moniteur* 110 (4 May 1858).
84 Ibid., Senoudebou and Bakel, 109 (27 April 1858); Rançon, *Bondou*, pp. 84–85; Lamartiny, *Etudes*, pp. 23–24.
85 Faidherbe, *Le Sénégal*, p. 214.
86 Rançon, *Bondou*, pp. 84–85; Lamartiny, *Etudes*, p. 24. Both claim that letters were falsely written, but they had no way of knowing that.
87 Ibid.
88 Ibid., *Le Moniteur*, Bakel, 117 (22 June 1858).
89 Faidherbe, *Le Sénégal*, pp. 214–15; *Le Moniteur*, Bakel, 117 (22 June 1858).
90 Ibid.; Bakel to Governor, 14 June 1858; ANF 13G 167 (200 Mi 925).
91 *Le Moniteur* 113 (25 May 1858).
92 Ibid., Bakel, 117 (22 June 1858).
93 Rançon, *Bondou*, p. 86; Lamartiny, *Etudes*, p. 24.
94 Robinson, *Holy War*, p. 231. Hanson estimates almost 50,000 returned to Nioro ("Umarian Karta," p. 56).
95 *Le Moniteur*, Senoudebou, 129 (14 September 1858); Fernand Dumont, *Le Anti-sultan ou Al-Hajj Omar Tal du Fouta combattant de la Foi* (Dakar, 1971), p. 113.
96 *Le Moniteur* 123 (3 August 1858).
97 Ibid., 126 (24 August 1858).
98 Ibid., Senoudebou, 164 (17 May 1859); Faidherbe, correspondence no. 6, ANF 3B 78 (200 Mi 186).
99 *Le Moniteur*, Senoudebou, 171 (5 July 1859).
100 Rançon, *Bondou*, pp. 85–86.
101 Faidherbe, "Notice sur la colonie," p. 53.
102 Rançon, *Bondou*, p. 88.
103 Ibid., pp. 86–87; Kamara, "Histoire," p. 810.
104 Kamara, "Histoire," p. 810.

105 *Le Moniteur*, Senoudebou, 154 (8 March 1859).
106 Ibid., Senoudebou, 164 (17 May 1859); Rançon, *Bondou*, p. 87; Kamara, "Histoire," p. 810.
107 Kamara claims that Bokar Saada went in person to Saint Louis ("Histoire," p. 810).
108 Rançon, *Bondou*, p. 87; *Le Moniteur*, 190 (15 November 1859); Faidherbe, *Le Sénégal*, pp. 225–27.
109 Rançon, *Bondou*, p. 88; Robinson, *Chiefs and Clerics*, p. 49; Rançon *Holy War*, p. 241.
110 Robinson, *Holy War*, p. 305.
111 Hanson, "Umarian Karta," pp. 12, 39–40, 58–65; Oloruntimehin, *Segu Tukulor Empire*, p. 98; Yves-J. Saint-Martin, *L'Empire Toucouleur et la France: un demi-siècle de relations diplomatiques (1846–1893)* (Dakar, 1967), p. 125.
112 These percentages were determined by following the careers of the *almaamies'* progeny. The assumption is that anonymous Sissibe followed either the *Shaykh* or Bokar Saada in similar proportions.

9: The age of Bokar Saada

1 Rançon, *Bondou*, p. 89.
2 Ibid., pp. 89–98; Bakel to Governor, 9 February 1861, ANF 13G 168 (200 Mi 925); Bakel to Governor, August 1874, ANF–OM, Senegal IV–44d; Bakel to Governor, 15 June 1873, ANF 13G 172 (200 Mi 927); Bakel to Governor, 18 December 1875, ANF 13G 173 (200 Mi 927); Issaga Opa Sy, Goudiry, 9 September 1988.
3 Rançon, *Haute-Gambie*, p. 64.
4 Issaga Opa Sy, Goudiry, 9 June 1988; Rançon, *Bondou*, pp. 90–91.
5 Rançon, *Bondou*, p. 91.
6 Faidherbe to Commandant at Bakel, 15 April 1865, ANF 3B 89 (200 Mi 187).
7 "Report on the State of the Upper Gambia," 13 December 1869, NAG 59: 1.
8 Rançon, *Bondou*, p. 91. Amadi Bokar Sy (Tambacounda, 13 June 1988) denies that Bokar Saada made slaves of the people of Wuli.
9 Saint Louis to Bakel, 15 March 1866, ANF 3B 90 (200 Mi 188).
10 D'Arcy to LaPrade, 16 April 1866, ANF 1F 6 (200 Mi 570) and 3B 89 (200 Mi 187).
11 LaPrade to D'Arcy, 21 April 1866, ANF 1F 6 (200 Mi 570).
12 "Tu ignores sans doute que la France et l'Angleterre sont alliés sur tous les points du globe." LaPrade to Bokar Saada, 21 April 1866, ANF 3B 89 (200 Mi 187).
13 Bokar Saada to Commandant at Bakel, 6 June 1866, ANS 13G 242.
14 Governor to Commandant at Bakel, 26 April 1866, ANF 3B 89 (200 Mi 187).
15 Ministère de la Marine et des Colonies, Paris, to Governor, 7 June 1866, ANF 1F 6 (200 Mi 570).
16 "Report on the State of the Upper River," 13 December 1869, NAG 59: 1. For more on this raid, see Gov. Blackall to Duke of Buckingham, June 1867; Merchants to Lord Carnarvon (Sec. of State for the Colonies), 23 April 1867; B. Tanner to Admiral Patey, 10 April 1867; B. Tanner to Col. Anton, 3 September 1867, PRO CO87 87.
17 D'Arcy to David Brown, 22 April 1866, *British Parliamentary Papers, 1845–87* (Shannon Island, 1971), p. 372.
18 Ibid., David Brown to Colonial Office, London, 8 February 1877, p. 364.
19 Cooper to Bokar Saada, 13 May 1876, ANF–OM, Senegal IV–45e.
20 "Mission Laude dans le Bondou et la Haute Falémé," ANF 1G 44 (200 Mi 651).
21 Rançon, *Bondou*, pp. 94–96; Bakel to Governor, 1 May 1868 and 11 May 1869, ANF 13G 170 and 13G 171 (200 Mi 926); Bakel to Governor, 14 May 1871, ANF 13G 171 (200 Mi 927); Bakel to Governor, 31 January, 30 March, 30 April, 1875; 28 April, 24 December 1879, ANF 13G 173 (200 Mi 927) and 13 G 175 (200 Mi 928); David Brown to Mr. Meade, 17 February 1877, PRO CO87 110 (1877); Cooper to Governor, 30 March 1875, PRO CO87 108 (1875).

22 Rançon, *Bondou*, pp. 93–95, 98–99; "Mission Laude," ANF 1G 44 (200 Mi 651). Although technically submitted to the *Almaami*'s authority at Timbo, Labe in reality often functioned as a sovereign entity. See P. Marty, *L'Islam en Guinee*, passim.
23 Rançon, *Bondou*, pp. 99–100; Valesius Skipton Gouldsbury, Chief of the Upper Gambia Expedition, 1881, NAG 1: 62.
24 Rançon, *Bondou*, pp. 100–101; Gouldsbury to Sierra Leone, 29 August 1879, PRO CO87 114 (1879); Amadi Bokar Sy, Tambacounda, 13 June 1988.
25 Idy Dia, 25 February 1966, trans. H. A. Sy, CC T2, side 2; Rançon, *Haute-Gambie*, pp. 491–92; Rançon, *Bondou*, pp. 92–93, 96–97; Bulletin from Bakel, July 1873, ANF 13G 172 (200 Mi 927).
26 Issaga Opa Sy, Goudiry, 9 June 1988; Rançon, *Bondou*, pp. 89, 90–91, 96; Rançon, *Haute-Gambie*, pp. 379–80.
27 Rançon, *Haute-Gambie*, pp. 376–77.
28 Ibid.
29 Rançon, *Bondou*, pp. 105–106.
30 No. 10, enclosure 2, *British Parliamentary Papers*, p. 366.
31 Fraser to Bundu, 10 December 1827, ANF–OM, Senegal IV–15.
32 No. 10, enclosure 3, Treaty of 13 April 1829, *British Parliamentary Papers*, p. 366.
33 Governor to Bakel, 9 February 1867, ANF 3B 89 (200 Mi 187).
34 No. 10, enclosure 6, Treaty of 12 November 1869, *British Parliamentary Papers*, p. 364.
35 No. 10, David Brown to Colonial Office, London, 8 February 1877, *British Parliamentary Papers*, p. 364.
36 Bakel to Governor, 30 April 1875, ANF 13G 173 (200 Mi 927).
37 Ibid.; Bakel to Governor, 31 January 1875, ANF 13G 173 (200 Mi 927); also in ANF–OM, Senegal IV–44d.
38 Bakel to Governor, 14 May 1875, ANF 13G 173 (200 Mi 927).
39 Cooper to Bokar Saada, 13 May 1876, ANF–OM, Senegal IV–45e. "King Amade Syhou" is Amadu Sheku.
40 "Mission Laude," 1879, ANF 1G 44 (200 Mi 651).
41 Saint-Martin, *L'Empire Toucouleur*, pp. 208–209.
42 "'J'aime tous ceux que vous aimez, et je deteste ceux que vous detéstez, tous les ordres que vous me donnez je les exécurai s'il plaît à Dieu. Je vous dirai que depuis que Bakel et Senoudebou existent, nos produits ont toujours été dirigés vers ces comptoirs'." Bokar Saada to Governor, 28 October 1863, ANS 13G 242.
43 Gallieni, ANF–OM, 1887, Senegal IV–87bis.
44 Lamartiny, *Etudes*, p. 54.
45 Saint-Martin, *L'Empire Toucouleur*, p. 205.
46 Barrows, "Faidherbe and Senegal," pp. 103–104.
47 Barrows, "General Faidherbe," p. 345.
48 Bakel to Governor, 16 October 1865, ANF 13G 169 (200 Mi 926).
49 Robinson, *Chiefs and Clerics*, p. 61.
50 Paul Marty, "Les groupements Tidiania, derivés d'Al-Hadj Omar (Tidiania Toucouleurs)," *Revue du monde musulman* 31 (1915–16): 275–365; Robinson, *Chiefs and Clerics*, pp. 61–62.
51 Marty, "Les groupements Tidiania," pp. 277–78; n.a., "Operations militaires dans la colonie du Sénégal et dependances pendant les années 1862, 1863 et 1864," *Revue maritime et coloniale*, (1864): 737–38.
52 Robinson, *Chiefs and Clerics*, pp. 67–69.
53 Ibid., p. 62; Bokar Saada was Jiba's guardian as well; Rançon, *Bondou*, p. 95.
54 ANS 13G 140, nos. 58 and 63; ANS 13G 157, no. 90.
55 Robinson, *Chiefs and Clerics*, pp. 67–69.
56 Governor to Bakel, 6 October 1866, ANF 3B 89 (200 Mi 187).
57 Robinson, *Chiefs and Clerics*, pp. 70–71. For more on Sidiya al-Kabir, see Stewart, *Islam*.

58 Robinson, *Chiefs and Clerics*, p. 78.
59 Bakel to Governor, 16 October 1865, ANF 13G 169 (200 Mi 926).
60 Bakel to Governor, 1 April 1869, ANF 13G 171 (200 Mi 926).
61 Robinson, *Chiefs and Clerics*, pp. 91–92.
62 *Le Moniteur*, 1872.
63 Bakel to Governor, 15 June 1873, ANF 13G 172 (200 Mi 928).
64 Ibid.
65 Rançon, *Bondou*, p. 95.
66 Ibid.; Robinson, *Chiefs and Clerics*, pp. 93–94.
67 Ibid.; Kamara, "Histoire," p. 811.
68 Rançon, *Bondou*, pp. 97–98.
69 Bakel to Governor, 12 May 1877, ANF 13G 174 (200 Mi 928).
70 Robinson, *Chiefs and Clerics*, p. 149.
71 L. C. Barrows, "Some Paradoxes of Pacification: Senegal and France in the 1850's and 1860's" in *West African Culture Dynamics*, ed. B. K. Swartz, Jr. and Raymond E. Dumett (New York, 1980), p. 530.
72 Bokar Saada to Bakel, 9 October 1867, ANF 13G 170 (200 Mi 926).
73 Saint-Martin, *L'Empire Toucouleur*, p. 208.
74 "Mission Laude," ANF 1G 44 (200 Mi 651).
75 Issaga Opa Sy, Goudiry, 9 June 1988; Rançon, *Bondou*, p. 169.
76 Faidherbe, "Notice sur la colonie," pp. 61–63.
77 Rançon, *Bondou*, p. 169.
78 Bulletin from Bakel, July 1873, ANF 13G 172 (200 Mi 927).
79 Rançon, *Bondou*, p. 169.
80 Lamartiny, *Etudes*, p. 54.
81 Report by Roux, April 1892, ANF 13G 192 (200 Mi 932); Hanson, "Umarian Karta," p. 91.
82 "Mission Laude," ANF 1G 44 (200 Mi 651).
83 Ibid.
84 Bulletin, August 1881, ANF 13G 181 (200 Mi 930).
85 Rançon, *Bondou*, p. 98.
86 Ibid., pp. 102–103.
87 Sanneh, *Jakhanke*, pp. 193–95.
88 "Boubakar n'est plus très-aimé de ses populations; il a des embarras domestiques, des sujets pressures qui ne demandent qu'a secouer le joug." "Mission Laude," ANF 1G 44 (200 Mi 651).
89 Bakel to Governor, 14 January 1871, ANF 13G 171 (200 Mi 927).
90 Bakel to Governor, 1 January 1867, ANF 13G 170 (200 Mi 927).
91 "Mission Laude," ANF 1G 44 (200 Mi 651).
92 "'Tout le monde m'abandonne à présent, je vais aller en Gambie'." Ibid. The current picture of Bokar Saada is very different. According to everyone with whom I spoke, he was greatly loved by the people of Bundu (e.g., Saada Denbele, Gabou, 7 September 1987; Hammadi Kouliabali, Naye, 8 September 1987; Issaga Opa Sy, Goudiry, 8 and 9 June 1988). I believe the nineteenth-century portrait is accurate.
93 Saada Denbele, Gabou, 7 September 1987, trans. Sire Sy; Rançon, *Bondou*, p. 106.
94 Bulletins, May and June of 1885, ANF 13G 185 (200 Mi 930).
95 Rançon, *Bondou*, p. 106.
96 Ibid., p. 108; Lamartiny, *Etudes*, p. 54; Kamara, "Histoire," p. 811; Saada Denbele, Gabou, 7 September 1987, trans. Sire Sy.
97 Kamara states that Bokar Saada reigned thirty years ("Histoire," p. 811). FC, nos. 4, 18, and 30 give a range from thirty-one and a half years to thirty-two years. Diakité gives thirty-three years ("Livre," p. 212). The second civil war obviously affected these calculations, except for Kamara's.

98 Lamartiny, *Etudes*, p. 53; Rançon, *Bondou*, p. 107.
99 Lamartiny, *Etudes*, pp. 53–54.

10: Mamadu Lamine and the demise of Bundu

1 Faidherbe, "Notice sur la colonie," p. 54.
2 Administrateur du Bondou to Directeur Affaires Politiques, 1893, ANS 13G 251.
3 Faidherbe, *Le Sénégal*, p. 416; Bakel to Governor, 12 November 1875, ANF 13G 173 (200 Mi 927).
4 B. O. Oloruntimehin, "Senegambia – Mahmadu Lamine," in Michael Crowder, ed., *West African Resistance* (New York, 1971), pp. 80–110; Humphrey Fisher, "The Early Life of al-Hajj Muhammad al-Amin the Soninke (d. 1887)," *JAH* 11 (1970): 51–69; Ivan Hrbek, "The Early Period of Mahmadu Lamine's Activities," in J. R. Willis, *Studies in West African Islamic History. Volume One: The Cultivators* (London, 1979), pp. 211–232; Abdoulaye Bathily, "Mamadou Lamine Drame et la resistance anti-imperialism dans le Haut-Sénégal (1885–1887)," *Notes africaines* 125 (1970): 20–32. Interestingly, Amadou Abdoul Sy, whose foreparents fought against Lamine, would agree with Hrbek's appraisal (Tambacounda, 12 June 1988).
5 Barry, *La Sénégambie*, pp. 306–10.
6 Telegram from Commandant Superieur to Governor, 14 August 1886, ANF 1D 81 (200 Mi 257). Manding populations may have always been in the majority in Bundu.
7 Bathily, "Mamadou Lamine," pp. 20–32; Daniel Nyambarza, "Le marabout el Hadj Mamadou Lamine d'après les archives françaises," *CEA* 9 (1969): 124–45; Rançon, *Bondou*, p. 107.
8 Smith, "Les diakhanke," p. 16; Sanneh, *The Jakhanke*, pp. 68–9; Rançon, *Bondou*, p. 107; Rançon, *Haut-Gambie*, pp. 383–84. Bathily and Nyambarza maintain he was born in Cocoumalla, just outside Safalou.
9 Rançon, *Bondou*, p. 108; Hanson, "Umarian Karta," pp. 215–17.
10 Henri Frey, "Campagne contre le marabout Mamadou Lamine," ANF 1D 81 (200 Mi 257); also in ANF–OM, Senegal IV–85.
11 Henri Frey, *Campagne dans le Haut-Sénégal et dans le Haut Niger (1885–1886)* (Paris, 1888), p. 251.
12 Samani Sy, "Wars of Mamadu Lamine," Bakel, 16 April 1966, trans. A. Bathily, CC T4, side 1; Rançon, *Bondou*, p. 109; Bathily, "Mamadou Lamine," p. 22.
13 Bathily, "Mamadou Lamine," p. 22. Rançon, (*Bondou*, p. 109) maintains that he did not go to Bakel until 1854, when he met *al-ḥājj* Umar.
14 Bathily, "Mamadou Lamine," p. 31; Mahmadou Alioum Tyam, *La vie d'el Hadj Omar*, trans. H. Gaden (Paris, 1935), p. 34.
15 A. LeChatelier, in *L'Islam dans l'Afrique occidentale* (Paris, 1899), p. 216, says that Lamine traveled to Cairo, then to Medina, then to Mecca for three years. It is Faidherbe (*Sénégal*, p. 420) who maintains that the cleric stayed at Constantinople for several years. Frey (*Campagne*, pp. 251–2) also claims that Lamine spent some years in Mecca. In contrast, Lamine does not claim to have visited Egypt or Constantinople.
16 Hrbek, "Early Period," p. 214; Nyambarza, "El Hadj Mamadou Lamine," p. 128.
17 Rançon, *Bondou*, pp. 111–15.
18 Frey, "Campagne."
19 Rançon, *Bondou*, pp. 115–16; Bathily, "Mamadou Lamine," pp. 22–23.
20 Ibid.; Frey, "Campagne."
21 "J'ai l'honneur de mettre à votre connaissance que je viens d'arriver d'un pèlerinage de la Mecque, après une absence dans mon pays natal de trente-six ans.
"Je suis l'ami des Français et ne suivra que leurs ordres partout où je pourrais être.
"Je viens donc vous prier Monsieur le Gouverneur de vouloir bien m'autoriser à suivre

mes traces dans la droiture et dans la sagesse et d'enseigner à tous mes gens qui seront sous mes ordres de marcher dans la meme voie." Mamadu Lamine to Governor, August 1885, ANF 1D 81 (200 Mi 257).
22 "Les infidèles sont très nombreux. Je ne peux même pas leur faire la guerre à tous, à plus forte raison faire la guerre aux Français, parce que ce sont ceux-ci qui peuvent amélior ma situation; car la poudre, les balles, les fusils, et munitions de guerre, ainsi que le papier sont tous des articles français, que nous ne pouvons nous procurer que chez vous et avec votre consentement; pour cela il faut être en paix." Mamadu Lamine to Governor, 24 September 1886, ANF (200 Mi 258).
23 Myambarza, "El Hadj Mamadou Lamine," p. 131.
24 Bathily, "Mamadou Lamine," pp. 22–23.
25 Rançon, *Bondou*, pp. 115–16; Frey, "Campagne,"; also see Hrbek, "Early Period," pp. 216–17.
26 Apparently Lamine had a similar experience in Gamon, where either he or his mother had been taken captive early in his life. Rançon, *Bondou*, p. 108; Bathily ("Mamadou Lamine," p. 22) and Nyambarza ("El Hadj Mamadou Lamine," p. 125) relate a different story. According to them, Mamadu Lamine was made a prisoner by Gamon at the age of twenty, after participating in a raid by Kamera on Gamon. He was able to escape later.
27 Frey, "Campagne."
28 Report by Brosselard, ANF–OM, Senegal III–11f.
29 Frey, "Campagne."
30 Nyambarza, "El Hadj Mamadou Lamine," pp. 131–32; Sanneh, *The Jakhanke*, p. 78.
31 Rançon, *Bondou*, p. 116.
32 Ibid., pp. 117–18; Frey, "Campagne."
33 Hrbek, "Early Period," p. 222; Nyambarza, "El Hadj Mamadou Lamine," pp. 138–39. According to Bathily, he went to Diawara, downstream from Bakel, not Balou ("Mamadou Lamine," p. 24).
34 Rançon, *Bondou*, p. 106; Rançon, *Haut-Gambie*, p. 384.
35 Hrbek is not convinced that Bokar Saada actually refused the cleric ("Early Period," pp. 217–18).
36 Frey, "Campagne."
37 Frey, *Campagne*, p. 270.
38 Amadou Abdoul Sy, Tambacounda, 12 June 1988; Hrbek, "Early Period," p. 222.
39 Frey, *Campagne*, p. 272; Faidherbe, *Le Sénégal*, p. 419.
40 Rançon, *Bondou*, p. 117.
41 Ibid., p. 118.
42 Ibid.
43 Frey, "Campagne."
44 Bathily, "Mamadou Lamine," p. 23.
45 Amadou Abdoul Sy, Tambacounda, 12 June 1988; Rançon, *Bondou*, pp. 118–19; Sanneh, *Jakhanke*, pp. 80–82.
46 Ibid., pp. 119–20. Hrbek ("Early Period," p. 222) says that Lamine entered Bundu on 1 February.
47 Hrbek, "Early Period," p. 223.
48 Rançon, *Bondou*, p. 120.
49 Ibid. Debou was a few kilometers south of Senoudebou.
50 Modi Seck, "The Story of Mamadou Lamine," Dakar, 17 April 1966; Dakar; trans, H. A. Sy, CC T9. side 2.
51 Rançon, *Bondou*, p. 120.
52 Ibid.
53 Ibid., pp. 120–21.

54 Frey, *Campagne*, p. 272. Rançon, (*Bondou*, pp. 124–25) was either given or manufactured for himself an explanation for Gassi's absence, which vindicated him of any wrong-doing. The story is highly suspect, and therefore untreated here.
55 Rançon, *Bondou*, pp. 121–23.
56 Ibid., p. 124; Frey, *Campagne*, p. 272.
57 Rançon, *Bondou*, p. 123.
58 Frey, *Campagne*, p. 272; Faidherbe, *Le Sénégal*, pp. 422–23.
59 Rançon, *Bondou*, pp. 123–25.
60 Frey, *Campagne*, pp. 272–74. that Mamadu Lamine took the title *Mahdi* is a most serious proposition, calling for a thorough examination of all the contemporary Arabic material that may shed light on the issue.
61 Rançon, *Bondou*, pp. 126–27.
62 Frey, *Campagne*, p. 274.
63 Frey, "Campagne."
64 Frey, *Campagne*, p. 274.
65 Lieutenant-Colonel Gallieni, *Deux campagnes au Soudan français, 1886–1888* (Paris, 1891), p. 51.
66 Rançon, *Bondou*, pp. 130–31.
67 Ibid.; Frey, *Campagne*, pp. 287–90.
68 Frey, *Campagne*, pp. 282–84. Bathily ("Mamadou Lamine," p. 24) gives the date for this as 13 March 1885; the cleric was still in Segu at that time, as was Bokar Saada.
69 Frey, *Campagne*, p. 293.
70 Ibid., pp. 280–81. Regarding the position of Commandant Supérieur, it had been created in September of 1880 for the purpose of expanding into the African interior. The post was independent of the colonial government in Senegal (Abun-Nasr, *Tijaniyya*, p. 134).
71 Frey, *Campagne*, p. 296; Rançon, *Bondou*, p. 131; Usuman Gassi to Sous-Secrétaire d'Etat au Ministère de la Marine et des Colonies, 3 October 1889, ANF–OM, Senegal IV–70a; Demba Simbalou Sock, Senoudebou, 14 March 1966; trans. H. A. Sy, CC T4, side 1.
72 Frey, *Campagne*, p. 299; H. Frey, *Côte occidentale d'Afrique* (Paris, 1890), p. 152.
73 Gallieni, *Deux campagnes*, pp. 13–14.
74 Frey, "Campagne."
75 Rançon, *Bondou*, p. 131; Report by Captain Mazillier, October 1893, ANF 13G 193 (200 Mi 932).
76 Frey, *Campagne*, p. 394.
77 Rançon, *Bondou*, p. 132.
78 Frey, *Campagne*, p. 416.
79 The villages were Sambakagny, Kemando, and Guemou (Frey, *Campagne*, pp. 416–17).
80 Frey, "Campagne"; Rançon, *Bondou*, pp. 132–33.
81 Rançon, *Bondou*, p. 133.
82 "La grande fatigue des troupes ne m'a pas permis de poursuivre le marabout dans le Diakha,..." Frey, "Campagne."
83 Rançon, *Bondou*, p. 132.
84 Frey, *Campagne*, p. 443.
85 Commandant Supérieur to Governor, 14 August 1886, ANF 1D 81 (200 Mi 257).
86 "Au nom de Dieu. O! habitant de Gadiaga et Guidimakha, défiez-vous la haine,... réunissez-vous entièrement au vrai religion, c'est-à-dire celle du bon Dieu, aussi bien de réunir tous pour faire la guerre contre les Chrétiens. Nottez bien que les Chrétiens sont mères des perfides et des démons. O! habitant Gadiaga [sic] et Guidimakha; je vous jure par Dieu si vous ne réunissez pas de faire la guerre contre les chrétiens, vous n'aurez jamais bonne religion de notre temps, c'est-à-dire celle du Dieu, et la religion de Chrétiens est celle de *satan*, connaissez-vous que *satan* est un ennemi de vous,..." ANS 13G 240.
87 Rançon, *Bondou*, p. 134.

88 Ibid.
89 FC, nos. 4 and 30 state that he reigned five months and ten days.
90 Rançon, *Bondou*, p. 134.
91 Ibid.; Kamara, "Histoire," p. 811.
92 Rançon, *Bondou*, pp. 134–37.
93 Ibid., pp. 137–38. Reported by Gallieni, 1886–87, ANF–OM, Senegal IV–87bis.
94 Briquelot, "Mission du Boundou et de la Gambie (1888–89)," ANF 1G 207 (200 Mi 668); Rançon, *Bondou*, p. 138; Sanneh, *Jakhanke*, pp. 84–90; Smith, "Diakhanke," pp. 247–57.
95 Mamadu Lamine to Governor, 24 September 1886, ANF (200 Mi 258).
96 "Je te fais connaitre, à toi gouverneur,..., et je te le jure deux fois devant Dieu, que je n'ai jamais voulu me battre avec toi, car je voulais vivre en paix avec les Français ... Sache que j'ai beaucoup d'ennemis, autres que les Français. Les infidèles sont très nombreux. Je ne peux même pas leur faire la guerre à tous, à plus forte raison faire la guerre aux Français; parce que ce sont eux qui peuvent seuls améliorer ma situation; car la poudre, les balles, les fusils et munitions de guerre, ainsi que le papier sont tous des articles français, que nous ne pouvons nous procurer que chez vous et avec votre consentement; pour cela il faut être en paix.

"Comment pourrais-je vous declarer la guerre, moi qui sait tout cela et qui le comprend bien. Non! Non! Non! Voice ce que Dieu a décidé entre nous:

"J'ai oublié tout ce que tu m'as fait ... Acceptez et oubliez aussi – c'est ce que je demande avec force et c'est plus mon grand désir – si je puis obtenir cela de dieu et de vous, je rendrai grace à Dieu." Ibid.
97 Gallieni, *Deux campagnes*, p. 14; Yves Saint-Martin, "Un fils d'El Hadj Omar: Aguibou, roi de Dinguiray et du Macina (1843?–1907)," *CEA* 8 (1968): 144–78.
98 Gallieni to Bonacorsi, 1 October 1886, ANF–OM, Senegal IV–87bis.
99 "Un mauvais homme, un imposteur, un menteur, un homme qui cherche à s'enricher a vois defens [*sic*] est venu dans vos pays demander des forces pour combattre les Français. Quelques uns de vous ont eu la faiblesse de le suivre et vous savez ce qui est arrivé. Des qu'ils ont été devant les Français, ils ont été tués ou obligés de fuir.

"Si vous êtes raisonnables écoutez mes conseils. Voici ce que je vous dis. Chassez loin de vous Mamadou Lamine, refusez lui l'accès de votre pays et le concours de vos armes.

"Si vous ne faites pas cela, si vous continuez à aider Mahmadou Lamine, il y aura de grands malheurs, les colonnes des mes soldats iront le chercher jusque chez vous et alors ce sera la ruine pour tous.

[Not in text] "Les Français seront vos amis, si vous écoutez mes conseils. Ils le sont déjà car vous savez que plusieurs d'entre eux sont déjà venus vous apporter des paroles de paix et d'amitie et vous proposer de faire le commerce avec eux. Mais ils deviendront des ennemis, si vous continuez à soutenir un imposteur et un traitre, qui ne cherche qu'à vous tromper. Reflechissez et écoutez les conseils des hommes sages, que je vous envoie et qui vous diront ce qu'il faut faire." Gallieni to Sirimana, Badon, Gamon, Tenda, Wuli, lands along the Faleme, and Dianna, 8 December 1886, ANF–OM, Senegal IV–87bis.
100 Paul Marty, "Les groupements Tidiania, derivés d'Al-Hadj Omar (Tidiania Toucouleurs)" *Revue de monde musulman* 31 (1915–16): 318.
101 Gallieni, *Deux campagnes*, p. 55.
102 Report by Gallieni, ANF–OM, Senegal IV–87bis. In his *Deux campagnes* (p. 55), however, he claims Saada Amadi had 200 cavalry.
103 Report by Gallieni, 19 November 1886, ANF–OM, Senegal IV–87bis. This column was composed of 108 Europeans, 455 "indigènes" and 21 officers.
104 Gallieni, *Deux campagnes*, p. 17.
105 Report by Gallieni, 22 November 1886, ANF–OM, Senegal IV–87bis. The second column consisted of 63 Europeans, 313 Africans, and 15 officers.
106 Report by Gallieni, n.d., ANF–OM, Senegal IV–87bis.

107 Gallieni, *Deux campagnes*, p. 55.
108 Report by Gallieni, n.d., ANF–OM, Senegal IV–87bis.
109 Ibid.
110 Sous-secrétaire (Paris) to Governor, 26 July 1888, ANF–OM, Senegal IV–70a.
111 Rançon, *Bondou*, p. 143.
112 Ibid., pp. 150–51; Gallieni *Deux campagnes*, p. 338.
113 Bulletin, August 1887, ANF 13G 187 (200 Mi 931).
114 Bulletin, April 1887, ANF 13G 187 (200 Mi 931).
115 Rançon, *Bondou*, pp. 148–49; Sabatié, *Le Sénégal*, p. 228. For a discussion of this ancient center, see Smith, "Les Diakhanke."
116 Rançon, *Bondou*, p. 153; Report by Fortin, 6 January 1888, ANF 2B 92 (200 Mi 259).
117 Gallieni, *Deux campagnes*, p. 345.
118 Ibid., pp. 348–60.
119 Ibid.
120 Gallieni, *Deux campagnes*, p. 365.
121 Ibid.; Gallieni states that he died on 9 December. However, other French materials indicate he died 11 December. See Communication on Mamadu Lamine's death, 26 December 1887, ANF–OM, Senegal IV–91a.
122 Rançon, *Bondou*, p. 158; Gallieni, *Deux campagnes*, p. 365.
123 Robinson, *Chiefs and Clerics*, pp. 149–59.
124 Briquelot, "Mission du Boundou," ANF 1G 107 (200 Mi 668).
125 Kamara, "Histoire," p. 811.
126 Marty, "Les groupements Tidiania," pp. 318–19; Rançon, *Bondou*, p. 159; Louis Archinard, *Le Soudan français en 1888–1889* (Paris, 1890), p. 6.
127 Saada Amadi to Commandant at Bakel, October 1888, ANF 15G 81 (200 Mi 1017).
128 Briquelot, "Mission du Boundou," ANF 1G 207 (200 Mi 668).
129 Ibid.
130 Ibid.
131 Dorr, ANF 1G 101 (200 Mi 657).
132 Briquelot, "Mission du Boundou."
133 Briquelot, to Commandant Supérieur, 14 May 1889, ANF 1G 207 (200 Mi 668).
134 'Ousman s'empressa de déclarer que s'il était l'almamy pour les Français, Amady Ciré serait toujours le véritable chef du Boundou." Report by Roux, April 1892, ANF 13G 192 (200 Mi 932).
135 Bakel Correspondence, 23 February 1891, ANF 13G 190 (200 Mi 931).
136 Report from Bakel, 1 May 1889, ANF 13G 189 (200 Mi 931).
137 Briquelot, "Mission du Boundou."
138 Bulletin, May 1890, ANF 13G 190 (200 Mi 932); Marty, "Les groupements Tidiania," p. 319.
139 Bulletin, June 1889, ANS 13G 189.
140 Robinson, *Chiefs and Clerics*, pp. 150–51.
141 Archinard, *Soudan français*, pp. 11–13. This contradicts Robinson's assertion that Abdul Bokar Kan failed to take any military initiatives on Saada Amadi's behalf (*Chiefs and Clerics*, p. 151).
142 Curiously, the *Annuaire du Sénégal et Dépendances* lists "Sando Amady," an obvious reference to Saada Amadi, as the *Almaami* of Bundu for 1888 and 1889. Apparently, the *Annuaire* was not very concerned with current events in Bundu.
143 "... ces contingents, peuvent nous être d'un grand secours lorsqu'ils seraient réunis dans la main d'un seul chef, l'Almamy du Boundou." Instructions from Archinard to Briquelot, 24 March 1889, in Briquelot, "Mission du Boundou."
144 Rançon, *Bondou*, p. 159.
145 Correspondence with Bundu, ANF 15G 81 (200 Mi 1017).

Notes to pages 172–173

146 Rançon, *Bondou*, p. 159.
147 Report by Roux, April 1892, ANF 13G 192 (200 Mi 932).
148 Rançon, *Bondou*, p. 3.
149 "... sans aucune idée nouvelle heureux de retourner sa cohorte de griots dont la privation lui avait été bien pénible." Report by Roux, April 1892, ANF 13G 192 (200 Mi 932).
150 Rançon, *Bondou*, p. 160.
151 Moussa Kamara maintains that he ruled one year (Kamara, "Histoire," pp. 811–12). Fulbe traditions record his reign lasted four years (Demba Simbalou Sock, Senoudebou, 14 March 1966, trans. H. A. Sy, CC T3, side 2). Only two of the three "kings'" lists collected by Curtin extend beyond Bokar Saada; neither recognized Usuman Gassi. Rather, both Saada Amadi and Amadi Cire are credited with having reigned one year (FC, nos. 4 and 30). Kamara also recognizes the latter two as having reigned (Kamara, "Histoire," p. 816).
152 Briquelot, "Mission du Bondou."
153 Report by Roux on Bakel, 1892, ANF 1G 135 (200 Mi 660).
154 Bulletin, March 1891 and 16 April 1891, ANF 13G 190 (200 Mi 932); Bakel Correspondence, 23 February 1891, ANF 13G 190 (200 Mi 931).
155 Report by Roux, April 1892, ANF 13G (200 Mi 932).
156 Bakel Correspondence, 28 March 1892, ANF 13G 192 (200 Mi 932).
157 Report by Roux, April 1892, ANF 13G 192 (200 Mi 932); Marty, "Les groupements Tidiania," p. 319.
158 Smith, "Diakhanke," p. 256; Sanneh, *Jakhanke*, pp. 86–88.
159 Hanson, "Umarian Karta," pp. 287–91; *Bulletin du Comité de l'Afrique française*, August 1893.
160 L. Faissole, Administrateur du Cercle de Bakel to Directeur des Affaires Indigènes, Saint Louis, April 1899, ANF 13G 202 (200 Mi 936).
161 Bakel to Saint Louis, 6 October 1898, ANF 13G 201 (200 Mi 935).
162 Bakel to Saint Louis, 1 May 1898, ANF 1G 201 (200 Mi 935).
163 Marty, "Les groupements Tidiania," pp. 319–20; FC, nos. 4 and 30 agree Malik Ture reigned fourteen years. Rançon's narrative ends before Malik Ture's death. Demba Simbalou Sock (CC T3, side 2) also gives his reign as fourteen years.
164 Brigaud, *Etudes sénégalaises*, p. 220; Marty, "Les groupements Tidiania," p. 320; Briquelot, "Mission du Boundou."
165 FC, nos. 4 and 30; A. Bonnel de Mezières, "Les Diakhanke de Banisiraila et du Boundou méridional (Sénégal)," *Notes africaines* 41 (1949): 20–25.
166 Ibid.

Bibliography

I. Unpublished sources

Archival documentation

Archives nationales de France, Paris.
Archives nationales de France, section Outre-Mer, Paris.
Archives nationales du Sénégal, Dakar.
National Archives of the Gambia, Banjul.
Public Record Office, London.

Oral and Arabic documentation

Curtin Collection of oral traditions of Bundu and Gajaaga, on deposit at IFAN, Dakar, and the African Studies Association, Center for African Oral Data, Archives of Traditional Music, Maxwell Hall, Indiana University, Bloomington. The Curtin Collection has a total recording length of close to 100 hours. The informants listed below proved to be the most important for the purposes of this study.

Diakité, Kadealy. Grand Dakar, 23 February 1966. The narrator was about seventy years old at the time of the interview, and was *Imām* of the mosque at Dielani. Generally recognized as having been the most eminent religious leader of the Jakhanke of southern Bundu. Conditions: changing audience (from two to six persons), basically family members. Translated from Pulaar into French by Hamady Amadou Sy, 5, 6 and 8 May 1966, Dakar.

Ly, Idrisa. Dakar, 27 February 1966. Narrator was 60 years old at the time of the interview, and was *Imām* of the mosque at Diarra. An adherent of the Tijaniyya *ṭarīqa*, he was the son of a famous *shaykh* of the past, Baba Ly. Conditions: in a mosque, with two others connected with the mosque. Translated from Pulaar into French by Hamady Amadou Sy, 12 May 1966, Dakar.

N'Diaye, Saki. Dakar, nine sessions (5, 6, 11, 21 and 23 May; 7, 10, 13 and 16 June 1966). Originally from Bundu, about seventy years old at the time of the interviews. A descendant of the chief *griot* (*farba*) of *Almaami* Saada Amadi Aissata. Conditions: small audience of family members at times, private recitations at others. Translated from Pulaar into French by Hamady Amadou Sy, 17–21 July 1966, Dakar.

Seck, Modi. Goudiry, 17 April 1966. A *gawlo*, Pulaar for "oral historian" or "praise-singer," he was fifty-five years old and blind at the time of the interview. A specialist in the praises and genealogies of the weavers (*maboude*). Conditions: unspecified. Translated from Pulaar into French by Hamady Amadou Sy, 12 and 13 July 1966, Dakar.

Sissoko, Sassana. Dakar, 19 May 1966. The narrator was not a *griot* but an ex-slave with close ties to the royal family of Damga, who were the *chefs d'arondissement* in 1966. Conditions: unspecified. Translated from Soninke into French by Abdoulaye Bathily, 25 and 26 June 1966, Dakar.

Sock, Demba Simbalou. Senoudebou, three sessions (12, 13 and 14 March 1966). *Griot* of Senoudebou, and principal historian and genealogist of the Sissibe. Conditions: small audience, including Sissibe notables of Senoudebou. Instrumental accompaniment at times. Translated from Pulaar into French by Hamady Amadou Sy. n.d.

Sy, Maimouna Mamadou. Grand Dakar, 20 February 1966. Narrator was the widow of Saada Abdul Sy (*chef de canton*, 1918–54). Conditions: private house, no audience. Translated from Pulaar into French by Hamady Amadou Sy, grandson of narrator, 30 April 1966, Dakar.

Sy, Samani. Bakel, 15 and 16 April 1966. Narrator from Bakel, born *c.* 1892, with family ties to the N'Diayebe of Bakel. Conditions: small audience in the home of one of the N'Diaye family. Translated from Soninke into French by Abdoulaye Bathily, 23 June 1966, Dakar.

In addition to the Curtin oral collection, the author conducted a series of interviews in 1984 and 1987–88. Of these interviews, the following are the most useful:

Denbele, Saada. Gabou, 7 September 1987. The informant was seventy-eight years old at the time of the interview. A Pullo, he is regarded as a leading authority on Bundunke history. Conditions: Sire Sy acted as interpreter; interview in the compound of Sire Sy; family members present.

Koulibali, Hammadi. Nayes, 8 September 1987. Of Bambara extraction, the 70-year-old informant is deferred to as the most knowledgeable man in the village. Conditions: interview conducted in the public reception area – about fifty men present. Baba Traore acted as interpreter.

Sy, Amadi Bokar. Tambacounda, 13 June 1988. Well-regarded as an expert on Bundunke history, the 56-year-old informant is a descendant of Bokar Saada. Conditions: interview in the office of the informant, two others present. Conducted in French.

Sy, Amadou Abdoul. Tambacounda, 11 June 1988. The younger brother of Amadi Bokar Sy, this 45-year-old is highly-esteemed by all in the Tambacounda area as a preeminent source of historical information on the Sissibe, notwithstanding his relative youth. Conditions: interview at the Ecole Elementaire Batou Diarra, where the informant is the Directeur. A total of three persons were present. In French.

Sy, Issaga Opa. Goudiry, 8 and 9 June 1988. The former *chef d'arondissement* of the region of Boundou, the 73-year-old descendant of Bokar Saada was recommended by all in "Sénégal orientale" as an accurate repository of information on Bundu's past. Conditions: interview progressively joined as it continued until nine people had gathered. On the subject of Futa Toro, joined by Abrahim (not Ibrahim) Keita, of Manding extraction. In French.

Fonds Curtin of Arabic materials from Bundu, on deposit at IFAN, Dakar, and available through the Cooperative Africana Microfilm Project and the Center for Research Libraries, Chicago.

Unpublished theses

Barrows, Leland C. "General Faidherbe, the Maurel and Prom Company, and French Expansion in Senegal." Ph.D. thesis, UCLA, 1974.

Bibliography

Boulège, Jean, "La Sénégambie du milieu du XVe au debut de XVIII siècle." Thèse de troisième cycle, University of Paris, 1968.
Brown, William. "The Caliphate of Hamdullahi c. 1818–1864: A Study in African History and Tradition." Ph.D. thesis, University of Wisconsin, 1969.
Hanson, John H. "Umarian Karta (Mali, West Africa) during the Late Nineteenth Century: Dissent and Revolt among the Futanke after Umar Tal's Holy War." Ph.D. thesis, Michigan State University, 1989.
Hawkins, Joye B. "Conflict, Interaction and Change in Guinea-Bissau. Fulbe Expansion and Its Impact, 1850–1900," Ph.D. thesis, UCLA, 1980.
Hunter, Thomas. "The Development of an Islamic Tradition of Learning among the Jahanka of West Africa." Ph.D. thesis, University of Chicago, 1977.
Johnson, James. "The Almaamate of Futa Toro, 1770–1836: A Political History." Ph.D. thesis, University of Wisconsin, 1974.
McDougall, E. Ann. "The Ijil Salt Industry: Its Role in the Precolonial Economy of the Western Sudan." Ph.D. thesis, University of Birmingham, 1980.
McGowan, Winston F. "The Development of European Relations with Futa Jallon and the Foundation of French Colonial Rule, 1794–1895." Ph.D. thesis, London University, SOAS, 1975.
Ould Cheikh, Abdel Wedoud. "Nomadisme, Islam et pourvoir politique dans la société Maure precoloniale (XIème siècle – XIXème siècle)." Thèse pour le doctorat en sociologie, University of Paris, 1985.

Official and semi-Official French Publications

Annales sénégalaises de 1854 à 1885 suivies des traités passés avec les indigènes. Paris. 1885.
Annuaire de la marine et des colonies, 1853–65.
Annuaire du Sénégal et Dépendances, 1859–70, 1872–84, 1886–1901.
Moniteur du Sénégal et Dépendances (also called *Feuille officielle du Sénégal et Dépendances* and *Journal officielle* at times).
Revue coloniale, 1848–59, and its successors, the *Revue algerienne et coloniale*, 1859–61, and the *Revue maritime et coloniale*, 1862 ff.

II. Published primary sources

Abd al-Rahman al-Sa'di, *Tā'rīkh al-Sūdān*, Translated by O. Houdas. Paris, 1900.
Adam, M. G., *Legendes historiques du pays de Nioro (Sahel)*. Paris, 1904.
Adanson, Michel, *Histoire naturelle du Sénégal*. Paris, 1757.,
Archinard, Louis. *Le Soudan français en 1888–1889*. Paris, 1890.
Barbot, John. *A Description of the Coasts of North and South Guinea*. N.p., 1732.
Bayol, Jean. *Voyage en Sénégambie*. Paris, 1888.
Bechet, Eugene. *Cinq ans de séjour au Soudan français*. Paris, 1889.
Bérenger-Feraud, L. J. B. "Etudes sur les soninkes." *Revue d'anthropologie* 1 (1878): 584–606.
   Les peuplades de la Sénégambie. Paris, 1879.
   Recueil de contes popularies de la Sénégambie. Paris, 1885.
Bluett, Thomas, *Some Memoirs on the Life of Job*. London, 1734.
Boilat, L'Abbe P.-D. *Esquisses sénégalaises*. Paris, 1853.
Boucard, Claude. "Relation de Bambouc." Edited by P. Curtin and J. Boulegue. *BIFAN* 36 (1974): 246–75.
Brigaud, Felix. *Etudes sénégalaises: Fascicule 9. Histoire traditionelle du Sénégal*. St. Louis du Sénégal, 1962.
Brossard de Corbigny, P. "Exploration hydrographique de la Falémé." *Revue coloniale* 3 (1858): 142–51.

Bibliography

Ca da Mosto, Alvise da. *The Voyage of Cadamosto*. Edited by G. R. Crone. London, 1937.
Caillé, Réné. *Travels Through Central Africa to Timbuctoo and Across the Great Desert, to Morocco, 1824–1828*. Translated. 2 vols. London, 1968.
Carrère, Frederic, and Holle, Paul. *De la Sénégambie française*. Paris, 1855.
Colin, G. "La population de Bambouck." *Revue d'anthropologie* 1 (1886): 432–47.
"Le Soudan occidental." *Revue maritime et coloniale* 78 (1883): 5–32.
David, Pierre. *Journal d'un voyage fait en Bambouc en 1744*. Edited by Andre Delcourt. Paris, 1974.
Diakité, Mamadou Aissa Kaba. "Livre renfermant le généalogie des diverses tribus noires du Soudan et l'histoire des rois après Mahomet, suivant les renseignements fournis par certaines personnes et ceux recueillis dans les anciens livres." *Annales d'académie des sciences coloniales* 3 (1929): 189–225.
Durand, J. B. L. *Voyage au Sénégal*. Paris, 1807.
A Voyage to Senegal. Translated. London, 1810.
Enduran, Ludoix. *La traite des nègres ou deux marins au Sénégal*. Paris, 1868.
Faidherbe, Louis Leon Cesar. "L'avenir du Sahara et du Soudan." *Revue maritime et coloniale* 8 (1863): 221–48.
"Notice sur la colonie du Sénégal et sur les pays qui sont en relation avec elle." In *Nouvelles annales des voyages*. Edited by V. A. Malte-Brun. Paris, 1889.
Filze, Louis. "Le Bambouk." *Le Moniteur* 51 (17 March 1857) and 52 (24 March 1857).
"Le Boundou." *Le Moniteur* 37 (9 December 1856).
"Le Boundou (Sénégal)." *Revue coloniale* 17 (1857): 175–78.
"Le Gadiaga." *Le Moniteur* 42 (January 1857).
Fox, William. *A Brief History of the Wesleyan Missions on the Western Coast of Africa*. London, 1851.
Frey, Henri. *Campagne dans le Haut Sénégal et le Haut Niger, 1885–86*. Paris, 1888.
Gaby, Jean Baptiste. *Relation de la Nigritie*. Paris, 1689.
Gallieni, Joseph S. *Deux campagnes au Soudan français, 1886–1888*. Paris, 1891.
Voyage au Soudan français, 1879–81. Paris, 1885.
Gray, Major William, and Dochard, Surgeon. *Travels in Western Africa in the Years 1818, 19, 20, and 21*. London, 1825.
Great Britain. Parliament. *Parliamentary Papers, The Gambia Papers, 1845–87*. Shannon, Ireland, 1971.
Hecquard, Hyacinte. *Voyage sur la côte et dans l'intérieur de l'Afrique occidentale*. Paris, 1855.
Ibn al-Mukhtar. *Tā'rīkh al-Fattash*. Translated by O. Houdas and M. Delafosse. Paris, 1913.
Isma'il Hamid. *Chroniques de la Mauritanie sénégalaise*. Paris, 1911.
Jobson, Richard. *The Golden Trade, or a Discovery of the River Gambia*. London, 1968.
Kamara, Moussa. "Histoire du Boundou." From *Zuhūr al-Basātin fī Tā'rīkh al-Sawādīn*. Edited and translated by Moustapha Ndiaye. *BIFAN* 37 (1975): 784–816.
Labarthe, P. *Voyage au Sénégal, pendant les années 1784 et 1785*. Paris, 1802.
Labat, Jean Baptist. *Nouvelle relation de l'Afrique occidentale*. 4 vols. Paris, 1728.
La Courbe. *Premier voyage du Sieur de La Courbe fait à la coste d'Afrique en 1685*. Edited by P. Cultru. Paris, 1913.
Lamartiny, J. J. *Etudes africaines: le Bondou et le Bambouck*. Paris, 1884.
Leblanc. "Voyage à Galam en 1820." *Annales maritime et coloniale* 1 (1822): 133–59.
LeChatelier, A. *L'Islam dans l'Afrique occidentale*. Paris, 1899.
Levtzion, N., and Hopkins, J. F. P., eds. *Corpus of Early Arabic Sources for West Africa*. Cambridge, 1981.
Lindsay, John. *A Voyage to the Coast of Africa in 1728*. London, 1759.
Ly, Djibril. "Coutumes et contes des Toucouleurs du Fouta Toro." *BCEHSAOF* 21 (1938): 304–26.
Mage, Eugene. *Voyage au Soudan occidentale, 1863–1866*. Paris, 1872.

Bibliography

Mollien, Gaspard Theodore. *Travels in Africa to the Sources of the Senegal and Gambia in 1818.* Translated. London, 1825.
Moore, Francis. *Travels into the Inland Parts of Africa.* London, 1738.
Noirot, Ernest. *A travers le Fouta-Diallon et le Bambouc.* Paris, 1882.
Park, Mungo. *Travels in the Interior Districts of Africa, 1795–1797, 1805.* London, 1817.
Pascal, S. L. "Voyage d'exploration dans le Bambouck, Haut-Sénégal." *Revue algerienne et coloniale* 3 (1860): 137–64.
"Voyage au Bambouk et retour à Bakel." *La Tour du Monde* 3 (1861): 39–48.
Pelletan, Jean-Gabriel. *Memoire sur la colonie française du Sénégal.* Paris, n.d.
Raffenel, Anne. "Le Haut Sénégal et la Gambie en 1843 et 1844." *Revue coloniale* 8 (1846): 309–40.
Nouveau voyage dans le pays des nègres. 2 vols. Paris, 1856.
"Rapport sur le pays de Galam, le Bondou, et le Bambouk, adressé le 17 mars 1844 au gouverneur du Sénégal." *Revue coloniale* 4 (1844): 1–22.
"Second voyage d'exploration dans l'intérieur de l'Afrique." *Revue coloniale* 13 (1847): 1–47.
Voyage dans l'Afrique occidentale en 1843 et 1844. Paris, 1846.
Rançon, André. *Le Bondou: Etude de géographie et d'histoire soudaniennes de 1681 à nos jours.* Bordeaux, 1894. Also in *Bulletin de la société de géographie de Bordeaux* 7 (1894): 433–63, 465–84, 497–548, 561–91, 593–647.
Dans la Haute-Gambie, 1891–1892. Paris, 1894.
Roux, Emile. *Notice historique sur le Boundou.* St. Louis du Sénégal, 1893.
Saugnier, M., and Brisson, M. *Voyages to the Coast of Africa.* London, 1792.
Soh, Sire Abbas. *Chroniques du Fouta sénégalais.* Translated by M. Delafosse and H. Gaden. Paris, 1913.
Sow, Alfa Ibrahim. *Chroniques et récits du Fouta Djalon.* Paris, 1968.
Usuman dan Fodio. *Bayān wujūb al-hirja 'alā al-'ibād.* Edited and translated by Fathi Hassan El-Masri. Oxford and Khartoum, 1978.
"Kitab al-Farq." Translated by M. Hiskett. *BSOAS* 23 (1960): 550–79.

III. Secondary sources

Abun-Nasr, Jamil. *A History of the Maghrib.* Cambridge, 1975.
"Some Aspects of the Umari Branch of the Tijaniyya." *JAH* 2 (1962): 329–31.
The Tijaniyya: A Sufi Order in the Modern World. New York, 1965.
Aghnides, Nicolas P. *Mohammedan Theories of Finance.* New York, 1916.
Ahayi, J. F. Ade, and Crowder, Michael. *A History of West Africa.* 2 vols. 2nd ed. New York, 1976.
Allen, Christopher, and Johnson, R. W. *African Perspectives.* Cambridge, 1970.
Aubert, A. "Legendes historiques et traditions orales recueillies dans la Haute Gambie." *BCEHSAOF* 6 (1923): 384–428.
Ba, Amadou Hampate, and Daget, Jacques. *L'Empire peul du Macina.* Dakar, 1955.
Ba, Oumar. "Le franc-parler toucouleur." *BIFAN* 30 (1968): 1581–1629.
La pénétration française au Cayor, vol. 1 (1854–61). Dakar, 1976.
"Vocabulaire de base. Introduction à l'étude du poular du Fouta sénégalais." *BIFAN* 30 (1968): 1271–82.
Ba, Tamsir Ousmane. "Essai historique sur le Rip (Sénégal)." *BIFAN* 19 (1957): 564–91.
Barrows, Leland C. "Faidherbe and Senegal: A Critical Discussion." *African Studies Review* 19 (1976): 95–117.
"The Merchants and General Faidherbe: Aspects of French Expansion in Senegal in the 1850's." *RHCF* (1974): 236–83.
"Some Paradoxes of Pacification: Senegal and France in the 1850's and 1860's". In *West

Bibliography

African Culture Dynamics. Edited by B. K. Swartz, Jr. and Raymond E. Dumett. New York, 1980.
Barry, Boubacar. "Le guerre des marabouts dans la région du fleuve Sénégal de 1673 à 1677." *BIFAN* 33 (1971): 564–89.
Le royaume du Waalo. Paris, 1972.
La Sénégambie du XVe au XIXe siècle: traite negrière, Islam et conquête. Paris, 1988.
Basset, Rene. *Mission au Sénégal.* Paris, 1909.
Bathily, Abdoulaye. "La conquête française du Haut-Fleuve (Sénégal), 1818–1887." *BIFAN* 34 (1972): 67–112.
Les portes de l'or: le royaume de Galam (Sénégal), de l'ère musulmane au temps des negrièrs (VIIIe – XVIIIe siècle). Paris, 1989.
"Mamadou Lamine Drame et la resistance anti-imperialisme dans le Haut-Sénégal (1885–1887)." *Notes africaines* 125 (1970): 20–32.
ed. "Notices socio-historiques sur l'ancien royaume soninké du Gadiaga." *BIFAN* 31 (1969): 31–105.
Beart, Charles. "Sur les Bassaris du cercle de Haute-Gambie (Sénégal)." *Notes africaines* 34 (1947): 24–26 and 35 (1947): 1–7.
Behrman, Lucy C. *Muslim Brotherhoods and Politics in Senegal.* Cambridge, 1970.
Bonnel de Mezières, A. "Les Diakanke de Banisraila et du Boundou méridional (Sénégal)." *Notes africaines* 41 (1949): 20–25.
Boulègue, Jean. "Contribution à la chronologie du royaume du Saloum." *BIFAN* 28 (1966): 657–62.
Bovill, E. W. *Caravans of the Old Sahara.* London, 1933.
Boyer, Gaston. *Un peuple de l'Ouest soudanais: les Diawara.* Dakar, 1953.
The Golden Trade of the Moors. New York, 1968.
Bradley, Phillip; Raynaut, C.; Torrealbe, J. *The Guidimaka Region of Mauritania.* London, 1977.
Bravmann, Rene. *Open Frontiers: The Mobility of Art in Black Africa.* Seattle, 1973.
Brevie, Jules. *Islamisme contre naturisme au Soudan français.* Paris, 1923.
Bulliet, Richard W. *The Patricians of Nishapur: A Study in Medieval Islamic Social History.* Cambridge, Mass., 1972.
Carson, Patricia. *Materials for West African History in French Archives.* London, 1968.
Charles, Eunice A. *Precolonial Senegal: The Jolof Kingdom, 1800 to 1890.* Boston, 1977.
Cissoko, Sékéné-Mody. *Contribution à l'histoire politique du Khasso dans le Haut-Sénégal des origines à 1854.* Paris, 1986.
"Les princes exclus du pouvoir royal (mansaya) dans les royaumes du Khasso (XVIIIe – XIXe siècles)." *BIFAN* 35 (1973): 46–56.
"La royauté (mansaya) chez les Mandinques occidentaux, d'après leurs traditions orales." *BIFAN* 31 (1969): 324–38.
Tombouctou et l'empire Songhay. Dakar, 1975.
Clarke, Peter. *West Africa and Islam.* London, 1982.
Colombani, F. M. "Le Guidimaka, étude géographique, historique et religieuse." *BCEHSAOF* 14 (1931): 365–432.
Colvin, Lucie. "Islam and the State of Kajoor: A Case of Successful Resistance to Jihād." *JAH* 15 (1974): 587–606.
Crowder, Michael. *Senegal: A Study of French Assimilation Policy.* London, 1967.
West Africa under Colonial Rule. London, 1968.
Cultru, Prosper. *Histoire du Sénégal du XVe siècle à 1870.* Paris, 1910.
Curtin, Philip D. *Africa Remembered.* Madison, 1977.
"The Archives of Tropical Africa: A Reconnaissance." *JAH* 1 (1960): 129–47.
Economic Change in Precolonial Africa. Senegambia in the Era of the Slave Trade. Madison, 1975.

Bibliography

"Field Techniques for Collecting and Processing Oral Data." *JAH* 9 (1968): 367–85.
Image of Africa. Madison, 1964.
"Jihad in West Africa: Early Phases and Interrelations in Mauritania and Senegal." *JAH* 12 (1971): 11–24.
"The Lure of Bambuk Gold." *JAH* 14 (1973): 623–31.
"Pre-colonial trading networks and traders: the Diakhanke." In *The Development of Indigenous Trade and Markets in West Africa*. Edited by Claude Meillassoux. London, 1971.
"The Story of Malik Sy." *CEA* 11 (1971): 467–87.
"The Uses of Oral Tradition in Senegambia: Maalik Sii and the Foundation of Bundu." *CEA* 15 (1975): 189–202.
Daniel, Fernand. "Etude sur les Soninkés ou Sarakolé." *Anthropos* 4 (1910): 27–49.
Davies, K. G. *The Royal African Company*. London, 1957.
Delafosse, Maurice. "Les confrèries musulmanes et le maraboutisme dans les pays du Sénégal et du Niger." *Bulletin du comité de l'Afrique française et renseignements coloniaux* (1911): 81–90.
Haute-Sénégal-Niger (Soudan français). 3 vols. Paris, 1912.
Delcourt, André. *La France et les établissements français au Sénégal, entre 1713 et 1763*. Dakar, 1952.
Deschamps, Hubert. *Le Sénégal et la Gambie*. Paris, 1964.
Désiré-Vuillemin, G. M. *Histoire de la Mauritanie*. Paris, 1964.
Diagne, Pathe. *Pouvoir politique traditionnel en Afrique occidentale*. Paris, 1967.
Diallo, Thierno. *Catalogue des manuscrits de l'Ifan*. Dakar, 1966.
Les institutions politiques au Fouta Dyalon au XIXe siècle. Dakar, 1972.
"Les Peuls avant le XIXe siècle." *Annales de la faculté des lettres et sciences humaines de Dakar* 2 (1972): 121–93.
Diop, Amadou Bamba. "Lat Dior et le problème musulman." *BIFAN* 28 (1966): 493–539.
Dodwell, H. "Le Sénégal sous la domination anglaise." *RHCF* 4 (1916): 267–300.
Dumont, Fernand. *L'Anti-sultan, ou Al-Hajj Omar Tal du Fouta, combattant de la Foi*. Dakar-Abidjan, 1971.
Dupire, Marguerite. *Organisation sociale des Peul*. Paris, 1970.
Equilbecq, Francois Victor. *Contes populaires d'Afrique occidentale*. Paris, 1972.
Faure, Claude. "Un politique méconnu: Duranton dans le Haut-Sénégal." *RHCF* 7 (1919): 293–99.
"Le premier séjour de Duranton au Sénégal (1819–1826)." *RHCF* 9 (1921): 189–263.
Fisher, Humphrey. "Early Arabic Sources and the Almoravid Conquest of Ghana." *JAH* 23 (1982): 549–60.
"The Early Life and Pilgrimage of Al-Hajj Muhammad al-Amin the Soninke (d. 1887)." *JAH* 11 (1970): 51–69.
Gaden, Henri. *Proverbes et maximes peuls et toucouleurs*. Paris, 1931.
Gamble, D. P. *The Wolof of Senegambia*. London, 1957.
Gibb, H. A. R. *Mohammedanism*. London, 1970.
Goody, Jack. "The Impact of Islamic Writing on the Oral Cultures of West Africa." *CEA* 11 (1971): 455–66.
ed. *Literacy in Traditional Societies*. Cambridge, 1968.
Grant, Douglas, *The Fortunate Slave: An Illustration of African Slavery in the Early Eighteenth Century*. London, 1968.
Gray, J. M. *A History of the Gambia*. Cambridge, 1940.
Gray, Richard and Birmingham, David, eds. *Pre-Colonial African Trade*. London, 1970.
Hallet, Robin. *The Penetration of Africa*. London, 1965.
Proceedings of the Association for Promoting the Discovery of the Interior Parts of Africa. London, 1967.
ed. *Records of the African Association, 1788–1831*. New York, 1964.

Bibliography

Hardy, Georges. *La mise en valeur du Sénégal, de 1817 à 1854*. Paris, 1921.
Harris, Joseph E. "Protest and Resistance to the French in Fouta Diallon." *Geneve-Afrique* 8 (1969): 3–78.
Hiskett, Mervyn. "An Islamic Tradition of Reform in the Western Sudan from the 16th to the 18th Century." *BSOAS* 25 (1962): 577–96.
  The Sword of Truth. New York, 1973.
Hodge, Carleton T., ed. *Papers on the Manding*. Bloomington, 1971.
Hodges, Cornelius. "The Journey of Cornelius Hodges in Senegambia." Edited by Thora G. Stone. *English Historical Review* 39 (1924): 89–95.
Hodgson, Marshall G. S. *The Venture of Islam*. 3 vols. Chicago, 1974.
Hopkins, A. G. *An Economic History of West Africa*. New York, 1973.
Hrbek, Ivan. "The Early Period of Mahmadu Lamin's Activities." In *Studies in West African Islamic History. Vol. I: The Cultivators of Islam*. Edited by J. R. Willis. London, 1979.
Hunwick, J. O. "Sālih al-Fullānī of Futa Jallon: An 18th Century Scholar and *Mujaddid*." *BIFAN* 40 (1978): 879–85.
Jah, Omar. "Source Materials for the Career and *Jihad* of Al-Hajj 'Umar al-Futi, 1794–1864." *BIFAN* 41 (1979): 371–97.
Jenkins, R. G. "The Evolution of Religious Brotherhoods in North and Northwest Africa, 1523–1900." In *Studies in West African Islamic History. Vol. I: The Cultivators of Islam*. Edited by J. R. Willis. London, 1979.
Johnson, James and Robinson, David. "Deux fonds l'histoire orale sur le Fouta Toro." *BIFAN* 31 (1969): 120–37.
Johnson, Marion. "The Economic Foundations of an Islamic Theocracy: The Case of Masina." *JAH* 17 (1976): 481–95.
Johnston, H. A. S. *The Fulani Empire of Sokoto*. London, 1967.
Kamara, Moussa. "La vie d'el-Hadji Omar." Edited and translated by Amar Samb. *BIFAN* 32 (1970): 44–135, 370–411, 770–818.
Kane, Oumar. "Essai de chronologie des satigis du XVIIIe siècle." *BIFAN* 32 (1970): 755–65.
  "Samba Gelajo-Jegi." *BIFAN* 32 (1970): 911–26.
Klein, Martin. *Islam and Imperialism in Senegal: Sine-Saloum, 1847–1914*. Stanford, 1968.
  "Social and Economic Factors in the Muslim Revolution in Senegambia." *JAH* 13 (1972): 419–41.
Kopytoff, Igor, ed. *The African Frontier: the Reproduction of Traditional African Societies*. Bloomington, 1987.
Labouret, Henri and Travele, Moussa. "Quelques aspects de la magie africaine. Amulettes et talismans au Soudan français." *BCEHSAOF* (1924): 477–545.
Lanrezac, Victor L. M. "Légendes soudanaises." *Revue economique francaise* 5 (1907): 607–19.
Last, Murray. *The Sokoto Caliphate*. New York, 1967.
Law, Robin. *The Horse in West African History*. New York, 1980.
Lawrence, A. W. *Trade Castles and Forts of West Africa*. London, 1963.
Levtzion, Nehemiah. *Ancient Ghana and Mali*. London, 1973.
  Conversion to Islam. New York, 1979.
  Muslims and Chiefs in West Africa. London, 1968.
  "Oral Traditions and Arabic Documents in the Muslim Historiography of Africa." *Congrès International des Africanistes*, deuxième session. Dakar, 1967.
  and Fisher, Humphrey J. *Rural and Urban Islam in West Africa*. Boulder and London, 1987.
Lewis, Bernard. *Race and Color in Islam*. New York, 1970.
Lewis, I. M. *Islam in Tropical Africa*. London, 1966.
Ly, Abdoulaye. *La compagnie du Sénégal*. Dakar, 1958.
Machat, J. *Documents sur les établissements français et l'Afrique occidentale au XIIIe siècle*. Paris, 1906.
Martin, Bradford. "A Mahdist Document from Futa Jallon." *BIFAN* 25 (1963): 47–65.

Bibliography

Muslim Brotherhoods in 19th Century Africa. Cambridge, 1976.

Marty, Paul. "Le comptoir français d'Albreda en Gambie (1817–1826)." *RCHF* 12 (1924): 237–72.

"La découverte des sources de la Gambie et du Sénégal: Mollien (1818–1819)." *RHCF* 9 (1921): 53–98.

L'Emirat des Trarzas. Paris, 1919.

"L'Establissement des Français dans le Haut-Sénégal (1817–1822)." *RCHF* 13 (1925): 51–118, 210–68.

Etudes sénégalaises (1785–1826). Paris, 1926.

Etudes sur l'Islam au Sénégal. 2 vols. Paris, 1917.

Etudes sur l'Islam et les tribus du Soudan. 4 vols. Paris, 1920.

Etudes sur l'Islam et les tribus Maures, les Brakna. Paris, 1921.

Etudes sur l'Islam Maure. Paris, 1916.

"Les groupements Tidiania derivés d'al-Hadj Omar (Tidiania Toucouleurs). *Revue du monde musulman* 31 (1915–16): 275–365.

L'Islam en Guinée. Paris, 1921.

Mauny, Raymond. *Tableau géographique de l'Ouest africain au Moyen Age*. Dakar, 1961.

McGowan, Winston. "Fula Resistance to French Expansion into Futa Jallon, 1889–1896." *JAH*, 22 (1981): 245–61.

Meillassoux, Claude, ed. *The Development of Trade and Markets in West Africa*. London, 1971.

L'Esclavage en Afrique procoloniale. Paris, 1975.

Miers, Suzanne and Kopytoff, Igor, eds. *Slavery in Africa: Historical and Anthropoligical Perspectives*. Madison, 1977.

Mitchinson, A. W. *The Expiring Continent: A Narrative of Travel in Senegambia*. London, 1881.

Monteil, Charles. *Les Bambara du Ségou et du Kaarta*. Paris, 1924.

Les Khassonké. Paris, 1915.

Monteil, Vincent. *Esquisses sénégalaises*. Dakar, 1966.

"Goundiourou." *Notes africaines* 12 (1966): 595–636.

Morgan, W. B. and Pugh, J. C. *West Africa*. London, 1969.

Niane, Djibril Tamsir. "A propos de Koli Tenguella." *Recherches africaines* 4 (1960): 33–36.

Norris, H. T. *Saharan Myth and Saga*. Oxford, 1972.

Shinqiti Folk Literature and Song. Oxford, 1968.

The Tuaregs: Their Islamic Legacy and Its Diffusion in the Sahel. Wilts, England, 1975.

"Znāga Islam during the Seventeenth and Eighteenth Centuries." *BSOAS* 32 (1969): 496–526.

Nyambarza, Daniel. "Le marabout El Hadj Mamadou Lamine d'après les archives françaises." *CEA* 9 (1969): 124–45.

O'Brien, Donald B. Cruise. *Saints and Politicians: Essays in the Organization of a Senegalese Peasant Society*. New York, 1975.

O'Brien, Rita Cruise. *White Society in Black Africa: The French of Senegal*. London, 1972.

Oloruntimehin, B. O. "The Idea of Islamic Revolution and Tukolor Constitutional Evolution." *BIFAN* 33 (1971): 675–92.

"Muhammad Lamine in Franco-Tukulor Relations, 1885–1887." *Historical Society of Nigeria* 4 (1968): 375–98.

"Resistance Movements in the Tukulor Empire." *CEA* 8 (1968): 123–43.

The Segu Tukulor Empire. London, 1972.

"Senegambia – Mahmadu Lamine." In *West African Resistance*. Edited by Michael Crowder. New York, 1971.

Pageard, Robert. "Un mystérieux voyage au pays de Bambouc (1789)." *Notes africaines* 1 (1961): 23–27.

Patterson, Orlando. *Slavery and Social Death: A Comparative Study*. Cambridge, 1982.

Person, Yves. *Samori: une revolution Dyula*. 3 vols. Dakar, 1968–75.

Peters, Rudolph. *Islam and Colonialism. The Doctrine of Jihad in Modern History.* New York, 1979.
Jihad in Medieval and Modern Islam. Leiden, 1977.
Quinn, Charlotte A., *Mandingo Kingdoms of the Senegambia.* Evanston, 1972.
"A Nineteenth Century Fulbe State." *JAH* 12 (1971): 421–40.
Rahman, Fazlur. *Islam.* 2nd ed. Chicago, 1979.
Riesman, Paul. *Société et liberté.* Paris, 1974.
Ritchie, Carson I. A., ed. "Deux textes sur le Sénégal." *BIFAN* 30 (1968): 289–353.
Roberts, Richard L. "Production and Reproduction of Warrior States: Segu Bambara and Segu Tokolor, c. 1712–1890." *IJAHS* 13 (1980): 389–419.
Robinson, David. "Abdul Qadir and Shaykh Umar: A Continuing Tradition of Islamic Leadership in Futa Toro." *IJAHS* 6 (1973): 386–403.
"Almamy Abdul Kader." *Les Africains* 10 (1978).
Chiefs and Clerics: Abdul Bokar Kan and Futa Toro (1853–1891). Oxford, 1975.
The Holy War of Umar Tal. Oxford, 1985.
"The Islamic Revolution of Futa Toro." *IJAHS* 8 (1975): 185–221.
"Un historien et anthropologue sénégalais: Shaikh Musa Kamara," *CEA* 28 (1988): 89–116.
Curtin, Philip D.; and Johnson, J. "A Tentative Chronology of Futa Toro from the Sixteenth through the Nineteenth Centuries." *CEA* 12 (1972): 555–92.
Rodney, Walter. *A History of the Upper Guinea Coast.* Oxford, 1970.
"Jihad and Social Revolution in Futa Djalon in the Eighteenth Century." *Historical Society of Nigeria* 4 (1968): 269–84.
Sabatié, A. *Le Sénégal: sa conquête et son organisation (1364–1925).* Saint Louis du Sénégal, 1925.
Saint-Martin, Yves-J. *L'Empire toucouleur et la France. Un demi-siècle de relations diplomatiques (1846–93).* Dakar, 1967.
Saint-Pere, J. H. *Les Sarakholle du Guidimaka.* Paris, 1925.
Samb, Amar. "Condemnation de la guerre saints." *BIFAN* 38 (1976): 158–99.
"L'Islam et l'histoire du Sénégal." *BIFAN* 33 (1971): 461–507.
"La vie d'El-Hadji Omar par Cheikh Moussa Kamara." *BIFAN* 32 (1970): 44–135, 370–411.
Sanneh, Lamin O. *The Jakhanke.* London, 1979.
"The Origins of Clericalism in West African Islam." *JAH* 17 (1976): 49–72.
"Slavery, Islam and the Jakhanke People of West Africa." *Journal of the International African Institute* 46 (1976): 80–97.
Saulnier, Eugene. *La compagnie de Galam au Sénégal.* Paris, 1921.
Schultz, Emily, ed. *Image and Reality in African Interethnic Relations.* Williamsburg, 1981.
Shefer, Christian, ed. *Instructions générales données de 1763 à 1870 aux gouverneurs et ordonnateurs des établissements français en Afrique occidentale.* 2 vols. Paris, 1921.
Simmons, William S. *Eye of the Night: Witchcraft among a Senegalese People.* Boston, 1971.
Smith, Pierre. "Les Diakhanke: histoire d'une dispersion." *Bulletin et memoire de la société d'anthropologie de Paris* 8 (1965).
Smith, Robert. "The Canoe in West African History." *JAH* 11 (1970): 515–33.
Stewart, Charles C. *Islam and Social Order In Mauritania.* Oxford, 1973.
"Political Authority and Social Stratification in Mauritania." In *Arabs and Berbers.* Edited by Gellner and Micaud. London, 1973.
"Southern Saharan Scholarship and the Bilad al-Sudan." *JAH* 17 (1976): 73–93.
Suret-Canale, Jean. *French Colonialism in Tropical Africa, 1900–1945.* Translated by T. Gottheimer. New York, 1971.
"Touba in Guinea: Holy Place of Islam." In *African Perspectives.* Edited by Christopher Allen and R. W. Johnson. Cambridge, 1970.
Tauxier, Louis, *Histoire des Bambara.* Paris, 1942.
Moeurs et histoire des Peuls. Paris, 1937.
Le noir de Bondoukou. Paris, 1921.

Bibliography

La religion Bambara. Paris, 1927.
Techer, H. "Coutumes des Tendas." *BCEHSAOF* 16 (1933): 630–66.
Trimingham, J. Spencer. *A History of Islam in West Africa.* London, 1962.
The Influence of Islam upon Africa. New York, 1980.
The Sufi Orders in Islam. London, 1971.
Vasina, Jan. *Oral Tradition as History.* Madison, 1985.
Walckenaer, Charles A., ed. *Collection des relations des voyages par mer et par terre, en differentes parties de l'Afrique.* 21 vols. Paris, 1842.
Wane, Yaya. "Etat actuel de la documentation au sujet des Toucouleurs." *BIFAN* 25 (1963): 459–77.
"De Halwaar à Degembere ou l'itinéraire islamique de Shaykh Umar Tal." *BIFAN* 31 (1969): 445–51.
Les Toucouleur du Fouta Tooro (Sénégal). Dakar, 1969.
Watt, W. Montgomery. *Islamic Political Thought.* Edinburgh, 1968.
Muhammad at Medina. Oxford, 1966.
Weber, Henry. *La compagnie française des Indes (1604–1875).* Paris, 1904.
White, Gavin. "Firearms in Africa: An Introduction." *JAH* 12 (1971): 173–84.
Wilkes, Ivor. "The Transmission of Islamic Learning in the Western Sudan." In *Literacy in Traditional Societies.* Edited by Jack Goody. Cambridge, 1968.
Willis, John Ralph. "Jihād fī Sabīl Allāh." *JAH* 8 (1967): 395–415.
Ed. *Studies in West African Islamic History: The Cultivators of Islam.* London, 1979.
"The Torodbe Clerisy: A Social View." *JAH* 19 (1978): 195–212.
Wood, W. Raymond. "An Archaeological Appraisal of Early European Settlements in the Senegambia." *JAH* 8 (1967): 39–64.
Works, John. *Pilgrims in a Strange Land.* New York, 1976.
Wright, Donald R. *Oral Traditions from the Gambia.* 2 vols. Athens, 1979.
Wurie, A. "The Bundunkas of Sierra Leone." *Sierra Leone Studies* 1 (1953): 14–25.
Yoder, John C. "Fly and Elephant Parties: Political Polarization in Dahomey, 1840–1870." *JAH* 15 (1974): 417–32.
Zeltner, Frantz de. *Contes du Sénégal et du Niger.* Paris, 1913.

Index

aaye (Qur'anic verse), 57
Abbas (son of *Almaami* Tumane Mudi), 99
Abd al-Rahman (son of *Almaami* Amadi Gai), 81
Abdul Bokar Kan (grand elector of Futa Toro), 145–51, 169–71
   marriage to Jiba, niece of *Almaami* Bokar Saada, 146, 148
Abdul Qadir, 4, 28–30, 75, 82–100, 136, 178–79
   in Bundu, 4, 14, 82–93, 98–100, 109
   in Futa Toro, 4, 81
   manner of death, 90
Abdul Salum (son of *Almaami* Tumane Mudi), 99
Abdul Sega (*chef de canton*), 173–74
Abdul Sega Sy, 9, 11, 33
'abīd army (of Morocco), 70
agriculture, 2–3, 21–22, 56–59, 64–69, 77–79, 100, 137–38, 149
   cereals, 2, 21
   cotton, 2–3, 21, 77, 79
   description in Bundu, 77
   groundnuts, 3, 21, 138
   gum, 3, 58–59, 68–69, 79, 100
   indigo, 3, 21, 77, 79
   kola nuts, 3, 58, 98, 100
   maize, 3, 21
   millet, 3, 21
   onions, 22
   pepper, 22
   rice, 3, 21
   sorghum, 3, 21
   sorrel, 22
   tobacco, 21
   under Bokar Saada, 137, 149
   watermelon, 22

Aissata Bela (*Almaami* Maka Jiba's second wife), 73, 76, 82
al-Bekkai, 123, 134
al-Bukhari (*see also Ṣaḥīḥ*), 28
alfa, 47
Alfa Hatib, 28
Alfa Nuh, 28
Alfa Raji, 28
al-Hariri (*see also Maqāmāt*), 28
Alium Bubu Malik, 63, 73
Alium Malik (son of *Almaami* Malik Kumba), 99
alkali (from *al-qāḍī*), 47
al-Kanemi, 1, 123
al-Kusun (son of *Almaami* Tumane Mudi), 99
almaamate
   in Futa Jallon, 72, 90
   in Futa Toro, 90
   in Bundu, 87, 90, 93, 99–110, 120
Almaami (in Bundu), *passim*
   final court of appeal, 108–109
   in Futa Toro, 87–88, 90
   question of piety, 80
   shift from *Eliman*, 80
Almoravids, 48, 50
al-Muslim (*see also Ṣaḥīḥ*), 28
al-Qāḍī 'Iyad (*see also Shifā'*), 28
Amadhie, Bokar Saada's defeat of, 129–30
Amadi Aissata, *Almaami*, 73, 87–100, 104–105, 121
   ascension, 87–90
   conflict with Kaarta, 90–93
   death, 93
   Koussan support, 111
   military under, 104–105
   policy towards Bakel, 93–95
   southern policy, 98–99

Index

Amadi Amadu (son of *Almaami* Amadu Sy), 118
Amadi Bokar (son of *Almaami* Bokar Saada), 150
Amadi Bokar Sy, 42
Amadi Cire, *Almaami*, 164, 170–72
Amadi Gai (son of *Almaami* Amadi Gai), 81
Amadi Gai (son of Usuman Kumba Tunkara), 121–22
Amadi Gai, *Almaami* (son of *Almaami* Maka Jiba), 73–76, 79–82, 88, 97, 100, 111
   need for firearms, 79–81
   regional policies, 79–81
   response to Futanke reform pressures, 76, 81–82
Amadi Kama (son of Tumane Bubu Malik Sy), 93
Amadi Makumba (son of *Almaami* Amadi Gai), 81.
Amadi Pate Gai, *Almaami* (son of Pate Gai), 84, 87–90
   civil war with Amadi Aissata, 88–90
Amadi Saada (son of *Almaami* Saada Amadi Aissta), 118
   leader of Boulebane, 118, 120–22, 127
Amadi Tumane (of Farabana), 67–68, 73
Amadi Usuman, 170, 172
Amadu Musa, 104
Amadu Sheku, 1, 83, 134, 155, 169
Amadu Sy, *Almaami* (son of *Almaami* Amadi Gai), 81, 102, 111, 118–22, 135
amulets, 8, 29–30, 37–39, 41, 66, 103
   Amadi Aissata covered with, 93
Arabic documents, 7, 10, 12
army (*see* '*abīd* army, military)
Arondou, 46–47, 55
   Battle of, 46–47
ash'ar (poetry), 37
assemblies (public), 103
asylum, 20, 43–44, 70
Awa Demba (of Khasso), 98
awlube (*see also griot*, oral historians), 8, 13–14, 23, 41
axes
   North–South, 2
   East–West, 3
Ayuba Sulayman Diallo, 47, 61–62, 68–70

Babawuamataguifama, 56–57
Bacili (*see also* Bakel, Gajaaga, Guey, Kamera, *Tunka*), 19, 30, 41–45, 55–58, 96–97, 112, 124

Badiar, 42–3, 56
Bakel (*see also* Gajaaga), 7–11, 18, 28, 76, 89
   and *al-ḥājj* Umar, 124–27
   assault of Mamadu Lamine, 162–63
   during Gajaaga civil war, 112–14
   establishment of French fort, 93–99
   struggle for control of, 87
   under the N'Diaybe, 80
Bakiri (*see* Bacili)
Bala Setai (son *Almaami* Musa Yero), 97
Balou, 157–58
Bambara (*see also* Kaarta, Segu), 19–20, 37, 52, 72
   and Amadi Aissata, 90–93
   and Bokar Saada, 126–27, 148–50
   and Sega Gai, 83–84
   conflict with Bundu, 97
   fear of British alliance, 94
Bambuk, 17, 20, 25, 42–43, 56–57, 69–70, 113
   alliance with Bundu, 116–18
   and Bokar Saada, 138–39, 150
   as part of anti-Kaartan alliance, 114
   as asylum, 20
   conflict with Bundu, 67–68, 73, 95–99, 105, 118
   French interest in, 114–15
   goldfields, 3, 20, 29, 53, 38–68, 76–77, 100, 137
   maroons in, 87, 98
Bani Israila, 66
Banjul (Bathurst), 12, 142–45
Banu Maghfar, 19
Banu Ma'quil, 19
Baol (Bawol), 19
Bassari, 42
bāṭin ("secret" sciences), 30
Battle of Dara Lamine, 73, 81, 89–90, 121
bay'a (fealty), from Sega Gai to Abdul Qadir, 83
Bayol, 53
"Belli," 128
Bofel, 147
Boila Mailk (son of *Almaami* Malik Kumba), 99
Bokar Saada, *Almaami*, 9, 29–31, 38, 45, 102–7, 115, 118, 120–21, 126, 137–38, 142–52, 179–80
   campaigns, 31, 138–42
   consolidation of power, 137–38
   death, 102, 150–52, 158
   domestic affairs, 148–51

Index

head of Senoudebou, 115, 118
  military under, 105
  parents, 126
  relations with Abdul Bokar Kan, 145–48
  relations with the British, 142–45
  relations with the French, 137–38, 143–51
  royal slaves of, 103
  taxation under, 106–7
Bokar Sane (son of *Almaami* Amadi Aissata), 93
booty, 107
Bordeaux wholesalers, 125
Bornu, 1–2, 4, 123
Bosseya (province in Futa Toro), 88, 90, 145
Boulebane, 42, 73
  al-ḥājj Umar's occupation of, 132–33
  Amadi Saada's headquarters, 127
  as center of northern Bundu, 100–101
  as residence, 88, 103
  branch of Sissibe, 86–87, 97, 100, 111
  description by Gray and Dochard, 92–93
  in First Civil War, 86–90
  Kaartan siege of, 91–92
  opposed to Amadu Sy, 118–19
  relations with the French, 86, 96
  relations with the Kaarta, 86
  Second Civil war, 120–24
  tension over Senoudebou, 114–17
boundaries (of Bundu), 17, 100–1
Brakna, 19
British (*see* Bokar Saada, commerce, commodities, Gambia River Valley, Koussan, merchants, Royal African Company, slaves, treaties, Wuli)
brotherhoods
  Qadiriyya, 1, 122–23
  Sidiyya, 146
  Tijaniyya, 122–24
Bubacar Malik (son of *Almaami* Malik Kumba), 99
Bubacar Sega (son of *Almaami* Sega Gai), 84
Bubacar Sidiq (son of *Almaami* Tumane Mudi), 99
Bubu Malik Sy, *Eliman*, 15, 17, 28, 37, 47–48, 52–64, 74, 101, 177
  death, 60–61
  early court, 55–56
  expansion, 58–60
  Kumba's well, 56–58
  return from Futa Jallon, 54–55
  sources, 54
Bubuya, 56–58, 63

Bugul (of Farabana), 129, 131–33, 138–39
Bundu, origin of the name (*see also* Kumba's well), 56–58
Bundunke, *passim*
Bundunkobe ("people of Bundu"), *passim*
Buur-ba-Jolof, 41–42, 49

cannon, 96, 115, 132, 135
Casamance, 21
caste, 8, 22–25, 42
Cayor (Kajor), 19
  detainment of Abdul Qadir, 90
  during *tubenan*, 49–51
ceddo (*see also* Wolof), 24
cercle, of Nioro, 9
children, as war captives, 83
cholera, 137
Cire Adama, 134–35
Cire Suma (son of *Almaami* Saada Amadi Aissata), 118
Cire Ture (son of *Almaami* Bokar Saada), 150
civil war (in Bundu), 5, 82, 86–90, 99, 120–24
Civil War of 1852–54, 99
clerics, 1, 8, 19, 27–31, 36
colonial period, 8
Combegoudou (early designation for southeastern Bundu), 57
commerce, 1–3, 14, 20, 52, 58–68, 76 80, 84–5, 110–19, 176–77
  British involvement in, 14, 20, 52, 60, 78–80, 110, 115–16
  "desert-edge" system, 77
  French involvement in, 14, 20, 52, 60, 78, 110
  importation of firearms, 58, 76, 78, 110
  long-distance, 2–3
  Moors participation in, 77
  networks, 2–3
  protection of trade routes, 104
  regional, 2, 20, 58–59, 115–17
  strategy for control, 64, 67–68, 76–80, 84–85, 110–19, 176–77
commodities
  amber, 58
  beads, 3, 58
  beeswax, 3, 59
  brandy, 3, 58
  brassware, 3
  calicoes and prints, 58
  cattle products, 2
  cereals, 2–3, 21

Index

commodities (*cont.*)
  copper basins, 58
  cotton, 2–3, 21, 77, 79
  east Indian cotton (or "baft"), 3, 58, 107
  firearms, 3, 58, 76, 93, 105, 107, 110
fish, 2
gold, 2–3, 59, 76–79, 97, 100, 137
  groundnuts, 3, 21, 138
  gum, 3, 58–59, 68–69, 79, 100
  gunpowder, 58
  horses, 3
  knives, 58
  kola nuts, 3, 58, 98, 100
  iron, 3, 58
  ivory, 59, 78
  rum, 3, 58
  salt, 2–3, 77, 106–107
  semiprecious stones, 3
  shea butter, 2
  silver, 3
  textiles, 2–3, 58, 77
  woolens, 58
Compagnie des Indes, 63
comptoir (*see also* posts), 53, 59–60, 86, 97–98, 100–11, 114
  as source of data, 86, 111
  increase in nineteenth century, 110
Coniagui, 42
"constitution" of Bundu (between Malik Sy, the N'Guenar, and the Fadube), 55, 60–61, 88
Contou (early designation for Faleme Valley), 57, 67, 79
correspondence
  between Hesse and LeCoupe, 96
  between Sule N'jai and Maka Jiba, 71–72
  from Colonel Gallieni, 165–66
  from Mamadu Lamine, 164–65
council of notables, 101
court,
  composition of, 103
  strategies, 86–87
cultivation (*see* agriculture)

Dakar, 8
Dalafine, 164–65
Damel (of Cayor), 90
Damga (Futa), 147
Dara (former capital of Bundu), 67–68, 76–77, 81–82
Darame (Soninke maraboutic family), 24, 28, 157

David, Pierre, 10, 53–54, 63, 67–69, 71, 73
Dawuda Hamet (father of Malik Sy), 35
Demba Musa (son of *Almaami* Musa Yero), 97
Dentilia, 29
Denyanke (*see also* Futa Toro), 36–38, 51, 60–64, 70–72, 81, 122
desert (*see also* commerce), 2
dhimmi, 31, 107
Diakha (province in Bundu), 29, 66, 101, 155, 163–67
  headquarters of Mamadu Lamine, 155, 163–67
Diakha Ba (Bambuk), 29, 65
Diamwali
  Abdul Qadir's alleged birthplace, 83
  and Mamadu Lamine, 160–61
  and the Second Civil War, 122
Dianna (*see* Diakha)
Diara, 35, 37, 39–41, 47, 51, 75
Diawara (ruling dynasty of Diara), 37, 39–41, 44
Didecoto, 18, 29, 60, 65
Dingiray, 123
divination (by Jakhanke), 66
Do-Maio, 101
Dongo (of Diara), 40
Duranton, 113
Dyunfung (former capital of Bundu), 42, 67–68, 76–77, 88

education (*see also* Islam, schools), 27, 28
electoral council, 102
Eli Amadi Kaba, 129–30
Eli Gitta (son of *Almaami* Tumane Mudi), 99
Eliman, 39–40, 47, 54–76, 81
  shift to *Almaami*, 81
  significance of title, 47
"Eliman" Salum (possibly Alium Bubu Malik, brother of *Almaami* Maka Jiba), 63, 73

factories (*see also* posts), 2
Fadube (*see also* Wolof), 24, 42–43, 48, 50, 55–57, 60–61
Faidherbe, 125–37
Faleme River, 3, 17–25, 42–47, 56–68, 76, 79–80, 87–98
  agriculture, 76, 87
  struggle for control of, 79–80, 89
Falou Falls, 21, 60, 95
fatwa, 90

244

Index

Farabana (*see also* Bambuk), 60, 63, 67–68, 72–3, 114–15
   conflict with *Almaami* Amadi Gai, 79–80
   visit of *al-ḥājj* Umar, 123
farḍ, 106
Fatima (daughter of Malik Sy), 29
Fatteconda (former capital of Bundu), 76, 82
fay' (*see* tribute)
Fena, 58, 63–64, 67, 104
fergo, 121, 130–35, 154
Ferlo, 17–18, 20, 59, 68–69
Ferlo-Baliniama, 101
Ferlo-Maodo, 101
Ferlo-M'Bal, 101
Ferlo-Nieri, 101
fiqh (jurisprudence), 27–28, 90, 106–107
   Maliki, 106–107
firearms (*see also under* commodities)
   British manufacture, 143–45
   Bundu's dependence upon, 78, 84–85, 105, 110–12
   requested by *Almaami* Amadi Aissata, 93
First Civil War, 86–90, 111
Fissa-Daro, 88, 122, 164
Fissa-Tamba, 56, 61–63
Fonds Curtin, 10
forest, 2, 3
French, *passim* (*see also* Abdul Bokar Kan, *al-ḥājj* Umar, Amadu Sheku, Bokar Saada, commerce, commodities, Futa Toro, Malik Ture, Mamadu Lamine, posts, Saada Amadi Aissata, Senegal River Valley, Senoudebou, slaves, treaties, Umar Penda, Umarins, Usuman Gassi)
frontiers
   Atlantic, 2–3, 6
   effect on Bundu's development, 50–51
   Sahara, 2–3
Fudi Gassama Gaku, 28
Fudi Mahmud Jawari, 28
Fudiya Ansura, 83
Fugumba (in Futa Jallon), 72
Fula (*see also* Fulbe, *Halpulaar'en*), 23
Fulani (*see also* Fulbe, *Halpulaar'en*), 23
Fulbe (*see also Haalpulaar'en*), 19, 35, 41
   in Bundu, 22–27, 55–74, 117–18
Fulbe-Malinke (of Khasso), 19
Futa Jallon, 4–6, 20–29, 38, 48, 52–56, 70–74, 79, 109, 122–24, 177–78
   al-ḥājj Umar in, 122–24
   jihād in, 72–74, 109, 177–78

Second Civil War in Bundu, 122
commerce, 79
Futa Toro, 4, 9, 12, 19–28, 36–39, 44, 48–51, 60–64, 70–73, 81–91, 94, 109, 122–23, 145–48, 177–78
   Abdul Bokar Kan, 145–48
   al-ḥājj Umar in, 122–23
   conflict with Bundu, 70–72
   during *tubenan*, 49–51
   government, 101
   jihād in, 70, 74, 81–82, 109, 177–78
   reform influence in Bundu, 76, 81–91
   Second Civil War in Bundu, 122

Gabou, 9, 18, 118, 120–22
Gajaaga (Gala; *see also* Bakel, Guey, Kamera), 6, 11, 19–28, 34–51, 54–61, 70–72, 78, 82–83, 89–99, 110–14, 124–27
   Abdul Qadir's influence in, 83
   and *al-ḥājj* Umar, 124–27
   as asylum, 38, 41, 49
   civil war in, 110–14
   conflicts with Bundu, 34, 46–47, 54–55, 58–59, 72, 80
   establishment of Bakel, 93–99
   French policy towards, 112–14
   Guey (Lower Gajaaga), 112–14
   Kamera (Upper Gajaaga), 112–14
   relations with *Almaami* Amadi Aissata, 89–93
Gallieni, 16
Gambia River Valley, 3, 11, 18–24, 53, 58–60, 78–82, 93, 97, 100, 110, 115–17
   Almaami Tumane Mudi's raids in, 98
   British presence in, 58, 68–69, 110
   commerce from, 78–79, 97, 100, 115–17
   Upper Valley, 3, 11, 18–24, 53, 93
Gamon (*see also* Tanda), 98, 142, 150, 153–60
ganimah (*see* booty)
gawlo (s. of *awlube*), 41
gayahke (leather worker), 8
gold (*see under* Bambuk, commodities)
goldfields (*see under* Bambuk, commodities)
Golmy (in Gajaaga), 55
Gooriel (in Futa Toro), 90
Goudiry, 9
Goumba-Koko (site of Malik Sy's death), 47, 55
Goundiourou
   in Bundu, 60, 132
   in Khasso, 28, 155

245

Index

government (in Bundu)
  dual nuclei, 87
  early court, 55–56
  executive, 100–103
  justice, 108–109
  legal treasury, 106–107
  military, 104–106
  provincial governors, 101
  role of Jakhanke, 65–67
  under reform, 81
Gray and Dochard, 11, 22, 92–93, 106–107
griot (*see also awlube*), 8, 33, 36, 103
groundnuts (*see under* commodities, Wuli)
Guemou, 134–35
Guey (Lower Gajaaga), 112–14
Guidimakha, 19–20, 59, 83, 91, 113–14, 126, 155–56
  alliance with Kaarta, 91, 113–14
  Mamadu Lamine in, 155–56
Guinea, 20
Guirobe (*see also* N'Guenar)
  town of, 42–43, 56
  inhabitants, 43, 48
gum (*see under* commodities)
gunboats, 126, 130–31, 135
guns (*see* firearms)

Haalpulaar'en (*see also* Fulbe), 23, 43–44
$\d{h}ad\bar{\i}th$, 27–28
Hamdullahi, 122–24, 134
Hamet (Malik Sy's grandfather), 35
Hamet (son of *Almaami* Tumane Mudi), 99
Hassaniya (in Mauritania), 49–50
Hesse, Commandant, 95–97
hijra (*see also fergo*), 131–34
Hodh, 3, 19, 77
holy war (*see jihād*)
hoodu, 3
horses, 22, 172
"hungry season," 116

Ibn Abu Zayd (*see also Risāla*), 28
Ibnu Morvan (Malik Sy's great-grandfather), 35–36
Ibrahim Jane, 28
Ibrahim Sori (*Almaami* of Futa Jallon), 72
Idaw 'Aish, 19
Ijil (salt mines), 77
imāms (*see also* clerics), 27, 47, 49
  and the *alaamate*, 81
  and the justice system, 108
  rightly-guided, 84

immigration
  to Bundu, 22–26, 70, 111, 117–18
informants, 8–17
interregnum, 52, 60–62, 64
Inter-Tropical Convergence Zone, 21
Islam (*see also sharī'a*), 11, 16
  and the state, 4
  conversion to, 1, 24, 38, 42–43, 66, 74, 100
  education, 27–28
  in Bundu, 26–28
  law, 1, 24
  militancy, 1–4, 20, 38, 48–52, 74, 99, 109
  militancy in Bundu, 75–76, 81–87, 176–77
  militancy under *al-ḥājj* Umar, 119–37, 179
  militancy under Mamadu Lamine, 136, 152–69
  platform of militants in Futa Toro, 75
  rural, 2, 6
  taxation, 106–107
  urban, 6
istikhāra, 66

Jakhanke, 6, 22, 27–31, 42–43, 50, 55–56, 64–67, 101, 149–50, 176–77
  agricultural activities, 65
  and Mamadu Lamine, 159, 165–69
  and the Sissibe, 29–31, 50, 65–67
  as *tamsirs*, 108
  commercial activities, 29, 50, 65–66
  council of notables, 101
  ideology, 29–30, 50
  in Bundu, 22, 27–28, 43, 50, 55–56, 64–67, 74
  relations with Bokar Saada, 149–50
  schools, 66
  slaves of, 65
  spiritual services, 66
James Island, 58
Jelia Gai (*Almaami* Maka Jiba's first wife), 73
Jenne, 3, 28
jeeri, 21
Jiba Hammadi (*Almaami* Maka Jiba's mother), 72
jihād, 1–6, 12, 24–25, 29–31
  in Futa Jallon, 52, 54, 72–73, 177–78
  in Futa Toro, 70, 81, 177–78
  in Niani, 117
  under *al-ḥājj* Umar, 75, 120–37
  under Mamadu Lamine, 136, 152–69
  under Nasir al-Din, 48–51
jihadists (*see jihād*)

jinn, 57
jizya, 56, 107
  paid by the French at Bakel, 95, 97, 126
Job Ben Solomon (*see* Ayuba Sulayman Diallo)
Jolof, 42–44
  during the *tubenan* period, 49–51
Juula (*see* merchants)
justice (*see also under* government, Islam, Jakhanke), 56, 108–109
  role of Jakhanke, 56, 65–66, 101, 108

Kaaba, 28
Kaabu, 98, 116
Kaarta (*see also* Bambara, Massassi), 3, 6, 20, 37, 40–44, 75, 83–93, 97–98, 110–14, 118, 123–37, 148–50
  alliance with *Almaami* Amadi Aissata, 87–90
  alliance with *Almaami* Sega Gai, 83–85
  conflict with Bundu, 86–87, 90–93, 97, 110–12
  connections with *Almaami* Bokar Saada, 126–27, 148–50
  in opposition to *al-ḥājj* Umar, 123–37
  involvement in Gajaaga, 112–14
  involvement in Senegambia, 75, 98, 118
  relations with Boulebane, 86
Kaedi, 9
kāfir, 82, 84
Kamera (*see also* Gajaaga), 112–14, 118, 124, 126
Kanem-Bornu (*see also* Bornu), 2, 4
Kantora, 104, 116–18
Karamoko Alfa (of Futa Jallon), 54, 72
Karamoko Ba (of Touba), 28–29
Kenieba, 129, 150
Keri Kafo, 41–42
khalīfa, 82, 122
Khalil b. Ishaq (*see also Mukhtaṣar*), 28, 37
Khasso, 6, 19–20, 28, 37–39, 72, 89–90, 98, 113–17, 126
  alliance with Bundu, 89–90, 98, 116–17
  alliance with Faidherbe, 126
  alliance with Kaarta, 91
  Duranton's residence, 113
Kidira, 9
Kingui (capital of Diara), 37
kola nuts (*see under* commodities)
Koli Mudi (son of *Almaami* Saada Amadi Aissata), 118, 127
Konko Bubu Musa (*Satigi* of Futa Toro), 70

kora, 8
Kotere (*see also* Gajaaga), 41
Kounguel (*see also* Gajaaga), 55, 60, 80, 112
Koussan, 11, 29, 33, 58, 60, 73
  branch of Sissibe, 86, 97, 100, 111
  capital under *Almaami* Amadi Gai, 77, 81
  center of southern Bundu, 100–101
  during First Civil War, 86–90
  relations with the British, 86
  Rubault's description, 92–93
  Second Civil War, 120–24
  tensions over Senoudebou, 114–17
  Almaami Tumane Mudi's home, 98–99
Kulubali (of Segu), 40
Kumba's well, 15, 34, 56–58
Kunta *shaykhs*, 1, 77
Kurubarai Kulubali, 89, 126

Lake Chad (*see also* Bornu, Kanem-Bornu), 1, 23
Le Grand-Bassam, 131
Le Serpent, 128–29, 131
Leze-Bundu, 101
Leze-Maio, 101
literacy (*see* Arabic documents, scholarship, schools)

Maasina, 1, 28, 118, 134
McCarthy Island, 110, 140–45
madrasa (*see* schools)
Maghrib, 2–3
Maka Jiba, *Eliman*, 48, 52–76, 87–88, 101, 104, 137, 176–77
  ascension, 62–64
  children, 73
  conflict with Futa Toro, 69–72
  death, 73
  effect of *jihād* in Futa Jallon, 72–73
  interregnum, 61–62
  military under, 104
  policy toward Faleme Valley, 67–69
  relations with Jakhanke, 65–67
  reputation, 72
Makhana (*see also* Gajaaga, Guey), 63, 91, 112–14, 124
  and *al-ḥājj* umar, 124
  struggle with Guey, 112–14
Mali (ancient), 2, 37, 40
Mali (contemporary), 1, 22
Malik Aissata (son of *Eliman* Maka Jiba), 73, 89

247

Index

Malik Kumba, *Almaami* (son of *Almaami* Amadi Gai), 81, 88, 98–100, 111
Malik Musa (son of *Almaami* Musa Gai), 82
Malik Samba Tumane, 93, 102, 127, 130
Malik Sy, *Eliman*, 8, 15, 25–58, 62–67, 73–74, 175–76, 180
 background, 35–36
 early years, 36–39
 creation of Bundu, 47–51
 death, 45–47
 in southern Gajaaga, 41–43
 sources, 32–35
 tale of the walk, 40, 43–45
 travels, 39–41
Malik Ture, *Almaami*, 101, 172–74
Maliki law (*see also fiqh*), 106–107
Malinke, 6–8, 20–25, 29, 40, 52–53, 56–60, 66, 79, 82, 96, 116–18, 121, 138–42
 and *al-ḥājj* Umar, 121
 and Bokar Saada, 138–42
 as sources of slaves, 98, 116–18
 conversion to Islam, 24
 in Bambuk, 96
 in Bundu, 22, 24–25, 43
 in Tenda, 79
Mamadou Ben Damankalla (*Fari* of Diara), 39
Mamadu Lamine, 5, 8, 12–13, 152–69
 against the Sissibe, 156–62
 and Amadu Sheku, 155, 157
 background, 152–53
 conception of *jihād*, 156
 conflict with the French, 153, 162–69
 in Bundu, 5, 8, 12–13, 118
 sources, 152–53
Mande (*see* Malinke)
Mandinka (*see also* Malinke), 20
Maqāmāt (*see also* al-Hariri), 28
Marmari Kulubari (of Segu), 52–53
Marsa, 83
Massassi (*see also* Bambara, Kaarta), 20, 40–41, 75
Maty-Hamet (Malik Sy's aunt), 35, 54
Maurel and Prom, 125
Mauritania, 6, 19, 22, 28, 35–38, 48–51, 98
Mawlay Isma'il, (Moroccan sultan), 19, 70
Medine (*see also* Khasso), 19
 establishment of French post in, 110
 Faidherbe in, 126–27
 Umarian siege of, 130–31
merchants (*see also* commerce, commodities)
 European, 2
 Juula, 2, 19

military (of Bundu),
 cavalry, 105
 recruitment, 104–105
 role of slaves, 104–105
 size, 104–105
 under Bubu Malik Sy, 55–56, 58–59
 under Maka Jiba, 64
 under Malik Sy, 46–47
moderates (*see also* Boulebane, pragmatism), 109
 Boulebane branch, 86–87
Moors, 19, 36, 41, 64, 76–77, 84, 98, 105, 128–29
 against the Umarians, 128–29
 combat tactics, 105
 commerce with, 76–7
 competition for control of Upper Senegal, 98
Moriba (of Kaarta), 91–92
mosques, 19, 88, 92, 124
Mudi Bubu Malik, 73
Mudi Malik (son of Malik Sy), 37, 61
Muhammad al-Kharashi, 28
Muhammad al-Taslimi, 28
Muhammad Fatima, 29, 65
Muhammad Fudi, 29, 65
Muhammad Ghali, 28
Muhammad Kumasat, 28
Muhammad Tumane, 28
Mukhtar Kudaije, *Shaykh*, 90
Mukhtar-uld-Buna, 84
Mukhtaṣar (*see also* Khalil b. Ishaq), 28, 37
multiethnicity, 14, 111
Musa Gai, *Almaami* (son of *Eliman* Maka Jiba), 73, 75, 78–80, 82
Musa Kurabo (of Kaarta), 90–1
Musa Makka, *Shaykh*, 82
Musa Yero, *Almaami*, 93, 95–98, 111, 135
 Bakel, 95–97
 campaigns, 98
 death, 97
Musa Yero (son of *Almaami* Amadu Sy), 118
Musa Yero (son of *Almaami* Bokar Saada), 150
Musa Yero Malik (son of *Almaami* Malik Kumba), 99
Muslims, 1–2, 16–17
 in Bundu, 26–28
 polities, 4, 50–1, 62
Muwaṭṭa' (of Malik b. Anas), 28

naḥwa (grammar), 37

Index

Nague-Hore-Bundu, 101
Nasir al-Din (*see also* Shurrbubba, *tubenan*), 48–51, 175–76
N'Diaybe (of Gajaaga), 80, 95
  Bundunke support of, 97
N'Diaye Gauki, 80
N'Diob-Hamet (Malik Sy's uncle), 35, 63
N'Dioum, 127
  Bokar Saada's defeat of, 129
  reorganization, 132
N'Guenar (*see also* Guirobe)
  in Bundu, 43, 50, 55, 60–64, 68, 73
  part of council of notables, 101
  province of Futa Toro, 43
Niani, 29, 116–18
  and Bokar Saada, 141–42
Nieri, 101
Niger River Valley (*see also* commerce, commodities)
  al-ḥājj Umar in, 120–37
  floodplain, 3, 19
  commerce in, 79
  Upper Valley, 2–3, 20, 53
Niocolo, and Bokar Saada, 142
Nioro, 9, 19, 124, 133
Njukunturu, 83
Ntiangulai (*Fari* of Diara), 39–41
Nyakhate (founding dynasty of Diara), 37

oral history (*see also* awlube, griot), 7–8
Ormankobe raids, 66, 70, 72

Park, Mungo, 10, 20, 27–28, 82, 92, 107
pastoralism, 19, 22–23, 36, 57
Pate Gai (son of *Eliman* Maka Jiba), 64, 67, 73
periphery (in Bundu; *see also* boundaries), 100–101
Peuls (*see* Fulbe, *Haalpulaar'en*)
police force (under Amadi Gai), 81
poll tax (*see jizya*)
population estimates, 26
  under Bokar Saada, 137, 148–52
posts, 13, 16
  British, 68–69, 110
  French, 11–12, 59–60, 94–99, 110
pragmatism (as a state policy), 1–2, 4, 14, 26, 30, 47–52, 58–59, 66, 74, 85–87, 109, 175–81
  components of the policy, 100
  definition of, 1–2
  development of, 47–51, 58–59
  response to Abdul Qadir, 85–87, 109

Pulaar, 2, 8, 22–23, 36, 81
punishment (*see* justice)

qāḍī, 65–66, 108
Qadiriyya (*see* brotherhoods)

rainfall, 20–21
Rançon, Andre, *passim*
reform, 5, 52
  in Bundu, 73–76, 81–87, 100, 136
Rio Grande, 28
Risāla (*see also* Ibn Abu Zayd), 28
Roux, Emile, *passim*
Royal African Company, 68–69

Saada Amadi, *Almaami*, 150, 164–66, 170–74
Saada Amadi Aissata, *Almaami*, 30, 89–90, 97–99, 111–22, 103, 137
  aftermath of reign, 121–22, 127
  ascension, 111–12
  end of reign, 117–19
  entourage, 103
  marriage to Kurubarai Kulubali, 89, 126
  regarding Senoudebou, 114–16
  relations with Gajaaga, 112–14
  southern campaigns, 116–17
Saada Bokar (son of *Almaami* Bokar Saada), 150, 170
Saada Dude (son *Almaami* Musa Yero), 24
Sambala (of Khasso), 138–42, 145–48, 156–57
Safalou (in Diakha province), 29, 155
Sahara, 70
sahel, 3, 22
Ṣaḥīḥ,
  of al-Bukhari, 28
  of al-Muslim, 28
Saint Joseph (fort), 59–63, 69–70, 78–80
Saint Louis, 8, 59, 93–96, 113–15, 124–25
Saint Pierre (fort), 60
Salif Amadi Gai (son of *Almaami* Amadi Gai), 81
Salim Suware, al-ḥājj, 22, 29
salt (*see under* commodities)
Salum, 116–18, 139, 167
Samba Gaissiri (son of *Almaami* Malik Kumba), 99
Samba Gangioli (of Guidimakha), 91
Samba Gelaajo Jegi, 68, 70–71
Samba Kumba Diama (of Tiyaabu-Guey; *see also* Gajaaga, Guey), 112–14
Samba Kongole (of Gajaaga), 91

249

Index

Samba Molaju, 80
Samba Tumane, *Eliman*, 73
Samba Yacine (of Makhana-Kamera; *see also* Gajaaga, Kamera), 112–14, 124
Sangalou affair (*see also* Sega Gai, *Almaami*), 83–85
Sansanding, 97
Satigi (of Futa Toro), 41, 49–50, 61, 70–71
savannah, 1–3, 22–3
scholarship, 1, 28
schools, 19, 22
   Jakanke, 27–28, 6
   Qur'anic, 27, 36–37, 92, 124, 155
Second Civil War, 120–24
seeno (*see jeeri*)
Sega Amadi Gai (son of *Almaami* Amadi Gai), 81
Sega Bokar (*Almaami* Bokar Saada), 150
Sega Gai, *Almaami*, 73, 75, 82–86, 90
   civil disorder under, 82–83
   execution of, 83–86
   Sangalou affair, 83–85
Sega Tumane (son of *Almaami* Tumane Mudi), 99
   leader of Koussan, 121–23
Segu, 3, 38, 40, 52–53, 66, 93
   Segovian merchants in Bundu, 87, 92–93
   Umarian defeat of, 130, 134
Senegal River Valley
   al-ḥājj Umar in, 120–37
   commodities from, 100
   establishment of Bakel, 94–99
   Faidherbe in, 126–37
   French presence in, 59–60, 69–70, 84–85, 93–99
   Kaartan influence in, 90–93
   lower valley, 4, 19
   middle valley, 19–26, 36–38, 50, 66–67
   struggle for control of, 5, 78, 80, 87, 89, 109–19
   upper valley, 1, 5, 11, 13, 19, 36, 48, 53, 59–60, 70–71, 88–89
Senegalese Riflemen's Corps, 12, 125, 134, 154, 162
Senegambia, *passim*
Senoudebou, 7, 11, 43, 46, 56, 60
   and Mamadu Lamine, 160–61, 164–65
   French fort at, 102, 110, 114–17
   population of, 117–18
   source of tensions within Sissibe, 114–17
   Umarian attack on, 128–29, 133
Serracolet (*see* Soninke)

Sereer, 22
Sevi Laya, 41
sharī'a (*see also* Islamic law), 1, 81, 175–76
   Abdul Qadir's observance of, 84, 90
   al-ḥājj Umar's position on, 124
   Bokar Saada's disregard for, 150–51
   on justice, 108–109
   on taxation, 106–107
   violation of, 83
shaykhs (*see also* Kunta; Umar, *al-ḥājj*), 1, 28
Shifā' (*see also al-Qāḍī* 'Iyad), 28
Shurrbubba, 48–51, 70
Sidiya al-Kabir, 146
Sidiyya (*see* brotherhoods)
Silla (polity of), 4
Silla (Soninke maraboutic family), 24
Sisse (Soninke maraboutic family), 24
Sissibe, *passim*
   as *Torodbe*, 35–6
   conflict between branches, 4–5, 73, 76, 86–87, 100–101, 114–17, 120–22
   relations with Jakhanke, 29–31, 50
   rules governing succession, 101–102
   succession disputes, 4, 73, 86–90, 98–99, 111
slaves (*see also* '*abīd* army)
   absconding, 87, 98
   armed, 64, 70, 104–105
   as payment for education, other services, 27–28, 37
   as resources for forced labor, 154
   commerce in, 6, 19, 38, 52–53, 58–59, 66–68, 87, 98
   from Samori, 149–50
   from Upper Senegal, 77–78
   from Wuli, 117, 139–41
   in Bundu, 23–25, 41–42, 56–58, 64–67, 70, 92, 98, 111
   procured by Bokar Saada, 138–42
   through Ormankobe, 70
society (in Bundu) 4, 22–26
Sokoto caliphate, 1, 23, 28, 40, 122–24
Somsom-Tata, 127, 130–31
Songhay, 2
Soninke, 8, 18–20, 29, 33, 40, 43
   and *al-ḥājj* Umar, 121, 124
   and Mamadu Lamine, 154–69
   conversion to Islam, 24
   in Bundu, 22–26, 43–44, 117–18
   in Gajaaga, 95

sources
  endogenous, 6–7, 8–10
  exogenous, 6–7, 10–11
  intermediate, 6–7, 11–12
  oral, 8
  reliability, 12–17
Sulayman Bal, 81
Sulayman Bokar (son of *Almaami* Bokar Saada), 150
Sule N'jai (*Satigi* of Futa Toro), 71–72
Suracoto (*Almaami* of Tumane Mudi), 99
Susu (and Aissata Bela), 73
Suyuma (Futa Toro), 35–38
"sword of power," 40–41
Sy (*see* Sissibe)
Sy Amadou Issaga, 9, 33

Tagant, 3, 77
Taim Sy Hamme-Mishin (*see* Ibnu Morvan)
Takrur, 4
tafsīr (Qur'anic exegesis), 27–28
Talansan, 72
ṭālibs (*see also* clerics), 27
"tale of the walk," 40, 43–45
Tamba (people of), 56
Tamba Kunte, 41
Tambacounda, 43, 67, 79
Tambadunabe, 43, 50
Tambu (of Makhana-Kamera), 113–14
tamsir (*see also* clerics), 27, 108
ṭarīqa (*see* brotherhoods)
tata, 58, 68
  along eastern Faleme, 76–77
  at Fena, 89, 63–64, 67, 104
  Gamon, 142
  of Koussan, 81
  Somsom-Tata, 130–31
tawba, 49
Tawdenni (salt mines), 77
tawḥīd (theology), 27–28
taxation, 56
  informed by *shari'a*, 81
  of caravans, 53, 58–59, 78–79, 103
  on commodities, 79
  on Jakhanke, 65
  under Bokar Saada, 148–50
  under Malik Sy, 48
Tenda, 20, 81
  and Bokar Saada, 142
  conflict with Bundu, 31, 97–98, 117–18
  emergence, 79

theocracy (*see also* militancy *under* Islam, *shari'a*), 26, 29, 61–62
Tiali, 101
Tieougue-Hamet (Malik Sy's aunt), 35
tierno, 37
Tierno Alium, 128
Tierno Brahim (of Futa Toro), 146–47
Tierno Samba, 72
Tillika, 78, 103, 107
Timbuktu, 1, 3, 28, 123, 134
Tirailleurs sénégalais (*see* Senegalese Riflemen)
Tishit (oasis), 77
Tiyaabu (*see also* Gajaaga, Guey, Kamera, *Tunka*), 41, 44–46, 51, 54
  conflict with Bakel, 95–96
  conflict with Kamera, 112–14
  Sangalou affair, 83
  struggle with Kounguel, 80
Tunka, 95–98
topography (of Bundu), 20–21
Torodbe, 25–176, *passim*
Toubacouta, 28, 167–68
Toucouleur (*see also* Fulbe, *Haalpulaar'en*), 23
trade (*see* commerce)
traitants (*see also* commerce, commodities, merchants), 125
Trarza (emirate), 19
traveler accounts, 7–8, 11–12
treaties
  Amadi and Wuli, 79
  Bokar Saada and the British, 143–45
  Bokar Saada, Bugul and Faidherbe, 132–33
  Malik Sy and the Fadube, 48, 55
  Malik Sy and the N'Guenar, 48, 55, 58
  Musa Yero and the French, 95–96
  Saada Amadi Aissata and the French, 114–16
tribute, 107
tubaab (foreigner), 13
tubenan, 41, 44, 48–51, 175–76
Tumane Bubu Malik Sy, 62, 64, 93
Tumane Malik (son of Malik Sy), 37, 61
Tumane Mudi, *Almaami*, 81, 88–89, 111, 121, 142–43
  ascension, 97
  death, 99
  representative of Koussan, 93
  southern campaigns, 98–99
Tumane Samba, 122

Index

Tunka (also see Gajaaga, Guey, Kamera, Tiyaabu), 19, 37–47, 54, 91
   and *al-ḥājj* Umar, 124
   of Tiyaabu, 95–98
   Sangalou affair, 83
   struggle between Guey and Kamera, 112–14
   under n'Diaybe, 80
Ture (Soninke maraboutic family), 24

Umar, *al-ḥājj*, 1, 4–14, 28–30, 83, 86, 97–99, 109, 118–37, 179
   against Kaarta, 123
   background, 122–23
   death, 134
   fight against the French, 124–37
   French arms embargo, 124–25
   hijra, 131–34
   in Bundu, 14, 120–37
   in Upper Niger, 130, 134
   jihād, 75, 120–37
   understanding with the French, 134–35, 137
Umar "the Grammarian," 28
Umar Musa (son of *Almaami* Musa Gai), 82
Umar Penda, *Almaami*
   ascension, 152
   at father's death, 118
   his death, 164
   inheritance, 102
   Mamadu Lamine, 158–64
   relations with Bokar Saada, 150
Umar Saada (son of *Almaami* Saada Amadi Aissata), 118, 124, 127, 129
Umar Sane (nephew of *Almaami* Bokar Saada), 170
Umar Sane, *Almaami*, 93, 121–24, 127, 130
Umarians, 118, 120–37
   composition of army, 123–24
'*ushr* (see *zakāt*)
Usuman dan Fodio, 30, 40
Usuman Gassi, *Almaami*, 150
   and Mamadu Lamine, 158–61, 166–67
   ascension and tenure, 170–72
   inheritance, 102
Usuman Kumba Tunkara (son of *Eliman* Maka Jiba), 73, 121

village organization and taxation, 103, 106–107

waalo (floodplain), 21, 58, 60
Walata, 77
waliyu, 39
Walo, 19
   during *tubenan*, 49–51
war (*see also* civil war, *jihād*), 46, 53, 71, 93
weapons, 105
well (*see also* Kumba's well), 57–58
Wolof (*see also* Fadube), 19
   conversion to Islam, 24
   in Bundu, 22–25, 42–43, 117–18
   groundnut cultivation, 138, 145
   revolt against *tubenan*, 49
Wopa Bokar (son of *Almaami* Bokar Saada), 150, 173–74
Wualiabe, 42–43, 56
Wuli, 20, 39
   and Bokar Saada, 139–41
   caravans from, 103
   conflict with Bundu, 31, 97–8, 116–18
   establishment of, 43, 67
   Second Civil War in Bundu, 122
   treaty with Amadi Gai, 79
Wuro-Alfa, 42, 44, 55, 57, 60

Yelimane (capital of Kaarta), 91
   Battle of Yelimane, 123–26
Yoro Kumba, 164–65

zakāt, 56
   collected during *tubenan*, 49
   collected for *al-ḥājj* Umar, 83
   collected in Bundu, 106–107
zwāya, 36, 48–49
   Kunta confederation, 77

OTHER BOOKS IN THE SERIES

6 *Labour in the South African Gold Mines, 1911–1969* Francis Wilson
11 *Islam and Tribal Art in West Africa* René Bravmann
14 *Culture, Tradition and Society in the West African Novel* Emmanuel Obiechina
18 *Muslim Brotherhoods in Nineteenth-century Africa* B. G. Martin
23 *West African States: Failure and Promise: A Study in Comparative Politics* edited by John Dunn
25 *A Modern History of Tanganyika* John Iliffe
26 *A History of African Christianity 1950–1975* Adrian Hastings
28 *The Hidden Hippopotamus: Reappraisal in African History: The Early Colonial Experience in Western Zambia* Gwyn Prins
29 *Families Divided: The Impact of Migrant Labour in Lesotho* Colin Murray
30 *Slavery, Colonialism and Economic Growth in Dahomey, 1640–1960* Patrick Manning
31 *Kings, Commoners and Concessionaires: The Evolution and Dissolution of the Nineteenth-century Swazi State* Philip Bonner
32 *Oral Poetry and Somali Nationalism: The Case of Sayyid Mohammed Abdille Hasan* Said S. Samatar
33 *The Political Economy of Pondoland 1860–1930: Production, Labour, Migrancy and Chiefs in Rural South Africa* William Beinart
34 *Volkskapitalisme: Class, Capital and Ideology in the Development of Afrikaner Nationalism 1934–1948* Dan O'Meara
35 *The Settler Economies: Studies in the Economic History of Kenya and Rhodesia 1900–1963* Paul Mosley
36 *Transformations in Slavery: A History of Slavery in Africa* Paul E. Lovejoy
37 *Amilcar Cabral: Revolutionary Leadership and People's War* Patrick Chabal
38 *Essays on the Political Economy of Rural Africa* Robert H. Bates
39 *Ijeshas and Nigerians: The Incorporation of a Yoruba Kingdom, 1890s–1970s* J. D. Y. Peel
40 *Black People and the South African War 1899–1902* Peter Warwick
41 *A History of Niger 1850–1960* Finn Fuglestad
42 *Industrialisation and Trade Union Organisation in South Africa 1924–55* Jon Lewis
43 *The Rising of the Red Shawls: A Revolt in Madagascar 1895–1899* Stephen Ellis
44 *Slavery in Dutch South Africa* Nigel Worden
45 *Law, Custom and Social Order: The Colonial Experience in Malawi and Zambia* Martin Chanock
46 *Salt of the Desert Sun: A History of Salt Production and Trade in the Central Sudan* Paul E. Lovejoy
47 *Marrying Well: Marriage Status and Social Change among the Educated Elite in Colonial Lagos* Kristin Mann
48 *Language and Colonial Power: The Appropriation of Swahili in the Former Belgian Congo 1880–1938* Johannes Fabian
49 *The Shell Money of the Slave Trade* Jan Hogendorn and Marion Johnson
50 *Political Domination in Africa: Reflections on the Limits of Power* edited by Patrick Chabal
51 *The Southern Marches of Imperial Ethiopia: Essays in History and Social Anthropology* edited by Donald Donham and Wendy James
52 *Islam and Urban Labor in Northern Nigeria: The Making of a Muslim Working Class* Paul M. Lubeck

Other books in the series

53 *Horn and Crescent: Cultural Change and Traditional Islam on the East African Coast, 500–1900*   Randall L. Pouwels
54 *Capital and Labour on the Kimberley Diamond Fields 1871–1890*   Robert Vicat Turrell
55 *National and Class Conflict in the Horn of Africa*   John Markakis
56 *Democracy and Prebendal Politics in Nigeria: The Rise and Fall of the Second Republic*   Richard A. Joseph
57 *Entrepreneurs and Parasites: The Struggle for Indigenous Capitalism in Zaire*   Janet MacGaffey
58 *The African Poor: A History*   John Iliffe
59 *Palm Oil and Protest: An Economic History of the Ngwa Region, South-eastern Nigeria 1800–1980*   Susan M. Martin
60 *France and Islam in West Africa, 1860–1960*   Christopher Harrison
61 *Transformation and Continuity in Revolutionary Ethiopia*   Christopher Clapham
62 *Prelude to the Mahdiya: Peasants and Traders in the Shendi Region, 1821–1855*   Anders Bjørkelo
63 *Wa and the Wala: Islam and Polity in Northwestern Ghana*   Ivor Wilks
64 *Bankole-Bright and Politics in Colonial Sierra Leone: The Passing of the "Krio Era", 1919–1935*   Akintola Wyse
65 *Contemporary West African States*   edited by Donal Cruise O'Brien, John Dunn, and Richard Rathbone
66 *The Oromo of Ethiopia: A History, 1570–1860*   Mohammed Hassen
67 *Slavery and African Life: Occidental, Oriental and African Slave Trades*   Patrick Manning
68 *Abraham Esau's War: A Black South African War in the Cape, 1899–1902*   Bill Nasson
69 *The Politics of Harmony: Land Dispute Strategies in Swaziland*   Laurel Rose
70 *Zimbabwe's Guerrilla War: Peasant Voices*   Norma Kriger
71 *Ethiopia: Power and Protest: Peasant Revolts in the Twentieth Century*   Gebru Tarket
72 *White Supremacy and Black Resistance in Pre-Industrial South Africa: The Making of the Colonial Order in the Eastern Cape, 1770–1865*   Clifton C. Crais
73 *The Elusive Granary: Herder, Farmer, and State in Northern Kenya*   Peter D. Little
74 *The Kanyok of Zaire: An Institutional and Ideological History to 1895*   John C. Yoder